The Reconstruction of the Church of Ireland

Thomas Wentworth landed in Ireland in 1633 – almost 100 years after Henry VIII had begun his break with Rome. The majority of the people were still Catholic. William Laud had just been elevated to Canterbury. A Yorkshire cleric, John Bramhall, followed the new viceroy and became, in less than one year, Bishop of Derry. This study, which is centred on Bramhall, examines how these three men embarked on a policy for the established church which not only represented a break with a century of reforming tradition but which also sought to make the tiny Irish church a model for the other Stuart kingdoms. Dr McCafferty shows how accompanying canonical changes were explicitly implemented for notice and eventual adoption in England and Scotland. However, within eight years the experiment was blown apart and reconstruction denounced as subversive. Wentworth, Laud and Bramhall faced consequent disgrace, trial, death or exile.

JOHN McCAFFERTY is Director of the Mícheál Ó Cléirigh Institute at University College Dublin. He has recently edited, with Alan Ford, *The Origins of Sectarianism in Early Modern Ireland* (2005).

Cambridge Studies in Early Modern British History

Series editors

ANTHONY FLETCHER
Emeritus Professor of English Social History, University of London

JOHN GUY
Fellow, Clare College, Cambridge

JOHN MORRILL
*Professor of British and Irish History, University of Cambridge,
and Vice-Master of Selwyn College*

This is a series of monographs and studies covering many aspects of the history of
the British Isles between the late fifteenth century and the early eighteenth
century. It includes the work of established scholars and pioneering work by a
new generation of scholars. It includes both reviews and revisions of major topics
and books, which open up new historical terrain or which reveal startling new
perspectives on familiar subjects. All the volumes set detailed research into our
broader perspectives and the books are intended for the use of students as well as
of their teachers.

For a list of titles in the series, see end of book.

THE RECONSTRUCTION OF THE CHURCH OF IRELAND

Bishop Bramhall and the Laudian Reforms, 1633–1641

JOHN McCAFFERTY
University College Dublin

CAMBRIDGE
UNIVERSITY PRESS

CAMBRIDGE UNIVERSITY PRESS
Cambridge, New York, Melbourne, Madrid, Cape Town, Singapore, São Paulo

Cambridge University Press
The Edinburgh Building, Cambridge CB2 8RU, UK

Published in the United States of America by Cambridge University Press, New York

www.cambridge.org
Information on this title: www.cambridge.org/9780521643184

© John McCafferty 2007

First published 2007

Printed in the United Kingdom at the University Press, Cambridge

A catalogue record for this publication is available from the British Library

ISBN 978-0-521-64318-4 hardback

In memoriam Pádraic McCafferty, 10 September 2006

CONTENTS

TABLES

ACKNOWLEDGEMENTS

When a book has been as long in the making as this one there are many people to thank. Very many things have come between this work and its completion over the years. Some of those things were wonderful and some banal but now it is finished. It has its flaws but it is less flawed than it would have been had not several friends read drafts. There is a custom which calls upon authors to thank the readers by name. I am not going to follow it because I do not wish to implicate my friends in any mistakes or enlist them in my stubbornness. You know who you are. Thank you so much.

I started researching John Bramhall in St John's College, Cambridge. Its fellows awarded me a Benefactors' scholarship, they even paid for microfilming through the Harry Hinsley memorial fund, and then they elected me to a title 'A' fellowship. All of which leaves me indebted to that society for some of the happiest years I have spent. John Morrill took care of me in Cambridge and never stopped believing in this project. He has been, and is, a wonderful and generous adviser and friend. He is a great advocate for Irish history in Britain and he delighted many people when he incorporated it into the title of his chair. I have been both medievalist and early modernist but the fact I have spent so much time on Stuart history is due to Brian Sommers, and to his brilliant seminars and endless support. James McGuire is the best of friends and he has shown how to keep to true scholarly values in all the storms and stresses of university affairs. Ciaran Brady is one of the best people I know to talk about history. Our meetings are always happy. Art Cosgrove was my first postgraduate supervisor and I am still grateful to him. Any ability I have to read historical documents thoroughly is due to the excellent training I received from Charlie Doherty.

There are others to thank. Gerald Bray for his remarkable generosity, Brendan Bradshaw for his insight and encouragement and Seán Hughes for patient theological advice and friendship over many years. A lot of other people helped in various ways and I thank them for it, especially Brian Jackson, Kate Breslin, Ivar McGrath, Eamon Ó Ciardha, Peter Gray,

Mícheál Mac Craith, Marc Caball, Brian Mac Cuarta, Mark Empey, Robert Armstrong, Patrick Little, Patrick Geoghegan, Alan Ford, Oliver Rafferty, Eamon Duffy, Fergus D'Arcy, Harry White, Rena Lohan, Elva Johnston, Andrew Carpenter, Alun Carr, Jane Ohlmeyer, Peter Marshall, James Murray, Arnold Hunt, Julia Merritt, David Smith, Richard Nolan, Howard Hughes, Peter Linehan, Nial Osborough, Maurice Bric, Bernadette Cunningham, Dave Edwards, Jebu Rajan, Liam Smith, Aishling Begley and Michael Clarke. Vincent Morley gave me some excellent advice which helped me overcome a block and move to finishing the book. Richard Aldous, Ronan Fanning and Michael Laffan have done me many favours at UCD, with some convivial times along the way. Pádraic Conway has been a good friend and helped me sharpen my understanding of ecclesiastical politics greatly. Mary Daly showed me great kindness and patience and forgave many disappearances from other duties. Máire Ní Mhaonaigh and Torsten Meissner gave me a home from home in Cambridge. Patrick Collinson and Anthony Milton helped this work develop from its earlier incarnation as did the late Conrad Russell. *Ar dheis Dé go raibh a anam uasal.*

I would also like to record my thanks to the British Academy for funding me as a PhD student. Librarians and archivists in many places have made much of what follows possible. If it had not been for a generous donor there would be no Mícheál Ó Cléirigh Institute, of which I have the great honour of being director. I want to thank very warmly all those who work with me in this happy project, especially Edel Bhreatnach, Colmán Ó Clabaigh, Emmett O'Byrne and Malgorzata Krasnodebska-D'Aughton, as well as our friends and partners, the Irish Franciscans.

Bill Davies has been a great friend to Irish historians and to me. Michael Watson has been more than patient and understanding. Isabelle Dambricourt has been unfailingly helpful and kind throughout all stages of this and another project.

Work on this 'dead bishop', as she once called him, commenced before I married Pádraicín and went on and on after the births of Máire, Aoife and Séamus. My debt to her and to them is just incalculable. My parents, Jim and Ann, and my sisters, Rachel and Audrey, never thought they would see the end but out of the goodness of their hearts they kept faith. I am more grateful to them than I can say. Máire and Aoife, with Séamus consenting, wanted this book to be called *Century after century of Irish history*. I am sorry it has not been possible (as it would violate description of goods legislation) but it is a worthy title to be saved for another time. The best is kept till last. So I dedicate this book to Pádraicín with great love.

NOTE ON THE TEXT

In the text, dates are Old Style but the year is taken to begin on 1 January. Of the printed works cited below, the place of publication is London unless otherwise stated. Spellings have been silently modernised. Unless otherwise stated, all references to statutes are to those passed by the Irish parliament.

ABBREVIATIONS

Bodl.	Bodleian Library, Oxford
BL	British Library
BW	A. W. Haddan (ed.), *The works of . . . Bramhall*, 5 vols. (Oxford, 1842–5)
Cal. SP Ire.	*Calendar of state papers relating to Ireland*
Clarke, *Old English*	Aidan Clarke, *The Old English in Ireland* (1966)
Commons' jn. Ire.	*Journals of the House of Commons of the kingdom of Ireland*, vol. I, 1613–66 (Dublin, 1796)
Cotton, *Fasti*	Henry Cotton, *Fasti ecclesiae Hibernicae*, 6 vols. (Dublin, 1848–78)
DOC	Duchy of Cornwall Office, Buckingham Gate, London
EC	English canons of 1603
Ford, *Protestant*	Alan Ford, *The Protestant reformation in Ireland, 1590–1641* (Frankfurt, 1985)
HA	Hastings manuscripts, Huntington Library, California
HJ	*Historical Journal*
HMC	Historical Manuscripts Commission
IC	Irish canons of 1634
IHS	*Irish Historical Studies*
JEH	*Journal of Ecclesiastical History*
Kearney, *Strafford*	Hugh Kearney, *Strafford in Ireland* (Cambridge, repr. 1989)
Knowler	W. Knowler (ed.), *The earl of Strafford's letters and despatches*, 2 vols. (1799)
Lib. mun Hib.	Rowney Lascelles (ed.), *Liber munerum publicorum Hiberniae*, 2 vols. (1824–30)

Lismore papers	A. B. Grosart (ed.), *Lismore papers*, 1st series 5 vols., 2nd series 5 vols. (1886–8)
Lords' jn. Ire.	*Journals of the House of Lords of the kingdom of Ireland*, vol. I, 1634–99 (Dublin, 1779)
NAI	National Archives of Ireland
NHI III	T. W. Moody, F. X. Martin and F. J. Byrne (eds.), *A new history of Ireland*, vol. III, *1534–1691* (Oxford, repr. 1991)
NLI	National Library of Ireland
ODNB	*Oxford dictionary of national biography* (Oxford, 2004)
P&P	*Past and Present*
PRONI	Public Record Office of Northern Ireland
Rawdon	E. Berwick, *The Rawdon papers* (1819)
RCB	Representative Church Body, Dublin
RIA	Royal Irish Academy
Rushworth	J. Rushworth (ed.), *The trial of Thomas, Earl of Strafford* (1680)
Shirley	E. P. Shirley (ed.), *Papers relating to the Church of Ireland, 1631–9* (1874)
Shuckburgh, *Two lives*	E. S. Shuckburgh (ed.), *Two lives of William Bedell* (Cambridge, 1902)
SO	Signet Office
SP	State Papers, Public Record Office, London
STC	W. A. Jackson, F. S. Ferguson and K. F. Panzer (eds.), *A short-title catalogue of books printed in England, Scotland and Ireland and of English books printed abroad, 1475–1640*, 3 vols. (1976–86)
Str P	Strafford Papers, Sheffield City Libraries
Tanner letters	C. McNeill (ed.), *The Tanner letters* (Dublin, 1943)
TCD	Trinity College Dublin
UWW	C. E. Elrington (ed.), *The whole works of . . . James Ussher*, 17 vols. (Dublin, 1847–64)
Vesey, *Athanasius Hibernicus*	John Vesey, *Athanasius Hibernicus* (1676)
WL	W. Scott and J. Bliss (eds.), *The works of . . . William Laud*, 7 vols. (Oxford, 1847–60)

Church of Ireland dioceses, *c.*1636

CHAPTER I

Prologue: Ireland's English reformation

In 1632 James Spottiswoode was rowed out into the middle of Lough Derg in Co. Donegal. He was a Scot, ordained in the Church of England, who had become Church of Ireland bishop of Clogher in 1621. He bore a mandate issued by the lords justices and privy council of Ireland which permitted him to break down, deface and utterly demolish 'the chapel and all the Irish houses now situate in that island called St Patrick's purgatory, all the buildings, pavements, walls, works, foundations, circles, caves, cells and vaults . . . called St Patrick's bed'. Spottiswoode had a miserable time. The secular arm, in the form of the high sheriff of Donegal, failed to turn up and a pilot could not be found. When one was eventually located, the bishop and his companions were nearly sunk and then narrowly avoided being marooned by a storm. Meanwhile onlookers, the 'country people', stood by and waited for a divine thunderbolt while Spottiswoode dashed about toppling hostels, chapels and other devotional structures erected by the Franciscans only a few years earlier. All of this took place just four years short of the first centenary of the passing of the Act of Supremacy by the Irish parliament. By that date, 1636, Lough Derg was once again open for business as Catholic Ireland's leading pilgrimage site.[1]

James Spottiswoode wasted his time and risked the lives of his servants. That this was so may have caused this younger brother of the archbishop of St Andrew's to ask himself, in private, a hard question: 'why did Ireland not become Protestant?' Historians of Ireland have, in one way or another, examined religious change in the sixteenth and seventeenth centuries and come to the conclusion that reformation failed. Some scrabble for slender examples of success or ambiguity. Others assert failure, but emphasise conditionality and imply that different administrators and a different administration could have led to a national establishment founded

---

[1] Henry Jones, *St Patrick's Purgatory: containing the description, original, progress and demolition of that superstitious place* (1647), p. 130.

on the 1536 statute.[2] Historians of England, by and large, have detected an overall success marred by instances of failure – delay, contingency, evasion, church papistry.[3] There is more here, though, then a ready contrast. There is an unexceptionable truth – Ireland got an English reformation. The pace might have been slightly different and the detail slightly varied, but constitutionally and canonically, the kingdom of Ireland got what the kingdom of England got. Ireland did not become Protestant because it underwent an English reformation. Or rather the Irish state-sponsored reformation faltered and failed for the very reasons that the English state-sponsored reformation, for all of its acknowledged slowness and mixed messages, succeeded.

From the very outset, writers in Ireland and writers on Ireland have used the vocabularies of success and failure.[4] Catholics came to argue that there was something definitive, something innate about the attachment of the people of Ireland to the faith. Their story was one of muscular resistance to any ploy to lure them away from the Apostolic See. Their

---

[2] Brendan Bradshaw, 'Edwardian reformation in Ireland', *Archivium Hibernicum* 24 (1976–7), 83–99; 'Sword, word and strategy in the reformation of Ireland', *HJ* 21 (1978), 475–502; 'The English reformation and identity formation in Ireland and Wales' in Brendan Bradshaw and Peter Roberts (eds.), *British consciousness and identity: the making of Britain 1533–1707* (Cambridge, 1998), pp. 43–111; Karl Bottigheimer, 'The failure of the Irish reformation: *une question bien posée*', *JEH* 36 (1985), 196–206; Nicholas Canny, 'Why the Reformation failed in Ireland: *une question mal posée*', *JEH* 30 (1979), 423–50; 'Protestants, planters and apartheid in early modern Ireland', *IHS* 25 (1986); Aidan Clarke, 'Varieties of uniformity – the first century of the Church of Ireland' in W. J. Sheils and Diana Wood (eds.), *The churches, Ireland and the Irish*, Studies in Church History 25 (Oxford, 1989), pp. 105–22; Steven Ellis, 'Economic problems of the church: why the Reformation failed in Ireland', *JEH* 41 (1990), 239–65; Ford, *Protestant*, pp. 105–15; G. A. Hayes-McCoy, 'The royal supremacy and ecclesiastical revolution, 1534–47', *NHI* III, pp. 39–67, 'Conciliation, coercion, and the Protestant Reformation, 1547–71', *NHI* III, pp. 69–92; 'The completion of the Tudor conquest and the advance of the Counter-reformation', *NHI* III, pp. 94–140; Henry A. Jefferies, *Priests and prelates of Armagh in the age of reformations, 1518–1558* (Dublin, 1997); Colm Lennon, 'The counter-reformation in Ireland, 1542–1641' in Ciaran Brady and Raymond Gillespie (eds.), *Natives and newcomers* (Dublin, 1986), pp. 75–92.

[3] For an accessible recent survey of the historiography, see Peter Marshall, *Reformation England* (2003). Given the great size of the field, this footnote lists only a selection of monographs: A. G. Dickens, *The English reformation*, 2nd edn (1989); Eamon Duffy, *The stripping of the altars* (1992); Christopher Haigh, *English reformations: religion, politics and society under the Tudors* (Oxford, 1993); Norman Jones, *The English reformation: religion and cultural adaptation* (Oxford, 2002); Diarmaid MacCulloch, *Tudor church militant: Edward VI and the English reformation* (1999); Peter Marshall (ed.), *The impact of the English reformation 1500–1640* (1997); Richard Rex, *Henry VIII and the English reformation* (Basingstoke, 1993); J. J. Scarisbrick, *The reformation and the English people* (Oxford, 1984); Lucy Wooding, *Rethinking Catholicism in reformation England* (Oxford, 2000); Alexandra Walsham, *Church papists: Catholicism, conformity and confessional polemic in early modern England* (Woodbridge, 1993).

[4] Alan Ford, '"Standing one's ground": religion, polemic and Irish history since the Reformation' in Alan Ford, J. I. McGuire and Kenneth Milne (eds.), *As by law established: the Church of Ireland since the reformation* (Dublin, 1995), pp. 1–14.

triumph was predicated on Protestant defeat. Protestant commentators, depending on their mood and inclination, saw anything from gullibility and pliability to malice and willful obduracy. Popery was superstition and Rome-running the proof of enduring incivility. This sectional analysis of affairs, which occasionally tumbled out in pulpit vitriol, jogged along for centuries. But from the 1960s onwards Irish historians increasingly replaced character with chronology and determinism with contingency. Religious change in early modern Ireland reverted to being the hard problem it had been for contemporaries. The confessional past regained its open future so that incidents such as that of Lent 1542, when Paschase Broet and Alphonse Salmeron became the first two Jesuits to set foot in Ireland, ceased being an early point in a long narrative thread which wound on until Catholic Emancipation in 1829 or Disestablishment in 1869.[5] The two harbingers of Catholic reformation abandoned their mission after five weeks. In the wake of a cool reception from Conn O'Neill and Manus O'Donnell, they concluded Ireland would follow its sovereign Henry VIII into schism.[6] Historians, like the legates, became concerned with trajectory. They retained the trope of success and failure while trying to discern whether the outcomes were due to economics or the interplay of colonisation with confessionalisation or even to theological styles. The hard problem has been rendered even harder by the destruction of swathes of records, which made it difficult to employ research strategies that have served other parts of Europe well in any meaningful way beyond broad generalisation. To take one small example, only very few cities, such as Dublin and Limerick, offer anything close to real narrative depth over any appreciable time span.[7]

Bishop Spottiswoode found his lakeside wait for the high sheriff of Donegal an unpleasant business. Had he been asked, he would have said there was only one bishop in Clogher and that was him. If he had been asked the difference between himself and the popish or 'pretended' or 'titular' bishop of Clogher, his answer would have almost certainly contained the phrase 'church as by law established'. As it happened, 'Church of Ireland'

---

[5] Edmund Hogan (ed.), *Ibernia Ignatiana* (Dublin, 1880), p. 6.
[6] Salmeron and Broet to Cardinal Cervini (Santa Crucis), Edinburgh, 9 April 1542, *Epistolae PP. Paschasii Broëti, Claudi Jaji, Joannis Codurii et Simonis Rodericii Societatis Jesu ex autographis vel originalibus exemplis potissimum depromptae, Monumenta Historica Societas Iesu 24* (Madrid, 1903), pp. 23–31. I wish to thank Brian Jackson for drawing this reference to my attention.
[7] Brendan Bradshaw, 'The reformation in the cities: Cork, Limerick and Galway, 1534–1603' in John Bradley (ed.), *Settlement and society in medieval Ireland* (Kilkenny, 1988), pp. 445–76; Colm Lennon, *The lords of Dublin in the age of reformation* (Dublin, 1989); *The urban patriciates of early modern Ireland: a case-study of Limerick, the 28th O'Donnell Lecture* (Dublin, 1999).

came far less readily to contemporary pens and lips than some variant of 'as by law established'. When, in 1603, Lord Deputy Mountjoy arrived outside Waterford city, he found himself looking at a improvised processional crucifix borne by a vested Dr James White, vicar apostolic of Waterford and Lismore. The viceroy promptly opened up dialogue by asking, 'what are you?'[8]

The Church of Ireland was the statutory expression of extension and ratification of English legislation in Ireland. A first glance at statutes for both kingdoms shows apparently identical lists with small intervals – Acts of Supremacy in 1534 and 1536, Acts of Uniformity in 1559 and then 1560. Ireland, and so it seemed to both lay and clerical contemporaries, was England with a little time lag. The more the smaller island proved to be different or difficult, the more it seemed the best solution was to make it England.

Ireland was seductively similar or deceptively different. Which of these it was depended on your point of view. The Irish 'reformation' parliament of 1536–7 put through Acts of Supremacy, Appeals, Slander, First Fruits, Against the authority of the bishop of Rome – all mirroring Westminster.[9] Apart from cosmetic changes such as replacing 'England' with 'Ireland' in the wording of bills and adjusting official titles, they were virtually identical.[10] The preamble to the Irish bill for supreme headship even remarked on the necessity of following developments across the water by virtue of the dependency of the Irish crown.[11] In the same session a snappy little bill (at least by Tudor standards) was passed and received royal assent as an Act for the English Order, Habit and Language. This kind of legislation was not at all unusual as insistence on the speaking of English, as well as English hairstyle and dress, had been parliamentary business in 1297, 1366 and afterwards.[12] If the other acts can be understood as the start of a process

---

[8] Anon. (ed.), 'After the death of Queen Elizabeth', *Duffy's Irish Catholic Magazine* (Nov. 1848), p. 275: 'Having presented ourselves before his excellency and paid to him all the customary honours in due form he instantly asked me, "what are you?". I answered that I was a Christian, a firm Catholic, a servant and most loyal subject of His Majesty King James. He interrogated me closely, not only on the meaning but on the etymology of that answer, but after having explained myself to the best of my power, I perceived that his passion was rising and he called me "traitor".'

[9] 28 Hen. VIII, c. 5, 6, 7, 8, 13.

[10] W. N. Osborough, 'Ecclesiastical law and the Reformation in Ireland' in R. H. Helmholz (ed.), *Canon law in Protestant lands* (Berlin, 1992), pp. 223–52.

[11] 28 Hen. VIII, c. 5: 'Forasmuch as this land of Ireland is depending and belonging justly and rightfully to the imperial crown of England'.

[12] 28 Hen. VIII, c. 15; Seán Duffy, 'The problem of degeneracy' in James Lydon (ed.), *Law and disorder in thirteenth-century Ireland: the Dublin parliament of 1297* (Dublin, 1997), pp. 87–106; James Lydon, 'The middle nation' in James Lydon (ed.), *England and Ireland in the later middle ages* (Dublin, 1981), pp. 1–26.

which eventually led to a Protestant establishment, then this Act can be seen as linking Ireland's medieval past to its future as a Protestant kingdom. The 1537 statute insisted that benefices be given to English speakers unless all efforts to locate one had failed. In that event, each priest was to take an oath at ordination to endeavour to learn the 'English tongue . . . to the uttermost of his power, wit and cunning'. Having done so, he was to instruct his flock in the same, so that the cleric now became an instrument of anglicisation in a church of which Henry and his heirs would be supreme heads. This church made the acquisition and spread of English language and manners a priority. The result was that evangelisation through Irish was regarded as at best maverick but more usually as suspect.[13] So, from the very outset, Westminster statutes were exported whole and then made law in a neighbouring kingdom which had a very different past and a very different present.

The 1541 Act for Kingly Title offered a new future by superseding the medieval Lordship. The snag was that the future on offer was predicated on England's, not Ireland's, past. Henry VIII attempted by strategy, by policy and by law to turn all of the inhabitants of Ireland into his obedient subjects *and* into Englishmen and Englishwomen *and* lead them into schism with Rome *all at once*. If, as seems the case, it was a 'habit' of obedience that turned English subjects into Protestants in the long term and made religious change there a success, then there was no comparable 'habit' to build on in Ireland. Here was a brand new synthetic kingdom, all head and no body, enjoying no coronation, no coronation oath and no separate proclamation. This made it different from the far older kingdom of England and, in time, the other older kingdom of Scotland. It also threw up another problem which grew steadily more acute over the next hundred years. The infant kingdom was neither fish nor fowl because Irish policy was neither purely domestic policy nor was it purely foreign policy. It was both rolled, maddeningly, into one. Pope Paul III had glimpsed this when he sent his two Jesuits on reconnaissance, and, when *Propaganda Fide* came into existence in 1622, it paid special attention to this overwhelmingly Catholic realm as a key European theatre. Yet dazzled by what was, in relative terms, stunning success in England, lords deputy, judges and clerics moving across the Irish Sea to impose the Henrician and its successor settlements could not usually get beyond the seductive similarity. This meant that a paper kingdom was to get a paper reformation.

---

[13] Nicholas Williams, *I bprionta i leabhar: na protastúin agus prós na Gaeilge, 1567–1724* (Baile Átha Cliath, 1986).

The kingdom of Ireland was at once a jewel of Cromwellian reform and an embarrassing little itch. The itch was an old one begun in the twelfth century as a kind present of the English pope Adrian IV, who was believed to have granted Ireland to Henry II in exchange for overhauling its anachronistic (barbaric, if you were John of Salisbury) church practices.[14] The 1541 statute rather lamely overcame Adrian's *Laudabiliter* by declaring that the 'king of England is and is of right' the king of Ireland. Otherwise English dominion over the smaller island might have been construed as dependent on papal grant. The catch was that the Old English population took *Laudabiliter* to be their charter, their mandate to 'tame' the wild Irish. To their mind, denial of the papal bull might be understood as denial of their right to exist as a community.[15]

The twelfth century had other claims on the attention of sixteenth- and seventeenth-century ecclesiastics and governors. Councils convened in 1111 and 1152 had, despite some later unions and amalgamations, given the island over twenty dioceses.[16] The number, size and boundaries of these sees made up a lovely still life of power relations in 1152, but had a deleterious effect on the new Tudor *Ecclesia Hibernicana*. Most bishoprics were poor and many had inchoate or almost vestigial parish structures. It turned into a poisoned chalice for the state church. Places like Killaloe, Cloyne, Ferns, Kilfenora, Leighlin, Dromore – indeed the vast majority of sites – were complete backwaters and usually ruinous by the early modern period. The claim to be a national church, the very title of the Church of Ireland, meant that civil and religious authorities shied away from proposals for extensive unions and relocations of cathedral churches to more populous centres.[17] Inherited canon law carried with it a claim to exclusive jurisdiction.[18] Impoverished bishops began to lease see lands with manic intensity. Residence in the hotspots of four centuries earlier was so unappealing that prelates gravitated to Dublin. Tudor and Stuart monarchs found it almost impossible to give away dioceses like Ardfert and Kilmore. Church of Ireland bishops,

---

[14] See J. A. Watt, *The church and the two nations in medieval Ireland* (Oxford, 1970), ch. 1, for an overview.

[15] James Murray, 'The diocese of Dublin in the sixteenth century: clerical opposition and the failure of the Reformation' in James Kelly and Dáire Keogh (eds.), *History of the Catholic diocese of Dublin* (Dublin, 2000), pp. 92–111.

[16] It is not surprising that 26 Hen. VIII, c. 14 (Eng.), the suffragan bishops Act of 1534, was not proposed for Ireland.

[17] See chapter 4 below and John McCafferty, 'Protestant prelates or godly pastors? The dilemma of the early Stuart episcopate' in Alan Ford and John McCafferty (eds.), *The origins of sectarianism in early modern Ireland* (Cambridge, 2005), pp. 54–72.

[18] Osborough, 'Ecclesiastical law', pp. 223–52.

faced with the erosion of landed endowments, proceeded to corrosive abuse
of jurisdiction and flagrant pluralism simply to make ends meet. Discredit
followed on dilapidation. Catholic commentators, as in the *Annals of the
Four Masters*, took delight in declaring that the reformation was propelled
by avarice and rapine.[19] Many of the patentee bishops who had no previous
Irish career, or had only a very brief one, found themselves strangers in a
strange land, disliked and alien. Their troubles were compounded by the
defiant existence of vicars apostolic and, worse, from the 1610s onwards,
a rival episcopate who used identical titles and had shadow officials and
courts all modelled on the exact same medieval structures. The Roman
bishops were often locals, sons of the well-connected, who were supported
by voluntary contributions; they were not shackled to crumbling cathedrals and were free to work in the towns that counted.[20] Many of the old
cities possessed chartered liberties which allowed corporations to hamper
the state church if they chose – and some chose to do so.[21] Examples of the
ways in which the medieval past turned out to be a noxious inheritance
for the Church of Ireland and a balm to the illegal counter-church can
easily be multiplied. The moral of the story is that what ended by working
well in England often backfired in Ireland. Elizabeth's achievement was, as
Conrad Russell has said, the creation of a church 'which looked Catholic
and sounded Protestant' by virtue of its resting on so many medieval foundations.[22] Her Church of England worked out to be a blend, but her Church
of Ireland curdled.

Even dissolution of the monasteries, the great fissure in English religious
life, which did so much to secure aristocratic and landed acquiescence,
played out in almost farcical reverse on the other side of the water. By
the 1570s, as Colm Lennon has shown, Old English impropriators were
siphoning off the profits of dissolution to pay for the upkeep of the new
seminary clerics. 'Massing' priests in the Dublin area were often better off

---

[19] John O'Donovan (ed. and trans.), *Annála ríoghachta Éireann: Annals of the kingdom of Ireland by the Four Masters from the earliest times to the year 1616*, 7 vols. (Dublin, 1851), p. 1445; RIA MS 23 P7 fols. 54v–55r.

[20] Tadhg Ó hAnnracháin, *Catholic reformation in Ireland* (Oxford, 2002), ch. 2, 'Development and reform in the Irish church, 1618–1645'; P. J. Corish, 'The reorganisation of the Irish Church, 1603–1641', *Proceedings of the Irish Catholic Committee* (1957), 9–14; Donal Cregan, 'The social and cultural background of a counter-reformation episcopate 1618–60' in Art Cosgrove and Donal MacCartney (eds.), *Studies in Irish history presented to R. Dudley Edwards* (Dublin, 1979), pp. 85–117.

[21] A. J. Sheehan, 'The recusancy revolt of 1603: a reinterpretation', *Archivium Hibernicum* 38 (1983), 3–13.

[22] Conrad Russell, 'The reformation and the creation of the Church of England, 1500–1640' in John Morrill (ed.), *The Oxford illustrated history of Tudor and Stuart Britain* (1996), p. 280.

than the established church incumbents. Here at least the pope did better from dissolution than the king.[23]

Recusants hugged Ireland's medieval practices to themselves. They contrived to 'disremember' the manifold abuses and bitter divisions and so adroitly turn past centuries into an age of faith. The literary expression of this medievalism deserves separate consideration. On the ground it was played out by persistent pilgrimage. A life of St Kevin of Glendalough (surviving in eighteenth-century recension) identifies '4 chief pilgrimages of Erin' – one for each province – St Patrick's Purgatory, Croagh Patrick, Inis na mBeo (the isle of the living) or Monaincha in Co. Tipperary and Glendalough. Gerald of Wales mentions several of them in his *Topographia*.[24] Custom and lack of state intervention kept them alive, but the counter-reformation episcopate adroitly colonised them and turned them into statements about survival as well as sanctity. Cornelius O'Devany of Down and Connor (executed in 1612) made his devotions at Monaincha and Francis Kirwan of Killala did the rounds at Lough Derg shortly after Spottiswoode's wrecking.[25] In response to lobbying by Irish exiles, popes Paul V and Clement VIII attached plenary indulgences to the four 'national' pilgrimages as well as highly localised ones such as St Gobnait in west Cork.[26] Prayers for the extirpation of heresy from Ireland were mandatory for successful receipt of the indulgence. Catholic apologists gleefully pointed out the island's prior freedom from stain of heresy and apparent lack of anticlericalism. In this view, not only was there no reformation from 'below' but the island also exhibited an exceptional purity of faith which deserved to be guarded at all costs.[27]

Protestant engagements with the earlier centuries were less assured. Dublin Castle could not erase older practices and readings of medieval authors were beguiling but harmful. Cambrensis remained required reading

[23] Lennon, *The lords of Dublin*, pp. 144–50.
[24] Charles Plummer, *Bethada náem na nÉrenn: Lives of Irish saints*, 2 vols. (Oxford, 1922), vol. 2, p. 156.
[25] P. F. Moran (ed.), *Analecta Sacra*, p. ciii; C. P. Meehan (ed.), *The portrait of a pious bishop; or the life and death of the Most Reverend Francis Kirwan, bishop of Killala. Translated from the Latin of John Lynch, archdeacon of Tuam* (Dublin, 1864), pp. 83–7.
[26] John Hagan (ed.), 'Miscellanea Vaticano-Hibernica', *Archivium Hibernicum* 3 (1914), 263–4; D. Ó hÉaluighthe, 'St Gobnet of Ballyvourney', *Journal of the Cork Historical and Archaeological Society* 72 (1952), 43–61 at p. 51, quoting from Lambeth Palace library, Carew MS, vol. 621.
[27] For typical expressions of this sentiment, see B. B. [Robert Rochford], *The life of the glorious S. Patricke apostle and primate together with the lives of the holy virgin S. Bridgit and of the glorious abbot Saint Columbe, Patrons of Ireland* (St Omer, 1625), pp. ii–xvi and I. C. [John Copinger], *The theatre of Catholique and Protestant religion diuided into twelue bookes* (St Omer, 1620). John McCafferty, 'Mirabilis in sanctis suis: the communion of saints and Catholic reformation in early seventeenth-century Ireland' in Robert Armstrong and Tadhg Ó hAnnracháin (eds.), *Community in early modern Ireland* (Dublin, 2006), pp. 199–214.

for administrators, soldiers and settlers, but his writings, especially translated, had a deleterious effect on those readers.[28] Gerald made it too easy –
too easy to read 'Catholic' for 'barbarian', too easy to believe the Irish
'problem' was one, the same, unchanging. Writing to Laud in winter
1633, Wentworth spelled out a list of ecclesiastical abuses which are so
similar to Archbishop Lanfranc's that there is a temptation to believe in
reincarnation.[29] The concluding sections of the *Expugnatio* (on how Ireland should be governed) made it far too easy to believe in a quick and
easy fix. Viceroy after viceroy read Gerald in Holinshed and Camden and
fell under the spell. By the time they had shaken it off they had usually
been recalled or burnt out.[30] Sir John Davies's cunning plan to use only
pre-reformation statutes in pursuit of the 'mandates' campaign did not
exactly evoke warm feelings about the ancient legitimacy of the Church of
Ireland.[31] James Ussher's sophisticated attempt in 1622 to recast Patrick as
Protestant and Irish monks as proto-dons caused no known conversions.
In 1632, a joint Old English and Gaelic Irish campaign, headed up by the
Franciscan scholar Luke Wadding, had Patrick placed in the Roman brev-
iary. Muirchú's seventh-century Moses of Armagh became a Tridentine
Moses for a seventeenth-century Catholic nation. Wadding's patriarch did
far better than Ussher's puritan.[32]

There is a grave temptation to ask when it was 'all over' for Protestantism
in Ireland. It was never 'all over', of course. There have been arguments that
the Church of Ireland sank into a state of sulky pessimism, but nobody

---

[28] Hiram Morgan, 'Giraldus Cambrensis and the Tudor conquest of Ireland' in Hiram Morgan (ed.),
Political ideology in Ireland, 1541–1641 (Dublin, 1999), pp. 22–44; Nicholas Canny, 'The attempted
anglicisation of Ireland in the seventeenth century: an exemplar of "British history"' in J. F. Merritt
(ed.), *The political world of Thomas Wentworth, Earl of Strafford 1621–1641* (Cambridge, 1996), pp. 157–
86; Richard Anthony McCabe, 'Making history: Holinshed's Irish *Chronicles*, 1577 and 1587' in David
J. Baker and Willy Maley (eds.), *British identities and English renaissance literature* (Cambridge, 2002),
pp. 51–67.

[29] Wentworth to Laud, 31 January 1634, Knowler I, p. 187.

[30] Ciaran Brady, 'England's defence and Ireland's reform: the dilemma of the Irish viceroys, 1541–1641'
in Brendan Bradshaw and John Morrill (eds.), *The British problem, c.1534–1707: state formation in
the Atlantic archipelago* (1996), pp. 89–117.

[31] John McCavitt, 'Lord Deputy Chichester and the English government's "mandates policy" in Ireland
1605–7', *Recusant History* 20 (1990), 320–55; Hans S. Pawlisch, *Sir John Davies and the conquest of
Ireland* (Cambridge, 1985), pp. 103–21.

[32] Bernadette Cunningham and Raymond Gillespie, '"The most adaptable of saints": the cult of St
Patrick in the seventeenth century', *Archivium Hibernicum* 49 (1995), 82–104; Alan Ford, 'James
Ussher and the creation of an Irish Protestant identity' in Brendan Bradshaw and Peter Roberts
(eds.), *British consciousness and identity: the making of Britain 1533–1707* (Cambridge, 1998), pp. 185–
212; Ute Lotz-Heumann, 'The Protestant interpretation of the history of Ireland: the case of James
Ussher's Discourse' in Bruce Gordon (ed.), *Protestant history and identity in sixteenth-century Europe*,
vol. II, *The later reformation* (Aldershot, 1996), pp. 107–20; John McCafferty, 'St Patrick for the
Church of Ireland: James Ussher's *Discourse*', *Bullán* 3 (1997–8), 87–101.

was ever going to say, or even think, the reformed future lay exclusively with immigrants, because to do so would have been to undermine its very existence as a Christian church. Timing is important but not as a means of determining *the* year of which it could be said that Ireland was not going to be Protestant. It is important to recall that when James VI acceded to the English throne in 1603 his arrival inaugurated a period of comparative peace lasting up to 1641 and for the first time the state could, if it chose to, contemplate a thorough reformation all across Ireland. It is, however, equally important to remember the relationship between timing and the Englishness of the reformation: England's reformation had its own velocity and its own critical junctures such as 1534, 1559, 1571 and 1611. The outcomes of those dates, the products of England's own journey to Protestantism, were then, respectively, introduced into Ireland at points in its own historical trajectory – 1536, 1560, 1634 and 1611. None of them – Henry's Act of Supremacy, the Prayer Book, the Thirty-Nine articles, the Authorised Version of the Bible – were designed for or were remotely in response to Irish conditions.

Ireland's binary life as foreign and domestic matter had an effect on legal enforcement of the religious settlement. More than once recusants had it both ways. During negotiations for the Spanish match in 1623 James permitted de facto toleration, yet in 1625, when his son went to war with Spain, threat of invasion made it imperative to compromise with Old English Catholics, so uniformity went out the window and talks began on concessions.[33] Even the 1607 mandates scheme, which rested on creative use of prerogative powers, was suspended for policy reasons and not for legal ones. As Church of Ireland clergy endlessly pointed out, political goals took precedence. If the Irish kingdom had been more real and the English church settlement less secure, things might have been different but, as it was, the gospel invariably lagged behind government. As a result, the Church of Ireland lacked definition, lacked form for far too long. By the time James began to fill up the vacancies left by Elizabeth, the Catholics had begun on their counter-hierarchy. Until 1615 the Church of Ireland had no formulary beyond a Dublin promulgation of Matthew Parker's Eleven articles of 1559. The Thirty-Nine articles were not received until 1634. Translations of scripture and service books were long delayed. A brief catechism was issued in 1567 (really as a response to the apparent Presbyterianism of John Carswell's Gaelic translation of the Book of Common Order). There was no Prayer Book until 1608 and no Old Testament until 1685. This compares, as

---

[33] Clarke, *Old English*, chs. 2–3.

many scholars have pointed out, woefully with Wales.[34] Endless squabbling over the secularisation of St Patrick's cathedral delayed the foundation of Dublin University as a Protestant seminary until 1591. By then, even as the royal charter admitted, wealthy Dubliners were sending their sons out to continental colleges.[35] As late as 1615 it was still necessary for the Church of Ireland to include an attack on private masses in their first formulary and the 1634 canons gave directions for the removal of monuments of superstition from churches.

Under Mary in England, churchwardens unwrapped and re-erected concealed rood crosses and other objects – there is almost no parallel in Ireland because nothing had been taken down. The vast majority of Marian bishops stayed on in Elizabeth's Church of Ireland.[36] Mary's Irish reign was so far from being the last gasp of Catholicism that her most enduring legacy to her successors was papal reconfirmation of the kingly title, which cut the Gordian knot as it superseded *Laudabiliter* and so paved the way for effective recusant allegiance to the crown. When the Spanish armada pushed Englishness and Protestantism into hypostatic union, those arriving from the 'beleaguered isle' had either no memory of Catholicism or a very dim one. They found a kingdom which bore a paper resemblance to their own to be nightmarish, alien, a scandal.

Those who made careers in the new kingdom and who were charged with reducing it to conformity found even the paper resemblance to be deceptive. The church was established by law differently and the means of 'compelling them in' was quite different too. Under the Irish Uniformity Act, non-attendance at parish churches meant only a fine of 12d.[37] Supplementary penalties did not make it through parliament, as Old English wrecking in 1585–6 and in 1613–15 clearly showed. There was the option of prerogative power – as in the 1605 proclamation against seminary priests – but this was always subject to political override. The Irish Uniformity Act of 1560 permitted Latin services in *all* parishes, allowed the 1549 Prayer Book and vestments, as at 2 Edward VI. Small wonder that the large Marian episcopate

---

[34] Bradshaw, 'The English reformation and identity formation', pp. 43–111; Ciaran Brady, 'Comparable histories? Tudor reform in Wales and Ireland' in Steven G. Ellis and Sarah Barber (eds.), *Conquest and union: fashioning a British state, 1485–1725* (1995), pp. 64–86; Philip Jenkins, 'The Anglican Church and the unity of Britain: the Welsh experience, 1560–1714' in Ellis and Barber (eds.), *Conquest and union*, pp. 115–38.

[35] James Murray, 'St Patrick's Cathedral and the university question in Ireland *c.* 1547–1585' in Helga Robinson-Hammerstein (ed.), *European universities in the age of reformation and counter-reformation* (Dublin, 1998), pp. 1–33.

[36] Henry A. Jefferies, 'The Irish Parliament of 1560: the anglican reforms authorised', *IHS* 26 (1988), 128–41.

[37] 2 Eliz. I, c. 2.

made legal services look as old-fashioned or, to English eyes, as popish as possible. Most of the new English were so hardwired to think in terms of England that they frequently assumed Westminster statutes were current in Ireland. In 1611 Andrew Knox of Raphoe (who was Scottish, as it happens) secured royal permission for imposing the oath of allegiance on prominent Catholics in each diocese. The snag was that the oath was based on an English Act of 1606 which had not been brought in by Dublin and so there were no statutory punishments for those who refused the oath. In 1604, after forty-six years' Irish service, Chief Justice William Saxey of the Munster Presidency Court urged enforcement of a statute of 27 Elizabeth for the deportation of Jesuits and seminary priests. It was not on the Irish statute book.[38] Old English recusants came to specialise in these very legal niceties. Even when action was correctly taken, juries failed to indict, and would not do so even after fining and imprisonment. Mayors and civic officers used their charter privileges and other cunning legal ploys to avoid oaths of supremacy. As Elizabeth's reign wore on, more and more of them stayed away from civic religious services. Law, legal process and civic bodies were motors of Protestantisation in England. In Ireland they were frequently turned on their heads.

Legal ambiguity was just one element in the miasma of confusion and rumour that hung over Dublin Castle and its servants. Rumour could be spectacular – such as in 1603 when many Munster towns decided James was about to tolerate Catholicism. They ejected Protestant clergy and refused to admit the lord deputy. In 1614, distance from the centre allowed a recusant delegation to report, on return from London, that James had, again, conceded toleration. It was some time before Lord Deputy Chichester could repair the damage done to his own position.[39] More niggling errors abounded. Archbishop Laud confused the Council of Cashel (1172) with Castle Chamber (the Irish Star Chamber).[40] Bernard Adams was offered Kilfenora and Dromore together in 1605, which was the Irish geographical equivalent of being granted Ely along with Bath and Wells. Only eleven years after the first Irish convocation in 1615, nobody appeared to be sure

[38] Alan Ford, '"Firm Catholics" or "loyal subjects": religious and political allegiance in early seventeenth-century Ireland' in D. George Boyce, Robert Eccleshall and Vincent Geoghegan (eds.), *Political discourse in seventeenth and eighteenth century Ireland* (2001), pp. 1–31 quoting BL Add. MS 4756, fol. 63v; Pawlisch, *Sir John Davies*, pp. 107–8. For a brief discussion of the applicability of English statutes to Ireland, see J. H. Baker, 'United and knit to the imperial crown' in D. S. Greer and N. M. Dawson (eds.), *Mysteries and solutions in Irish legal history* (Dublin, 2001), pp. 51–72.
[39] John McCavitt, *Sir Arthur Chichester: lord deputy of Ireland, 1605–16* (Belfast, 1998), pp. 190–5.
[40] Laud to Bramhall, 1 October 1634, HA 15156.

whether their 101 articles had been licensed or approved by the king.[41] Much of this is trivial, the fruit of distance, bad record keeping and cursory research but, in a magisterial reformation which commanded almost no popular support, confusion and delay were deadly dangerous.

While the crown employed politic drifts with little in the way of sober persuasions, Catholicism just would not go away. William Prynne would argue that the sight of habited friars on Irish streets was proof of Wentworth's laxity and leanings. Had he visited Ireland at any time he would have learnt that they had never gone away. Donegal friary, a key Franciscan house, functioned up to 1607. By the end of Henry VIII's reign only 55 per cent of 140 monasteries and 40 per cent of about 200 mendicant houses had been suppressed. Chantries and guilds were never abolished. While some guilds, like St Anne's in Dublin, as Colm Lennon has shown, did go through a neutral 'mercantile investment club' phase, many of these surviving medieval institutions were ready to dock with the sodalities and dynamic lay pieties of imported Tridentine Catholicism.[42] Writing to Walsingham in June 1580, Marmaduke Midleton of Waterford and Lismore complained that 'the windows and walls of the churches [are] full of images. They will not deface them, and I dare not for fear of tumult.'[43] Official iconoclasm more or less began and ended in 1540–1 and focused on high-profile relics such as the *Bachall Ísu* in Christchurch and the image of Our Lady of Trim. The fabric remained intact in many parish churches for many years. As late as 1631, there were churches in the Dublin area which were in Catholic hands.[44] The dead began to declare allegiance as burials switched to ruined abbeys and friaries. The living openly pullulated about holy wells even on the very outskirts of Dublin, the royal capital. Others ostentatiously celebrated Easter according to the new Gregorian calendar.[45] In the heart of cities mass houses were opulently fitted out, barely discreet.[46] On St Stephen's Day 1629 a raid on a Carmelite house on Cook street ended with Lancelot Bulkeley, Church of Ireland archbishop of Dublin, and a

---

[41] James VI & I to Chichester, 4 October 1605, *Cal. SP Ire.* 1603–6, p. 331. See chapter 3 below.

[42] Colm Lennon, *Sixteenth-century Ireland: the incomplete conquest* (Dublin, 1994); 'The chantries in the Irish reformation: the case of St Anne's Guild, Dublin, 1550–1630' in R. V. Comerford, Mary Cullen, Jacqueline R. Hill and Colm Lennon (eds.), *Religion, conflict and coexistence in Ireland* (Dublin, 1990), pp. 6–25.

[43] W. Maziere Brady (ed.), *State papers concerning the Irish church in the time of Queen Elizabeth* (1868), p. 40.

[44] Myles Ronan (ed.), 'Archbishop Bulkeley's visitation of Dublin, 1630', *Archivium Hibernicum* 8 (1941), 56–98.

[45] Hiram Morgan, '"Faith & fatherland" in sixteenth-century Ireland', *History Ireland* 3:2 (1995), 13–20.

[46] Meehan (ed.), *Portrait of a pious bishop*, pp. 73–4.

detachment of musketeers fleeing for the safety of the castle under a hail of stones from furious worshippers. Four aldermen stood by and watched.[47]

Catholicism could never become 'old-time' religion in Ireland because it never went away, not even for a little. Timing played a large part in the sense that old late medieval ways persisted long enough to be transformed into new Tridentine ways. Yet the majority did more than 'keep the faith' – they created, over time, an equation of 'Ireland' and 'Catholic'.

Foxe's Book of Martyrs infused the blood of the saints into the veins of English Protestantism. The blood of Edmund Campion and Margaret Clitheroe was a sign of the seriousness of the state-sponsored ecclesiastical settlement. Public executions in Ireland, as Clodagh Tait has shown, were very often the outcome of treason legislation and turned what was supposed to be a salutary public spectacle on its head in an environment in which it was a minority hanging members of the religious majority.[48] Bishop Conor O'Devaney's 1612 martyrdom was amongst the last. Thousands turned out to watch his procession to the gallows and so to express their hostility to the government: 'and the Catholics despising the danger, cast themselves upon their knees to ask the bishop's blessing, which he gave them to satisfy their devotion and the blows and kicks of the heretics not sufficient to deter them'. They came not to mock but rather to be humble pilgrims and the authorities were powerless to stop the open rush for relics. The new martyr cults became a badge of orthodoxy for Catholics in Ireland and abroad.[49]

The gallows also became a venue for the display of sectarian sentiment. On 18 November 1581 the Baltinglass rebels approached the scaffold, reciting the Ave Maria. When approached by Thomas Jones, Church of Ireland minister, they shouted 'vade satana, vade satana, vade post me satana'.[50] Once choices had been made early in Elizabeth's reign, there were very few conversions either way as sectarian identity froze out religious choice. Irish Protestants were saturated with the apocalyptic anti-Catholicism of their English origins. At the same time, many Catholics in Ireland began to articulate an anti-Protestantism which insisted on these very same English origins. In their entry for 1537, Mícheál Ó Cléirigh and his associates noted: 'a heresy and new error sprang up in *England* through pride, vain-glory,

---

[47] P. F. Moran, *History of the Catholic archbishops of Dublin* (Dublin 1864), pp. 317–19; Brendan Jennings (ed.), *Wadding Papers 1614–38* (Dublin, 1953), pp. 331–2.

[48] Alan Ford, 'Martyrdom, history and memory in early modern Ireland' in Ian Mcbride (ed.), *History and memory in modern Ireland* (Cambridge, 2001), pp. 43–66; Clodagh Tait, 'Adored for saints: Catholic martyrdom in Ireland c.1560–1655', *Journal of Early Modern History* 5 (2001), 128–59.

[49] Tait, 'Adored', pp. 155–9.   [50] M. V. Ronan, *Irish martyrs of the penal laws* (1935), p. 50.

avarice and lust . . . so that the men of *England* went into opposition to the Pope and Rome [and] they also appointed bishops for themselves'.[51]

Most of those who went to see O'Devaney and his companion die were Old English descendants of the medieval colonists. They were defiantly recusant and frenziedly pious, yet the object of their devotion was a Gaelic Irish bishop. Less than a hundred years previously, in 1518, the Dublin provincial synod banned clergy from Connacht and Ulster – Gaelic Irish zones.[52] This shift at the very heart of the Pale, place of ancient English settlement in Ireland, was important. It pointed to a break with centuries of history.

The Old English, *Anglo-Hibernici*, ancient and loyal subjects of the crown, remained predominantly recusant. Much has been written about why this happened and why they drifted away from even church papistry at an early stage. The main arguments can be condensed as follows. Apart from lower clergy, most of the political community of the Englishry welcomed Henry's reforms. Over time, and as the new kingdom failed to get off the ground, Mary's then Elizabeth's government drifted towards coercion, confiscation, plantation and general conquest. All of these measures were not necessarily distasteful to the Old English as they had all been advocated by the English in Ireland since Richard II's failed settlement.[53] Conquest was expensive and much of the cost fell on the ancient subjects. At the same time a further class of subject – the New English – sprang into being. They treated the kingdom, it appeared, as their own particular booty. When the old interest blocked parliamentary subsidy, viceroys desperate for 'spectacular' fixes resorted to prerogative powers and cessed the landed Palesmen heavily. The Old English were compelled to defend their rights. In this way, English reformation administered by New English Protestants worked its particular alchemy by causing the ancient subjects to identify their ancient religion with their ancient liberties.

While the Old English prosecuted what Ciaran Brady has called a strategy of 'conservative subversion' through legal devices and appeals direct to the monarch, the history of sixteenth-century Ireland is not merely one of brinkmanship. Crown policy provoked rebellion from both Gaelic Irish and Old English lords and as soon as it was possible to do so, confessional

---

[51] O'Donovan (ed. and trans.), *Annála ríoghachta Éireann*, p. 1445; RIA MS 23 P7 fols. 54v–55r.

[52] *Red Book of Ossory*, fol. 15v. I am grateful to Gerald Bray for a copy of this text, which forms part of his project to publish convocation records covering Britain and Ireland from the Middle Ages to the nineteenth century, *Records of the Irish Councils, synods and convocations 1101–1704*, unpublished edn (Birmingham, AL, 2001), p. 155.

[53] Dorothy Johnston, 'The interim years: Richard II and Ireland, 1395–1399' in James Lydon (ed.), *England and Ireland in the later Middle Ages* (Dublin, 1981), pp. 175–95.

polemic was deployed as a weapon. When Silken Thomas Fitzgerald began his baronial revolt in 1534, he dispatched his chaplain to Rome with instructions to present him as a crusader against a heretical king.[54] In 1579, James Fitzmaurice Fitzgerald explained his insurrection was against a queen who had deprived herself: 'thus, then, we are not at war against the honourable and legitimate crown of England but against a she-tyrant who, by refusing to hear Christ in the person of his vicar and even by daring to subject the church of Christ to a woman in matters of faith, on which she has no right to pronounce has deservedly forfeited her royal authority'.[55] When James, second Viscount Baltinglass, took up arms shortly afterwards he asserted: 'he is no Christian man that [can] think and believe that a woman uncap of all holy orders should be supreme governor of Christ's church a thing Christ did not grant unto his own mother'.[56] Lord Grey's ferocious reaction to the Baltinglass revolt led to a shocking wave of arrests, executions and even confiscations within a Pale which had not turned out in support of the insurgents. By 1599, Hugh O'Neill was demanding complete restoration of Catholic church properties and that 'the Church of Ireland be wholly governed by the pope'. Robert Cecil scratched 'utopia' on his own copy of O'Neill's articles.[57] Fulminations against Elizabeth and the fantastical demands of her government may have had little currency beyond the immediate political situations that generated them, but they also contributed to a sense that not only was Catholicism visible but that it was also violently visible. Gradually a split emerged between those who advocated dual loyalty and hoped for tacit toleration with some guarantees or, in their wilder moments, official toleration and those who pushed for a more sweeping change. This position, usually urged by émigrés, consisted of handing Ireland over to the Spanish crown and was based on the union of Philip and Mary. The Catholic primate, Peter Lombard, first went for the Spanish option but gravitated to the other after the death of O'Neill and accession of James I.[58]

---

[54] Micheál Ó Siochrú, 'Foreign involvement in the revolt of Silken Thomas, 1534–5', *Proceedings of the Royal Irish Academy*, section C, 96 (1996), 49–66.

[55] M. V. Ronan, *The reformation in Ireland under Elizabeth 1558–1580* (1930), p. 620.

[56] James Eustace, Viscount Baltinglass, to Ormond, July 1580, PRO SP 63/74/64(i); Lambeth Palace Library MS 597, fo. 406; *Cal. Carew MSS*, 1575–88, no. 443.

[57] Morgan, '"Faith & fatherland"'; Hiram Morgan, 'Hugh O'Neill and the Nine Years War in Tudor Ireland', *HJ* 36 (1993), 21–37.

[58] Thomas O'Connor, 'A justification for foreign intervention in early modern Ireland: Peter Lombard's *Commentarius* (1600)' in Thomas O'Connor and Mary Ann Lyons (eds.), *Irish migrants in Europe after Kinsale* (Dublin 2003), pp. 14–31; John J. Silke, 'Later relations between Primate Peter Lombard and Hugh O'Neill', *Irish Theological Quarterly* 22 (1955), 15–30; 'Primate Lombard and James I', *Irish Theological Quarterly* 22 (1955), 124–50.

Lombard's changeover reflects a deeper movement. All the sixteenth-century rebels had different aims and all their revolts had different causes and none, of course, was just about religion. Yet one thing did become more manifest over time. They were concerned about the position of Catholics in Ireland – not just the Old English alone or Gaelic Irish alone – but all Catholics in all of Ireland. Catholic Ireland had arrived. Like Protestant England, it took time in the coming and it was never absolute but it had, nonetheless, arrived.

The Irish language was as instrumental in the birth of Catholic Ireland as conservative subversions and outright rebellions. Because Protestant reformers were generally hostile to the Gaelic vernacular and because the language collapsed so spectacularly in later centuries it has often been tempting to dismiss it or treat it as a spent force. No one denies that the vernacular was the star of the English reformation from Cranmer to the Authorised Version. Just as it triumphed in England, it was a damp squib in Ireland where Gaelic became the star of Catholic reform. Europe's oldest written vernacular was far from being an ebbing tide. It allowed completely new connections that helped guarantee that Ireland would remain Catholic.

There was a reactive quality to Catholic apologistics. Historians, annalists and genealogists sought to deny the equation of Catholicism with barbarity – itself a confessional twist on a long-established manner of writing about Ireland.[59] They unleashed a torrent of publications – in Latin for an international audience – and in Irish for the domestic and emigrant readers and hearers. They presented the country to themselves and to Catholic Europe as an island of saints and scholars and as an ancient, civilised and irreducibly Catholic kingdom. The 'four masters' structured their annals as a compendium of the history of the entire island as a single unit.[60] The secular priest Seathrun Céitinn offered his refutation of Giraldus as *Foras feasa ar Éirinn*, which translates as 'collection of wisdom about Ireland'. In order to make the case, they had to remake the language. Three neologisms stand out – *náisiun* (nation) used along with Catholic;

---

[59] Bernadette Cunningham, 'The culture and identity of Irish Franciscan historians at Louvain 1607–1650' in Ciaran Brady (ed.), *Ideology and the historians* (Dublin, 1991), pp. 11–30; Clare Carroll, *Circe's cup: cultural transformations in early modern writing about Ireland* (Cork, 2001), pp. 104–34; Brendan Jennings, *Michael O Cleirigh, chief of the Four Masters, and his associates* (Dublin, 1936); Colm Lennon, 'Taking sides: the emergence of Irish Catholic ideology' in Vincent Carey and Ute Lotz-Heumann (eds.), *Taking sides: colonial and confessional mentalités in early modern Ireland* (Dublin, 2003), pp. 78–93; Canice Mooney, 'Father John Colgan, OFM, his work, times and literary milieu' in Terence O'Donnell (ed.), *Father John Colgan OFM, 1592–1658* (Dublin, 1959), pp. 7–40; Richard Sharpe, *Medieval Irish saints' lives: an introduction to Vitae Sanctorum Hiberniae* (Oxford, 1991), ch. 2.

[60] In both the Annals and the *Genealogiae regum et sanctorum Hiberniae* completion dates were indicated by Mícheál Ó Cléirigh using the regnal years of Charles I.

creideamh agus athartha (faith and fatherland) and finally *Éireannaigh* (Irish)
to denote all of the inhabitants of the island regardless of their descent: an
Irish Catholic nation able to fuse Old English loyalism with the Gaelic passion for genealogy when James Stuart took the throne. Aodh MacAingil,
Lombard's successor in Armagh, extolled James as 'ar rí uasal óirdheirc' (our
noble illustrious king). He even went on to prove by convoluted casuistry
that James was not, in fact, a heretic at all. Gaelic poets alluded to the three
crowns in James VI & I's charter and supplied him with lavish genealogies.
So the kingdom of Ireland itself had arrived but in a Catholic guise and
with a Gaelic tongue. This deep engagement between Catholics and Stuarts
was destined to be amazingly enduring as recusant thinking came to settle
firmly on securing rights under this Scottish dynasty.[61]

The language was not exclusively kept for political theory and praise
poetry; it also bore directly on the competition for souls in the early modern
period. By turning their backs on Gaelic, Church of Ireland theologians
engaged with Catholicism exactly as if they had been in Cambridge, Oxford
or the king's Chelsea College.[62] The Dublin printing press churned out
apologetical and polemical pamphlets which were in every respect identical
to those printed across the Irish Sea. The Gaelic typeface at Louvain stamped
out Bonabhentura Ó hEoghusa's uncompromisingly counter-reformation
Teagasg Críosdaidhe (catechism); Flaithre Ó Maolconaire's *Desiderius* was
based on a popular Spanish text of the *devotio moderna* and Mac Aingil's
tract on confession *Scáthán Shacramuinte na Aithridhe* was based on the
teaching on the fourteenth session of the Council of Trent.[63] Apart from

---

[61] Brendan Bradshaw, 'Geoffrey Keating: apologist of Irish Ireland' in Brendan Bradshaw, Andrew
Hadfield and Willy Maley (eds.), *Representing Ireland: literature and the origins of conflict 1534–
1660* (Cambridge, 1993), pp. 166–90; Marc Caball, *Poets and poetry: continuity and reaction in Irish
poetry, 1558–1625* (Cork, 1998); 'Innovation and tradition: Irish Gaelic responses to early modern
conquest and colonization' in Hiram Morgan (ed.), *Political ideology in Ireland, 1541–1641* (Dublin,
1999), pp. 62–82; Bernadette Cunningham, *The world of Geoffrey Keating* (Dublin, 2000); Mícheál
Mac Craith, 'The Gaelic reaction to the Reformation' in Steven G. Ellis and Sarah Barber (eds.),
Conquest and union: fashioning a British state, 1485–1725 (1995), pp. 139–61; 'Creideamh agus athartha:
idéoloaíocht pholaitíochta agus aos léinn na Gaeilge i dthús an seachtú haois déag' in Máirín Ní
Dhonnchadha (ed.), *Nua-léamha: gnéithe de chultúr, stair agus polaitíocht na hÉireann, c1600–c1900*
(Baile Átha Cliath, 1996), pp. 7–19; Breandán Ó Buachalla, 'Annála Ríoghachta Éireann agus Foras
Feasa ar Éirinn: an comhtheacs comhaimseartha', *Studia Hibernica* 22–3 (1982–3), 59–105; *Aisling
ghéar: na Stíobhartaigh agus an t-aos léinn* (Baile Átha Cliath, 1996).

[62] Declan Gaffney, 'The practice of religious controversy in Dublin, 1600–1641' in W. J. Sheils and D.
Wood (eds.), *The churches, Ireland and the Irish*, Studies in Church History 25 (Oxford, 1989), pp.
145–58; Brian Jackson, 'The construction of argument: Henry Fitzsimon, John Rider and religious
controversy in Dublin, 1599–1614' in Ciaran Brady and Jane Ohlmeyer (eds.), *British interventions
in early modern Ireland* (2005), pp. 97–115; Anthony Milton, *Catholic and Reformed: the Roman and
Protestant churches in English Protestant thought, 1600–1640* (Cambridge, 1995), pp. 32–3.

[63] Old English Catholics also had access to the large English-language output of the Douai, Rouen
and St Omer presses.

Seaán Ó Cearnaigh and William Bedell's short and basic catechisms, the Church of Ireland had no indigenous pastoral publications.

Irish poetry also played its part in deploying sectarian invective and strengthening the resolve of the hearers. In these poems there is the same attitude encountered by Thomas Jones at the scaffold and by William Lyon, bishop of Cork and Ross, who lamented that his people called 'the divine service appointed by her majesty in the Church of England and Ireland the devil's service, and the professors thereof, devils'. Here is a verse from the late 1570s:[64]

> An chliar-sa anois tig anall
> Cliar dhall ar a ndeachaidh ceo,
> ní mó leo muire ná *dog*,
> dar by *God* ní rachaidh leo

> These clergymen who have come from the
> Other side – blind clergy enveloped in
> Fog, respect a dog more than Mary. And,
> By God, they shall not get away with it.

The same poet called on Ireland to resist Captain Luther and Captain Calvin through adherence to 'General' St Patrick and so to avoid becoming an inferior replica of England.[65] This is a very nice demonstration of bardic understanding of reformation impulses in Ireland. Those few Gaelic clerics who did conform, such as Maol Muire Mac Craith (or Miler McGrath), archbishop of Cashel from 1571 to 1622, invited particular spleen:

> You empty, befogged churchmen, you shall live in hell;
> Whilst Mary's clergy shall flourish fruitfully, high up in God's heaven
> Maol-without-Mary you are a fool. You journey not towards heaven.
> A Maol-without-Mass, a Maol-without-canonical hours is a
> Maol destined for hell with its savage pain

> An archbishop and his wife, and a suffragan of unclean
> Life, who breaks the fast and burns statues, shall have only bitter
> Fire for ever and ever

> Your woman-folk have ruined the people. Your titles have
> Been obtained by sorcery – so it has been whispered abroad,
> Obsequious clergy of colossal pretentiousness[66]

---

[64] Cuthbert Mhág Craith OFM, *Dán na mBráthar Mionúr*, 2 vols. (Dublin, 1967), Gaelic text of the poem by Eoghan Ó Dubthaigh, vol. I, pp. 127–50; English translation vol. II, pp. 58–67.

[65] Mhágh Craith, *Dán*, vol. I, p. 152. Aodh MacAingil accused Luther of having the devil as his father and teacher: Mhágh Craith, *Dán*, vol. I, p. 178.

[66] Mhágh Craith, *Dán*, vol. II, pp. 58–67.

Even allowing wives to the notoriously unchaste Gaelic clergy was not a sufficient draw to conformity, which is not surprising when this kind of bitter invective was the response. In a sense, too, the ambivalence with which the early stages of English reformation treated clerical wives probably lessened any potential appeal to Irish clergy.

The Church of Ireland was, from the very outset, blinded by the English experience, handcuffed to the claim inherent in its title and hobbled by its medieval inheritance. Almost everything that ultimately made state reform in England a success – the language, the old ecclesiastical structures, the law, the towns, the aristocracy and gentry, the lawyers, the habits of obedience – had the opposite effect in Ireland. In critical ways pressures caused by the extension of that reformation to the neighbouring island helped create a notion of Ireland that had not existed before: that Ireland was a Catholic kingdom and its inhabitants were Catholics and obedience to Rome was vital to its existence. That kingdom never did become Protestant. This book is about one attempt to alter that outcome.

CHAPTER 2

Raising up the Church of Ireland: John Bramhall and the beginnings of reconstruction, 1633–1635

THE TEMPORAL ESTATE OF THE CHURCH OF IRELAND UNDER JAMES I AND CHARLES I

There is little agreement about what actually happened at James VI & I's Hampton Court conference of January 1604. One thing is certain: the king used Ireland as a rallying cry. It was scary, it was irreligious, it made him but 'half a king' and it needed preachers.[1] By March of 1610, in the wake of the previous year's rebellion, James was telling the English parliament that a plantation was the only way to solve the great problem.[2] As it turned out, the Ulster plantation was the first great opportunity to radically revive the fortunes of the Church of Ireland. In these escheated counties the prospect of sweeping away the pre-reformation jumble and starting afresh presented itself. Endowing the church handsomely was to prepare it for serving the expected influx of Protestant settlers who themselves would act as leaven in the dough of the 'benighted' natives.

James had reached these conclusions largely because of a series of reports compiled by George Montgomery, then bishop of Derry, Clogher and Raphoe. This Scot, who, tellingly, retained his deanship of Norwich for most of his episcopate, saw Ulster as the chance to start afresh.[3] He envisaged a church firmly founded on a generous allotment of lands to a vigorous British episcopate whose prosperity would be assured by excision of all unassimilable Gaelic customs and structures.[4] In almost every respect the king followed his recommendations and, into the bargain, made Montgomery

---

[1] William Barlow, *Summe and substance of the conference . . . att Hampton Court* (1638 edn), p. 98.

[2] J. P. Sommerville (ed.), *King James VI and I: political writings* (Cambridge, 1994), pp. 196–7.

[3] Henry A. Jefferies, 'George Montgomery, first Protestant bishop of Derry' in Henry A. Jefferies and Ciarán Devlin (eds.), *History of the diocese of Derry from earliest times* (Dublin, 2000), pp. 140–66.

[4] The vast number of parishes and livings in each diocese represented a great problem for the Church of Ireland. Sporadic efforts were made to unite parishes and to do as Montgomery proposed. However, the most common solution was pluralism. For his proposals, see Shirley, pp. 25–38. See also Ford, *Protestant*, pp. 127–54 and Nicholas Canny, *Making Ireland British 1580–1650* (Oxford, 2001), pp. 167–205. Montgomery saw to it that the older parochial structure of rector, vicar and erenagh was collapsed

a plantation commissioner. Since his arrival in Ulster in 1606 he had been busy suing for recovery of temporalities and he put his knowledge of the terrain to excellent use. The church was allocated 74,852 acres or 16 per cent of all of the escheated land. Its handmaidens in the work of civility also did well – 2,645 acres for the county freeschools and 12,400 acres for Trinity College.[5]

But the Ulster plantation turned out to be no simple transfer of land – and the church suffered badly as a result of its defects. The confusion over place names and the inaccuracy of surveys left many of the glebe lands, generous as they were on paper, distant from the churches and on poorer upland soils.[6] The church had also been stripped of its cathedral land, much of which had been passed in patents as monastery land.[7] Lords deputy Chichester and St John bore the brunt of the king's annoyance and frequent outrage at the progress of the entire enterprise. As far as the church was concerned, his logic was simple. As engines of reformation, the bishops had been given much, and much was expected of them. News that these prelates were leasing without apparent regard to their successors and without apparent regard to their mission was greeted by him as the most egregious kind of disobedience. It was, of course, easy to chastise the episcopate as a way of letting off steam about the plantation as a whole, but their manifest failure to lead was a blemish on the king's own self-image as the Constantine of the British Isles.[8] The horde of Protestant settlers never materialised. Those planters who remained were forced to deal with the 'natives' and seek derogations from the original conditions in order to retain Gaelic Irish as farmers, small tenants and labourers. Planter interest became focused on survival, then on profit, and religious reformation was, at best, an aspiration.[9]

into a single incumbent. This, in turn, meant that the older families were swept away by newcomers so that by 1622 there was almost a complete change of personnel. See Henry Jefferies, 'Bishop George Montgomery's survey of the parishes of Derry diocese: a complete text from c. 1609', *Seanchas Ard Mhacha* 17 (1996–7), 44–76.

[5] Philip Robinson, *The plantation of Ulster: British settlement in an Irish Landscape 1600–1670* (Belfast, repr. 1994), pp. 69–71, 82–4, 195, 211. See also *Cal. SP Ire.* 1611–14, p. 205.

[6] *Cal. SP Ire.* 1611–14, p. 296. The 1622 visitation, TCD MS 550, gives many examples of inconvenient glebe lands.

[7] James I to Oliver St John, 24 September 1616, *Cal. SP Ire.* 1615–25, p. 138.

[8] For a typical outpouring, see James I to Chichester, 29 April 1612, *Cal. SP Ire.* 1611–14, p. 264. The bishops had no resources with which to develop their vast lands and, as the plantation progressed, middling undertakers either sold out or left, leaving a number of larger planters who sought to maximise the size of their holdings in order to wrest what profit they could out of the lands. Given this, it is understandable that many of them had no alternative but to let their lands go for derisory rents. For a useful discussion of these and associated problems, see Canny, *Making Ireland*, pp. 205–42.

[9] The literature on the Ulster plantation is vast; for a convenient introduction see Aidan Clarke, 'Pacification, plantation and the Catholic question, 1603–23' in *NHI* III, 187–231.

Despite all its shortcomings, Montgomery's plantation scheme had a persistent appeal for churchmen. Its seductive simplicity concealed a profound evangelical flaw in that he had only conceived of full Protestantisation when the entire structure of an existing church and society was overturned.[10] For the rest of his reign, James showed marked favour to the church but made no further move towards systematic overhaul and simply tried to improve the material condition of the church by orders, commissions and investigations. In 1611, following a report from Andrew Knox which restated the link between the plantation scheme and promotion of Protestantism, he issued orders enjoining residence upon bishops, annual diocesan visitations, re-edification of churches and the appointment of able ministers.[11] Later still, he tried to fix some of the smaller problems by ordering that parish bounds be established, and glebes clearly named and assigned to more convenient places.[12] Another batch of remedies was proposed in a list of Acts intended for the parliament of 1613–15.[13] All cathedral churches would be repaired or rebuilt. The possibility of unification for some bishoprics was to be investigated. An Act which anticipated two of those passed in the 1634 parliament was also featured – a limitation on leases made by churchmen in accordance with Elizabeth's English statutes, and a proviso for Ulster plantation bishops to make longer leases.[14] The parliament collapsed but it is likely that the records were dug out a decade later under Wentworth.[15] In the meantime the sole safeguard against destructive leasing remained a proclamation of 21 October 1609 which was more honoured in the breach than the observance.[16]

The regal visitation of 1615 aimed to ascertain the numbers of clergy, their competency and the condition of their churches. While it aimed to

---

[10] Ford, *Protestant*, chs. 4 and 6; *Cal. SP Ire. 1615–25*, pp. 235, 275 ff. Ussher hoped that tithes in any projected Connacht plantation would be settled as they had been in Ulster: Ussher to Laud, 22 September 1613, SP 63/252/2025; *Cal. SP Ire. 1611–14*, pp. 630–1.

[11] James I to Chichester, 26 April 1611, *Cal. SP Ire. 1611–14*, pp. 31–2. Knox's activities are discussed in Ford, *Protestant*, pp. 140–7.

[12] James I to Oliver St John, 24 September 1616, *Cal. SP Ire. 1615–25*, p. 138.

[13] J. S. Brewer and William Bullen (eds.), *Calendar of the Carew manuscripts preserved in the archiepiscopal library at Lambeth, 1515–1624*, 6 vols. (1867–73), vol. VI, pp. 154–7.

[14] See below, pp. 46–53, for the church statutes in the 1634 parliament.

[15] Victor Treadwell, 'The House of Lords in the Irish Parliament of 1613–1615', *English Historical Review* 80 (1965), 92–107; John McCavitt, 'An unspeakable parliamentary fracas: the Irish House of Commons, 1613', *Analecta Hibernica* 37 (1995–6), 223–35. A number of bills concerning church temporalities were introduced, *Commons' jn. Ire.*, pp. 14–17, 24–6, 33, 41–2, 49–50.

[16] This proclamation was reissued on 17 March 1617, Str P 20/141; 17 March 1621, TCD MS 580, fols. 27r–28r. Wentworth to Laud, 29 January 1634, Str P 6, p. 13, suggests using it to commence prosecution of the earl of Cork in Youghal.

provide the information necessary to implement change and improvement it was, without the intended legislation, a dead letter.[17]

Due to the manifest failure of the planters to comply with the conditions imposed on them, the paralysis of government in Ireland, and continuing financial woes of the kingdom, not to mention the apparent missionary failure of the church, a commission of inquiry into the state of Ireland was launched in 1622. For the church this meant a much more searching regal visitation.[18] Now impropriations came under serious scrutiny and the commissioners were empowered to remind impropriators to ensure that vicars received their due proportion (one-third) of the income of the living.

Unsurprisingly, the report of the commissioners highlighted the poverty of the clergy and the failure of impropriators to pay the vicars a decent stipend; once again it condemned the allotment of glebes in the plantation areas. It recommended challenging the titles of some of the impropriators and the extension of English laws on leasing to Ireland.[19] The outcome of the commission was the issue of 'Orders and Directions concerning the state of the Church of Ireland' of 1623.[20] Incumbents on the plantation lands were restricted to 21-year leases and of no more than 60 acres at a time. No patents of impropriation would be renewed or confirmed without a bond agreeing a competent salary for the curate. There were detailed instructions on the re-edification of churches and cathedrals, lands given for charitable uses and the vexed question of 'customary' tithes. Clergy were enjoined to use the Book of Common Prayer and the New Testament in Irish where appropriate and there was to be stricter supervision of those presented as masters in the freeschools.

These 'Orders and Directions' are noteworthy for two reasons. The first is that there is no evidence that they were much complied with. The second is that when taken with the legislative proposals they encompass most of the programme Wentworth and Bramhall were to embark upon just a decade later. The crucial difference lay in the tactics used. James made scores of orders for individual bishops: making grants, commanding special hearings, permitting some bishops longer leases, instigating special commissions for

[17] P. B. Phair, 'Visitations of the seventeenth century', *Analecta Hibernica* 28 (1978), 79–102; M. V. Ronan, 'The royal visitation of Dublin, 1615', *Archivium Hibernicum* 8 (1941), 1–55.

[18] There are two recent accounts of the work of the commission, Victor Treadwell, *Buckingham and Ireland, 1616–28* (Dublin, 1998), pp. 186–248 and Canny, *Making Ireland*, pp. 243–58. Victor Treadwell, 'The survey of Armagh and Tyrone, 1622', *Ulster Journal of Archaeology* 23 (1960), 126–37, has some remarks on the 1622 commission as a whole; TCD MS 806, fol. 119r ff., 'Remembrances to the Commissioners 1615 [*recte* 1622]'.

[19] TCD MS 808, fols. 41r–45r.   [20] BL Add. MS 4756, Marsh MS Z3.1.3 (30–8).

their lands and so on.[21] While such actions were helpful for some bishops in the short term, they had no lasting impact. The overall numbers and quality of the clergy went on growing in the first two decades of the century and the strain on a church rich in resources but much poorer in revenue grew and grew.[22] The result was more pluralism, more disadvantageous leasing and more unwise alienation. Unstinting as James had been in his plantation settlement, a bare three weeks before his death the bishops whose dioceses fell within the escheated counties petitioned him to complain that their clergy had been deprived of the greater part of their maintenance.[23]

Anxiety about the state of the church was not just the preserve of the bishops and of the government. Lay commentators emphasised the connection between money and ministry. Richard Hadsor's 1623 tract, *Advertisements for Ireland*, is a useful Old English counterpart to the reports of the 1622 commissioners and a record of the kind of impact the Church of Ireland's established status could make.[24] He complained of the excessive fines exacted by the Protestant clergy for marriages, burials and churchings (known as clandestines) performed by papist priests: 'this they perform very punctually and all this goes to their own private purse and nothing to the king's'. He condemned commissary officials who paid great rents to bishops for their positions and then vexed the country 'with their too frequent courts'.[25] From the erosion of endowments proceeded abuse of ecclesiastical jurisdiction in order to make up missing income. Discredit followed on dilapidation. Hadsor suggested that the reason why so many of the estates of the clergy had been 'dismembered' was because in the disturbances of the past decades 'most of their records, charters and evidences were . . . embezzled and lost'.[26] Overcoming this dearth of reliable information would later account for a chief part of Bramhall's early activities in Ireland. Overall, the tract shows that the church was most vulnerable to the shifting patterns of landholding in Ireland. Others might gain great estates, but the church was a consistent loser. As it became poorer, then its own clergy began to devour what was left themselves.

The 'Graces' of 1627 echoed many of the concerns of the *Advertisements*.[27] The excessive fees of the ecclesiastical courts and the fines levied on

---

[21] *Inter alia: Cal. SP Ire.* 1611–14, pp. 106, 130, 181, 248, 311, 315, 346, 478.   [22] Ford, *Protestant*, ch. 4.
[23] SP63/240/30; *Cal. SP Ire.* 1615–25, p. 568. Ussher to Laud, 2 August 1631, Bodl. Sancroft 18, p. 13.
[24] The authorship of the tract has been attributed to Hadsor by Victor Treadwell, 'Richard Hadsor and the authorship of "Advertisements for Ireland"', *IHS* 30 (1997), 305–53. For a modern edition see George O'Brien (ed.), *Advertisements for Ireland*, Royal Society of Antiquaries of Ireland, unnumbered volume (Dublin, 1923).
[25] O'Brien (ed.), *Advertisements*, pp. 16, 54.   [26] O'Brien (ed.), *Advertisements*, p. 53.
[27] A list of the 'Graces' will be found in Clarke, *Old English*, pp. 242–54.

'clandestine' marriages, burials and christenings were still a matter for concern. The encroachments of undertakers on Ulster glebe lands were adverted to once again. Redress was also sought for 'the bestowing of plurality of benefices upon unqualified persons, who are unable or unworthy ministers'.[28] The mixture of complaints in the 'Graces' shows that both Protestant and Catholic laity were dissatisfied with, respectively, the condition of the established church and the behaviour of its clergy.

In 1620, Thomas Ryves, former judge of faculties in the prerogative court of Ireland, had published *The poor vicar's plea*.[29] This was an attempt to redress the 'miserable plight our poor Church of Ireland stands [in] at present'.[30] There were historical reasons for this indigence – there had been more monasteries in Ireland so the creation of large numbers of lay impropriators was even more catastrophic than it had been in England. The bulk of the pamphlet is taken up with a closely argued disquisition on the rights of bishops to sue impropriators for a decent maintenance for the incumbent clerks. However, the main interest of the pamphlet lies not in this exhibition of legal knowledge but in the fact that Ryves specifically eschewed the use of royal prerogative as a remedy since sufficient legal mechanisms were in existence.[31] The *Plea* ends on a bleak note:

If this course be legal, and may be taken for the better maintenance of the poor clergy in this miserable kingdom, well and good. If not, God grant some other may; for if none be, farewell religion: and what can then ensue but the abomination of desolation in the highest places of this kingdom? Which God forbid.[32]

Here Ryves put his finger on a substantive point – legal strategies or even prerogative strategies were nothing without consistent application. There was no dearth of plans for Ireland; there was, instead, a dearth of successful application of them.

Shortly after becoming bishop of London, William Laud began to correspond with Ussher about Irish church matters. As he did elsewhere, Laud adopted the voice of king's representative in his dealings with Ussher.

---

[28] Clarke, *Old English*, p. 249. They also showed how patentees of dissolved monasteries and priories had claimed the monastic liberties from military cesses and other public charges yet, despite their increased profits, had withheld competent maintenance from vicars and curates. This was also a dodge of impropriators in England.

[29] Ryves had been judge of faculties in the prerogative court of Armagh. He resigned after a dispute with Archbishop Hampton of Armagh and Bishop Montgomery of Meath. Returning to London, he published *The poor vicar's plea*. According to Heylyn, Ryves informed Laud of the deplorable state of the Church of Ireland; see *Cyprianus Anglicus* (1668), p. 268. 'Ryves, Sir Thomas (d.1652)', *ODNB*, http://www.oxforddnb.com/view/article/24434, accessed 13 December 2005.

[30] *Poor vicar's plea*, sig. A3.   [31] *Poor vicar's plea*, sig. A4.   [32] *Poor vicar's plea*, p. 152.

The earlier letters are concerned with men rather than measures but very rapidly Ussher began to make suggestions for further reform, suggesting, for instance, that the king issue letters on the scandal of drunken ministers but very rapidly working up to episcopal revenues and ecclesiastical jurisdiction.[33] Laud's first concern was to garner accurate information on the state of the church.[34] He also began to propose modest guidelines for the Church of Ireland which were distinct from previous schemes. He suggested that deaneries should not be held as commendams and that young men (under forty) should not be candidates for bishoprics.[35] These restrictions were eminently applicable to the Church of Ireland, but they clearly sprang from Laud's own beliefs about the dignity of the church and clergy. Such a ban on deaneries *in commendam* is very striking given that the practice was still current in the far wealthier Church of England.[36] The hybrid produced by the joining of Laud's wider goals for the established churches of these islands and the remedies devised in Ireland for the Irish church itself was, as we shall see, highly important through the 1630s.

Ussher, for his part, was happy to cooperate with a patron who had influence at the highest levels in England. He relished the effect Laud's name had at the privy council in Ireland: 'you strike such a terror into the hearts of those who wish to despoil the church, that if I merely mention your name at the Council table it is like the Gorgon's head to some of them'.[37] Laud's interest in Ireland became known beyond castle circles, though, because in early 1633 he was petitioned by a Kilmore clergyman about a tithe dispute.

The chief project on which the two men laboured over these years was a scheme to have the royal impropriations restored to the church. To this end, they compiled valuations of the affected benefices and mulled over the best course to take. To add weight to their case, Ussher drew up a 'horror report' of the condition of the church in Co. Louth. They fought off attempts to cripple the scheme by interested parties in Ireland and England

---

[33] Laud to Ussher, 29 January 1629, *WL* 6, p. 258; Ussher to Laud, 6 May 1629, Bodl. Sancroft 18, p. 8; Ussher to Laud, 11 September 1629, SP 63/249/1485, *Cal. SP Ire.* 1625–32, pp. 481–3. For a general discussion of Laud's interest in the Irish church, see J. S. Morrill, 'A British patriarchy? Ecclesiastical imperialism under the early Stuarts' in A. Fletcher and P. Roberts (eds.), *Religion, culture and society in early modern Britain* (Cambridge, 1994), pp. 226–31.

[34] He requested a list from Ussher of 'the names and values of all the bishoprics and deaneries in Ireland, and what bishoprics are joined to others, that I may be better able to serve that church'. Laud to Ussher, 16 June 1632, *WL* 6, p. 262. The list is in *Cal. SP Ire.* 1625–32, pp. 481–3.

[35] For the age bar on appointments, see also chapter 4, p. 117 below.

[36] For example, Laud's rival, John Williams, had managed to hold on to Westminster in 1621 when elevated to Lincoln.

[37] Ussher to Laud, 11 July 1631, SP 63/252/1991, *Cal. SP Ire.* 1625–32, p. 622.

and secured the requisite letters from Charles.[38] Despite all this effort, the Irish council saw to it that the scheme was sunk through a combination of legal reservations and a proposition made for improvement of royal rents.[39] This outcome spoke volumes about a church whose control of its own holdings and, indeed, its autonomy had been subverted by the influence of powerful interests who continued to profit from those weaknesses.

This experience of cooperation and failure with Ussher taught Laud two lessons. The first was a recognition of the critical importance of the *method* by which solutions (of which there was no shortage) were applied to the Church of Ireland. In the midst of the impropriations campaign Ussher had become distracted by an argument similar to Thomas Ryves's for getting existing impropriators to meet their legal obligations.[40] This lack of single-minded commitment to a more comprehensive change convinced Laud that the primate was not the kind of ally he sought. The second lesson was that the ability of the Irish council to sink the scheme showed nothing could be done for the church until the influence of figures such as lord justice the earl of Cork, who had extracted most from its endowment, was curbed.

Any plans for the effective reconstruction of the Church of Ireland had to be carried out by independent agents in Ireland who enjoyed strong English support. Laud could provide that support. In Thomas Wentworth there was a viceroy who was committed to restoring the patrimony of the church and who was strong enough to subdue the ruling élite in Ireland. Wentworth would quickly ascertain which of the many schemes for the restoration of the church could be effective. In Wentworth's chaplain, John Bramhall, there was someone prepared to undertake the enormous labour of turning all these advantages into real gains for the church and clergy of Ireland.

JOHN BRAMHALL: AGENT OF RECONSTRUCTION

While Laud and Wentworth are chiefly remembered for their actions in the 1630s, John Bramhall's posthumous fame rests mainly on his exchanges

---

[38] Laud to Ussher, 23 February 1630, *WL* 6, p. 270 and 5 July 1630, *WL* 6, p. 272. Ussher to Laud, 5 April 1630, Bodl. Sancroft 18, p. 10; 17 April 1630, Bodl. Sancroft 18, p 11; 2 May 1630, Bodl. Sancroft 18, p. 13; 23 December 1631, SP 63/252/2054, *Cal. SP Ire.* 1625–32, p. 638; 24 March 1632, SP 63/253/2100, *Cal. SP Ire.* 1625–32, p. 653; 19 November 1632, Bodl. Sancroft 18, p. 14. Ussher to the lords justices, 3 April 1630, SP 63/250/1638, *Cal. SP Ire.* 1625–32, p. 527. List of churches in Co. Louth, 5 April 1630, SP 63/250/1642, *Cal. SP Ire.* 1625–32, p. 529.

[39] Ussher to Laud, 25 August 1630, Bodl. Sancroft 18, p. 12. Report on petition of the clergy of Ireland for the restoration of royal impropriations, 1635, Str P 6, p. 158.

[40] This was presented to Ussher by William Noy. In great excitement, the primate wrote to Laud that this was 'a matter of as great (if not greater) moment for the repairing of the wastes of this poor church as that we have in hand', Ussher to Laud, 2 August 1631, Bodl. Sancroft 18, p. 13.

with Thomas Hobbes during the 1650s. Bramhall's reputation as an Anglican 'father' of the *via media* was first established by Jeremy Taylor in his funeral sermon on 16 July 1663, elaborated by John Vesey in his *Athanasius Hibernicus* (1676), canonised in the nineteenth-century Library of Anglo-Catholic theology and later elegised by T. S. Eliot.[41] His early life and Irish career up to 1641 have, comparatively speaking, remained obscure. John Bramhall was born in Pontefract and baptised in St Giles's church on 18 November 1594.[42] He was the first of six children of Peter Bramhall, who died in 1635.[43] Bramhall was admitted to Sidney Sussex College, Cambridge, on 21 February 1609, took his BA in 1612, MA in 1616 and BD in 1623. His tutor there was Richard Howlett, whom he later preferred in Ireland, and the Master was Samuel Ward.[44] Bramhall later praised Ward, with whom he occasionally corresponded about college finances, for recommending the study of patristics and scholastic theology as key guides in resolving controversies.[45]

Archbishop Toby Matthew ordained him deacon in York minster on 24 December 1615 and priest on 22 December 1616. His first pastoral appointment was as assistant curate at St Martin's Micklegate in York, where he succeeded as rector in August 1617.[46] On 24 June 1618 he was presented to the rectory of South Kilvington, near Thirsk, by Christopher Wandesforde, and on 10 November he married Eleanor Collingwood (née Halley), the widow of his predecessor. It was probably the patronage of Wandesforde which brought Bramhall to the notice of Wentworth and included him as one of the Yorkshire mafia promoted by the future lord deputy.

In the decade before his move to Ireland his career proceeded smoothly. He was promoted to a prebend of Ripon in March 1623 and rose to be sub-dean about 1627.[47] In 1625 he became Master of the Hospital of St John the Baptist near Ripon.[48] When appointed to Derry in May 1634, Bramhall resigned all of these preferments.

---

[41] T. S. Eliot, *Selected essays* (1951), p. 361. See John Spurr, *The restoration Church of England, 1646–1689* (New Haven, 1991), ch. 3, for his apologetical works. John McCafferty, 'Bramhall, John (*bap.* 1594, *d.*1663)', *ODNB*, http://www.oxforddnb.com/view/3237, accessed 29 September 2005.

[42] J. B. Leslie, *Derry clergy and parishes* (Enniskillen, 1937), p. 309.

[43] W. Ball Wright, *A great Yorkshire divine of the 17th century* (York, 1899), p. 4.

[44] Howlett's first Irish preferment came in 1635 when he was presented by the king to the rectory of Aghalurgher in the diocese of Clogher, NAI MS 2/446/34, fol. 96r.

[45] *BW* III, pp. 567–8. Ward to Bramhall, 24 August 1635 and n.d. (*c.* 1636) – both in unsorted Hastings Irish papers (boxes 5–8), Huntington Library, California.

[46] Ball Wright, *A great Yorkshire divine*, pp. 6–7.   [47] Ball Wright, *A great Yorkshire divine*, p. 9.

[48] *Victoria County History*, Yorkshire III (1913, 1974), pp. 327–8. Bramhall to Laud 26 May 1634, HA 14043.

In July 1632, Bramhall, a member of the York High Commission since 1630, received his first royal preferment in the shape of the prebendary of Husthwaite in York cathedral.[49] A letter from Laud to Wentworth of 30 July 1632 is the first evidence of links between the three men: 'Now, my Lord, what do you or have you done about Dr Bramhall for the prebend? For my Lord of Durham [Moreton] is actually translated so out of it.'[50] While the connection between Bramhall and Wentworth was most likely Wandesforde, it is not clear how he came to Laud's attention. Vesey mentions almost casually that Bramhall stood 'in good esteem with Archbishop Neile – then lately in the beginning of 1632 removed from Winton to York'.[51] There is a fair possibility that Neile introduced the future bishop of Derry to the future archbishop of Canterbury.[52] Vesey also stresses that Bramhall did not make the decision to come to Ireland lightly, which accords with Bramhall's own comment that 'it was not my seeking'.[53] However, there is no confirmation of Vesey's further remark on his future English career: 'besides he was offered by some noble men to be made his majesty's chaplain in ordinary'.[54]

Bramhall's reputation as an able disputant and preacher rested mainly on an unlicensed public disputation with two Catholic priests at Northallerton in 1623. The debate covered well-trodden theological ground – transubstantiation, utraquism and the visibility of the church. John Vesey claimed that he drove his opponents to affirm 'that eating was drinking and drinking was eating in a material or bodily sense'.[55] Vesey was gilding the lily a little here because the phrase was, in fact, Bramhall's own.[56] In his own very brief account of the dispute he attributed his zeal to the Spanish match

---

[49] Le Neve, *Fasti ecclesiae anglicanae*, IV (York diocese), compiled by J. M. Horn and D. M. Smith (1975), p. 43.

[50] *WL* 6, 302. Andrew Foster in his unpublished Oxford D.Phil. thesis, 'A biography of Archbishop Richard Neile (1562–1640)' (1978), p. 238, suggests that Bramhall's appointment to this prebend was part of the initial reform of his administration.

[51] Vesey, *Athanasius Hibernicus*, [p. 7]. Vesey's biography is, in fact, unpaginated and there are no useful printer's marks. The page numbers used here were arrived at by counting the pages from the start of the biography proper and omitting the dedicatory matter.

[52] Another possibility is that contact was made through Harsnett's work on the 1629 Instructions; see Julian Davies, *The Caroline captivity of the church* (Oxford, 1992), p. 28. Neile and Bramhall had similar views on a variety of theological and liturgical issues, Andrew Foster, 'Neile, Richard (1562–1640)', *ODNB*, http://www.oxforddnb.com/view/article/19861, accessed 29 September 2005.

[53] HA 16064.

[54] Vesey, *Athanasius Hibernicus*, [p. 7]. There is, however, one ambiguous reference to Bramhall being known to Charles: 'The King will not admit of the stranger as long as he has choice of men known to him by services done; upon which ground only he took notice from you of the service done and expected from Dr Bramhall', Laud to Wentworth, 23 June 1634, *WL* 7, p. 79.

[55] Vesey, *Athanasius Hibernicus*, [p. 3].   [56] Bodl. MS Rawlinson D 320, fols. 33r.–45v.

controversy, when 'religion in England seemed to our country people (though without any ground) to be placed in *aequilibrio*'.[57] After some light rebuke by Toby Matthew, he was employed by the archbishop, who provided him with an opportunity to display his skills in ecclesiastical administration, which became one of the dominant concerns of his life.[58] In 1621, Bramhall preached before the northern synod on the subject of 'the Pope's unlawful usurpation of jurisdiction over the Britannic Churches'. He returned to this theme for his doctoral disputation: 'that the Papacy . . . was either the procreant or conservant cause, or both procreant and conservant cause of all the greater ecclesiastical controversies in the Christian world'.[59] There is little doubt that he would have continued to flourish in the Church of England, but Wentworth's appointment as viceroy ensured that he would be associated with the Church of Ireland for the rest of his life.

Most of Bramhall's subsequent Irish career will be traced below, so for the moment it is only necessary to give a rough outline. Arriving with Wentworth in July 1633, he became treasurer of Christchurch on 3 September.[60] Bramhall got straight down to business, appearing in deeds from December 1633 and February 1634.[61] On 1 October 1633 he succeeded by royal patent to the archdeaconry of Meath, where he later purchased his Irish estate.[62] Finally, by 24 May 1634 the upward curve was complete upon his appointment to Derry. Bramhall's consecration took place in the chapel of Dublin Castle on 24 May 1634 and was performed by Ussher, Anthony Martin of Meath, Echlin of Down and Connor and Richard Boyle of Cork.[63] Bramhall's early Irish career demonstrates two things. The first is a close association with Wentworth's pet project and his undoubted diligence. The second is the speed at which a hard-working and approved English clergyman could advance. Of the 'fast-track' clergy of the 1630s, Bramhall's progress was the fastest of all.

Despite his unquestioned influence in the Church of Ireland: 'The Earl of Strafford, then Lieutenant of Ireland, did commit much to my hands the political regimentation of that Church for the space of eight years', Bramhall never became privy councillor.[64] Early advancement was ruled out by Laud in June 1634, though he asked the lord deputy to remind him about it after

---

[57] *BW* III, p. 540. [58] Vesey, *Athanasius Hibernicus*, [pp. 3–4].

[59] *BW* III, p. 540. [60] NAI MS 2/446/13.

[61] NAI MS 12/448/13, 2647–69. Through this work Bramhall first encountered John Atherton.

[62] Ball Wright, *A great Yorkshire divine*, p. 11. This was the equivalent of a deanery since Meath had none. NAI 2/446/34, fols. 6v, 17r.

[63] Cotton, *Fasti*, vol. V, p. 254; NAI 2/446/34, fol. 45r; Bodl. MS Carte 67, fol. 9r.

[64] *BW* II, p. 124.

parliament was over.[65] Wentworth never did so. One reason may have been that it was more convenient to refer church matters from the council board to Bramhall rather than have him on it. This prevented the possibility of debate since the reports came back without discussion, to be adopted or rejected. It also helped to concentrate ecclesiastical affairs into the hands of Wentworth and Bramhall alone. The lord deputy's clear personal backing for the bishop meant that the added prestige of being a privy councillor was unnecessary.[66] On 17 June 1638 a new option appeared to open up with the disgrace of lord chancellor Loftus.[67] This time, Laud pressed: 'I hope you will take advantages to make my lord of Derry Chancellor in case things go right. My assistance you shall have in it in the utmost.'[68] Just a month later, though, Laud agreed with Wentworth that it was most politic not to recommend anyone for the present.[69] A spiritual lord treasurer in England and a spiritual lord chancellor in Ireland would have been further proof in many minds of the *hubris* of the revived clerical estate.

Bramhall was, throughout the 1630s, the chief negotiator, arbitrator and enforcer of the policy of restoring and guarding the temporalities of the established church. While Laud's correspondence with Ussher declined into generalities and peevishness, his letters to Bramhall were busy, detailed and precise. The bishop of Derry leased a house in Christchurch close and, when not travelling about on commission or visiting his diocese, he stayed close to the viceroy.[70] Laud brought influence, a pan-insular vision and royal approbation to their project.[71] Wentworth made it an essential part of his ambitious plans for himself and for Ireland. Bramhall brought endless diligence, a flair for invoking higher authority and extraordinary command of detail.

PLANNING THE RESUMPTION CAMPAIGN

Bramhall's biographers have tended to recount his work for the temporal estate of the church in a form not far removed from a fable. They begin with

---

[65] Laud to Wentworth, 23 June 1634, *WL* 7, p. 79: 'I cannot hold it fit so suddenly without any trial to make him of the council, but when Parliament is over, and that he has done some good service, I will move it, so you take it on you to put me in mind.'

[66] But it also made Bramhall vulnerable when Wentworth was dislodged in 1640.

[67] Laud to Wentworth, 17 June 1638, *WL* 7, p. 445.

[68] Rumours to this effect were circulating as early as November 1637: George Gerard to Wentworth, Knowler II, p. 130: 'I see your Bishop of Derry here Dr Bramhall, a very able man I hear he is, one told me he shall be Lord Chancellor of Ireland.' Thomas Jones, archbishop of Dublin, had been lord chancellor of Ireland from 1605 to 1619.

[69] Laud to Wentworth, 30 August 1638, *WL* 7, p. 469.

[70] M. J. McEnery and Raymond Refaussé (eds.), *Christ Church deeds* (Dublin, 2001), p. 313.

[71] See Kenneth Fincham, 'William Laud and the exercise of Caroline ecclesiastical patronage', *JEH* 51 (2000), 69–93.

the wicked dilapidations of the church, and move on to the heroic stage of Bramhall's activity and adventure, to the happy ending (ignoring 1641): 'many a poor vicar now eats of the trees the bishop of Derry planted'.[72] This happy post-Restoration fairytale makes him a hero but occludes the extent to which Irish church business was an important part of the wider policies of both Canterbury and Dublin Castle.

Letters written by Bramhall, Laud and Wentworth between August 1633 and March 1634 combine an analysis of the problems of the church with an ambitious determination to resolve all of its defects with little delay. There was, of course, an element of posture in such decisiveness, yet it is worth examining each of these letters in some detail since the concerns they exhibited were to inform the approach taken by the three men in the six years that followed.

Bramhall's letter, dated 10 August 1633, is a litany of disrepair and decay familiar from the complaints of churchmen and administrators under James: 'it is hard to say whether the churches be the more ruinous and sordid, or the people irreverent'. He then proceeded to a brief considera-tion of the orthodoxy of the clergy, but quickly passed on to the problems of pluralism and clerical indigence:

the inferior sort of ministers are below all degrees of contempt, in respect of their poverty and ignorance: the boundless heaping together of benefices by *commen-dams* and dispensations in the superiors is but too apparent; yea, even often by plain usurpation, and indirect compositions made between the patrons (as well ecclesiastic as lay), and the incumbents.

He rounded off his diagnosis by adding dryly: 'generally their residence is as little as their livings'. All staple stuff, yet the passing reference to 'orthodoxy' struck a new note. Here was an equivalence being made between order, decency and conformity, not for recusants but for the clergy of the established church itself. Furthermore, the perceived cause of such shoddiness was not moral, nor was it even financial, but because power relations were not right: 'and it is a main prejudice to His Majesty's service and a hindrance to the right establishment of this Church, that the clergy have in a manner no dependence upon the Lord Deputy, nor he any means left to prefer those that are deserving amongst them'.[73]

---

[72] Jeremy Taylor in his *Funeral Sermon*, *BW* I, p. lxi. Bramhall's biographers have been Vesey, *Athanasius Hibernicus*; Ball Wright, *A great Yorkshire divine*; W. E. Collins, 'John Bramhall, 1594–1663' in W. E. Collins (ed.), *Typical English churchmen from Parker to Maurice* (1902), pp. 81–119; W. J. Sparrow Simpson, *John Bramhall* (1927). His apologetics are examined in H. R. McAdoo, *John Bramhall and Anglicanism: 1663–1963* (Dublin 1964).

[73] Bramhall to Laud, 10 August 1633, *BW* I, pp. lxxix–lxxxii, SP 63/254/54.

This concern to create a new network of patronage was central to Wentworth's administration and the church was to be one of the principal means of doing so. It was typical of the more pragmatic and anglocentric concerns of Bramhall that the conventional concern with clerical residence as a means of disseminating 'piety and civility' did not feature in his early letters.[74] While neither his descriptions nor his proposed remedies were particularly new or insightful, what is striking is his confidence that the process of reformation had been restarted and that it would continue unhindered. Such assured prediction of efficacious reform ahead was an important shift in tone from the more querulous and beleaguered writings of the past twenty years. Bramhall trotted out the plan of action without any hesitation, culminating in a remark which epitomised the new approach – that the lord deputy intended 'to settle as much as in present is possible the whole state of the church'.[75]

Wentworth's letter was written a few months later, on 31 January 1634. It began, in contrast to Bramhall, with an allusion to the grand scheme of bringing Ireland to 'civility': 'the reducing of this kingdom to a conformity in religion with the Church of England, is no doubt deeply set in His Majesty's pious and prudent heart'.[76] However, Wentworth immediately qualified this by adding: 'But to attempt it before the decays of the material churches be repaired, an able clergy provided, that so there might be wherewith to receive, instruct and keep the people, were, as a man going to warfare without ammunition or arms.'[77] For Wentworth, the restoration of the temporal estate of the church as the first step towards the eventual goal of a Protestant Ireland was paramount. This is not to say that every step he took in relation to the Church of Ireland was in pursuit of this particular grail. For instance, his suspension of various penal proceedings, including clandestines, was undeniably part of his wooing of the Old English in the months before parliament.[78] Nonetheless his belief in reconstruction allowed him to argue that even a temporising restraint on the jurisdiction

---

[74] But it can be seen later on, Bramhall to Laud, 23 February 1638, Shirley, p. 53.

[75] Bramhall to Laud, 10 August 1633, *BW* I, p. lxxxii.

[76] Wentworth to Laud, 31 January 1634, Knowler I, p. 187. In his *Caroline captivity of the church*, p. 38, Julian Davies interprets this phrase as meaning conformity of the Church of Ireland to the Church of England. However, the context of the letter makes it clear that he is referring to the Catholics. For Wentworth's preparations for his deputyship, see Nicholas Canny, 'The attempted anglicisation of Ireland in the seventeenth century: an exemplar of "British History"' in J. F. Merritt (ed.), *The political world of Thomas Wentworth, earl of Strafford, 1621–1641* (Cambridge, 1996), pp. 157–86, especially pp. 182–4. For the extent to which he was a 'programmatic' viceroy, see Ciaran Brady, 'England's defence and Ireland's reform: the dilemma of the Irish viceroys, 1541–1641' in Brendan Bradshaw and John Morrill (eds.), *The British Problem, c. 1534–1707* (1996), pp. 89–117.

[77] Knowler I, p. 187.   [78] Wentworth to the judges of assize, 21 August 1634, Knowler I, p. 293.

of the established church fitted the larger plan. Wentworth took no refuge in protests about the obduracy of the natives because, in his view, it all boiled down to a simple matter of obedience from every subject: 'It being therefore most certain that this to be wished for reformation must first work from ourselves, I am bold to transmit over to your grace these few propositions.'[79]

The lord deputy's litany was similar to the bishop's: the clergy were unlearned, non-resident, their glebes and houses despoiled and ruined, too much church land was in lay hands, bishops were busy alienating what was left to their families and associates, ecclesiastical jurisdiction was discredited, crown patronages had been usurped and the potential for the taxation of livings was damaged by the lack of proper records.[80] Wentworth knew exactly how to win Laud's approbation: 'The Crown did not only lose what belonged unto it, but the church a protection and safety, which ever follows it, where her interest, and the interest of the crown are thus woven together.'[81] His remedy was simple – irregularities must be dealt with by the application of English norms and standards imposed by a series of commissions which would attend to every aspect of church business and organisation. Every resource and device of government would be utilised in order to achieve the desired end. There was to be no doubt that the era of underhand deals was closed.[82] Such sentiments did not mean that he would support the church to the exclusion of all other considerations. Wentworth saw no aspect of government in isolation, he explained that while his aim was 'to bring the people there to a conformity of religion', it might be possible 'in the way to all these, [to] raise perhaps a good revenue to the Crown'.[83] In a letter to Laud of 29 January 1634, he had spelled out his understanding of the links between church and crown even more clearly: 'it is almost never seen that the church and crown suffer alone but by secret consent of parties, betwixt God's portion and the portion of God's anointed, they mutually prosper and decrease together'. For him, any erosion of the rights or diminution of the means of either the crown or church precluded all possibility of the people of Ireland being led out of their 'prophaneness and barbarism'.[84] Naturally this rhetoric did appeal

---

[79] Wentworth to Laud, 31 January 1633, Knowler I, p. 187.   [80] Knowler I, p. 188.

[81] *Ibid*. The lord deputy's account also took in the failure of the educational system as an instrument of reformation, occasioned by the stripping of freeschool lands and weak government in Trinity College.

[82] Wentworth to Laud, December 1633, Str P 6, p. 4: 'The church was . . . dearer and carried more prerogative with me than any one person whatsoever.'

[83] Wentworth to Laud, 31 January 1634, Knowler I, p. 188.

[84] Wentworth to Laud, 29 January 1634, Str P 6, p. 13.

to Laud, but it is also true to say that the church had been incorporated into Wentworth's overall political vision of a fiscally independent Dublin Castle governing an obedient, anglicised and prosperous kingdom.[85]

Laud's response came in a letter of 11 March 1634. He accepted Wentworth's contention that the material welfare of the church demanded immediate attention but qualified it: 'I would set upon the repair of the material and spiritual church together.' Laud added recommendations for the orderly celebration of divine service and a ceiling on pluralism. 'If these two were settled', he wrote, 'the rest would follow in order.'[86] Expressions of 'decency' and 'order' found ready sympathy with Wentworth. He took steps to see that some reformation of the liturgy was set in train. This was easily incorporated into his belief, which echoed that of King James, that religious reformation was a prerequisite for the truly effective government of Ireland: 'Undoubtedly, till we be brought all under one form of divine service, the Crown is never safe on this side.'[87]

Taken together this early correspondence spelt out a plan which combined the old and new. The old bit was almost a century old – Ireland was to be reformed in order to spread the Protestant gospel and to secure the English crown. Repair of the clerical estate would allow it to act as an effective servant of the crown with which it was in a near hypostatic union. This too was an old idea, but with a new spin, because this resumption would not just be at the expense of a handful of Gaelic lords. Simultaneously, in a completely new initiative, the Church of Ireland would be conformed as closely to a particular Laudian version of the Church of England as possible.

One specifically religious concern was manifest in this blend of statecraft and high ecclesiastical politics. Speaking in the opening stages of his campaign to reduce the earl of Cork, Wentworth declared: 'for my own part I held it one of the crying sins of this nation that men had laid sacrilegious hands upon the patrimony of the church'.[88] By the 1630s there was a fairly sizeable literature on sacrilege, partly because the misappropriation

---

[85] Terence Ranger, 'The career of Richard Boyle, 1st earl of Cork, in Ireland 1588–1643', unpublished D.Phil. thesis, University of Oxford (1959), pp. 290–3, expresses a similar view and demonstrates how Wentworth wove many existing demands for reform and recovery into his unified plan.

[86] Laud to Wentworth, 11 March 1634, *WL* 6, pp. 352–8. In his concern to prove his thesis of 'Carolinism', Julian Davies overlooks this part of the letter, *Caroline captivity*, p. 38. See also J. Sears McGee, 'William Laud and the outward face of religion' in R. L. DeMolen (ed.), *Leaders of the Reformation* (1984), pp. 318–44 especially pp. 332–4, for a handy summary of Laud's views on temporalities and the material well-being of the clergy.

[87] Wentworth to Coke, 28 November 1636, Knowler II, p. 39. See also BL Add MS 34, 253 for Ussher's testimony that Wentworth had said to him: 'that the crown of England could not be well secured in that kingdom without reducing them to conformity in religion to the Church of England'.

[88] Wentworth to Laud, December 1633, Str P 6, p. 4.

of church revenues was connected with the debate on whether tithes were due *iure divino*. Along with this went a growing belief that there was a curse on 'sacrilegious' landowners based on an argument that impropriations had been wrongly acquired by the monks and ought to have been returned to pastoral use at the time of the dissolution.[89] John Selden in his *History of tithes* endorsed the view that appropriated tithes could not be enjoyed by laymen in good conscience.[90] Sir Henry Spelman marshalled scriptural, moral and historical arguments to excoriate those laity who diverted tithes to their own use. In the posthumously published *History of sacrilege* he furnished an extensive catalogue of attendant ill fortune.[91] Edward Brouncker, in his *Curse of sacrilege*, thundered against landowners who believed they were sanctioned by statute: 'O, let no man hood-winke himself with a conceit of the infallibility of a state met in parliament . . . especially when fear and covetousness are the Speakers, as they usually were in Henry the 8th his parliaments.'[92]

Wentworth took up this trope of ill fortune when he condemned Boyle's lease of Lismore lands:

it is no more for the most part then a building up and finishing of the rotten sacrilegious foundation, set by Sir Walter Raleigh who first laid his unhallowed hands upon those church possessions . . . yet I cannot cho[o]se, but in this first period of the case, [to] observe the judgement which fell upon Sir Walter Raleigh.[93]

Spelman's reminders of the purposes for which churches had been endowed in *De non temerandis ecclesiis* found an echo in Laud's cynicism about Boyle's projected restoration of the cathedral church of Lismore: 'none so fit to build a new one by repentance, as he that pulled down the old by sacrilege'.[94] The language of sacrilege and profanation peppers the correspondence of the three, and Bramhall further applied it to his great bugbears, the Scots.[95] These expressions served to give the campaign an

---

[89] Keith Thomas, *Religion and the decline of magic* (1973), pp. 112–21, attributes it partly to Catholic influence. Ian Atherton, 'Viscount Scudamore's "Laudianism": the religious practices of the 1st Viscount Scudamore', *HJ* 34 (1991), 567–96.

[90] John Selden, *The history of tithes* (1618), pp. 471, 486.

[91] His sole Irish reference was lord deputy Leonard Gray who presided over the passage of the Act of Suppression for Ireland. Gray had been beheaded. Wentworth's zeal for the church did not preserve him from the same fate. Henry Spelman, *De non temerandis ecclesiis* (1616), *Larger treatise concerning tithes* (1647) and *The history and fate of sacrilege* (1698).

[92] B. E., *Curse of sacrilege* (Oxford, 1630), p. 20.

[93] Wentworth to Laud, 29 January 1634, Str P 6, p. 10.

[94] *De non temerandis*, pp. 43–4. Laud to Wentworth, 14 May 1634, WL 6, p. 375.

[95] Bramhall to Laud, 7 August 1639, Shirley, p. 71. See also Henry Leslie, *A full confutation of the covenant* (1639). This anxiety about the fate of church lands in non-episcopal churches was shared by others in the 1630s; see Anthony Milton, *Catholic and Reformed: the Roman and Protestant churches in English Protestant thought, 1600–1640* (Cambridge, 1995), pp. 500–2.

enhanced moral tone, further equating the work of the state and the work of God.[96]

The 1622 commissioners had reported that of the 2,492 parishes in Ireland, there were 1,289 impropriate churches. This comes to just over 50 per cent. There are varying figures for the levels of impropriations in England in the range of 3,227–3,849 out of around 8,880 parishes, which gives a range of about 36–43 per cent.[97] Alan Ford gives the Irish figure at about 60 per cent for 1615 and 51 per cent for 1622, and points to levels of 62 per cent for the Dublin province and up to 80 per cent in Tuam.[98] A brief comparison of the 1622 and 1634 visitations for the Armagh province indicates a slight fall in impropriations between the two visitations, but a concomitant rise in pluralism.[99]

Conditions in the provinces of Canterbury and York were themselves variable.[100] It is true to say that Bramhall, in his early letters, like Ussher before him, verged on titillating Laud's sense of shock and outrage with details of the dire condition of Irish bishoprics. As far as Canterbury and Derry were concerned, raising the value of benefices had a highly practical purpose alongside its function in the grand plan for the Irish kingdom. This was, very simply, to attract a well-qualified and motivated clergy from England. By leaving, as they did so strikingly, the prevalence of recusancy in Ireland to one side and by focusing on the overwhelming legal similarities, the Church of Ireland appeared as a very dilapidated version of the Church of England.[101] A programme to remedy these defects was, as we know, actively pursued in England in the 1630s. Similar solutions were tried out in Ireland but, because the options for implementation of these solutions

---

[96] The rhetoric of sacrilege appears to have considerable currency. It is to be found in petitions to the privy council, such as one made by Francis Hill, a rector in Leighlin in July 1634, BL Harl. 4297 (77). The dean of Leighlin from 1638 to 1644, and later Benedictine, Hugh Cressy, used the bad fortune of 'sacrilegious' landowners as an example of where the English reformation had gone wrong in his *Exomologesis* (Paris, 1647), pp. 16–23.

[97] Christopher Hill, *Economic problems of the church, from Archbishop Whitgift to the Long Parliament* (Oxford, 1956), pp. 144–5.

[98] The lower rate for 1622 is explained by the addition of the Ulster plantation dioceses to the visitation records, which were initially relatively free of impropriations. Ford, *Protestant*, p. 68.

[99] 1622 visitation in TCD MS 550 and 1634 in TCD MS 1067. See the tables on numbers of clergy, impropriations and the condition of church fabrics in Ford, *Protestant*, pp. 81–9, 113–15.

[100] Laud's account of his province for 1638 says that the bishop of Bangor had drawn his attention to two matters: 'The one concerns his bishopric, where everything is let for lives by his predecessors to the very mill that grinds his corn. The other concerns the diocese in general, where, by reason of the poverty of the place, all clergymen of hope and worth seek preferment elsewhere.' WL 5, p. 359. This could have been anywhere in Ireland.

[101] The view that in church temporal matters Ireland was like England, only worse, is shared by Hugh Trevor Roper in *Archbishop Laud*, 3rd edn (1988), p. 238 and Hill, *Economic problems*, pp. 334–5.

were somewhat different, what took place in the Church of Ireland in the 1630s was truly distinct. Distinct, but apparently familiar, and so enough to cause glee in some quarters and dismay in others.

MAKING EXAMPLES, 1633–4

Laud's repeated exhortations to Bramhall to keep Wentworth in mind 'of the great business of impropriations' sprang not so much from any anxiety that he would neglect the affairs of the church but rather from the speed and zeal with which he attended to it. Bramhall informed Laud in February 1634: 'For the restoring of the impropriations, yet not alienated from the Crown, my Lord *de facto* confers them daily upon the church but I doubt nothing can be done *de iure* until there be several acts of parliament for that purpose.'[102] From the very start the two prelates were concerned about the legality and permanence of any settlement.[103]

Ussher praised the incoming viceroy as 'a new Zerubbabel raised by God for the making up of the ruins of this decayed church' and he lost no time in procuring a commission of inquiry for the lands of his bishopric.[104] However, in those letters to Laud which date from the months after Wentworth's arrival, he makes no mention of the scheme to restore royal impropriations to the church.[105] The fact that at this point Ussher was not abreast with the latest developments, while Bramhall, Wentworth's domestic chaplain, was, indicates that whereas relations in these early months were polite they were not intimate. When Wentworth finally conferred with Ussher it was to insist on imposing the Thirty-Nine articles.[106]

Wentworth reassured Laud about the durability of the impropriations settlement while insisting on the usefulness of existing powers: 'precepts will not work the reformation, examples must'.[107] Information on the actual state of the Church of Ireland was making an impression because, in response to Laud's call for a ceiling on the number of benefices held by

---

[102] Bramhall to Laud, 19 February 1634, HA 15154. See also Wentworth to Laud, December 1633, Knowler I, 172.

[103] Laud to Bramhall, 16 August 1633, HA 15153; 11 March 1634, HA 15155; 1 October 1634, HA 15156.

[104] Ussher to Laud, 12 February 1634, *UWW* XV, p. 574; Ussher to Laud, ?late 1633/early 1634, *UWW* XV, p. 571; for the commission see *Cal. SP Ire.* 1633–47, p. 10.

[105] The last mention of it by Ussher was in the April before, and he merely expressed his hope that *Laud* would be able to do something for the Irish church when he was promoted to Canterbury. Ussher to Laud, 26 April 1633, SP 63/254/23: *Cal. SP Ire.* 1633–47, p. 8.

[106] Chapter 3, pp. 73–84.

[107] So 'as neither [the clergy] themselves, nor any other shall have it in their power to hurt the churches thereafter'. Wentworth to Laud, 7 March 1634, Str P 6, p. 29.

each clergyman, he pointed out that the poverty of some livings was so acute that even six together would not keep a minister in clothes.[108]

Scarcity of accurate records is the bane of all revenue raising. Bramhall complained of the omission of about 300 livings out of the book for the taxation for first fruits and twentieth parts.[109] The *Valor beneficiorum ecclesiasticorum Hibernia* published in 1741 contains no taxation figures of a later date than 5 Charles I (1629/30), with some assessments stretching as far back as 1537/8.[110] The obvious response in 1633–4 was a regal visitation. To achieve this, and as a first step towards a prosecution against Boyle, Bramhall was sent off with William Hilton, judge of the prerogative court, on the regal visitation of Munster.[111] His mission was not only to inform himself of the state of the clergy and church there, especially in Lismore and the College of Youghal, but also to work at persuading the bishops of Cork and Waterford to join in the complaint against their cousin the earl. Bramhall's other task was to compile an accurate list of royal impropriations for practical use in Ireland and for tactical use by Laud in England. By February 1635, he was able to send Laud the 'return concerning the impropriations and the true state of them which with a great deal of labour I discovered and reduced into form'.[112]

The articles drawn up for the visitation explicitly mentioned the deficiencies of previous inquiries and broadcast the state's determination that the church should not be deprived of its property.[113] Half of the eight articles dealt with revenues and incumbents. The very first article raised the hare of usurpations while popish schoolmasters were second to last, coming

---

[108] Wentworth to Laud, 12 April 1634, Str P 6, p. 44. To another proposal that benefices under £6 might be exempted from subsidies as in England, Wentworth again responded by putting him in mind of the lower values and suggested that exemptions be fixed at a lower rate.

[109] Bramhall to Laud, 10 August 1633, SP 63/254/54. An undated list of untaxed livings 'presented unto' since 1630, consisting of 201 benefices with a note that Kilfenora and Clonmacnoise were also untaxed, is probably a copy of notes compiled in the wake of this visitation. See Marsh MS Z3.2.6 (92).

[110] *Valor beneficiorum ecclesiasticorum Hibernia* (Dublin, 1741). Cashel's figures dated back to 1537/8 as did figures for Ferns, Ossory and Waterford. Dublin's were from 1538/9 followed by Meath's for 1539/40. Emly's were from 1583 and the Ardagh, Leighlin and Tuam figures were from 1585/6. Cork, Cloyne, Lismore and Ross were recorded from 1588–91. The north followed in 1618: Armagh, Clogher, Down, Connor, Derry, Raphoe, Kilmore and Dromore. During 1629/30, the following dioceses were completed: Limerick, Killaloe, Elphin, Clonfert, Achonry and Kilmacduagh. Kildare had been assessed 'tempore Regis Hen. VIII' and Ardfert 'incerto tempore'.

[111] Wentworth to Laud, 7 March 1634, Str P 6, p. 30; Phair, 'Visitations of the seventeenth century', 84.

[112] Bramhall to Laud, 21 August 1634, HA 14040; 13 February 1635, HA 14048.

[113] *Cal. SP Ire.* 1633–47, pp. 90–1, SP 63/254/190; Str P 20/154. Wentworth proposed the visitation in his letter to Laud of 31 January 1633, Knowler I, p. 187.

only before an invitation to add any other relevant details. The sixth article, on ecclesiastical jurisdiction, was the most detailed and requested a full account, probably to ensure that embarrassed bishops made a true return. Laud had Thomas Ryves and John Lambe cast their eyes over the articles. Ryves's opinion shows some irritation at a direction different to the one he had suggested. Nonetheless there was a touch of prescience in his wariness at blurring distinctions between crown and church: 'to put the bishops to inquire into laymen's estates, would draw an excess of hatred upon them'.[114]

The extent to which the 1634 visitation was a harbinger of a new phase in church affairs can be seen by contrasting it with a report on the state of the kingdom sent to Wentworth by the lords justices in July 1632. They pronounced that they had 'principally taken the state of the church into consideration' and painted the usual grim picture of ruinous churches, diversion of funds, lack of clergy and popish schoolmasters.[115] They clearly hoped their antidote of a commission with power to call in the 'principal inhabitants of every parish' would prove attractive to Wentworth. Measures would be taken for repairs and to ensure that every church was furnished 'with a Bible, a Book of Common Prayer, a communion table and all other decent ornaments fit and needful for that church, and (in those churches where the inhabitants are most of them Irish) for furnishing them with the New Testament as it is translated and published by authority in the Irish tongue'.[116] They further proposed chastising negligent impropriators, insistence on the Prayer Book, suppression of recusant schoolmasters and better scrutiny of parish officers. A committee of the privy council would monitor progress.[117] In fairness, this was a comprehensive programme but it utterly ducked the land question.

By contrast, the new Irish administration made church lands the headline. Directions for the liturgy were not mediated through a commission but put directly to the bishops through Ussher, and proceeded from Laud's prompting.[118] Schoolmasters slid down the list and no standing committee was established. Wentworth himself would oversee church reform and, through Bramhall, work directly on the bishops.

---

[114] SP 63/254/90–1, also printed in Shirley, pp. 38–40.
[115] Lords justices and council to Wentworth, 7 July 1632, Str P 1, fols. 47r–49v.
[116] This part of the proposal resembles a condensed version of English canons 80–2 of 1603. De facto use of the 1603 canons as a standard in Ireland is discussed in chapter 3 below. Archbishop Daniel published his Irish New Testament in 1602.
[117] Of the eight proposed members of this committee, only one was a bishop, Lancelot Bulkeley of Dublin.
[118] Wentworth to Laud, 12 April 1634, Str P 6, p. 44.

Wentworth and the 1632 report did agree over repair of fabric:

Commissions for repair of churches are issued over the whole kingdom and all the life shall be given to it that possibly I can; and yet it may be that some hot-headed prelate may think there is no good intent to religion . . . I must answer them, that his brainsick zeal would mark a goodly reformation, to force a conformity to religion, whereas yet there is hardly to be found a church to receive, or an able minister to teach the people.[119]

There is good reason for giving this quotation *in extenso* because it needs to be understood at a variety of levels. Wentworth's allusion to forced conformity was a clear reference to the struggle he had been engaged with before his arrival in Ireland with the administration of the lords justices concerning the imposition of the 12d recusancy fine. His opponents (supported by a good number of the bishops) had argued that the imposition of the fine was not only a godly act but would also cover current financial exigencies without any need for the subsidies he was proposing.[120] So, making the material church a priority had immediate political resonance and effect as a central part of Wentworth's initial drive to establish himself in Dublin Castle. By connecting his church policy with his goal of parliamentary subsidies, he also encouraged a perception of his diverse aims as one seamless garment.

There were other reasons why Wentworth anticipated clerical resistance to a scheme for the re-edification of churches. It is likely that the commission took a similar form to those established by a proclamation of 11 October 1629 for England. In that case, the new commissioners effectively bypassed presentment by churchwardens as the instrument of detection.[121] This, in turn, would have upset the delicate balances established between clergy and laity with regard to the disposal and leasing of ecclesiastical properties. Local churchwardens (some of whom may have been beneficiaries of those property arrangements) were less likely to present impropriators for the derelict state of churches than commissioners appointed from Dublin, who were under pressure to be accountable. William Bedell levied £1,000 in Co. Cavan for the repair of churches.[122] He did, however, have to take local feeling into account and he joined in a petition with the gentry of the county protesting against a new contribution for

---

[119] Wentworth to Laud, December 1633, Knowler I, p. 172.

[120] See Clarke, *Old English*, chs. 4–5, and Ford, *Protestant*, ch. 9.

[121] *By the King: a proclamation for preventing the decays of churches and chapels for the time to come* (1629).

[122] Bedell to Ward, 2 February 1634, *Tanner letters*, p. 107. A list of these churches and the amounts levied on them is to be found in Str P 20/117.

the army and seeking a return to recusancy fines as a means of raising the revenue.[123] As a result of this action, Bedell found himself almost immediately out of favour with the new administration and was in repeated collision with Wentworth, Laud and Bramhall over the ensuing years. Local loyalties and conditions were at no more of a premium under Wentworth and Bramhall in Ireland than under Laud in England.

It is difficult to gauge what kind of overall effect the commission may have had, but given the large sum mentioned by Bedell and what is known of Neile's active policies in York, there is no doubt that it was prosecuted from the centre with the promised vigour.[124]

Even before parliament was called, Wentworth was keen 'to trounce a bishop or two' for infringement of the 1609 Act of State.[125] Opportunities for making salutary examples were in abundance. In December 1633, the privy council considered a lease of lands in Killaloe for sixty years made by a previous bishop 'reserving about the hundredth part of the yearly value in rent to his successors'. It was a tricky case since the tenant who now held the lease pleaded that he was no way acquainted with the original 'fraud'. Wentworth was wary of the precedents admitting such pleas might create. He resolved the dilemma by ordering an investigation into the lease and the profits enjoyed by the tenant in which he made it abundantly clear that he did not believe it was reasonable that any lay person should profit so handsomely from church lands.[126] He then ordered an accompanying commission of inquiry into the value of the lands and laid down guidelines for a favourable rent to the bishop on a lease of twenty-one years. Nonetheless, as he explained to Laud, what worried him most was that the bishop would simply abuse any recoveries to turn in a quick profit. He soon got wind of the fact that the bishop, Lewis Jones, who was in Dublin for the

---

[123] See Knowler I, p. 150. See also Clarke, *Old English*, for the 'humiliatingly short shrift' given to a series of such petitions. Bedell tried to comfort himself with the thought that he had helped to moderate the tone of the Cavan petition, and that their representatives, unlike others, had not been imprisoned. James Ussher was himself a supporter of the recusancy fines: Ussher to Laud, 26 April 1633, SP 63/254/22.

[124] Andrew Foster, 'Church policies of the 1630s' in Richard Cust and Ann Hughes (eds.), *Conflict in early Stuart England* (1989), p. 202. A number of cases concerning church repairs came to the council board: BL Harleian 4297, pp. 1–101.

[125] Wentworth to Laud, December 1633, Knowler I, 173. For a similar sentiment from Laud, see his letter to Wentworth of 15 April 1634, *WL* 7, p. 71.

[126] Wentworth to Laud, December 1633, Knowler I, p. 171: 'if upon the return, it appeared he had not been fully satisfied for the money laid out, it should be recompensed to him forth of the premises, if the profits answered him his money, then the bishop should have the land'. The investigation followed on a royal commission requested by the bishop himself to examine all of the see's temporalities: Charles I to lords justices of Ireland, March 1633, SP 63/254/12; Wentworth to Coke, 8 November 1633, Knowler I, p. 151.

hearing, had compounded secretly with Sir Daniel O'Brien for lands worth £500 a year for a rent of £26 per annum. He was livid: 'I got notice of it, sent to the bishop, told him roundly he had betrayed the bishopric; that he deserved to have his rochet (setting the dignity of his calling aside) pulled over his ears.' The effect of this incident was to make Wentworth swear to Laud that he would hedge all his judgements in favour of bishops with strict conditions.[127]

This case has an added interest since it is one of the rare occasions on which Bramhall left a relatively detailed account of his proceedings.[128] Arriving in Killaloe, Bramhall was less than impressed by the squalid state of the bishop's seat but immediately set about his task, which was to act as a devil's advocate 'to clear Sir Daniel O'Brien's title'. He rapidly set about interviewing the oldest clergy and 'the most intelligent laity', and finally found a key witness with whom he dealt through an interpreter. Not surprisingly, he found that witnesses and records testified 'point-blank against Sir Daniel'. He confronted the bishop directly with accusations of an oath taken for secrecy, and obtained a promise of good behaviour in the future. Characteristically, he pressed home his advantage by reclaiming an impropriate rectory to make up a commendam for the archbishop of Tuam under the terms of an agreement made in February 1634.[129] It was this combination of assurance, diligence and thoroughness which made Bramhall so effective an agent. The letter from Killaloe was written on St Patrick's day and the case was in train by 15 May.[130] Therefore, within six months, a secret deal made between a bishop and a landowner had been exposed, rebuked, investigated and annulled. Such swiftness and publicity served to show clergy and laity alike what was on the agenda for the church.[131]

Recent abuses were not the only focus of attention. In June 1632, Robert Dawson of Clonfert wrote a long letter to Laud in which 'he did much bemoan himself and the state of his poor bishopric'.[132] The letter

---

[127] Wentworth to Laud, 7 March 1634, Str P 6, p. 28. Furious at the attempted sleight of hand, he also stipulated that the money would be employed 'either for building of the bishop a good house, or some other pious work, for this beast deserves it not'. He had to endure a second verbal barrage from Bramhall a few months later: Bramhall to Wentworth, 17 March 1634, HA 14042.

[128] Bramhall to Wentworth, 17 March 1634, HA 14042.

[129] McEnery and Refaussé (eds.), *Christ Church deeds*, p. 313. He also surveyed the diocese, discovering a high level of impropriations, and recommended that many parishes were fit for union, thereby laying the foundation for future action. He also rebuked those clergy who had recusant wives.

[130] Wentworth to Laud, 15 May 1634, Str P 6, p. 57.

[131] Other bishops, such as Archibald Adair of Killala, requested privy council involvement to recover see lands: Charles I to lord deputy of Ireland, 13 October 1633, Knowler I, pp. 122–3.

[132] Dawson's letter to Laud, 18 June 1632, SP 63/253/2137, *Cal. SP Ire.* 1625–32, p. 668. Kenneth Nicholls, 'The episcopal rents of Clonfert and Kilmacduagh', *Analecta Hibernica* 26 (1970), pp. 130–57. Laud's comment in his letter to Wentworth of 13 January 1634, *WL* 7, p. 58.

complained of the low rents of his lands and the hostility of clergy and laity, which he attributed to a plot to root the English out of the area by destroying the church. Above all he pleaded that the abbey of Clonfert or Portu Puro be restored to the see.[133] Henry VIII had united the abbey to the bishopric but later on Sir John King had sued successfully for it in the Connacht presidency court and it was lost to the see.[134] Yet a little over two years after the bishop's plea to Laud, the Irish privy council had cut through all the previous litigation, ordered the restoration of the abbey, and laid out future rental arrangements.[135] The signal here was that recovery of the rights of the church would not just be prompt but there would be no hesitation about going back a century or more to find in its favour.[136]

Bramhall very quickly established his position as chief business agent for the Church of Ireland. Writing to Laud in December 1634, he gave an account of his activities since he had been made bishop of Derry in August.[137] Here was an impressive opening series of bargains and agreements about impropriations with a Mr Stawton (in Ardfert), Sir Robert King in Connacht, the earl of Ormond and the countess of Tyrconnell and Lord Cromwell in Down. Four months earlier he informed Laud: 'I am also in a treaty with the greatest farmer of the king's impropriations – £400 a year very easily rented and the lease sixteen years in being. He demands six years value but I suppose would take five.'[138] The identity of the greatest of impropriators remains a mystery, though the most likely candidates are Ormond and Clanricard. The latter, according to Wentworth, had 'engrossed as many parsonages and vicarages as he has mortgaged for £4,000 and £80 rent'.[139] It was a mark of the support Wentworth enjoyed at this

[133] For a close analysis of this letter, see Ford, *Protestant*, pp. 113, 122–3, and J. C. Erck, *Ecclesiastical register* (1830), pp. 244–6, for the full story of Portu Puro.

[134] Brendan Bradshaw, *The dissolution of the religious orders in Ireland under Henry VIII* (Cambridge, 1974), pp. 197–205.

[135] Wentworth to Laud, 23 August 1634, Knowler I, p. 300; BL Harl. MS 4297, pp. 25–6. The king's letter to Wentworth making the regrant specifically drew attention to the way in which dearth of proper records had been used to usurp church property, 24 September 1634, Knowler I, p. 302.

[136] Laud to Wentworth, 20 October 1634, WL 6, p. 400; Wentworth to Laud, 9 December 1634, Str P 6, p. 120. Wentworth remarked that the bishop was so poor that he was hardly able to afford a rochet. In addition, when the warrant and letters were finally issued in the winter of 1634, administrative fees were waived both in Dublin and London. Wentworth satisfied himself with the thought that both the exchequer and the church had benefited from the case and that 'this matter shall I trust for ever peaceably rest in the bosom of the church'. Clearly encouraged by this success, Dawson went on to lodge a further petition for recovery of lands in August 1634, BL Harl. 4297, p. 66. Nonetheless, he was still experiencing revenue problems in 1638 and 1639; see Nicholls, 'The episcopal rentals', pp. 131–3, and 'Petition of Dr Robert Dawson', Shirley, pp. 69–70.

[137] Bramhall to Laud, 20 December 1634, Shirley, pp. 41–5.

[138] Bramhall to Laud, 21 August 1634, HA 14040.

[139] Wentworth to Laud, 23 August 1634, Knowler I, p. 299.

point and in this matter that Laud could write back to report that he had shown that part of his letter to Charles 'who bids you to be sure your ground is good, and then spare none'.[140] Wherever a weakness in a title could be ferreted out, it would be exploited to the full. The lord deputy was turning the culture of 'discovery' against those who had profited so much from it.

The first year of the new viceroyalty set the scene for what was to come. Through his personal direction of a number of highly public church cases and in insistence on his own style of church management, Wentworth had made it starkly obvious that revivifying the clerical estate was a key concern of his government. In the same period, the prominence of Bramhall's labours and his promotion to Derry established him as Wentworth's prime agent.[141] Yet declaration of intent was not enough and measures were afoot to prosecute the recovery of the church even more effectively.

MAKING STATUTES, 1634–5

Mr Stawton of Clonfert made his composition with Bramhall on the basis of 'the act that is now passing for the purpose'.[142] As the 1634–5 parliament progressed and the shape of the intended legislation could be discerned, landowners were positioning themselves to extract the best advantage from the new state of affairs. Since it appeared that the commission for defective titles and the drive for the church would put pressure on those whose lands or leases had anything less than the securest of foundations, there was an advantage in approaching Bramhall, the lord deputy, or the local bishop and negotiating now, protesting devotion all the while, rather than waiting to be at the receiving end of a petition or complaint.

Statutory provision, especially when combined with executive action, was bound to make the incidence of 'voluntary' submission higher. On 15 July, both houses were assured that only the temporal estate of the church would be touched on in the current parliament. Whatever doubts there might be about some of the lord deputy's other remarks, making adequate legislation in this area fitted well with overall strategy. Wentworth wished to buy his government freedom of action and assisting the established church did so in two satisfying ways. Firstly, turning landed resources into real revenue promised to break down clerical poverty and its unpopular offshoot of punitive revenue raising, such as clandestines, and grant to the

---

[140] Laud to Wentworth, 20 October 1634, *WL* 6, p. 398.
[141] Wentworth pointed out that Bramhall's elevation would make him a useful agent in the House of Lords for the church programme: Wentworth to Laud, 23 April 1634, Str P 6, p. 48.
[142] Bramhall to Laud, 20 December 1634, Shirley, p. 42.

church a real and unfaltering supply. Secondly, a more affluent and grateful clergy would provide a better subsidy revenue for the crown. Parliamentary confirmation of their vote of eight double tenths (4s in the £) was prefaced with a fawning address of gratitude and explicit references to the state's recent pains to repair their collective fortune.[143]

Temporalities featured in the first and second sessions only to the extent that they were mentioned in the 'Graces'. When all the manoeuvring was over, article 35 on pluralities was left to the care of the bishops, article 41 on impropriations was to be legislated for and article 39 on undertaker encroachments on glebe lands was the sole grace to drop completely out of sight. Seven bills concerning church revenues are referred to in the journals. Three of these – on parochial boundaries, on 'misemployment' of lands and goods for charitable uses and against 'unreasonable customs of tithings, mortuaries and other obventions' – did not pass into law. A letter from Ussher to Bramhall, in October 1634, suggesting changes to one of the four bills that did pass and thanking him for a glance at the draft indicates that, while not a member of the privy council, the bishop of Derry was heavily involved in framing the statutes and may well have been the main author.[144] Years later Bramhall summarised the overall intent of this legislation as being to: 'tie their (the clergy's) hands from alienation of anything, but [to] enlarge them and give them a capacity . . . to receive the bounty of devout Christians'.[145]

Towards the end of the second session of parliament in November 1634, Wentworth indicated that he would have the draft church bills ready for transmission within the week.[146] The bills on parochial boundaries and misemployments of charitable uses were introduced in February and spluttered out in committee stages by early March. Their loss was a minor setback because the statutory pillars of reconstruction were all complete by dissolution on 18 April 1635.

As bishop of Derry, Bramhall recognised the need for special arrangements for the Ulster plantation lands. The Act 'for the confirmation of leases made by the Lord Primate and other bishops in Ulster' permitted Armagh, Derry, Raphoe, Clogher and Kilmore to make leases of up to sixty years for a single five-year period. This was deemed a sufficient term to get these bishoprics fully settled and a suitable prompt to bishops and tenants

---

[143] 10 Charles I, sess. 3. c. 23: 'that as no church under heaven did ever stand more in need, so none did ever find more royal and munificent patrons and protectors than the poor Church of Ireland'.

[144] Ussher to Bramhall, 23 October 1634, HA 15949.

[145] Bramhall to Laud, 22 January 1638, Shirley, p. 6.

[146] Wentworth to Laud, 19 November 1634, Str P 6, p. 102.

alike to come to arrangements.[147] In addition, the Act confirmed the grants of termon and erenagh lands which James I had settled on the bishops out of his royal bounty. The Act also served as the ecclesiastical counterpart to the general Act for securing plantation estates.[148]

When the drafts were considered at the English privy council, Laud was not at all impressed with the sixty-year clause.[149] But letters had crossed and Laud had missed Bramhall's explanation of plantation patents held by bishops whose lands came within the six escheated counties. All the lands of Derry were in lease for fifty-nine years and 'these tenants will never surrender or improve their rents for a term of twenty-one years'. Should the act for sixty years not be passed it would 'leave the poor bishops in a miserable labyrinth of troubles and suits'.[150] This was the kind of language which appealed to Laud, who wanted to ensure that the Irish church, now it had the opportunity, would be freed from some of the legal shackles which he found so chafing in the Church of England. Wentworth offered similar arguments and was even able to hold out an equally enticing carrot in the shape of estimates of possible improvements: 'if you do pass this law, I dare say you shall improve the Primacy of Armagh £1,500 by year, the bishopric of Derry £700 by year and the rest of the bishoprics in Ulster *pro rata*'.[151] When all the correspondence had finally caught up, Laud was able to assure Wentworth that at the meeting of the Irish Committee on 14 March he would press the Act for Ulster with all his might.[152]

---

[147] Ussher who urged modifications that bishops should have sole discretion to make these leases without having to refer to the dean and chapter: Ussher to Bramhall, 23 October 1634, HA 15949.

[148] The Act for Ulster bishops is 10 Charles I, sess. 3, c. 5. The other was 'An Act for Securing of the Estates of Undertakers, Servitors, Natives and Others & c'. 10 Charles I, sess. 3, c. 2. There had been a brief discussion of the status of these lands in the 1613–15 parliament, *Commons' jn. Ire.*, pp. 49–50. Termon lands were those church lands held by laymen in a hereditary capacity as erenaghs. This arrangement, which resembled impropriation (though with greater rights for the erenaghs) was a relic of the structure of the Irish church before the eleventh- and twelfth-century reforms introduced a diocesan structure. See Katherine Simms, 'Frontiers in the Irish church – regional and cultural' in T. Barry, R. Frame and K. Simms (eds.), *Colony and frontier in medieval Ireland* (Woodbridge, 1995), pp. 177–200; Henry A. Jefferies, 'Erenaghs in pre-plantation Ulster: an early seventeenth-century account', *Archivium Hibernicum* 53 (1999), 16–19, 'Erenaghs and termonlands: another early seventeenth-century account', *Seanchas Ard Mhacha* 19 (2002), 55–8. Ussher himself was interested in this subject and wrote *Of the original and first institution of Corbes, Herenaches and Termon lands*, UWW XI, pp. 419–46.

[149] Laud to Bramhall, 16 January 1634, HA 15157.

[150] We do not have the letters which changed Laud's mind, but Bramhall restated his position in his next letter to the archbishop on 18 February 1635, HA 14048.

[151] Wentworth to Laud, 19 February 1634, Str P 6, pp. 132–3.

[152] Laud to Wentworth, 4 March 1634, WL 6, p. 414. Laud confessed to having entertained the thought that perhaps Bramhall was out to feather his own nest. As it happened, the delay caused over this alteration nearly ended in the failure of the bill to pass at all. If a letter had not arrived extending the third session for a month at the very time the bill was in passage, it would have to have been

The arguments used by Bramhall and Wentworth to justify their proposal show that behind so much of their brittle rhetoric lay an acknowledgement of practicalities. Although Wentworth waxed lyrical about the Act, 'it is the best that has been done for them since they were bishoprics', it was little more than a concession to plantation exigencies.[153]

The Act for the bishops in Ulster passed through parliament on a single day, 21 March, as 'the Protestants obediently and unconditionally helped to defeat the relentless opposition of the Old English'.[154] Two other church bills, the long-desired Act 'to Enable Restitution of Impropriations and Tithes and other Rights Ecclesiastical to the Clergy' and an Act 'for the Preservation of the Inheritance, Rights and Profits of Land Belonging to the Church and Persons Ecclesiastical', first introduced on 24 February and 2 March respectively, had much bumpier passages through the Commons but both scraped in just before the close of the fourth session.[155] The Lords' journal notes laconically, though not surprisingly, that the bill for impropriations was put to the vote after a long debate.[156]

The Act 'for the Maintenance and Execution of Pious Uses' experienced some drift in the Lords after a speedy run through the Commons but then passed on 21 March. This Act allowed archbishops and bishops to be compelled by trial at chancery or petition to the council board 'to execute trusts and uses of conveyances to them for lawful and charitable uses'.[157] While this statute aimed to restrict the kind of damage bishops could do to the church, it also reflected the desire to build up an orderly civic

---

abandoned: Wentworth to Laud, 13 April 1635, Str P 6, p. 162. One alteration made to the Act in Whitehall did stick. The clause which required the consent of deans and chapters had already been taken out at Ussher's suggestion, yet the bishops would still require the consent 'of the Lord Deputy and six of the Council'. Laud was not impressed. Consequently, the final version of the Act reads 'with the consent and approbation of the Lord Deputy or other chief governors of this kingdom for the time being', 10 Charles I sess. 3, c. 5.

[153] Wentworth to Laud, 13 April 1635, Str P 6, p. 162.

[154] Clarke in *NHI* III, p. 251. For the politics of this parliament, see Kearney, *Strafford*, ch. 5, and Clarke, *Old English*, ch. 5.

[155] 10 & 11 Charles I, c. 2 and 10 & 11 Charles I, c. 3. Both became tangled up with the rejected gunpowder bill which was provided for by Act of State: Wentworth to Coke, 19 May 1635, Str P 9, fol. 30; Clarke, *NHI* III, p. 251; Kearney, *Strafford*, p. 65.

[156] *Lords' jn. Ire.*, pp. 69–70.

[157] 10 Charles I, sess. 3, c. 1. An undated but contemporaneous petition of Sir Maurice Williams, the state physician, gives some idea of the situation: 'there are in this kingdom many hospitals and lazar houses or leper houses, which by the charity of former times have been well endowed yet of late sundry persons have invaded the same', BL Sloane MS 2681, p. 268. There had been some talk, too, of setting up a commission to inquire into how money for charitable uses had been bestowed: Laud to Wentworth, 13 January 1634, *WL* 7, p. 58; Laud to Wentworth, 12 January 1634, *WL* 7, p. 108; Wentworth to Laud, 12 April 1634, Str P 6, p. 45; Laud to Wentworth, 11 March 1634, *WL* 6, p. 355.

society found in the Acts against 'profane swearing', against the abduction of heiresses, usury, bigamy and buggery.

The 'Act for the Preservation of the Inheritance' essentially formalised, without need for commissions and investigations, the sort of action that the lord deputy had taken in the case of Killaloe. The Act made all leases, alienations and other demises of church lands made by ecclesiastical persons void as from 1 June 1634. From that point only 21-year leases would be permitted.[158] In order to prevent the total rapine of the past, there was a qualification that dwelling houses in use for the past forty years and their demesnes could not be demised. In addition, there should be no other lease in being at the time of the making of these new leases, unless it would expire within the year. To prevent the undervaluation so notorious in Ireland, where the excuse of 'late wars and rebellions' was frequently used, values would be determined by four or more 'honest, equal or indifferent persons' on a commission under the great seal or by a common law jury. It was possible to procure a licence, under certain circumstances, to make leases between twenty-one and sixty years, but only by permission of the lord deputy and council. Finally, rents were to be paid to the lessors and their successors and could not be aliened to anyone else.[159]

At a stroke, this Act sought to bring to an end over a hundred years of reckless and disadvantageous leases on the part of Irish bishops. The stringency of the clauses was as much to make bishops incapable of denuding their sees as it was to force tenants to come to reasonable terms. The commission for valuation and the licence gave the state a continuing supervisory role with the option of intervening if deemed necessary. Since all other forms of lease were now illegal, as each old one fell in, tenants were now constrained to enter a uniform system in which the lessor had certain basic protections and re-entry fines and realistic increases were guaranteed every two decades. In most respects, this was the long-awaited formal application of various English Elizabethan Acts to Ireland by repeating the little-heeded Irish Act of State of 1609 in statutory form.[160] But Bramhall went one step further by adding the commission or jury which could now strike at the heart of the system of undervaluation and not just tinker with the outward accidents. There was another crucial divergence. The English Acts permitted twenty-one

---

[158] Ecclesiastical dignitaries and governors of colleges and hospitals were permitted to grant 'ancient offices' with the pensions or grants that had been accustomed.

[159] The very last clause of the act reserved the right of James Ussher to make leases according to his previous letters patent.

[160] 1 Eliz. I c. 19 (Eng); 13 Eliz. I c. 10 (Eng); 18 Eliz. I c. 11 (Eng). For a discussion of the Act of State by Ussher, see Ussher to Laud, 26 April 1633, SP 63/254/22. Irish canon 24, 'Of the ordering of the revenues of ecclesiastical persons', is a highly condensed version of the main points of this statute.

years or three lives, but the Irish twenty-one years only. As Felicity Heal
has shown, Laud favoured the fixed-term leases as opposed to the uncer-
tainties of three lives.[161] So, the Church of Ireland was not simply being
brought into line with English legislation but also with what happened to
be Canterbury's preferred option.

The Act to enable restitution of impropriations and tithes had no direct
counterpart in English law, though it might be understood as an expression, in statute form, of the kind of restitutions being made by Viscount
Scudamore and others.[162] The preamble explained the purpose of the Act
as being 'for the due maintenance for such as shall teach and instruct the
people in the worship of God, and the better to enable them to keep hos-
pitality and relieve the poor', but was silent on specifically Irish conditions.
The core provision of the statute allowed lay owners by deed or by will to
restore appropriations to the church, that is, dissolve them, without need-
ing licence to alien in mortmain. The revenues would then be for the sole
use of the incumbent.[163] The former owners retained rights of presentation
based on the extent to which the new conveyance made up the endowment
of the minister.[164]

Various other provisions designed to improve the conditions of the
church at parish level were tacked on to the Act. The sixth section addressed
the very widespread problem of the multiplicity of small and poor livings.
Bishops were permitted to unite rectories and vicarages where the one parish
had been endowed with both.[165] The seventh section imposed a minimum
requirement of eighty days' residence for validity of leases and charges made
by the incumbent upon the benefice and decreed that new clergy could not
be encumbered with the leases or charges of their predecessors.[166] The

---

[161] Felicity Heal, 'Archbishop Laud revisited' in Rosemary O'Day and Felicity Heal (eds.), *Princes and paupers in the English church, 1500–1800* (Leicester, 1981), pp. 129–52.

[162] See White Kennett, *Impropriations* (1704), appendix xii; Atherton, 'Viscount Scudamore's "Laud-ianism"', pp. 567–96. Richard Bancroft unsuccessfully attempted to secure this kind of legislation between 1604 and 1610; see Kenneth Fincham, *Prelate as pastor: the episcopate of James I* (Oxford, 1990), pp. 139–40.

[163] If there was no incumbent, which was quite likely in many of these benefices, the bishop would hold the revenues in trust until one was presented.

[164] Laud was initially nervous about the draft bill: 'it may give a great blow to some of your bishoprics, and by way of example, quite undo some of the best of ours' but immediately changed his mind: Laud to Bramhall, 16 January 1635, HA 15157. It is hard to say what was worrying him but he may have been fearful that the scheme might be twisted in such a way as to produce something along the line of the English feoffees.

[165] This process had already been carried out to some extent in the Ulster plantation diocese. For wretchedly poor livings of this type, see Kilmore and Ardagh in the 1634 visitation, TCD MS 1067. There was a further attempt in the 1640 parliament to introduce the failed bill for 'the real union and division of parishes'; see chapter 6, p. 198 below. Irish canon 36 repeats most of this clause.

[166] 13 Eliz. I c. 20 (Eng).

intention here was to boost residency by making it legally necessary for
profit and more attractive by lifting the accumulated burdens of the past.
The eighth section made provision for leasing of glebe lands in any future
plantation and, indeed, Bramhall was anticipating significant gains in the
projected Connacht scheme.[167] The ninth and last section stipulated that
those parsons whose livings had been increased by means of the statute
were to be charged with the repair of the chancels of their churches.

Bramhall makes reference to two other planned bills. The first 'mutilated'
legislation dealt with simony which he believed, if pursued in its altered
form, would serve only 'to dull the edge of the ancient canons, which
include all the punishment'. It was never even transmitted to England.
It was a mark of the increasing confidence of the church that Bramhall
finished by declaring that 'what we want in a law we intend to supply by
a canon'. In the event, Irish canon 35 significantly extended the concept
of simony found in English canon 40 of 1603. For his part, Wentworth
promised to use his licence to make an Act of State for simony to punish
patrons as well as clergy and so 'be a better remedy . . . for that disease than
you have in England'.[168] A draft Act for residency of beneficed persons
was also prepared but, according to Bramhall, 'written in blood'. Again he
proposed a canon and killed two birds with the one stone in Irish canon
36 by adapting English canon 41 on pluralities to repeat the provisions
of clause 6 of the impropriations Act and enjoining residency on licensed
pluralists.

The new laws of 1635 brought Ireland substantially into line with England
and from certain angles even improved on the situation there. The breadth
and precision of the legislation represented an attempt by Wentworth and
Bramhall to address all of the main defects in ecclesiastical revenues. The
hands both of bishops and of the laity were fairly well tied and the more
enthusiastic among the clergy had the opportunity of turning the legislation
to real advantage. Bramhall and Laud were highly pleased with the outcome,
and Wentworth jubilantly described the parliament as 'the happiest this
kingdom ever had, having done more for the church and the settling and
securing of the state than any ten of them'.[169] This body of legislation not
only brought James's efforts to much fuller fruition, it was greater in scope

---

[167] Bramhall to Laud, 18 February 1635, HA 14048.
[168] Bramhall to Laud, 20 December 1634, Shirley, p. 44. See also Irish canon 35 of 1634, *Canons and constitutions ecclesiastical* (Dublin, 1635). Wentworth's authorisation to draw up a simony statute arrived too late, Wentworth to Laud, 18 May 1635; he was then ordered to make the Act of State on 8 June 1635, SP 63/255/39; StrP 20/ 124. Laud himself was associated with a whole series of prosecutions for simoniacal presentations in England; see Fincham, 'William Laud', 85.
[169] Wentworth to the earl of Danby, 21 April 1635, Knowler I, p. 414.

and better in design. Yet these statutes were still only one of the marks of favour shown to the church.

FAVOURING THE CHURCH, 1634–5

The convocation of 1634–5 was not entirely consumed by its wrangling over the English articles and canons. Despite all the other dissensions in the house, Bramhall was able to report in late December 1634 that he had introduced a motion urging a petition to the king and the lord deputy 'for the effecting of that long-intended work of piety'.[170] The work was the restoration of crown appropriations. Although the matter was formally referred to a committee of three bishops and three clerks, Bramhall himself had the petitions already drawn up. He also had accurate valuations of both crown and concealed appropriations which ensured that once the business was in train, it would not be buried by a long inquiry.

There was also another incentive to proceed with expedition. Wentworth had heard from London that someone had approached the queen with a suit 'to get a grant of all the impropriations here in the crown'. Unsurprisingly, he suspected Portland and he hinted to Laud that the plan might be part of a general ploy 'to disease the queen' towards Laud.[171] Months later, when preparations were being made to draw up the documentation to implement the king's grant, Laud was urging haste on the Irish side as he claimed Cottington was putting increased pressure on the queen through Sir Richard Wynn.[172] Plans for the Church of Ireland were always vulnerable when sent over to England, whether through court intrigue or before the Irish committee. In such cases, Laud's ability to secure the approbation of Charles was critical in ensuring that they did not come back so altered or compromised as to have the opposite effect to the original design.[173]

Convocation's petition addressed Charles as defender of the clergy and a potentially great architect of reformation in Ireland.[174] It opened on a grandly lachrymose note: 'in the whole Christian world, the rural clergy

---

[170] Bramhall to Laud, 20 December 1634, Shirley, p. 43.

[171] Wentworth to Laud, 9 December 1634, Str P 6, p. 125.

[172] Laud to Wentworth, 31 July and 3 August 1635, *WL* 6, p. 421 and *WL* 7, p. 159. Laud had feared that the moneys would then find their way into the hands of priests and friars: Laud to Wentworth, 12 January 1635, *WL* 7, p. 106.

[173] See Laud's comment that 'my desire is for all the king's impropriations and to make them certain, and past power of alienation, while we have a gracious king that is willing to do it', Laud to Wentworth, 13 January 1634, *WL* 7, p. 61. For more on this, see John McCafferty, 'John Bramhall and the Church of Ireland in the 1630s' in Alan Ford, James McGuire and Kenneth Milne (eds.), *As by law established: the Church of Ireland since the reformation* (Dublin, 1995), pp. 100–11.

[174] The petition, dated 15 January 1634, is in Str P 6, p. 153.

have not been reduced into such an extremity of contempt and beggary as in this your Highness' kingdom'. Such great emiseration was caused by the extent of appropriations and commendams as well as the 'many times of confusion' which had resulted in the violation of the 'undoubted rights' of the clergy. Invocations of lost or eroded power or property of the clerical estate were bound to be favourably entertained under Charles. Yet there was another note to strike in the Irish context. Ministers, convocation pointed out, were unable to reside 'whereby the ordinary subject has been left wholly destitute of all possible means to learn true piety to God, loyalty to their Prince and civility towards one another'. Piety, loyalty and civility – all elements of a vision of the Church of Ireland of coming with the gospel in one hand and English rule and manners in the other. Resident incumbents would expel 'barbarism and superstition' and promote obedience to the crown and church. The date on which Bramhall made his motion is unknown but it may well have been just after Wentworth's order to convocation to vote directly on acceptance of the Thirty-Nine articles on 10 December. He had cleverly produced a formula which not only appealed to Charles's image of himself as the gracious benefactor of the clergy but which all clergy of the Church of Ireland, whatever misgivings they had about the direction of Wentworth's administration, could not but support. The new strategy of building up the clerical estate first was now shrewdly couched in the language of reformation and evangelisation. Being seen to take some of the sting out of a doctrinal defeat by delivering royal bounty was not only good as a general tactic but it also allowed Bramhall room for manoeuvre in his dealings with his fellow clergy.

The accompanying petition to the lord deputy hammered home the point that the clergy would endeavour to make adequate compensation to the crown for such a generous grant.[175] A detailed schedule of the values of the appropriations still in the crown 'not made according to the present rents but the best surveys' was attached.[176] This estimated that the rent to the crown from these livings was in the order of £1,100 per annum. The snag was that the bulk of them were leased out and would fall in haphazardly over the next two to one hundred years. Roughly half of that figure would not fall in for either twelve to twenty years (£235) or about fifty years (£265). In words which perfectly encapsulated Bramhall's views on the importance of conspicuous example, the report contended that despite the timescale it would, in conjunction with the statute, encourage a wave

[175] This petition, also dated 15 January 1634, is in Str P 6, p. 154.
[176] For this see Str P 6, pp. 155–8. It may have been partly based on SP 63/253/2100, *Cal. SP Ire.* 1625–32, p. 653.

of lay beneficence.[177] As with the various statutes, regular revenue would be enhanced since as the leases fell in, the livings would become liable for first fruits and twentieths.

Five lay referees, Richard Bolton, William Parsons, George Radcliffe Christopher Wandesforde and James Ware, submitted their report on the schedule at the end of February.[178] They confirmed that the taxation of benefices would augment revenue and stressed the advantages of an increase in the number of donative benefices in the hands of the crown. They estimated that the church would clear £3,360 above the rent to be paid to the king, but acknowledged that it would take many years to do so. The impropriations would be settled on vicars where they already existed and if there were only stipendiary curates, then a vicarage should be endowed. These last measures were central to the whole purpose of the project because they laid the foundations for a resident clergy. In April 1635, the king granted the petition and Wentworth had George Radcliffe draw up the documents with all possible speed.[179]

With the statutes and the grant in place, the flow of revenue from the church was now staunched, leaving no scope for destructive alienations or leases by clergy from archbishop down to curate. In addition, the income of the clergy was itself secured and protected from the laity, which would leave no excuse for non-residence. The time was now ripe to press on with the main business of turning the church into a flourishing ally of the state. The chosen route was a prerogative so vigorous that it eventually lay open to the accusation of arbitrary government.

Work on land and revenue continued throughout Wentworth's entire viceroyalty but his personal involvement varied. The first phase, from his arrival until about the middle of 1635, was highly visible and in keeping with his pose as the personification of reform. Bramhall later identified this as the key period when each public case caused twenty private settlements.[180] During the second phase, which continued on to the winter of 1640, Bramhall directed his fellow bishops into settlements and cases using procedures and ploys developed while the lord deputy was in the driving seat.

---

[177] 'The example would be as conducible to the Church as the Act. And a great part of the benefit would be an opportunity to purchase in the leases by the assistance of pious and devout Christians', Str P 6, p. 157.

[178] 'A Certificate of the Referees appointed to deliver opinions upon the schedule', Str P 6, pp. 158–9. Bramhall noted that Radcliffe and Wandesforde had been made referees to make sure that the whole thing would not take 'seven years': Bramhall to Laud, 18 February 1635, HA 14048.

[179] Charles I to lord deputy of Ireland, 20 April 1635, SP63/255/28. Wentworth was given permission to give the resumption statutory basis if there was time: Wentworth to Laud, 18 May 1635, Str P 6, p. 181.

[180] Bramhall to Laud, January 1639, Shirley, pp. 6ff.

In order to make them an estate in their own right rather than the adjuncts of landed proprietors, ordinary parochial clergy needed to be made sensible of the opportunities on offer. Typically, Wentworth found a case which did just that in a very public way and offered a chance to niggle at Richard Boyle. In October 1633, George Beresford, vicar of Kilteny in Co. Kerry, petitioned for arrears of his stipend due from the earl as impropriator. Cork naturally pressed for a private hearing but then, as Wentworth wrote to Laud afterwards, 'considering that lapping the matter thus up in silence, I lost a great part of my end, which was by open example to lead on and encourage the poor clergy to exhibit their just complaints against persons how great soever', he sent Bramhall to 'steel' Beresford into requesting that his cause might be heard at the council table.[181] Cork and his lawyers attempt to put a brake on proceedings with legal exceptions, but the lord deputy seized the opportunity to deliver his message to the clergy in a trenchant speech against sacrilege, castigating those who took from ministers their livelihood 'making themselves thus guilty not only of shedding the blood but even the souls of men'.[182] Satisfying as all this was, Wentworth wanted more than an opportunity to declaim, and was casting about for ways to make the trial of church suits at the council board not only attractive to the clergy but, in certain cases, automatic.

Most of the records of the Irish privy council from this period have been lost. An order book, consisting of about 220 entries, survives for 1634. A brief analysis of the book makes it clear why, after parliament had finished, doubts were beginning to be cast on the overall legality of Wentworth's procedures. Between 6 May and 18 September 1634, there were at least sixty-eight distinct matters dealt with or in process of hearing. Of these, the largest single category consisted of twenty-three tithe cases. There were also eight cases involving vicars who were unable to secure possession of their benefices or where the impropriator failed to provide a sufficient stipend and five cases concerning the maintenance and repair of churches. Of the total of sixty-eight, eighteen were referred to Bramhall for investigation or composition (most of these involved tithes) as opposed to three to the justices of the peace and one to the diocesan – a reflection of the extent to which church affairs were supervised by him. Business ranged from great matters such as pretended fee farms in Ferns and Leighlin and usurped episcopal lands in Clonfert, down to the blockading of carts of tithe corn and squabbles over the cost of repairs of small parish churches. Yet, in every

---

[181] Wentworth to Laud, 22 October 1633, Str P 8, pp. 34–5; 31 October 1633, Str P 8, pp. 43–5; December 1633, Str P 6, pp. 3–5; 29 January 1634, p. 9.
[182] *Ibid.*, 4. See also Laud to Wentworth, 13 January 1634, *WL* 7, p. 57. Ranger, 'Boyle', pp. 330–1.

case where the plaintiff was a clergyman and where we know the verdict, the outcome was in his favour.

A petition presented by James Kian, vicar of Malahide, Co. Dublin, against one Patrick Strong for interfering with the collection of tithes reveals something about the way in which clergy were starting to respond to the encouragement that Wentworth had been so keen to give. Kian declared he was making petition to the council because if he had gone before a common law judge and jury 'there will be but slight damages recovered against him [Strong]'.[183] Appeal from the board was the natural response to all of this. It was the tack that Cork decided on in early 1635 when, after a successful prosecution by Arthur Gwyn (again encouraged by Bramhall), the lord deputy presented the cleric to livings in Tipperary. Presentation without proven lapse not only created the desired atmosphere of rough justice but also released a whiff of arbitrary government. The Gwyn case went on, in fact, to feature in Strafford's trial. By the end of March royal letters were issued forbidding appeal from the board in ecclesiastical causes.[184] The obvious drawback was that a growing perception of almost automatic victory for the clergy could only serve to fuel resentment in the long term as it transformed perception of church resumption from a woolly but morally pleasing endeavour into a mercilessly administered bitter pill. The Beresford case demonstrates that while most clergy loved the revenue, they hated the notoriety. Even Bramhall admitted it: 'even some of mine old friends are as averse as any when they can do it in private'.[185] He was writing in 1639 when tensions were building, but it is likely that once the initial euphoria at having their income taken seriously by Dublin Castle wore off, ordinary parochial clergy saw the need to soft-pedal.

Archbishop Miler McGrath, the longest-lived and most rapacious of Elizabeth's bishops, crippled his string of dioceses through a web of leases, grants and alienations.[186] His successor, Archibald Hamilton, took up the invitation proffered by Wentworth and began a suit 'to redeem that church from . . . the ugly oppressions of that wicked bishop Milerus'.[187] Examination began in the winter of 1633 and it was hoped that at least £400 per annum would be recovered to the see. Laud begged Wentworth to hasten

---

[183] BL Harl MS 4297, p. 88. In this case, a counter-petition against Bramhall's ruling was unsuccessful. The brusque manner in which it was rejected copperfastens the impression of overt partiality towards the church; see BL Harl. MS 4297, p. 90.

[184] Wentworth to Laud, 10 March 1635, Knowler I, pp. 378–80.

[185] Bramhall to Laud, 22 January 1639, Shirley, p. 64.

[186] Lawrence Marron, 'Documents from the state papers concerning Miler McGrath', *Archivium Hibernicum* 21 (1958), 73–189, gives a flavour of his machinations.

[187] Wentworth to Laud, December 1633, Knowler I, p. 171.

matters as far as possible while still exhibiting his customary scepticism about Irish bishops: 'look to him (Hamilton) that if he be once well settled, he prove not so good at it as Melerus was'.[188] Initially the case, which partially hinged around whether the deanery was in the gift of the king or the bishop, was to go into the court of common pleas and Wentworth wished to reserve the equity to the council board.[189] This became a contentious matter at the Irish committee in London which moved to refer the equitable matters to the Irish chancery. Laud was undaunted, though, and assured Wentworth that 'we shall have our letter'. He was as good as his word, and the letter for Cashel also allowed for suits at council table for 'the general of the patrimony of the church'. Wentworth acted quickly to sweep away 'all those sacrilegious grants made by old Magrath to his children' but he was more elated that a matter which would have dragged on interminably in chancery could now be resolved so speedily.[190] The combination of this royal letter and the bar on appeals made a speedy bypass around legal procedure.

Wentworth's overall governance was characterised by the use of a formidable array of other prerogative instruments, most of which were drawn into service of the church.[191] High Commission, for example, ordered that the salaries of curates of impropriated churches should be raised 'from three pounds or some other contemptible allowance, to the third part of the true value of the benefice'.[192] Wentworth took steps to stop undervalued royal impropriations passing at the commission for defective titles and Bramhall reached a secret agreement with the commissioners that no appropriation would pass until he was consulted.[193] The outcome of all of this, together with the Act of State for simony and the tight drafting of the temporalities statutes, was that in a space of less than two years Thomas Wentworth had put all of the resources of the state at the service of the state church for the first time in the history of that institution.

---

[188] Laud to Wentworth, 12 January 1634, *WL* 7, p. 107.
[189] Wentworth to Laud, 9 December 1634, Str P 6, pp. 125–6.
[190] Laud to Wentworth, 27 March 1635, *WL* 7, p. 115; Wentworth to Laud, 18 May 1635, Str P 6, p. 178; Laud to Wentworth, 12 June 1635, *WL* 7, p. 141; Wentworth to Laud, 14 July 1635, Str P 6, p. 204.
[191] See Kearney, *Strafford*, ch. 8.   [192] Bramhall to Laud, January 1639, Shirley, p. 6.
[193] Bramhall to Laud, 1 April 1636, Shirley, p. 46 and 23 February 1638, Shirley, p. 52.

CHAPTER 3

English codes and confession for Ireland, 1633–1636

THE CONSTITUTION OF THE CHURCH OF IRELAND, 1541–1632

In November 1638, Wentworth was directed by Laud to answer those Scots in Ireland looking for the same concessions as their countrymen that 'whatsoever he [the king] has indulged to Scotland, is because they have had there sometime a church government, such as it was, confused enough without bishops; but for Ireland, it has ever been reformed by and to the Church of England'.[1]

This response was, broadly speaking, correct. A reading of Meredith Hanmer's recently published translation of Giraldus Cambrensis's account of the last canon of the council of Cashel, 'that all the divine service in the Church of Ireland shall be kept used and observed in the like manner and order as it is in the Church of England',[2] would have lent a gratifyingly ancient tone to Laud's argument. The Henrician statutes did declare 'the King's Majesty to be only supreme head on earth of the *church* of England and Ireland' and they did endorse the validity of Irish canons, constitutions and other instruments of church government until 'such time as the King's highness shall order and determine according to his laws of England'.[3] While the Act for Kingly Title of 1541 caused the term 'Church of Ireland' to be used on its own, the titles and contents of statutes tended to mirror those of their Westminster equivalents. They did this so completely that some statutes ended up with inappropriate references to York and Canterbury. Consequently, appellate jurisdiction caused problems for

---

[1] Laud to Wentworth, 2 November 1638, *WL* 6, pp. 543–4.
[2] And continues: 'for it is meet and right that as by God's providence and appointment Ireland is now become subject and under the king of England: so the same should take from thence, the order, and rule, and manner how to reform themselves, and to live in better sort', James Ware, *The history of Ireland, collected by three learned authors viz. Meredith Hanmer Doctor in Divinity: Edmund Campion sometime fellow of St Johns College in Oxford: and Edmund Spenser Esq.* (Dublin, 1633), p. 135.
[3] The italics in the quotations are mine. 28 Hen. VIII c. 13.

many years because of the ambiguities opened up by legislating for Ireland by bare extension of English arrangements.[4]

Distance and different circumstances did leave a mark on the Irish establishment. Ireland's own Act of Uniformity of 1560 attempted to address the problems of a church where most of the Marian episcopate did not resign.[5] Irish uniformity now became somewhat distinct from the English variety. For example, article 15 claimed that while the sacraments should be administered in 'such language as they might best understand', yet 'the same may not be in their native language' because, it claimed, printing up books was too difficult and far too few people could read 'Irish letters'. Latin was authorised for all parishes.[6] There was no suggestion that this was a temporary measure until such time as an Irish translation could be procured. It seems likely that the production of the *Liber Precum Publicarum* was simultaneously a reflection of Old English 'antipathy towards a vernacular Irish liturgy' and a concession to the conservatives, especially when coupled with permission for the ornaments used in 2 Edward VI.[7]

Universal Latin liturgy was a contravention of article 24 of 1563.[8] But then the Thirty-Nine articles would have to wait over seventy years before becoming official doctrine of the Church of Ireland. In 1566, Henry Sidney used his authority to issue a set of twelve articles in conjunction with the bishops and High Commission. Like Wentworth, Sidney's aim was to give the established church greater institutional solidity, and to do so he simply imported Parker's Eleven articles of 1559.[9] These had no doctrinal intent beyond assertion of royal supremacy and a basic Protestant assault on Catholic sacrificial theology and traditional liturgical and devotional practises. Like their English counterparts, Irish ministers were expected to read and assent to them twice yearly as well as on first entry to a living. There is no indication that anyone was deprived or suspended for failure to do so.

---

4 Alan Ford, 'Dependent or independent? The Church of Ireland and its colonial context, 1536–1649', *The Seventeenth Century* 10 (1995), 163–87.

5 Henry A. Jeffries, 'The Irish Parliament of 1560: the anglican reforms authorised', *IHS* 26 (1988), 128–41, for an account of different views.

6 2 Eliz. I c. 2, article xv. The second Edwardian Book of Common Prayer was never authorised in Ireland.

7 Jeffries, 'Irish Parliament of 1560', 128–41.

8 'It is a thing plainly repugnant to the Word of God . . . to have the public prayer in the church, or to minister the sacraments in a tongue not understanded of the people', Gerald Bray (ed.), *Documents of the English reformation* (Cambridge, 1994), p. 298.

9 Ford, *Protestant*, p. 194; *UWW* I, p. 42. The only reason there were twelve articles in the Irish set is because the last exhortatory paragraph of the Eleven articles was turned into an article. See Bray (ed.), *Documents*, pp. 349–51.

In 1594 Trinity College Dublin, which had recently been granted a charter stressing its role in combating Catholic reformation and study on the continent, opened its doors to the first students. Constitutionally modelled on Emmanuel College, Cambridge, Trinity aimed to produce a learned graduate clergy for service in the parishes.[10] The 'puritan' ethos of Trinity was reflected not only in its constitution but in the choice of heads – the first acting provost was Walter Travers who was succeeded by Henry Alvey and William Temple, who reinforced the Cambridge link and the godly aspect of the college. James VI & I re-endowed the university in the hope that it would attract native Irish students. In this respect, the college was not successful. Only a small number of the students, even in the late 1610s, were of native or of Old English extraction, and as Alan Ford remarks, 'the extent to which the college sought to equip these students as Irish-speaking evangelists can be in doubt'.[11] Trinity's performance as a seminary was also disappointing – in 1622 there were only thirteen of its graduates throughout all eight of the Ulster dioceses despite generous endowment from the plantation lands.[12]

So what was going on in this Pale-based, anglocentric institution? Trinity ended up acting as an Irish version of the king's favourite, Chelsea College. A special professorship of Theological Controversies was held successively by Ussher followed by Joshua Hoyle, who spent the bulk of their lectures on a detailed refutation of Bellarmine, between them pummelling the cardinal for a total of thirty-four years.[13] Ussher's youthful determination to read the Fathers of the early church reflects that of Chelsea College's Thomas James. Polemical works accounted for a large proportion of Dublin books in the first three decades of the seventeenth century.[14] On his arrival as provost in 1627, William Bedell found that 'the worship of God' had been 'much neglected as appeared by the very ill array of the chapel itself, and omitting of the communion these many years'.[15] Bedell attempted to restore the college to its original purpose by re-establishing the Irish lecture. He also shrewdly identified the fatal narrowing of curriculum which had deflected

---

[10] Ford, *Protestant*, p. 77.   [11] Ford, *Protestant*, p. 105.   [12] Ford, *Protestant*, p. 78.

[13] Anthony Milton, *Catholic and reformed: the Roman and Protestant churches in English Protestant thought, 1600–1640* (Cambridge, 1995), pp. 32–4. Declan Gaffney, 'The practice of religious controversy in Dublin, 1600–1641' in W. J. Sheils and Diana Wood (eds.), *The churches, Ireland and the Irish*, Studies in Church History 25 (Oxford, 1989), pp. 145–58.

[14] Gaffney, 'Practice of religious controversy', p. 149; A. M. Pollard, *Dublin's trade in books, 1550–1800* (Oxford, 1989); Brian Jackson, 'The construction of argument: Henry Fitzsimon, John Rider and religious controversy in Dublin, 1599–1614' in Ciaran Brady and Jane Ohlmeyer (eds.), *British interventions in early modern Ireland* (Cambridge, 2005), pp. 97–115.

[15] Bedell to Ussher, 10 September 1627, *UWW* XVI, p. 458. He had to arrange for the purchase of a table, linen, cloths and utensils.

from the mission to 'civilise': 'it has been an error all this while, to neglect the faculties of law and physic, and attend only to the ordering of one poor college of divines'.[16] Bedell's efforts met with considerable internal opposition and when he was leaving to take up Kilmore and Ardagh, the theologian Joshua Hoyle 'prayed publicly in his church that God would send to the college a good head, no Arminian, no Italianated man'.[17]

It would be wrong to suggest that the Protestant church turned its liturgical back entirely on the Gaelic Irish. In 1608, William Daniel, Gaelic Irish by birth and a product of Emmanuel and Trinity College, published his *Leabhar na nUrnaightheadh gComhchoidchiond*. This was more than an Irish version of the Prayer Book because his translation moved beyond bare liturgical provision to a particular vision of the church as by law established. The English-language preface contrasted the 'ancient flourishing state of religion in Ireland' with a country which now 'does generally sit in darkness', a decline caused by the corruptions of the papacy.[18] Daniel's avowed purpose in translating the Prayer Book was polemical. His mission to 'undeceive' the Irish was itself a cause for optimism, 'though Satan do now rage more among us than ever heretofore. His rage argues his desperate estate, and the utter ruin of his kingdom.' William Daniel wanted to move the Church of Ireland away from statute into the realm of salvation.[19]

Away from the grand scheme of things, this translation tweaked at Cranmer's text. For example, the suffrage 'that it may please thee to illuminate all bishops, pastors and ministers of the church, with true knowledge and understanding of the word' became '*Go madh toil leat gach uile easpag, aoghaire spioritálta agus mhinisdir da bhfuil ad t'eaglais do dheallrughadh le héolus fírindeach, agus lé tuigsidh dhíongmhala do bhréithir*'. Which translates back into English as 'that it may be thy will to illuminate every bishop, spiritual shepherd and minister in thy church, with true knowledge and *suitable* understanding of thy word'. Where 'priest' occurs in English, it is consistently replaced by *minisdir*. While he uses Irish phrases for various saint's days (such as *lá fheile Muire na féile Brigdhe* for the Purification of Mary), the almanac has nowhere near the same number of feast days as the English book of 1604, and it mentions no Irish saints at all, not even

---

[16] Bedell to Ward, 14 November 1636, *Tanner letters*, p. 100.

[17] Bedell to Ward, 14 November 1636, *Tanner letters*, p. 100. T. W. Jones, *The life and death of William Bedell* (1872), pp. 28–9, gives an account of the origin of the dispute between Bedell and Hoyle.

[18] *Leabhar na nUrnaightheadh gComhchoidchiond* (Dublin, 1608), sig. A2. F. R. Bolton, *The Caroline tradition of the Church of Ireland* (1958), p. 8; Ford, *Protestant*, pp. 125–6.

[19] William Reeves, *The Book of Common Prayer according to the use of the Irish Church, its history and sanction* (Dublin, 1871), pp. 35–6; Nicholas Williams, *I bprionta i leabhar: na protastúin agus prós na Gaeilge, 1567–1724* (Baile Átha Cliath, 1986), chs. 3 and 9, *passim*.

Patrick. The same desire to define the established church as an antithesis to Catholicism is to be found in the use of *comhchoidhchiond*, 'common', throughout rather than *catoiliceach* whenever the word 'catholic' occurred. He omits the psalter of 1604 and also the ordinal.[20] Strikingly, the English Uniformity Act of 1559 was translated rather than the Irish one of 1560.

The veneration of the early Irish church in Daniel's preface gave the Church of Ireland a long historical pedigree, allowing ancient disputes such as the dating of Easter to be interpreted as proof of the Celtic church's original independence from Rome.[21] The second feature of this Prayer Book is its emphasis – the uniform substitution of 'minister' for priest, the paring away of holy days and the silent omission of the form of ordering bishops and priests, while following the 1604 book in all other respects. If the *Liber Precum Publicarum* used after 1560 pushed in one direction, this pushed in the other. Both show the small but sometimes significant margin Ireland allowed in the reception of English reformation.

Ireland had no tradition of convocation. In England convocations came to be called automatically with parliaments, whereas in Ireland the existence of a house of clerical proctors prevented the evolution of an analogous arrangement. The 104 articles compiled by the Church of Ireland in the first national convocation of 1613–15 have often been regarded as the constitution of a spacious and flexible Protestant church. Beyond a transcription of the preamble to a bill for clerical subsidies, no contemporary records of the assembly survive.[22] In 1717, Archbishop King claimed to have seen the royal licence to hold convocation but even then he had mislaid it.[23] A tradition that James Ussher was the author of the Irish articles exists but does not appear even its most rudimentary form until at least twenty years after events.[24] While some later commentators believed King James or Lord Deputy Chichester to have ratified or approved the articles, this cannot be verified or disproved either.[25] What can be said without hesitation is that

---

[20] This parallels the omission of English article 36 in 1615.

[21] Alan Ford, 'James Ussher and the creation of an Irish Protestant identity' in Brendan Bradshaw and Peter Roberts (eds.), *British consciousness and identity: the making of Britain 1533–1707* (Cambridge, 1998), pp. 185–212; Ute Lotz-Heumann, 'The Protestant interpretation of the history of Ireland: the case of James Ussher's Discourse' in Bruce Gordon (ed.), *Protestant history and identity in sixteenth-century Europe*, vol. 2: *The later reformation* (Aldershot, 1996), pp. 107–20; John McCafferty, 'St Patrick for the Church of Ireland: James Ussher's *Discourse*', *Bullán* 3 (1997–8), 87–101.

[22] TCD MS 1062, pp. 356–8.

[23] William King to William Wake, 12 September 1717, BL Add. MS 6117, fol. 46r–v.

[24] For two opposing views, see Ford, *Protestant*, pp. 156–64, and Amanda Capern, 'The Caroline church: James Ussher and the Irish dimension', *HJ* 39 (1996), 57–85 esp. n. 69.

[25] Contemporaries were themselves confused on this point. Peter Heylyn declared that they were passed by 'His Majesty's Commissioners [who] were employed about the settling of that Church Anno 1615'

these articles prefigure the Westminster confession of 1647 by having as a cornerstone article 80 with its ringing affirmation that the pope was 'that man of sin foretold in the holy scriptures whom the Lord shall consume with the spirit of his mouth and the brightness of his coming'.[26]

This new convocation was a predominantly English affair. Of the twenty-three bishops only three were Scots, and of the approximately 156–8 members of the lower house it is unlikely that more than twenty to twenty-five were Scottish.[27] The Irish articles were not framed to accommodate any Scottish opinion or preferences, though there was much in them that tallied with confession drawn up by the Aberdeen general assembly of 1616.[28] It is very likely that had English convocations met in 1614 and had they been at liberty to draw up a confession of faith they would have done something quite similar. These Irish articles were a mainstream Jacobean repointing of the 1562 structure. The Dublin assembly yoked together the last set of articles approved by bishops of the Church of England, the Lambeth articles, and most of the Thirty-Nine.[29] They also reflect the polemical bias of the Church of Ireland – articles 59 and 60 denied the deposing power of the pope, and article 67 condemned equivocation. The omission of English article 36 on the consecration of bishops and ordination of priests and deacons is frequently taken as a mark of the desire of Irish churchmen to preserve Protestant unity in the face of an obdurate Catholic mass. But there are *three* English articles omitted in 1615–32 (on clerical marriage), article 35 (on the Book of Homilies) and article 36 itself. So, does the absence of article 32 indicate a concession to a pro-celibacy rump in the Church of Ireland? Highly unlikely, of course, which shows that the omissions might

---

in *History of the Sabbath* (1636), p. 258. Nicholas Bernard in his *Judgement of the late Archbishop of Armagh* (1657), p. 108, berated Heylyn for his credulity: 'there having been no such commissioners here at that time'. Heylyn, writing anonymously, believed that James had 'recommended' the articles to Ireland and then to Dort in *Observations on the history of the reign of King Charles* (1656), p. 77. The belief that James 'sent over' articles appears to have been quite widespread. For instance, in May 1625, George Carleton, bishop of Chichester, wrote to Ussher asking for a copy of certain articles which 'the late King' had sent into Ireland, *UWW* XVI, pp. 430–1. Bernard had earlier claimed that Ussher had told him that after the articles had been framed they were signed by Archbishop Jones, who was lord chancellor and speaker of the house of bishops, by the prolocutor of the house of clergy 'and also signed by the then lord deputy Chichester by order from King James in his name', *The life and death of the most reverend and learned father of our church Dr James Ussher* (1656), pp. 49–50.

[26] Bray (ed.), *Documents*, pp. 437–52.

[27] These figures are based on Gerald Bray's unpublished 'Records of the Irish convocations', containing his transcription of TCD MS 668 for the lower house in 1704 taking into account the number of dioceses in 1613.

[28] I wish to thank Gerald Bray for drawing this resemblance to my attention. T. Thomson (ed.), *Acts and proceedings of the Kirk of Scotland from the year 1560 collected from the most authentic manuscripts, part third, 1593–1618* (Edinburgh, 1845), pp. 1132–9.

[29] For a breakdown, see Bray (ed.), *Documents*, pp. 662–3.

be viewed from a different angle. The absence of both articles 32 and 36, which are really more about the ordinal than ordination, might point to an uneasiness about set forms rather than to antipathy to hierarchy. The Irish church was not especially puritan because it sought to accommodate all shades; it was puritan because so many of its clergy, being English, were themselves puritan, reformed, godly, desirous of minimal conformity. The Irish church simply did what many oathbound conformists in England would have done had they had the same margin for action. The kind of hindsight provided by the adoption of so many of the Irish articles by the 1647 divines has acted to further obscure the motives of the 1613–15 clergy. John Vesey dismissed the Irish articles as a simple by-product of their environment, 'a little sour and Calvinistical, of which I can give no better reason than that some good men have sometimes more zeal than judgement, and like burnt children so much dread the fire that they think they can never be far enough from their fear'.[30] Peter Heylyn seized his opportunity by taking the view that subscription to the Irish articles meant easy subscription to the 'articles of all the reformed (or Calvinian) churches' but subscription to the English articles allowed no such continental drift.[31] The snag was that there was, in reality, no subscription before 1634.

Because of their undeniable significance the 1615 articles have often been treated as if they were the sole law binding the Church of Ireland. There is no evidence to suggest that the 'Decree of the Synod' which is tacked on to the end of the articles had any positive force in law or that any attempt was ever made to apply it.[32] What may well be in question, then, is no more than a particularly solemn theological exercise. Ireland had no national canons until after 1634–5 but it can be shown that the 1603 canons were used *de facto* as a standard of discipline. The royal *Orders and Instructions* of 1623 might have been widely ignored but they incorporated a number of the 1603 canons in their provisions. James ordered that tables of fees be set up in ecclesiastical courts (English canon 136), ruled on the use of the writ *de excommunicato capiendo* (English canon 65), gave guidelines on pluralities (based on English canon 41), and ordered that churchwardens should not be pressed to present more than twice a year (English canon

---

[30] Vesey, *Athanasius Hibernicus* (1676), [p. 27]. His view is shared by Heylyn in *Observations on the history . . . King Charles*, p. 78, and *Cyprianus Anglicus* (1668), p. 270.

[31] Heylyn, *Respondet Petrus* (1658), p. 128.

[32] 'If any minister, of what degree or quality soever he be shall publicly teach any doctrine contrary to these Articles agreed upon, If, after due admonition, he do not conform himself, and cease to disturb the peace of the church, let him be silenced, and deprived of all spiritual promotions he doth enjoy', Bray (ed.), *Documents*, p. 452.

116).[33] Penetration of the 1603 canons is even more apparent in sets of articles issued by Christopher Hampton in 1623 and reissued by Ussher in 1626 and 1629 for metropolitical visitations.[34] These articles, which appear to have been composed in Ireland, were undoubtedly framed with English canons in mind.[35] Article 1 on the use of the Prayer Book by ministers is drawn from English canons 14, 45 and 56, article 2 on the provision of curates comes from English canon 47, article 3 on the behaviour of clergy is based on English canon 75. Of the remaining twenty-eight articles, all but eight make reference to, or are based on English canons.[36] Indeed, the only article of the entire set which makes any direct reference to Ireland is 26, which mentions holy days appointed by order of the 'Churches of England and Ireland'.[37] When two successive archbishops of Armagh wished to examine the state of their province, they turned to Richard Bancroft's codification.

Even if they had no teeth, the very composition and publication of the Irish articles in 1615 was an important act, but it is very unlikely that a distinctive church settlement was on the minds of those who sat in Dublin. There may be a hint of convocation's intent in Irish article 77, which takes up English article 34 of 1562. On ceremonies, the English confession speaks of 'every particular or national church's' right to alter ceremonies, while the Irish article modestly reads 'every particular church'.[38] This tiny omission may provide a fleeting glimpse of an element, possibly a very large element, in the assembly who were uncomfortable with the notion of the Church of Ireland as a 'national' church and who preferred to think of it as standing in a similar relation to the Church of England as the crown of Ireland did to the crown of England. In short, they understood the Church of Ireland to be at heart a *dependent* church. The existence of the 1615

---

[33] Marsh MS Z3.1.3 (30, 33, 35, 36).

[34] *Anno Domini M.DC.XXXIII [i.e. M.DC.XXIII] articles given in charge to be inquired upon and presented too, by the churchwardens, side-men, quest-men, and inquisitors in every parish within the province of Ardmagh*, STC (2nd edn) 14265.3. The 1626 issue is *STC* (2nd edn) 14265.5 and the 1629 issue, 14265.1.

[35] Gerald Bray notes some resemblance to Thomas Dove's articles for Peterborough in 1617: Kenneth Fincham (ed.), *Visitation articles and injunctions of the early Stuart church*, vol. I (Woodbridge, 1994), pp. 142–8.

[36] These are as follows: article 6: EC 26; article 7: ECs 67, 68; article 8: EC 41; article 9: EC 14; article 10: EC 46; article 11: EC 59; article 12: EC 77; article 14: EC 14; article 15: EC 110; article 16: EC 109; article 17: EC 109; article 18: EC 109; article 20: ECs 82, 83, 85; article 21: EC 28; article 22: injunction 34 of 1559; article 23: EC 100; article 24: EC 62; article 26: EC 13; article 27: EC 127; article 28: EC 134; article 29: EC 107.

[37] On the evidence of Daniel's Prayer Book, Irish speakers would be treated to fewer holy days than those in English-speaking areas.

[38] Bray (ed.), *Documents*, pp. 305, 449. It is worth noting, too, the manner in which Irish article 91 on baptism (Bray (ed.), *Documents*, p. 450) avoids any potential conflict with English canon 30 of 1604: Gerald Bray (ed.), *The Anglican canons 1529–1947* (Woodbridge, 1998), pp. 303–7.

articles tempted some contemporaries and still tempts historians to see the Irish church as more elastic, but there is a likelihood that subscription to the English articles was, in fact, widespread. James Ussher's sermon to the English House of Commons in 1621 is often read as proof that even if he was author of the Irish articles, he had no antipathy to the Thirty-Nine: 'we all subscribe to the articles of doctrine agreed upon in the Synod of the year 1562'.[39] In 1632 the Scottish bishop Robert Echlin attempted to have Robert Blair and his friends subscribe.[40] Their very proper answer was: 'to what?' Many Irish bishops made the very common assumption that English law was *de facto* Irish law and so may have asked clergy for subscription. Added to that is the certain fact that a large number of clergy with Irish livings had commenced their careers in England after 1603 and so most came, as it were, pre-subscribed.

A romantic view of Ireland as a nearby land of liberty only began to take off a decade after the publication of the Irish articles. The theologically agitated English parliaments of 1626 and 1628 called for joint confirmation of the Irish alongside the Thirty-Nine.[41] The Church of Ireland was, at bottom, the church by law established, so even without any deliberations of the Dublin convocation there was a statutory conformity. The Irish Uniformity Act of 1560 made the Prayer Book a distinguishing mark of the church.[42] In the absence of any mandatory subscription there is good reason to believe use of the prescribed liturgy was the test in Ireland. While English article 36 may have been dropped in 1615, the Act of Supremacy made mention of archbishops and bishops and the same Irish parliament of 1560 had also passed an Act 'for the conferring and consecrating of archbishops and bishops'.[43] No matter how much anyone may have tried to fudge it, the constitution of the early Stuart Church of Ireland was that of the English church. Any latitude allowed in Ireland was mostly a reflection of the latitude, that is, the cocktail of subscription and minimal ceremonial conformity, that prevailed in the Church of England. When conditions changed in England they also changed across the Irish Sea with the roughest of jolts. The new hierarchs and conformists who came trailing

---

[39] *UWW* II, p. 421.

[40] Thomas McCrie (ed.), *The life of Mr Robert Blair, containing his autobiography from 1593 to 1636* (Edinburgh, 1848), p. 91.

[41] Nicholas Tyacke, *Anti-Calvinists: the rise of English Arminianism, c.1590–1640*, paperback edn (Oxford, 1990), pp. 154–5; S. R. Gardiner, *The constitutional documents of the puritan revolution 1625–1660*, 3rd edn (Oxford, 1906), p. 81.

[42] Jefferies, 'The Irish parliament of 1560', 128–41.

[43] 2 Eliz. I c. 4 which is itself mostly a repetition of 1 Edw. VI c. 2 (Eng.). Despite the omission of homilies from the 1615 articles, the Irish council considered, on at least one occasion, bringing in use of them for 'unpreaching ministers', *Cal. SP Ire.* 1606–8, p. 241.

in the wake of Wentworth after 1633 were appalled because in many respects they found the mirror of their own native English church as it had been in the past.

DECENCY AND ORDER IN DUBLIN, 1633–4

Bramhall's earliest Irish letter explicitly recommended the English settlement:

> I doubt much whether the clergy be very orthodox and could wish both the Articles and Canons of the Church of England were established here by Act of Parliament or State; yet as we live all under one king, so we might both in doctrine and discipline deserve an uniformity.[44]

In 1676 John Vesey glossed Bramhall's inquiries into the doctrine amongst the Irish clergy in order to present him as one who sought to confine theological discussion to the academic realm 'that those nicer accuracies that divide the greatest wits in the world might not be made the characteristics of the reformation'.[45] From the vantage point of 1676 this line is hardly surprising but Vesey may also have hit on something.[46] Bramhall's wish to conform Ireland to the Church of England was motivated as much by an ambition to create internal unity in the Church of Ireland through applying the ban on contentious debates (and so pave the way for English clergy) as it was by a desire to create outward conformity. Wentworth, writing to Laud some months later, explicitly alluded not to the lack of uniformity but to the apparent expression of autonomy: 'It is true indeed these Articles were changed here, which are such the Primate disavows and myself rest amazed that they ever slipped themselves in amongst us.'[47] Imposition of the Thirty-Nine articles would solve an English problem and an Irish problem simultaneously.

Accounts of the 1634 convocation have tended to focus on the English articles as the main event and downgrade the drive to canonical uniformity to an epilogue or, at best, a mildly successful counter-attack on the part of Ussher and the Church of Ireland. Yet the canons and a canonically inspired

---

[44] Bramhall to Laud, 10 August 1633, *BW* I, pp. lxxx–lxxxii.

[45] Vesey, *Athanasius Hibernicus* [p. 9].

[46] Vesey went on to suggest that Bramhall 'saw that the Church of England constituted both Calvinists and Arminians (as we have learned to abuse and nick name one another) subscribe the same propositions and walk to the same house of God as friends, and he from that time began to meditate how to have the same confession here', Julian Davies, *The Caroline captivity of the church* (Oxford, 1992), pp. 296–301.

[47] Wentworth to Laud, 5 May 1634, Str P 6, p. 56.

set of church reforms were an essential and significant counterpart to the articles, and fundamental to the drive for temporal reform: 'the repair of the material and spiritual church together', as Laud had put it.[48] Doctrine is a tiny part of Bramhall's first letter. His examination of the state of the Irish church was carried out with a decidedly canonical eye. Churches were in use as stables, dwelling houses and tennis courts. In Christchurch, where he was shortly to become treasurer: 'the vaults, from one end of the Minster to the other, are made into tippling-rooms, for beer, wine and tobacco . . .', contravening English canons 85 and 88.[49] 'The table used for the administration of the blessed Sacrament in the midst of the choir made an ordinary seat for the maids and apprentices', a violation of English canon 82, the breaking of the statutes of St Patrick's cathedral in the presence of the 'glorious tomb of the Earl of Cork at the east end', and 'in the heaping together of benefices', along with non-residence, were all in contravention of English canons 41, 46 and 47.[50] It is very unlikely the Bramhall ticked off Irish abuses against his copy of the English canons. Nonetheless his first impressions argued for canonical resolution of the excoriated 'evils'.[51]

Wentworth's letter of 31 January 1634 'anatomising' the 'Irish ecclesiastical disease' built on Bramhall's briefing. Most of his proposals were intended to, as the draft version of the letter put it, find 'the best method for settling this church'.[52] His remedies were visitation, regulation and supervision. Regulation meant that:

all the canons now in force in England should be imposed upon this clergy and the Church altogether governed under those rules for the future, for as yet they have no canons set by public authority at all.[53]

High Commission would act as supervisor of clerics and their courts as well as curbing 'foreign jurisdiction so far as shall be thought requisite by the state'.[54] Although popery is identified as the root cause of abuse of jurisdiction, the revived Commission's real function was to work as a tribunal to enforce reconstruction rather than to compel conformity. This was a programmatic response to Irish affairs and the first item was reform of the establishment.

For Laud, the aim of any programme was to guarantee 'the reformation of that church to the Church of England'.[55] He thought that two steps would set things in motion. The first, a strict direction to:

---

[48] Laud to Wentworth, 11 March 1634, *WL* 6, p. 354.
[49] Bramhall to Laud, 10 August 1633, *BW* I, p. lxxix.   [50] *BW* I, p. lxxx.   [51] *BW* I, p. lxxxi.
[52] Str P 20/149.   [53] Wentworth to Laud, 31 January 1634, Knowler I, p. 188.
[54] See Knowler I, p. 188 and Str P 20/149.   [55] Laud to Wentworth, 11 March 1634, *WL* 6, p. 354.

every minister . . . [to] read all divine service wholly and distinctly, in a grave and religious manner, to their people; and this, I take, may be presently done without any noise, because they have the English liturgy already.[56]

The second would consist of a ban on holding more than two benefices without cure simultaneously. His emphasis on the Prayer Book is unsurprising but within it lay a desire to begin the repair of the Church of Ireland by working explicitly on what it had in common with the Church of England.[57] He made no initial response to Wentworth and Bramhall's proposals for the Thirty-Nine articles and English canons, but did let them know on 11 March 1634 that he was still consulting with the king on these matters.[58]

Initially Wentworth was effusive about Laud's two steps, promising that he would speak to the primate and have the directions for services carried out within ten days, but by June the imminence of parliament and the importance of recusant support had made him more cautious.[59] Laud had no choice but to agree that 'two months' stay is to great good purpose' and make do with the prospect of good supply and statutory provision for the state church.[60]

There was still room for manoeuvre with convocation because by April the modalities of bringing in the English canons had already been dealt with:

[the king] requires your Lordship to prepare a draft there, such as may best fit the constitutions and customs of the country, for the reception and establishment both of the Canons and the Articles of the Church of England.[61]

The code was not to be referred to parliament and there was no anxiety that the Irish assembly would kick up in the same way that its English counterpart had done thirty years earlier.[62] Charles was, reportedly, especially pleased at measures to end clandestine marriage. This, of course, was only one of many abuses mentioned in Wentworth's original letter and suggests that the king was attracted not just by ecclesiastical congruence but also by

---

[56] *Ibid.*
[57] Davies, *Caroline captivity*, p. 67; also Str P 20/111; Alan Ford notes that Laud insisted on use of 'the English rather than Irish prayer book in the revised statutes for Trinity of 1637. The archbishop was perhaps being overcautious here since there was no distinct Irish Prayer Book and Daniel's translation gave the English Act of Uniformity of 1559 rather than the Irish Act of 1560, '"That bugbear Arminianism": Archbishop Laud and Trinity College, Dublin' in Ciaran Brady and Jane Ohlmeyer (eds.), *British interventions in early modern Ireland* (Cambridge, 2005), pp. 135–61 at p. 149.
[58] Laud to Wentworth, 11 March 1634, *WL* 6, pp. 357, 358.
[59] Wentworth to Laud, 12 April 1634, Str P 6, p. 44. Wentworth to Laud, 30 June 1634, Str P 6, p. 75: 'if that should give them an apprehension that a conformity in religion is so much as thought of'.
[60] Laud to Wentworth, 23 June 1634, *WL* 7, p. 78.
[61] Laud to Wentworth, 12 April 1634, *WL* 7, p. 66.   [62] Bray, *Anglican canons*, pp. liv–lxi, 258.

the prospect of engaging in a reform of Irish manners. In the private and frank correspondence of Laud and Wentworth, the canons are important in themselves and not just, as they have often been viewed, as a vehicle, through canon 1, for the imposition of the Thirty-Nine articles. Convocation was initially agitated by the Irish articles of 1615, but in the preceding months discipline and order had been the essence of official strategy for Ireland.

On 21 June 1633, or just over a month before Wentworth arrived, the communion table at Christchurch was set up altarwise.[63] Bramhall had marked Dublin as the place 'where the reformation will begin', and preached on 4 August 1633 on Matthew 16, xviii, 'tu es Petrus', declaring 'the church of Rome to be only schismatical and the pope to be a patriarch'.[64] Within a month of his arrival in Dublin, Wentworth had 'pulled down the deputy's seat in his own chapel, and restored the altar to its ancient place . . . the like is done in Christ's Church'.[65] The lord deputy and council issued orders for Christchurch which not only dealt with the misuse of the vaults and encroachments upon the churchyards but also regulated attire and behaviour within the cathedral.[66] Furthermore, the 'Dean, dignitaries and prebendaries' were to 'keep their proper seats', wear their surplices and hoods, the vicar and choristers were to wear surplices and no graduate was to preach without his hood.[67] Lay vicars choral were to seek ordination within six months or face dismissal.[68] These orders anticipated several of the provisions of the canons, but they were part of a greater whole. Christchurch was just a start and Laud wished to see the directions extended to every cathedral.[69] Change was not universally popular. Bedell, according to his biographer Clogie, was 'much displeased with the pompous service at Christ's Church in Dublin, which was attended and celebrated with all manner of instrumental music . . . as if it had been at the dedication of Nebuchadnezzar's golden image in the plain of Dura'.[70] Bedell 'discovered his dislike to a leading prelate', most likely Bramhall (who acts as a foil throughout that biography), who told him they 'served much to the raising of affections'.[71] Bedell allegedly made a suitably evangelical reply.

[63] Dublin City Library, Gilbert MS 169, p. 211.

[64] *Ibid.*   [65] Bramhall to Laud, 10 August 1633, *BW* I, pp. lxxix, lxxxi.

[66] SP 63/254/88, *Cal. SP Ire.* 1633–47, pp. 31–2; Raymond Gillespie (ed.), *The first Chapter Act Book of Christ Church cathedral, Dublin, 1574–1634* (Dublin, 1997), pp. 187–8, 202–4.

[67] See also Wentworth to Laud, December 1633, Knowler I, p. 172. These were similar to the orders issued for St Paul's and the Scottish parliament of 1633 required surplices and rochets for bishops: Macinnes, *Charles I*, pp. 136–7.

[68] Barra Boydell, *Music at Christ Church before 1800* (Dublin, 1999), pp. 68–9; Gillespie (ed.), *First Chapter Act Book*, pp. 205–6. Laud's Trinity statutes also placed considerable emphasis on ordination of fellows and students: Ford, '"That bugbear Arminianism"', p. 151.

[69] Laud to Wentworth, 13 January 1634, *WL* 7, p. 61.   [70] Shuckburgh, *Two lives*, p. 154.

[71] Kneeling for communion was also commanded.

The highly ornate Boyle family monument erected at the east end of St Patrick's was an immediate target of Wentworth's biting scorn: 'It is one of the most scandalous pieces that was ever – stands just in the altar place. The ten commandments taken down to make way.'[72] Wentworth had been forced to focus his attention on the removal of the Decalogue rather than the altar, following Ussher's insistence that the altar had never been near there in the first place. Laud, for his part, remained firmly outraged at the insult to the altar. The lord deputy judged the removal of the tomb a crucial prelude to motivating the two Boyle bishops to inform against their kinsman over his land deals. There was also a question of status intermixed with this part of the drive for decency in Dublin's cathedrals. Wentworth declared that he did not want to 'do reverence to God before his altar . . . lest men might think the king's deputy were crouching to a Dr Weston, to a Jeffrey Fenton, to an earl of Cork and his lady'.[73]

Cork procured letters of approbation from both Ussher and Lancelot Bulkeley, the archbishop of Dublin. Wentworth claimed that these had been written by Cork himself and approached Ussher to try to dissuade him from any further act of support.[74] He went on to claim that Ussher confessed his error and admitted he had been abused by Boyle. Laud's highly peremptory letters on the subject to Ussher and Bulkeley are amongst his most aggressive of all.[75] Wentworth, of course, tended to believe that others were inevitably dazzled by his logic and persuaded by his arguments. It is very likely that Ussher was highly affronted by this dual ticking off and viewed it as a slight on his primatial dignity. His earlier enthusiasm for Wentworth as a 'new Zerubbabel' was on the wane.[76]

As Ussher was lectured, Bramhall was promoted.[77] On 17 April 1634, Downham of Derry died.[78] Ussher's favoured candidate was John Richardson, bishop of Ardagh, though Wentworth wrote to Laud claiming that the primate preferred Bramhall. In turn, the provost (Robert Ussher) would be given Bramhall's archdeaconry of Meath and the dean of Cashel (Chappell)

---

[72] Wentworth to Laud, 29 January 1634, Str P 6, p. 14; Clodagh Tait, 'Colonising memory: manipulation of death, burial and commemoration in the career of Richard Boyle, First Earl of Cork (1566–1643)', *Proceedings of the Royal Irish Academy*, section C, 101, no. 4 (2001), 107–34.

[73] Wentworth to Laud, 18 March 1634, Str P 6, p. 35.

[74] Wentworth to Laud, 18 March 1634, Str P 6, p. 34: 'in a very respective and faithful manner . . . represented unto him . . . how far below it is a person of his estimation and place in the church to suffer himself to be wrought upon meanly to serve terms'.

[75] Ussher to Laud, *c.* August 1633, *UWW* XV, p. 573; Laud to Wentworth, 11[31] March 1634, *WL* 6, p. 358; Laud to Lancelot Bulkeley, March 1634, *WL* 6, pp. 361–3; Laud to earl of Cork, 21 March 1634, *WL* 6, pp. 364–5; 'The Lord Archbishop of Canterbury his answer to that branch of the Lord Primate of Armagh's letters concerning the Earl of Cork's tomb', Str P 6, pp. 62–3.

[76] Ussher to Laud, 12 February 1634, *UWW* XV, p. 574 [date from Bodl. Sancroft MS 18, p. 15].

[77] He had already been dean of Christchurch and archdeacon of Meath.

[78] Ussher to Laud, 30 April 1634, Bodl. MS Sancroft 18, p. 14.

the provostship.[79] This series of appointments was what Wentworth, not Ussher, desired. Wentworth not only supplanted Ussher with Bramhall but he even misrepresented him to Laud.[80] This was not conducive to good relations.

On Laud's elevation to Canterbury, Ussher offered him the chancellor-ship of Dublin University.[81] In his letter of 31 January 1634, Wentworth identified Trinity College as one of the key areas of the Church of Ireland in need of reform, suggesting that the provost be preferred out of the college and the statutes reviewed.[82] As it happened, Laud's involvement in Trinity College Dublin gave rise to some of the bitterest complaint.[83] Along with moves to investigate episcopal abuses of freeschool lands, to reform teaching in them and to compile a list of clergy with recusant wives and children, the wider campaigns for the cleansing of churches and the reorganisation of Trinity were begun in the months before convocation and served as continuing irritants of the wounds opened there.

In the meantime, Wentworth wholeheartedly agreed with Laud about keeping the matter of canons and articles away from the parliament 'which I confess I never held infallible, scarce orthodox in their decisions upon matters of faith'.[84] He had consulted with the nettled Ussher who had clearly decided to play a waiting game and see if convocation could provoke a crisis.[85] In a letter of 12 August, Samuel Ward wrote to Ussher praying that: 'God bless your meeting, both in the parliament and convocation; and that still the doctrine established both in the Kingdom and here may obtain.'[86] Laud and Wentworth allowed themselves to believe that given Ussher's 'disavowal', the convocation would simply settle, but Ward's tone was a hint that the Irish articles would not go without a struggle.

ADOPTING THE THIRTY-NINE ARTICLES, 1634

The greatest difficulty in discussing the Irish convocation of 1634 is that the journals are missing.[87] Retrospective accounts written in the 1650s are

---

[79] Wentworth to Laud, 23 April 1634, Str P 6, p. 49. Alan Ford, 'Richardson, John (1579/80–1654)', *ODNB*, http://www.oxforddnb.com/view/article/23558, accessed 19 September 2005.

[80] This manoeuvre gives the lie to Wentworth's claim in his letter to Laud of December 1633, Knowler I, p. 173, that he was keeping Ussher informed.

[81] Ussher to Laud, *UWW* XV, p. 572. 　　[82] Wentworth to Laud, 31 January 1634, Knowler I, p. 188.

[83] Ford, '"That bugbear Arminianism"', p. 158. 　　[84] Wentworth to Laud, 15 May 1634, Str P 6, p. 56.

[85] Wentworth appears to have understood the Irish articles as an altered version of the English ones: 'it is true indeed these Articles were changed here, which are such the Primate disavows'. Laud said he was glad to hear of Ussher's disavowal, see his letter of 25 June 1634, *WL* 7, p. 75.

[86] Ward to Ussher, 12 August 1634, *UWW* XVI, p. 520.

[87] They were extant amongst Clarendon's Irish manuscripts but dropped out of sight after the sale of the Chandos library and did not reappear in the British Museum or the Rawlinson collection.

unreliable. All of the remaining evidence is to be found in the correspondence of Laud, Wentworth, Ussher and Bramhall.[88]

Parliament opened on 14 July with a sermon in St Patrick's by Ussher on the text of Genesis 49, x: 'The Sceptre shall not depart from Judah, nor a lawgiver from between his feet, till Shiloh come, and to him shall the gathering of the people be.'[89] Wentworth praised the sermon and recommended its publication, but strained relations later on probably account for the fact that it never appeared in print.[90] After this apparently amicable start, convocation first sat on 21 July, and a week later gave the necessary example to the Commons by voting eight subsidies.[91]

There has been some confusion about what Ussher knew of Wentworth's intentions before the start of convocation.[92] Bramhall was definitely committed to the sole confirmation of the English articles.[93] The first hint of real trouble came towards the end of August.[94] Bramhall's regular letter to Laud began with news of William Chappell's election as provost of Trinity and the impropriations campaign before moving on to a skeleton account of convocation. He related that on 2 August, the last day of the session, there had been a bid to have the Irish articles confirmed along with the English a mere two hours after they had been proposed to a thinly attended

TCD MS 1062, p. 65; William Nicholson *The Irish historical library* (Dublin, 1724), p. 28; Bolton, *Caroline*, p. 11; William O'Sullivan, 'A finding list of Sir James Ware's manuscripts', *Proceedings of the Royal Irish Academy*, section C, 97, no. 2 (1997), 69–99.

[88] A version of this narrative account of convocation has appeared in John McCafferty, '"God bless your free Church of Ireland": Wentworth, Bramhall and the Irish convocation of 1634' in J. F. Merritt (ed.), *The political world of Thomas Wentworth, Earl of Strafford, 1621–1641* (Cambridge, 1996), pp. 187–208.

[89] Bernard, *The life of Ussher*, p. 92.

[90] *Tanner letters*, pp. 111–12. For Ussher's sermon on Wentworth's inauguration, see Alan Ford, 'James Ussher and the godly prince in early seventeenth-century Ireland' in Hiram Morgan (ed.), *Political ideology in Ireland, 1541–1641* (Dublin, 1999), pp. 203–28. From what Wentworth said in his speech to parliament it seems as if it dealt with the duty of the subject but may have included some allusions to the lord deputy's zeal for the church.

[91] TCD MS 1062, fols. 60–1. The subsidy was four shillings in the pound: 10 Charles I, sess. 3, c. 23.

[92] R. Buick Knox argues that Wentworth 'did not at first discuss with Ussher his plan to bring about uniformity with the Church of England', *James Ussher Archbishop of Armagh* (Cardiff, 1967), p. 48. Yet we know that in May Wentworth claimed to have secured a 'disavowal' of the Irish articles from the primate. Amanda Capern claims that Ussher and Bramhall had been working together, without telling Wentworth but with Laud's knowledge, to have both sets of articles received in the Irish church, '"Slipperye times and dangerous dayes": James Ussher and the Calvinist reformation of Britain 1560–1660', unpublished PhD thesis, University of New South Wales (1991), p. 237. This is a misreading of Bramhall's letter to Laud of 21 August 1634, HA 14040. While we know that Bramhall kept Laud abreast of Irish church affairs, there is no instance of him being commissioned by Laud to do anything (let alone enter into highly important negotiations) without consulting the lord deputy. Ussher knew what was in the wind from before the start of the convocation and it is reasonable to assume that he spent the time beforehand considering ways to protect the Irish articles.

[93] Bramhall to Laud, 21 August 1634, HA 14040.   [94] *Ibid.*

house 'without consulting his majesty or his deputy'.[95] He expressed his plain disapproval of the Irish articles and offered a historical solution to the emergent problem: 'the canon at the council of Cashel that the Irish church should be in all points conformed with the English'.[96] He also proposed that the Thirty-Nine articles could be brought in quietly through adoption of English canon 36 of 1603. He was optimistic about easy success on the confessional side and so had gone on to draw up the heads of several canons for Irish conditions which had been approved by Ussher. It seems that at this stage Bramhall, like Wentworth, had been lulled by Ussher's reassurances.

Wentworth's brief report on 23 August gave a somewhat less harmonious picture of events: 'it is true my Lord Primate seemed to disallow these Articles of Ireland, but when it comes to the upshot, I cannot find he does so absolutely as I expected'.[97] He went on to reassure Laud that he would 'carry it so as to have the Articles of England received in *ipsissimis verbis* leaving the other as no ways concerned in the state they now are, either affirmed or disaffirmed'. He could not afford, even if he wanted, to become embroiled in open conflict on Irish articles. Opposition in convocation had most likely accepted that the Thirty-Nine would be authorised for Ireland but aimed to give the 1615 confession equal status. Wentworth also hinted that Bramhall and Croxton were under considerable pressure in their respective houses during a first session of delicate skirmishing, in which Ussher gradually dropped his pretence of acquiescence but avoided a clash.[98]

On 1 October Laud responded to Bramhall in congratulatory tones, but reminded him to 'keep as close to the English canons as you can'.[99] Out of session Wentworth was preparing the church bills for transmission while Ussher bothered him about his primatial status and by recommending Dean George Andrews for the vacant see of Limerick.[100] Laud replied to

---

[95] Bramhall's agent in the lower house was James Croxton, who had been recommended to Mount-norris as a chaplain by Laud.

[96] The second council of Cashel, 1171–2: 'Item quod omnia divina ad instar sacrosanctae ecclesiae, juxta quod Anglicana observat ecclesia, in omnibus partibus amodo tractentur', John Wilkins, *Concilia Magnae Britanniae et Hiberniae*, 5 vols. (1737), vol. I, p. 473. Nial Osborough, 'Ecclesiastical law and the reformation in Ireland' in R. H. Helmholz (ed.), *Canon law in Protestant lands* (Berlin, 1992), pp. 223–52.

[97] Wentworth to Laud, 23 August 1634, Knowler I, p. 298.

[98] Wentworth's almost casual allusion to 'some little trouble there had been in it, and we are all bound not to advertise it over' evokes an image of opposing sides with strong views endeavouring to avoid a major incident. Given the delicate state of the Commons, none wished this more fervently than the lord deputy.

[99] Laud to Bramhall, 1 October 1634, HA 15156.

[100] Wentworth to Laud, 1 October 1634, Str P 6, p. 100; Wentworth castigated Andrews to Laud as a 'very covetous man' who had despoiled the diocese of Killaloe during the illness of its elderly

Wentworth's two letters on 20 October.[101] Either he had had his suspicions or was wise after the event as he wrote: 'I knew how you would find my Lord Primate affected to the Articles of Ireland; but I am glad the trouble that has been in it will end there without advertising of it over to us.' An apparently internal Irish solution averted any immediate political trouble or publicity in England. It also allowed Laud, if he chose, to argue that there had been no procedural irregularities or interference on his part. He was also careful to tell Charles about the strategy of having the English articles received without affirmation or denial of the Irish confession.[102] Tantalisingly, convocation politics occupy only a small part in this letter, which was far more concerned with demolition of the Boyle tomb, the assault on the earl's holdings at Youghal and in Lismore, a stock to buy in impropriations, and the overhaul of Trinity through Chappell's provostship.

The deceptive calm soon came to an end. On 31 October, Laud wrote to Wentworth to inform him of how, while visiting relatives in England, Theophilus Buckworth of Dromore (Ussher's brother-in-law) maintained that by sending for the Trinity statutes Laud meant to 'spoil' or 'overthrow' the college. Furthermore, he alleged that Canterbury favoured Arminians.[103] Buckworth had neatly associated recent events in Ireland with the theological brushfires of the last English parliament. His outburst gives an impression of how the church campaign was affecting sections of Irish clerical opinion for whom college and the 1615 articles were key expressions of identity. Again, the fallout from the Richard Montague affair and the royal declaration on controversies prompted Laud to urge, 'I heartily pray you make no public noise of it.'[104]

Six weeks later the storm heralded by Buckworth had broken:

it is true my Lord Primate did himself yield to the tacit way of burying the Articles of Ireland, and raising those of England forth of their ashes. But upon our meeting again this session he seems to be more diffident, pretending that he finds this Lower House of convocation more averse than he imagined, that they pressure the Articles of Ireland; so as I fear I shall be forced to speak loud amongst them.[105]

---

bishop; moreover 'he was in this last convocation as peevishly set for the Articles of Ireland and that as gravely and magisterially as any man in the company, for which I confess I like him not one jot'. Wentworth's opposition to Andrews, partly based on his behaviour in convocation, belied the picture of amity painted by Bramhall and was a sign of things to come. Bramhall was more circumspect and tended to support Andrews.

101 Laud to Wentworth, 20 October 1634, *WL* 6, pp. 396–402.
102 Laud to Wentworth, 20 October 1634, *WL* 6, p. 397, indicating that Charles approved of this course of action.
103 Laud to Wentworth, 31 October 1634, *WL* 7, p. 94: 'he delivered *in terminis* that in the late parliament I had set up men to maintain Arminianism'.
104 Laud to Wentworth, 31 October 1634, *WL* 7, p. 95.
105 Wentworth to Laud, 9 December 1634, Str P 6, p. 116.

The action had shifted to the clergy house in a bid to push the Irish articles through by pressure from below.[106] This move offered Ussher the chance to use the intransigence of the lower clergy as an excuse while, typically, refraining from expression of his personal feelings. There were two good motivations for this. Firstly, any apparent opposition to the Thirty-Nine articles would be politically suicidal for an archbishop of Armagh. Secondly, he too wished to avoid a public and potentially corrosive conflict.

Wentworth did raise the possibility of imposing the English articles and canons 'by the King's immediate pleasure' without the assent of convocation but only if all else was lost.[107] On 10 December Wentworth's patience broke. As he later avowed, Ussher's airing of his doubt about getting the English articles through the lower house put him on guard.[108] He claimed to have been preoccupied with the intricacies of parliament and so more reliant on Ussher. In fact, Wentworth had completed his last manoeuvre against the Old English on 27 November so his energies were not as fully engaged during the final days of the session. Bramhall, for his part, contended that it was he who had alerted Wentworth to the danger in convocation and, given the speed with which the latter acted on 9 and 10 December, this is likely.[109] Therefore Wentworth was magnifying his own part and placing the blame more squarely on Ussher.

What happened? The lower house of convocation had formed a select committee which proceeded to examine the English canons 'without conferring at all with their bishops'.[110] In the margins of the book they marked those they allowed with an 'A' and others with a 'D', which stood for *deliberandum*. In itself this was disquieting enough for the lord deputy and his allies but their draft Irish canon 5, in which 'they had brought the Articles of Ireland to be allowed and received under the pain of excommunication', really set off the alarm.

The proposed Irish canon gave the 1615 articles equal status. As the comments preserved in TCD MS 1038 (and they are most likely by Laud) point out, 'subscribe' in English canon 5 is changed to 'received and allowed', excommunication is not *ipso facto* and it does not speak of the public

---

[106] Wentworth identified the opposition in convocation as a group filled with 'a contradicting spirit of Puritanism', Str P 6, p. 123.

[107] 'I will still endeavour to obtain it with their own consents and thereby free your grace and his majesty from further appearing or trouble in it, and bring all ends together a more ecclesiastical way and with less noise', Wentworth to Laud, 9 December 1634, Str P 6, p. 116.

[108] Wentworth to Laud, 16 December 1634, Knowler I, p. 342: 'I rested secure upon the Primate, who all this while said not a word to me of the matter. At length I got a little time, and that most happily too, informed myself of the state of affairs.'

[109] Bramhall to Laud, 20 December 1634, Shirley, p. 43.

[110] Wentworth to Laud, 16 December 1634, Knowler I, p. 343; Bramhall to Laud, 20 December 1634, Shirley, p. 43.

Table 3.1 *Canon 1, 1634: a comparative table*

Canon 5, 1603	Canon 5, Hib: Manu: [TCD MS 1038, fols. 112v–113r]	Ussher's draft [WW20(172)]	Constitutions and canons ecclesiastical (Dublin, 1634)
Whosoever shall hereafter affirm, that any of the nine and thirty articles agreed upon by the archbishops and bishops of both provinces, and the whole clergy, in the convocation holden at London in the year of our lord God MDLXII for the avoiding of diversities of opinions, and for the establishing of consent touching true religion are in any part superstitious or erroneous, or such as he may not with a good conscience subscribe unto; let him be excommunicated *ipso facto*, and not restored, but only by the	Those which shall affirm any of the articles agreed upon by the clergy of Ireland at Dublin 1615, or any of the 39 concluded of in the convocation at London 1562 and received by the convocation at Dublin 1634 to be in any part superstitious, or such as may not with a good conscience be received and allowed, shall be excommunicated and not restored but only by the archbishop.[a]	For the manifestation of our agreement with the Church of England in the confession of the same Christian faith and the doctrine of the sacraments: we do approve the book of articles of religion agreed upon by the archbishops and bishops, and the whole clergy in the convocation holden at London in the year of our lord God 1562 for the avoiding of diversities of opinions, and for the establishing of consent touching true religion. So that hereafter any minister shall presume to teach anything contrary to the doctrine	For the manifestation of our agreement with the Church of England in the confession of the same Christian faith, and the doctrine of the sacraments; we do receive and approve the book of articles of religion agreed upon by the archbishops and bishops, and the whole clergy in the convocation holden at London in the year of our lord God MDLXII for the avoiding of diversities of opinions, and for the establishing of consent touching true religion. And therefore if any hereafter shall affirm that any of these articles are

archbishop, after his repentance, and public revocation of such his wicked errors.

delivered therein; upon refusal of the correction of his error, he shall be deprived of his ecclesiastical benefices as he doth enjoy.[b]

in part superstitious or erroneous, or such as he may not with a good conscience subscribe unto, let him be excommunicated, and not absolved, before he make a public revocation of his error.[c]

---

[a] There are marginal comments attached to the draft Irish canons in TCD MS 1038 fols. 112v–117r and PRONI Dio 4/10/2, pp. 149–61. They are most likely by Laud: 'And your book with A and D, I have sent it back to you, and with it some sudden animadversions guessing at the reasons of that reverend Dean's deliberations or doubtings of those canons so marked', Laud to Wentworth, 12 January 1635; WL 7, pp. 110–11. The comment on the draft Irish canon reads: 'Here the term of subscribing in the English canons is changed into receiving and allowing; for what reason I see not, except they suppose men that truly receive and allow would be loath to subscribe. I should think "erroneous" and "such as many not with a good conscience to be received and allowed" to differ very little from a tautology. It would be considered here whether these articles of Dublin 1615 agree substantially with those of London or confirmed equally by the King's authority else I see no reason of establishing them under one penalty.'

[b] Declaration of the synod affixed to the Irish articles of 1615: 'If any minister, of what degree or quality soever he be, shall publicly teach any doctrine contrary to these Articles agreed upon. If, after due admonition, he do not conform himself, and cease to disturb the peace of the Church, let him be silenced, and deprived of all spiritual promotions he doth enjoy', UWW I, appendix IV, p. 1.

[c] TCD MS 1038 fol. 112r gives: 'Let him be excommunicated *ipso facto* and not restored only by the archbishop after his repentance and public revocation of such his wicked errors', as the form sent to the prolocutor.

revocation of 'wicked errors'. This canon was more than a defence of the Irish articles: it harked back to the stresses and antipathies of the start of James VI & I's reign. By the same token, English canon 36, which included an article of subscription to the Thirty-Nine articles as 'agreeable to the word of God', was one of those canons *ad deliberandum*.[111] For Wentworth, the draft was the worst of both worlds – a defiant authorisation of the Irish articles combined with a direct challenge to his authority in its rejection of what he believed to be his politic drifts.

He hauled George Andrews, the chairman of the committee, before him and proceeded to examine the annotated canons with dramatic anger.[112] There would be no report from the committee. The next morning, Ussher, Anthony Martin of Meath, Bedell, John Leslie of Raphoe, Bramhall and Henry Leslie (as prolocutor of the lower house) and the other members of the committee were summoned to appear before him.[113] Acting as much the martinet as lord deputy, Wentworth admonished the clergy for their temerity: 'how unheard a part it was for a few petty clerks to presume to make articles of faith, without the privity or consent of state or bishop'. He lambasted them for their 'Brownism', for subversion of hierarchy. He also forestalled any response by warning them that he would not 'suffer them to be either mad in the convocation or in their pulpits'. He reiterated his ban on the report and ordered Henry Leslie to break up the house if any member of the committee attempted a question, moreover 'he should put no question at all, touching the receiving or not of the Articles of the Church of Ireland'. Reception of the English articles alone would be put to the house. There would be a straight ballot, without debate, and each vote recorded by name. In order to avoid any query (and to give Ussher a rap on the knuckles) the primate was instructed to draft a canon which, when inspected by Wentworth, would then be sent to the prolocutor.[114]

Convocation was now at the edge of an abyss. Internally, Bramhall, Croxton and others worked for the viceroy and, externally, it had no willing friends. For both of these reasons Wentworth had no need to invoke any particular powers and, like Henry Sidney before him, he simply acted in person as chief governor. Behind the façade of outrage, though, he worried he might have acted *ultra vires* and while he tried to trivialise his anxieties,

[111] TCD MS 1062, fol. 116r.

[112] 'I confess I was not so much moved since I came into Ireland. I told him certainly not a dean of Limerick but an Ananias had been there in spirit, if not in body, with all the fraternities and conventicles of Amsterdam.'

[113] Wentworth told Laud he was sending him a list of those on the committee; this too is no longer extant.

[114] Wentworth to Laud, 16 December 1634, Knowler I, p. 343.

he repeatedly pressed Laud for a letter from the king 'either of allowance of what I have done or for my absolution'.[115] Some interpretations of the Irish Acts of Supremacy and Uniformity tended to support his position but, in the end, royal approbation or absolution was the only sure defence.[116] His bluster even gave way to a kind of politic piety in his protestation that he had gone with 'an upright heart to prevent a breach, seeming at least, betwixt the churches of England and Ireland', along with a rather shrill promise that he would oversee the confirmation of the Irish articles with a canon if required.

Ussher's hastily drafted canon represented a last ditch effort to salvage something from the wreckage. He began with a 'manifestation of our agreement', an attempt to soften the blow by portraying the acceptance of the English articles as the agreement of one free church with another. He went further and tried in the final clause to sneak in a form of the 'Decree of the Synod' attached to the end of the 1615 articles. This last clause spurred Wentworth, who disliked both the sanction and the evocation of 1615, to draw up his version 'more after the words of the canon in England'. This new draft brought Ussher rushing to Wentworth to press for his own version as 'he feared the canon would never pass in such form, as I had made it'.[117] He got short shrift because, as Wentworth explained to Laud, he felt he could no longer trust the primate to be frank with him.[118] He now gave free voice to his suspicions of Ussher, but still added 'he is so learned a prelate, and so good a man, as I do beseech your Grace it may never be imputed unto him'.[119] Once again, Wentworth avoided openly personalising the conflict. Like Boyle, Ussher was not meant to become a focus for opposition. His standing in England meant any controversy would have more than domestic implications. If no dire offence was given, the cautious primate would hold his peace.

Despite his assertion that he would put his canon to convocation 'in those very words', there is a slight discrepancy between Wentworth's draft of the canon in his letter to the prolocutor in TCD MS 1038 and the final printed version. Wentworth's letter reproduces the last clause of English

---

[115] Wentworth to Laud, 16 December 1634, Knowler I, p. 344: 'I am not ignorant that my stirring herein will be strangely reported and censured on that side, and how I shall be able to sustain myself against your Prynnes, Pinns and Bens, with the rest of that generation of odd names and natures, the Lord knows'. For pressure on Laud to have his letter, see Knowler II, p. 381; *WL* 7, pp. 118, 122, 280. Even when the latter said there was no need of one – *WL* 7, p. 99.
[116] 28 Hen. VIII c. 5; 28 Hen. VIII c. 13; 2 Eliz. I c. 1.   [117] Knowler I, p. 344.
[118] 'Having taken a little jealousy that his proceedings were not open and free to those ends I had my eye on', Wentworth to Laud, 16 December 1634, Knowler I, p. 344.
[119] Knowler I, p. 343.

canon 5 exactly, but the printed version omits *ipso facto* excommunication, replaces 'restored' with 'absolved', makes no mention of archbishops or bishops, and changes 'wicked errors' to plain 'error'. There may have been, despite all the posturing, some small final concession to take a fully English gloss off canon 1.

The letter to the prolocutor was dispatched on the afternoon of 10 December and was put first to the bishops, where it carried unanimously. The clergy recorded one or two negative votes.[120] Wentworth mentions one unidentified opponent whereas Bramhall maintained there were two: 'Dr Hoyle and Mr Fitzgerald'.[121] The only resort now was to argue, as some did later on, that since the Irish articles had not been touched on one way or another, double subscription or rather a combination of double subscription and affirmation was a valid option.[122] By avoiding dissolution, convocation remained sitting and capable of affecting the shape of the canonical settlement.

Bramhall's account of proceedings, written on 20 December 1634, differed from Wentworth's in detail and in emphasis.[123] He maintained there had been another bid to force the Irish articles through the House of Bishops even before Andrews's committee had been due to make its report. 'I was the means to stay it', he claimed. Next he alerted the lord deputy to the danger. Bramhall collapsed all of the committee activity into one terse sentence: 'my lord deputy hath so ordered it that the articles of England solely are received by all the clergy'.[124] Instead he drew attention to 'underhand packing and *tacitorum inimicorum genus*' in the first session and, as ever, passed optimistically into the future: 'there is now no doubt of the canons'. His only other comment was to suggest that George Andrews had been more pawn than player and to beg Laud to forget 'some unbeseeming passages' since 'peace and perfect amity' now reigned.[125]

---

120   Wentworth to the prolocutor, 10 December 1634, TCD MS 1038, fol. 111v; Str P 20/173; Knowler I, p. 344. Writing about this around 1659, Bramhall claimed: 'My lord primate himself being president of the convocation, did send for the prolocutor of the house of clerks, and the rest of the clergy, and declare unto them the votes of the bishops, and move them to assent thereunto, which they did accordingly: all which the Acts and Records of that convocation do sufficiently testify', BW V, p. 82.

121   Bramhall to Laud, 20 December 1634, Shirley, p. 43. Heylyn, *Cyprianus Anglicus*, p. 272, follows Wentworth 'one man'. James Seaton Reid (*History of the Presbyterian Church in Ireland*, new edn, 3 vols. (Belfast, 1867), p. 174) suggests that this was one 'Hamilton of Ballywalter' which Reeves hotly refutes in TCD MS 1062, p. 63. Joshua Hoyle had his revenge by alleging Wentworth's part in an Arminian plot to subvert the Irish church. William Prynne, *Canterbury's doom* (1646), pp. 178, 359. The 'Mr Fitzgerald' might possibly be John Fitzgerald, dean of Cork.

122   See below, p. 111, for a discussion of this point.

123   Bramhall to Laud, 20 December 1634, Shirley, pp. 41–4.

124   Bramhall to Laud, 20 December 1634, Shirley, p. 43.   125   *Ibid.*

Wentworth's account excused his strong-arm tactics on grounds of the folly of convocation. Bramhall, however, impugned neither convocation nor primate and pointed the finger at an unnamed faction as the irritant. While Wentworth lambasted Andrews and suggested he be given Ferns and Leighlin without any commendams as a punishment, Bramhall was much more moderate.[126] Bramhall cast no aspersions at the deputy but neither did he risk cutting himself off from the rest of the clergy by appearing too triumphant or vengeful. It was obvious to everyone he was the agent of Laud and Wentworth but he was diplomatic enough to remember he had to work with other bishops in the recovery of the church's rights.[127] Overlooking the wrangles of the past months was the best hope of moving towards the united and disciplined church he hoped for in Ireland. When writing about it all in 1659, Bramhall was far less circumspect. He claimed that Ussher and Martin of Meath had opposed reception of the English articles in the initial debate in the upper house mainly out of 'love to the Irish'.[128] He wheeled out a 'precedent found of the ancient synod of Cashel' as the defining moment and elevated himself to a position as sole mediator between convocation and the lord deputy.[129]

Laud accepted Wentworth's assessment of the trouble which confirmation of the Irish articles would have caused, shared in his criticisms of Andrews, and castigated Ussher in cipher as one 'you had no reason to trust so far whom you had so good cause to suspect had not dealt openly with you in a business of such consequence'.[130] He agreed there had been an intention to surprise the castle with a snap confirmation but undertook to be circumspect.[131] He reported that he had given an edited account of proceedings to the king and council ostensibly because Wentworth's language had been a bit strong in places.[132] He reassured him that Charles was never better satisfied and would issue a 'letter of allowance'.[133]

---

[126] Wentworth to Laud, 16 December 1634, Knowler I, p. 344. Bramhall described Andrews as 'a grave cathedral man, well befriended and able to subsist of himself. I confess he has been a great deliberator this parliament, but surely rather as an instrument to others than a principal agent', Shirley, p. 44.

[127] In fact, Bramhall had just steered a motion through convocation for a petition for the restoration of royal impropriations: Shirley, p. 43. Bramhall probably also felt it was not his place to criticise Ussher.

[128] *BW* V, p. 81.   [129] *BW* V, p. 82.   [130] Laud to Wentworth, 12 January 1635, *WL* 7, p. 99.

[131] Laud to Wentworth, 12 January 1635, *WL* 7, p. 98: 'since you desire it, it shall not be imputed to the Primate'.

[132] 'I related the sum of the business to the King before the Lords but because we are not all one woman's children, I did forbear to read all your letters, lest some to whose pains you are beholden, might check at Ananias, and some other very good expressions; and especially to conceal the Primate', Laud to Wentworth, 12 January 1635, *WL* 7, p. 99.

[133] Laud to Wentworth, 12 January 1635, *WL* 7, p. 99.

The problem of George Andrews turned into an opportunity to mollify Ussher. Despite the king's reported annoyance at the dean's behaviour, Laud persuaded him to grant him Ferns and Leighlin. In explaining this, Laud made a crucial distinction: 'And since he is a bishop, I can be content to maintain his place, though I value not his person; and therefore have obtained of the King that he might hold *in commendam* that which he now has.'[134] Upholding the dignity of the church took precedence over revenge, in the same way that alienating Ussher, the chief dignitary of the church, was to be avoided even at the cost of seeing Andrews strut about in a rochet (or in his case not in a rochet).[135] Laud also implied that pleasing Andrews and through him appeasing Ussher was done in order to fit in with Bramhall's strategy for the rest of convocation.[136]

When discussing convocation with Bramhall, Laud was again entirely tactical, noting that one advantage of the whole affair was that it had forced the 'enemies' into the open and made them easier to deal with in the future.[137] The English canons were next and here the prime objective was to bring the Church of Ireland 'up' to standard.[138] Irish canon 1 was a first step towards a conformist reconstruction of the Church of Ireland.

JAMES USSHER, PRIMATE OF ALL IRELAND, AND THE ENGLISH CANONS, 1635–6

The third session of parliament began on 26 January 1635 but there was to be no easy passage in convocation. By mid February Bramhall was embroiled once more. On 18 February Bramhall reported to Laud that he knew well who the members of the 'faction' were, but he would keep going.[139] A new book of canons composed 'of the English and Irish Canons never yet allowed and the Injunctions' was being offered to convocation 'upon a pretence that the English canons will not pass freely unless they be brought in by a wile'. He admitted, grudgingly, that some special canons might be needed 'for this meridian', but expressed his opposition to some of the propositions.

---

[134] *Ibid.*   [135] See Wentworth to Laud, 9 December 1634, Str P 6, p. 121, for Andrews and the rochet.
[136] Laud to Wentworth, 12 January 1635, *WL* 7, p. 104.
[137] 'I gave my Lord Deputy a doubtful intimation of it [a faction] before, but it is no matter now, since all is well passed what the opposition was.' Laud suggested that Bramhall could use his knowledge of who the members of this faction were upon 'like occasions': Laud to Bramhall, 16 January 1635, HA 15157.
[138] Laud to Wentworth, 12 January 1635, *WL* 7, p. 109: 'though some of them perhaps will not presently fit that church, yet better it is that church should grow up to them, than that such confusion should continue as hitherto been among them'.
[139] Bramhall to Laud, 18 February 1635, HA 14048.

Here was an important difference in perception between Bramhall and his opponents. For him, any discrete Irish canons would merely allow for the specifics of the Irish situation, but the overall thrust of legislation would establish and even improve on the English standard – this was his principle of congruence. His adversaries were motivated partly by what had happened before Christmas and partly by a sense of a distinctiveness which was of recent vintage.

Skirmishing started again and again Ussher's sensibilities were the pivot. Bramhall pressured the primate into sending the drafts to Laud for his 'advice'.[140] Laud had a chaplain review the canons, treating the question of Ussher gingerly.[141] Armagh chose to needle, by attacking Laud's protégé Croxton, by backing Andrews, by giving spiky sermons, and in all summoning up the spectre of a public breach. Wentworth got the message. In his next letter to Laud he acknowledged the desirability of a full set of English canons but added:

> the Primate is hugely against it . . . lest Ireland might become subject to the Church of England, as the province of York is to that of Canterbury: needs forsooth we must be a church of ourselves, which is utterly lost unless the canons here differ, albeit not in substance, yet in some form from yours in England.[142]

Although resigned to concessions, Wentworth kept up a stream of complaint – these objections were 'punctilio', a mere 'crotchet', he had been put up to it by 'puritan correspondents of his' who took advantage of his desire to please everybody. Ussher appears to have hoped for a revival in the old spirit of cooperation since he had broached writing to Laud on the subject of canons.[143] Even if Laud had been inclined to be gracious, he would have hardly understood the subtleties of Ussher's position since his argument for identical codes was based on an assumption that all secular law was the same in both jurisdictions.[144]

The final session of parliament began on 24 March.[145] By 13 April Wentworth reported that a book of canons had been passed even though Ussher had threatened to resign 'least forsooth, the Church of Ireland should

---

[140] Though Bramhall was beginning to apprehend the opportunities – a chance to make up canonically for some of the losses in parliament such as the failed bills on simony and for residence of beneficed persons: Bramhall to Laud, 20 December 1634, Shirley, p. 44.

[141] Laud to Bramhall, 4 March 1635, HA 15158: 'I have pressed the English Canons to be received *formaliter*, a little softer to my Lord Primate . . . I leave the further care of this business to you'.

[142] Wentworth to Laud, 10 March 1635, Knowler I, p. 381.   [143] Knowler I, p. 381.

[144] Laud to Wentworth, 27 March 1635, WL 7, p. 118: 'what hurt were it more that the canons of the Church should be the same, than it is that the Laws are the same?'

[145] Parliament was dissolved on 18 April 1635.

be held subordinate to the Church of England'.[146] He did not because the new book of canons was a compromise. Wentworth was sure to gratify Canterbury with altars at the east end, or sacramentalised confession, but had to concede defeat on bowing to the name of Jesus.[147] Bramhall was instructed to write to Laud detailing how the canons had been finally formulated, but since this crucial letter is no longer extant only John Vesey's account remains.[148]

According to this narrative, based on the testimony of Thomas Price, Ussher expressed his desire to extend the 'right hand of fellowship' and give 'due honour' to the Church of England, but cautioned against surrendering all self-determination and ending up with the canonical equivalent of Poynings' Act.[149] Some 'discrepancy' must continue because

there is no necessity of the same in all churches that are independent, as these are, of one another; that Rome and Milan might have different canons and modes and yet the same faith and charity and communion.

Bramhall's response was crisp: 'they would no more resign their privileges and authority in receiving of their canons, than of their faith in the Articles'.[150] After a heated debate and conference of both houses only a minority voted for a plain adoption of the English code and Bramhall was appointed chief compositor of a new Irish book. Laud was sarcastic, 'God bless your free Church of Ireland, though for my part I do not think the canons of the Church of England would have shot any of the freedom of it.'[151] Some near contemporary and many later accounts of the convocation of 1634–5 have chosen to represent it as a credal conflict. This works nicely for a narrative in which the Westminster assembly is all the more triumphant because its harbingers – Lambeth and Ireland – were rejected or suppressed. Ussher may well have had theological anxieties in 1634–5, but he was also undoubtedly concerned with possible implications for the primatial status he had so assiduously cultivated over the previous decade.

---

[146] Wentworth to Laud, 13 April 1635, Str P 6, p. 162.

[147] 'But as for bowing at the name of Jesus it will not down with them yet. They have no more joints in their knees for that than an elephant', Wentworth to Laud, 18 April 1635, Str P 6, p. 164. See also Bernard, *Judgement* (1657), p. 147, and Bramhall's response, *BW* V, p. 77.

[148] John Vesey claimed to have been given an account of the convocation by Thomas Price, then archbishop of Cashel, who had been the archdeacon of Kilmore in 1634–5. Vesey, *Athanasius Hibernicus*, [pp. 18ff]. See also Laud to Wentworth, 31 July and 3 August 1635, *WL* 7, p. 156; Wentworth to Laud 14 July 1635, Str P 6, p. 20; Heylyn, *Cyprianus Anglicus*, p. 272; *BW* V, p. 77.

[149] Vesey, *Athanasius Hibernicus*, [p. 19]: 'that nothing shall be law here that were not first allowed there, and afterward, that we must refuse nothing here, that there had obtained a confirmation'.

[150] Vesey, *Athanasius Hibernicus*, [p. 19].   [151] Laud to Bramhall, 11 May 1635, HA 15159.

On 21 March 1625 James Ussher received his letters patent making him archbishop of Armagh and primate of all Ireland. Armagh had enjoyed mixed fortunes since Henry's reformation. The first two reformation archbishops had been of intermittent conformity, recognised by crown and pope.[152] The first demonstrably Protestant archbishop, Adam Loftus, was translated to Dublin in 1567 (technically a demotion) after only four years in Armagh. From then until the advent of Henry Ussher (Ussher's uncle) in 1595, the see was served by a series of undistinguished and politically uninfluential men. In addition, until the plantation of Ulster, the diocese continued to be divided *inter anglicos* and *inter hibernicos*, thus reducing the authority and income of the archbishops.[153] Such weakness caused the dispute for precedency between Dublin and Armagh (which had been running since the twelfth century) to flare up again.[154] John Allen of Dublin and George Cromer clashed in 1533 and in 1551 George Browne of Dublin procured letters from Edward VI annexing the primacy of all Ireland to his own see. While Mary passed the primacy back to Armagh, the matter was still unresolved at the time of Ussher's promotion.

Christopher Hampton, Ussher's immediate predecessor, began not only to improve the temporal fortunes of the primacy but also to rebuild its status.[155] In 1616, he secured the office of almoner of Ireland for the primacy, giving Armagh sole power of collecting and spending recusancy fines.[156] In 1620, he procured a grant of the offices of prerogative and faculties.[157] The recovery of Armagh provoked jealousy in Dublin and matters reached such a pitch that James had to order the lord deputy to hear the claims of each party as he disapproved of them 'jostling one another at public meetings'.[158] Lancelot Bulkeley succeeded in recapturing prerogative jurisdiction for his own province in 1621 though he was quickly repulsed.[159]

---

[152] George Cromer 1521–43 and George Dowdall 1543–51 and 1553–8.

[153] Loftus, for instance, was unable to go to Armagh itself as it was in the hands of Shane O'Neill. The income was pitiful – perhaps as low as £20 a year.

[154] *UWW* I, p. cxxix; J. A. Watt, 'The disputed primacy of the medieval Irish church' in Peter Linehan (ed.), *Proceedings of the Seventh International Congress of Medieval Canon Law, Cambridge, 1984*, Monumenta Iuris Canonici, ser. C, Subsidia, 8 (Vatican City, 1988), pp. 373–83.

[155] Christopher Hampton, 1613–25. He commissioned Ussher to write a treatise on the archbishops of Armagh: Ussher to Camden, 8 June 1618, *UWW* XV, p. 135.

[156] James to Oliver St John [Grandison], 12 June 1621, *Cal. SP Ire.* 1615–25, p. 328.

[157] *Cal. SP Ire.* 1615–25, p. 296; Osborough, 'Ecclesiastical law and the Reformation in Ireland', p. 236.

[158] James to Oliver St John [Grandison], 12 June 1621, *Cal. SP Ire.* 1615–25, p. 328.

[159] *Cal. SP Ire.* 1615–25, pp. 332, 344. It was called in twice, in July 1621 and again in February 1622; Bulkeley finally surrendered it in April, *Cal. SP Ire.* 1615–25, p. 328.

On his promotion, one of Ussher's first acts was to petition for the maintenance of the rights and dignities of his see.[160] While this was prompted as a result of a dispute with Thomas Ryves, the registrar of the court of prerogative and faculties, it also reflected Ussher's concern to continue on in the same way as his predecessor.[161] After some struggle he was confirmed in the office of prerogative and faculties, with the power to 'appoint surrogate, register &c, *as is done by the Archbishop of Canterbury*'.[162] Gratifyingly for the antiquarian Ussher, this fitted with his perception of himself as successor to Patrick, entitled to rank with the successor of Augustine in equal dignity. All that remained was to secure the primacy irrevocably to Armagh. While Charles had directed lord deputy Falkland to determine the question in 1626, nothing happened until June 1634 when Wentworth summoned Ussher and Bulkeley to appear before the board.[163] Ussher produced a meticulously researched statement and emerged victorious as 'sole primate of Ireland'. A fortnight later, he took the primate's place in the procession to parliament.[164]

His ambition for Armagh went beyond national precedence. In a letter to Laud of August 1634, he expanded out his account of the primacy hearings to wonder, after a display of erudition, 'whether it would not make somewhat for the dignity of his majesty's kingdoms and the splendour of our church that we should have not only metropolitans, but patriarchs also within ourselves as in the days of old'.[165] When Ussher congratulated Laud on his appointment to Canterbury, he presented him with a treatise 'touching the

---

[160] Ussher to Secretary Conway, 15 July 1625; Edward Clark to William Boswell, 24 August 1625; Ussher to Conway, 27 September 1625; *Cal. SP Ire.* 1625–32, pp. 24, 31, 41.

[161] William Clerk to Ussher, 16 April 1625, *UWW* XVI, pp. 421–4; Ussher to the Lord Keeper and Lord High Treasurer, 20 August 1635, *UWW* XV, p. 300; Buick Knox, *Ussher*, pp. 42–4.

[162] SP 63/247/1066, *Cal. SP Ire.* 1625–32, p. 364 (my italics). Ussher also put much energy into reorganising the cathedral chapter in Armagh itself, *Cal. SP Ire.* 1625–32, pp. 416, 587, 674. He also used the cathedral for the consecration of bishops for the first time in living memory: Ussher to Laud, *c.* late 1633, *UWW* XV, p. 571.

[163] *UWW* I, p. 161. Ussher's *Religion anciently professed* makes many references to Armagh employing terms such as 'the city apostolic', *UWW* IV, p. 18.

[164] Wentworth's judgement is printed in *UWW* I, pp. 161–2. Ussher's notes on the primacy are to be found in TCD MSS 580–2 and 786, some of these are printed in *UWW* I, appendix vi. There is no evidence to support Capern's view that Ussher was determined to settle the primacy in case a 'Laudian' succeeded Bulkeley in Dublin: Capern, '"Slipperye times and dangerous dayes"', p. 228. Ussher seized every opportunity to further enhance the dignity of the primacy. So, while he was the only notable figure in communication with Lord Chancellor Loftus when the latter fell from power in 1638, he still wrote to Laud proposing the reduction of the chancellor's rank to that of the same officer in England. This entailed the archbishop of Armagh taking precedence: Ussher to Laud, 9 July 1638, *UWW* XVI, p. 36. See also *BW* V, p. 84; Str P 7, pp. 114–15; Richard Parr, *Life of Ussher* (1686), p. 41.

[165] Ussher to Laud, 20 August 1634, Bodl. MS Sancroft 18, p. 15. A row about precedence in the convocation between the dean of Armagh and the deans of Christchurch and St Patrick's was

ancient dignity of the see of Canterbury'.[166] For Ussher, Armagh was the equal of Canterbury, so he and Laud were brother primates, even brother patriarchs. If Ussher was angry, even somewhat alienated, on account of his treatment in winter 1634 and spring 1635 it was in a good part because he felt he had not been treated as a co-equal primate of a national church.[167]

In the dedication to his *Discourse of the religion anciently professed*, he had asserted that 'the religion professed by the ancient bishops, priests and monks and other Christians in this land, was for substance the very same with that which now by public authority is maintained therein'.[168] This was 1631 and the religion maintained by authority included the 1615 articles. In a letter to Samuel Ward just after convocation he lashed out at Robert Shelford's *Five pious and learned discourses* complaining 'while we strive here to maintain the purity of our ancient truth, how comes it to pass that you in Cambridge do cast such stumbling blocks in our way by publishing unto the world such rotten stuff'.[169] The purity of ancient truth was included in the Irish articles because, as he said elsewhere, 'we bring in no new faith, no new church'.[170]

While he conferred the Church of Ireland with its own distinct pedigree, Ussher made no pretension to autonomy. He strongly defended the claim of the kings of England to the dominion of Ireland independent of any papal authority.[171] Ireland was undeniably part of the *imperium* vested in

---

to be decided on the practice used between the dean of Canterbury and those of St Paul's and Westminster.

[166] Ussher to Laud, undated, late 1633, *UWW* XV, p. 573. This may well be *De antiquitate Britannicae ecclesiae et privilegiis ecclesiae Cantaurensis cum archiepiscopus eiusdem 70* (1572) which as Anthony Milton points out in *Catholic and reformed*, p. 337, had a very limited print run.

[167] Ussher never rejected the English articles. In his sermon to the English House of Commons in 1621 he declared 'we all agree that the Scriptures of God are the perfect rule of our faith, we all consent in the main grounds of religion drawn from thence: we all subscribe to the articles of doctrine agreed upon in the Synod of the year 1562', *UWW* II, p. 421. See also *UWW* I, p. 43 and *BW* V, p. 81. It seems likely that he saw the Irish articles as a more perfect explanation of the English. Yet the Irish articles were bound up with his belief in the Church of Ireland as the true successor of the church of Patrick. See Randolph Holland to Ussher, 1 June 1623, *UWW* XVI, p. 403, and Ussher to anon., 8 December 1628, *UWW* XVI, p. 439. See also Philip Schaff, *The creeds of Christendom* (1877), pp. 665, 743, 761.

[168] Ussher, *Discourse*, sig A3r.

[169] Ussher to Ward, 15 September 1635, *UWW* XVI, p. 9. Shelford's denial of the pope as Antichrist fits well with Ussher's insistence that the 1615 articles still stand later in the letter: Milton, *Catholic and reformed*, p. 118.

[170] *An answer made to a challenge made by a Jesuit in Ireland* (1625), *UWW* III, p. 493.

[171] He pushed back the existence of the kingdom of Ireland three centuries before the Henrician statute, maintaining that Ireland in the twelfth century 'was esteemed a kingdom, and the kings of England accounted no less than Kings thereof', Ussher, *Discourse*, p. 118. Ussher rejected the notion of Canterburian primacy out of hand in a letter to Spelman of 4 September 1639, TCD MS 3659 (draft version MS 545): 'to infer a primacy of the see of Canterbury over the British and

the crown of England. The Church of Ireland, for its part, could share in the type of 'government of the Church of England', it could use the English Prayer Book and could accept 'fraternally' the doctrine of the neighbouring church.[172] This attitude lay behind his comparison with Rome ('great dunghill of errors' though it might be) and Milan.[173] The outright failure of Wentworth and Laud to appreciate the need for some 'discrepancy', even just as a means of acknowledging status, was a large part of what motivated Ussher to opposition. In defeat, he ended by taking comfort in a variant of the position he had initially rejected:

the articles of religion agreed upon in our former synod anno MDCXV we let stand as they did before. But for the manifesting of our agreement with the Church of England, we have received and approved your articles also.[174]

Ussher wrote to Samuel Ward announcing the outcome of convocation from his house at Drogheda.[175] His withdrawal from Dublin has been subject to varying interpretations. One is that of scholarly exile to prepare for *Immanuel* (1638) and *Antiquities of the British churches* (1639). Another is of angry retreat, a protest against what had happened in convocation and his gradual eclipse by Bramhall.[176]

In 1631, Ussher had reluctantly agreed to a recall of George Downham's *Covenant of grace* at Laud's request but he persisted in the publication of his own *Gotteschalcus* which was, he said, designed to 'bring either side to some better temper'.[177] This study of Gotteschalk was a historical work, published in Latin, but its account of the rise of Pelagianism and its concern with double predestination skated on the thinnest of ice. Only Ussher's sheer erudition prevented a serious crack.[178]

Irish churches standeth with little reason'. This point has been discussed in J. S. Morrill, 'A British patriarchy? Ecclesiastical imperialism under the early Stuarts' in Andrew Fletcher and Peter Roberts (eds.), *Religion, culture and society in early modern Britain* (Cambridge, 1994), pp. 209–37.

172 Ussher used the term government of the Church of England with reference to Ireland in a letter to an unknown English correspondent on 28 January 1630, *UWW* XIV, p. 511.

173 *An answer*, *UWW* III, p. 10.   174 Ussher to Ward, 15 September 1635, *UWW* XVI, p. 9.

175 Ussher to Ward, 15 September 1635, *UWW* XVI, pp. 9–10. In an undated letter, Ward had this to say to Bramhall on the subject of canons: 'I understand by your lordship's letters that the Scottish church has set forth canons which I did not hear before. It is much to be wished that there were an uniformity in the churches within His Majesty's dominions. I received the Irish canons from my Lord Primate of Armagh which are much conformable to the English', HA Irish Manuscript Unsorted Papers, Boxes 5–8.

176 Buick Knox, *Ussher*, pp. 52–3, Parr, *Life of Ussher*, p. 46; *UWW* I, p. 17; Str P 6, pp. 363, 271; *WL* 7, p. 212.

177 Ussher to Laud, 30 June 1631, SP 63/252/1978, *Cal. SP Ire.* 1625–32, p. 618: 'I thought it fitter to publish it in the Latin tongue than in the vulgar, because I held it not convenient that the common people should be tangled with questions of this nature.'

178 Ussher to Laud, 8 November 1631, SP 63/252/2035, *Cal. SP Ire.* 1625–32, p. 633. Prynne, *Canterbury's doom*, prints a version of this letter, which is denounced by Elrington in *UWW* I, pp. 129–30.

So while Laud urged Wentworth to cooperate with Ussher, he still had periodic misgivings.[179] In response to the lord deputy's question whether the primate had 'all that goes to a good bishop, and a good governor? I must needs answer, No.'[180] He went on to warn Wentworth to be vigilant as Ussher's 'frequent' letters had ceased 'since your lordship went thither'.[181] It must have rankled that the drafts of the statutes for church lands passed through Bramhall's hands first and, worse still, so did the new statutes for Trinity, and that Derry enjoyed the consistent favour of the lord deputy over longer-serving clergy as well as the ready ear of Laud.

On Wentworth's side, Ussher's silences, prevarication, alliance with Boyle in the tomb affair, defence of 'transgressors' and hurt disposition drove him to exasperation.[182] Only the old familiar explanation made sense – the primate was a good-natured but impractical academic, inclined to be churlish at times and easily led by others.

Ussher's own excuse for withdrawal from the capital was exhaustion, need for recuperation and meditation, and to save on the expense of life in Dublin.[183] His biographers, and indeed Bramhall himself, have been at pains to show that he was not of a vindictive disposition and did not seek revenge.[184] This is true, it was not his style, but absence of overt recriminations does not mean that he was happy. Long absences in Drogheda spoke for themselves especially at a time when much was being asked of a freshly endowed and heavily supported episcopate. Even before convocation was over, Ussher was attacking James Croxton for preaching Arminianism.[185] Hugh Cressy, another of Laud's protégés, gave the primate offence with 'some Arminian points touched in his sermons'. In his own sermons before the lord deputy, Ussher was giving 'gentle touches' against bowing.[186] Ussher resented the changes being made in Trinity, eventually accusing Chappell of Arminianism and 'idolatrous bowing'. He pointedly seized upon

---

179 Laud to Wentworth, 30 April 1633, *WL* 6, p. 307.
180 Laud to Wentworth, 15 November 1633, *WL* 6, p. 332.   181 *WL* 6, 332.
182 Ussher's defence of Sutton, 'the genius of this country', Wentworth to Laud, 18 March 1634 Str P 6, pp. 43–4; Wentworth to Laud, 19 November 1634, Str P 6, p. 100.
183 Ussher to Ward, 15 September 1635, *UWW* XVI, p. 9; Ussher to Laud, 4 January 1636, Bodl. Sancroft 18, p. xvi. His library was in Drogheda but he may have been thinking of a shift because in 1632 he petitioned to have a garden around a newly purchased house in Rathfarnham: J. T. Gilbert (ed.), *Calendar of the ancient records of Dublin*, 5 vols. (Dublin 1889–95), vol. III, p. 260. In the garden he had built a study at a good distance from the main house in order to work undisturbed; see William Brereton, *Travels in the United Provinces, England, Scotland and Ireland*, ed. Edward Hawkins (1844), p. 143: 'although there be not very many books, yet those that are, much used and employed'.
184 *BW* V, p. 83; *UWW* I, p. 176; Parr, *Life of Ussher*, p. 46.
185 Laud to Bramhall, 4 March 1635, HA 15159; Wentworth to Laud, 14 July 1635, Str P 6, p. 200.
186 Wentworth to Laud, 14 July 1635, Str P 6, p. 201.

Wentworth's absence in England to close down the licensed theatre in Dublin.[187] He even teased. When a vacancy arose for a baron of the exchequer, Ussher petitioned on behalf of his brother-in-law, William Hilton, one-time judge of the prerogative court. This man had earlier been targeted as the exemplar of all that was corrupt about Irish officials. Ussher wrote deadpan:

I have a brother in law not altogether unknown unto your honour . . . generally reputed of all that know him, to be a most honest man, and to have carried himself most diligently and faithfully in those employments wherewith he had been entrusted.[188]

Even his reclusive disgruntlement found a public platform. By November 1635 a story began to circulate that Ussher had 'given over preaching and is turned papist'. Wentworth attributed Ussher's decision to retire to Drogheda to his inability to 'digest' the reception of the English articles.[189] In a reply which showed how deep the rift could have become, Laud remarked 'if the Articles of England be the cause of it, I had rather lose him than them'.[190] But he did not believe Ussher could have turned recusant. Ussher's defence was indignant but cleverly barbed: 'whatsoever others do imagine of the matter, I stand fully convicted that the pope is Antichrist'.[191] This was not just a conventional piece of anti-popery but also a deliberate allusion to Irish article 80 – a clear message to Laud that not only had he not apostatised but that he stood firmly by the 1615 articles.

While Wentworth and Laud were at pains to keep up an appearance of general amity, they privately acknowledged that the Irish primate was prickly and alienated. Bramhall was strictly enjoined to show all due respect.[192] Correspondence between the two archbishops was guttering down by 1633 and appears to have extinguished itself completely from 1636 to 1638. Laud complained a number of his letters went unanswered. Ussher's absence and his barbs and teases were publicly interpreted as opposition and so tarnished the image of a revivified Church of Ireland. Irish Catholics

---

[187] Laud to Wentworth, received 14 September 1637, *WL* 7, p. 280; Wentworth to Laud, 10 July 1637, Str P 7, p. 39. Alan Fletcher, *Drama, performance and polity in pre-Cromwellian Ireland* (Cork, 2000), pp. 262–3.

[188] Ussher to Wentworth, 5 January 1637, Str P 20, p. 131.

[189] Wentworth to Laud, 2 November 1635, Str P 6, pp. 271–2.

[190] Laud to Wentworth, 30 November 1635, *WL* 7, p. 213.

[191] Ussher to Laud, 4 January 1636, Bodl. Sancroft 18, p. 16.

[192] Laud to Wentworth, 8 September 1636, *WL* 7, pp. 280–1; 26 September 1636, *WL* 7, p. 287; Wentworth to Laud, 14 September, Str P 6, p. 357; Laud to Bramhall, 11 May 1635, HA 15159.

gleefully seized, with deliberate exaggeration, on something which offered further proof of the disunity of the established church. Observers in England who were hostile to William Laud's reconstructions in the Church of England were less free to speak out than Irish Catholics, but Ussher's demeanour allowed them to recast him as a protomartyr when their tongues were unleashed some years later.

A NEW BOOK OF CANONS FOR IRELAND

Authorship of the Irish canons has been attributed to Bramhall and Ussher respectively.[193] In reality, the Irish canons were hammered out during March and April of 1635 and their final published form reveals a complicated compromise.[194] Before they were halted, the lower house produced draft versions of thirty English canons, having worked their way up to canon 71.[195] Canon 5 was altered, as seen, to include the 1615 articles, while each of the others was rewritten in such a way as to lessen its impact or make it less specific.[196] Out of the thirty English canons touched upon by the committee of convocation, eight were omitted from the final version. Overall 141 English canons became 100 Irish – thirty English canons were dropped entirely and there were seven uniquely Irish canons. Twenty Irish canons incorporated anything from two to four of the English ones. The Irish book also betrays some signs of haste. Irish canon 49 on marriage licences repeats English canon 102 (with only a small addition), beginning: 'the security mentioned shall contain these conditions'. The problem is that this is a reference to English canon 101 (which concerns licences to marry without banns and the security to be provided for the issue of the licences), but that canon was dropped from the Irish code, making the start of Irish canon 49 a nonsense.

The alterations made to the 1603 book were far more than the raggedness of a deal worked out in a hurry. In their final form the Irish canons were the product of a clash between Bramhall, trying not only to ensure the greatest conformity with England but also to target specific Irish abuses

---

[193] Nicholas Bernard, *Clavi trabales* (1661), p. 63; *UWW* I, p. 177.

[194] Unlike the official Latin version of the 1571 and 1603 canons, the Irish canons seem to have been only in English: *Ecclesiastical law: being a reprint of the title ecclesiastical law from Halsbury's laws of England*, 3rd edn (1955), p. 13. I would like to thank Gerald Bray for drawing this to my attention and for his generosity in allowing me see the drafts of his book *Anglican canons* prior to its publication.

[195] English canons 5, 13, 14, 15, 17, 18, 24, 25, 26, 27, 28, 30, 31, 32, 33, 34, 35, 36, 37, 38, 40, 41, 44, 55, 62, 71.

[196] Eleven of the twenty-nine English canons were eventually omitted in the range ECs 72–141.

Table 3.2 *English canons deliberated, TCD MS 1038 fols. 112v–117r*[a]

Canon	Irish canons 1634
4 Impugners of public worship of God established in the CofE	3
5 Impugners of articles of religion censured	1
6 Impugners of rites and ceremonies . . . censured	–
11 Maintainers of conventicles censured	5
12 Maintainers of constitutions made in conventicles censured	–
13 Due celebration of Sundays and holydays	6
14 Prescript form of divine service to be used Sundays & holydays	7
15 Litany to be read on Wednesdays and Fridays	–
17 Students in colleges to wear surplices in time of divine service	–
18 Reverence and attention to be used within church	7
24 Copes to be worn in cathedral churches	–
25 Surplices and hoods to be used in cathedral churches	7
26 Notorious offenders not to be admitted to communion	20
27 Schismatics not to be admitted to communion	–
28 Strangers not to be admitted to communion	95
30 Lawful use of the cross in baptism	–
31 Four solemn times for making of ministers	29
32 None to be made deacon and minister both in the one day	29
33 Titles of such as are to be made ministers	30
34 Quality of such as are to be made ministers	31
35 Examination of such as are to be made ministers	32, 1–4
36 Subscription of such as are to be made ministers	32, 1–4
37 Subscription before the diocesan	32
38 Revolters after subscription censured	–
40 Oath against simony	35
41 Licences for plurality	36
44 Prebendaries to be resident as benefices	28
55 Form of prayer to be used before all sermons	–
62 Ministers not to marry any persons without banns or license	52
71 Ministers not to preach or administer communion in private houses	21

[a] Also PRONI Dio 4/10/2, pp. 149–61.

and 'improve' on the English canons, and Ussher who was seeking to preserve a degree of 'discrepancy' and greater elasticity on preaching. A closer
examination of the Irish canons offers further insight into the dynamics of
the convocation as well as the reconstruction project. Two different under-
standings of establishment were at work over these months. In the event,
Bramhall went far beyond his initial grudging acceptance of a few canons
for 'that meridian' and Ussher secured something more than a facsimile of
the Church of England.

Table 3.3 *Comparison of 1603 and 1634 canons*

Irish 1634	English 1603	Irish 1634	English 1603
I	5, 36	51	104
2	1, 2, 36	52	62, 63
3	4, 36	53	105
4	7, 8, 36	54	106
5	9, 11	55	107, 108
6	13	56	92, 93
7	14, 18, 25	57	95
8	–	58	96
9	45	59	97
10	53	60	65
11	59	61	109
12	–	62	110
13	56	63	112
14	68	64	113
15	69	65	115
16	29	66	116
17	60, 61	67	117
18	21	68	119
19	22	69	120
20	26	70	–
21	71	71	122
22	73	72	123
23	127	73	124
24	–	74	125
25	–	75	126
26	42	76	127, 128
27	43	77	129
28	44	78	132
29	31, 32	79	133
30	33	80	–
31	34	81	134
32	35, 37	82	135
33	39	83	136
34	–	84	137
35	40	85	138
36	41	86	91
37	46, 47	87	89
38	48	88	90, 85
39	50, 51	89	118
40	66	90	–
41	67	91	18, 85, 111
42	74, 75	92	88
43	–	93	85
44	87	94	80, 81, 82
45	–	95	83
46	70	96	20, 28
47	99	97	84
48	100	98	–
49	102	99	78, 79
50	103	100	139, 140

Table 3.4 *English canons omitted in their entirety from the Irish code*

---

3. The Church of England a true and apostolical church
6. Impugners of rites and ceremonies . . . censured
10. Maintainers of schismatics . . . censured
12. Maintainers of constitutions made in conventicles . . . censured
15. Litany to be read on Wednesdays and Fridays
16. Colleges to use the prescript form of divine service
17. Students in colleges to wear surplices in time of divine service
23. Students in colleges to receive communion four times a year
24. Copes to be worn in cathedral services by those that administer communion
27. Schismatics not to be admitted to communion
30. The lawful use of the cross in baptism explained
38. Revolters after subscription censured
49. Ministers, not allowed preachers, may not expound
52. The names of strange preachers to be noted
54. The licences of preachers refusing conformity to be void
55. The form of a prayer to be used by all preachers before their sermons
57. The sacraments not to be refused at the hands of unpreaching ministers
58. Ministers . . . to wear surplices and graduates therewithal hoods
64. Ministers to solemnly bid holydays
72. Ministers not to appoint public or private fasts or prophecies &c.
76. Ministers at no time to forsake their calling
86. Churches to be surveyed, and decays certified to the High Commissioners
94. None to be cited into the Arches or Audience but dwellers &c.
98. Inhibitions not to be grant to factious appellants
101 By whom licences to marry without banns shall be granted & to what sort of person
114 Ministers shall present recusants
121 None to be cited into several courts for one crime
130 Proctors not to retain causes without the counsel of an advocate
131 Proctors not to conclude in any case without the knowledge of an advocate
141 Depravers of the Synod censured

A good starting point is Irish canon 7 because it reproduces many of the features of the wider canonical settlement.[197] It was an amalgam of three

---

[197] Irish canon 7: '*The prescript form of divine service to be used on Sundays and Holydays with all decency and due Reverence*: Every Sunday and holyday, vicars and curates shall celebrate divine service at convenient and usual times of the day, and in such place of ever church, as the bishop of the diocese or ecclesiastical ordinary of the place shall think meet, for the largeness or straitness of the same, so as the people may be most edified. All the ministers shall use and observe the orders, rites, and ceremonies prescribed in the Book of Common Prayer and in the Act for Uniformity printed therewith, as well in reading the holy scriptures, and saying of prayers, as in the administration of the sacraments; without either diminishing in regard of preaching, or in any other respect, or adding anything in the matter or form thereof. And in the cathedral and collegiate churches, all deans, masters and heads of collegiate churches, canons and prebendaries, being graduates, shall daily at the times both of prayer and preaching, wear with their surplices such hoods as are agreeable to their degrees. No man also shall cover his head in any church or chapel in the time of divine service,

English canons – 14, 18 and 25 – but a close reading of this canon reveals interesting alterations to its progenitors.

English canon 14 begins 'the Common Prayer shall be said or sung distinctly and reverently upon such days as are appointed to be kept holy by the Book of Common Prayer'. Irish canon 7 specifies that 'parsons, vicars and curates shall celebrate divine service at convenient and usual times'. So while the Irish canons do not enjoin the use of the litany (English canon 15), the rules for the timing of litanies are transferred to the celebration of divine service. The Irish canons specify 'Sundays and holydays', again corresponding to English canon 15 rather than English canon 14, which merely specifies the days appointed by the Prayer Book. English canons 14 and 15 were on the list of those 'doubted' by the Irish committee, but while the litanies of English canon 15 were dropped, its provisions were imported to strengthen English canon 14.

English canon 18, again one of those 'doubted', was heavily cut. It omits the English preamble 'let all things be done decently and according to order' but keeps the provisions for behaviour during services – headgear, walking about and so on. But it then proceeds to completely omit the directions on kneeling and standing and, of course, bowing to the name of Jesus. English canons 16 and 17 regulating behaviour in university chapels were omitted from the Irish canons, looking very much like a victory for Trinity.[198] English canon 24 on the use of copes fell, but English canon 25 on surplices survived.

The omission of English canons 16, 17 and 24 as well as the mutilation of English canon 18 looked very much like a victory for Irish amendators. But this was not so clear-cut, because Bramhall had contrived to alter one line of English canon 14 which now read: 'All ministers likewise shall use and observe the orders, rites, *ornaments* and ceremonies prescribed in the Book of Common Prayer and in the *Act for Uniformity printed therewith.*'[199] The Irish committee had recommended that the next phrase in the 1603

---

except he have some infirmity, in which case he may wear a night cap or coif. Neither shall any person be otherwise at such times busied, than in quiet attendance to hear, mark and understand that which is read, preached or ministered; using all such reverent gestures and actions, as by the Book of Common Prayer are prescribed in that behalf, and the commendable use of this church received; and not departing out of the church during the time of service and sermon without some urgent or reasonable cause.'

[198] But short-lived as the new statutes would regulate on these matters. J. P. Mahaffy, *An epoch in Irish history* (1903, repr. New York, 1970), pp. 228–63; Ford, '"That bugbear Arminianism"', pp. 135–60.

[199] My italics. This was a typical ambiguity of the Irish settlement because the Act of Uniformity printed therein was 1 Eliz I c. 2 (Eng.) of 1559 not 2 Eliz. I c. 2 (Ire.) of 1560. This phrase is to be found in Irish canon 13, *Preachers and lecturers to read divine service and administer the sacraments twice a year at least.*

book, 'without either diminishing in regard of preaching, or in any other respect, or adding anything in the matter or form thereof', should be altered to read 'without adding to the form thereof'.[200] By averting this change and by inserting the references to 'ornaments' and the Act of Uniformity, Bramhall had clawed back considerable ground. The standard of vestments as well as the orders, rites and ceremonies were to be those of 1549.[201] Only a royal command (or, under the Irish Act of Uniformity, that of the lord deputy and council) could now make any alteration, which was not about to happen. Irish canon 7 was not an unqualified victory for the anglicisers but neither was it an Irish triumph. It was a compromise which allowed both sides to believe that they had won the argument.

Two of the canons dealing with the sacrament of communion, numbers 19 and 94, directly legislated for what could only be enquired after by enthusiasts in England.[202] Directions for 'the special ministry of reconciliation' were tacked on to English canon 22.[203] The signal was to be a special tolling of church bells on the eve of services, after which parishioners 'finding themselves extreme dull or much troubled in mind', may 'resort unto God's ministers' to receive advice and counsel 'as the benefit of absolution likewise for the quieting of their consciences, by the power of the keys which Christ has committed to his ministers for that purpose'.[204]

Irish canon 94 was composed of English canons 80, 81, 82 and 83 but with key changes. It ordered a 'fair table to be placed at the east end of church or chancel' and it also stipulated 'a cup of silver for the celebration of the holy communion'. As the table moved east the Word took a blow since Irish canon 94 omitted the direction to place the Decalogue on the east wall.[205] Irish canon 43 stated: 'As often as churches are newly built, where formerly they were not, or church yards appointed for burial, they shall be dedicated and consecrated.'[206] This was more than just a preparation

---

[200] TCD MS 1038, fol. 113r, Laud's remark: 'so they are free to diminish what they list'.

[201] This meant that he also saved the use of the sign of the cross in baptism so ostentatiously missing from the Irish canons. The undated 'considerations touching the state of the church', in Str P20/149, raise the possibility of bringing in the 1549 Prayer Book in Ireland as a means to attract recusants.

[202] Kenneth Fincham, 'Clerical conformity from Whitgift to Laud' in Peter Lake and Michael Questier (eds.), *Conformity and orthodoxy in the English church, c. 1560–1660* (Woodbridge, 2000), pp. 125–58.

[203] EC 22, 'Warning to be given beforehand for the communion'; Fincham, 'Clerical conformity', p. 148.

[204] See Scottish canons (1636), 18.9; Bray (ed.), *Anglican canons*, p. 551.

[205] It also dropped the requirement of EC 80 for parishes to have a copy of the Book of Homilies. For Laudian criticisms of the Book, see Milton, *Catholic and reformed*, p. 332.

[206] J. Sears McGee ('William Laud and the outward face of religion' in R. L. De Molen (ed.), *Leaders of the reformation* (1984), p. 328) describes Laud's pleasure in consecrating churches, for which he was attacked at his trial, *WL* 4, pp. 247ff. A proposal for a form of consecration of churches was put to the English convocation of 1640 but not passed: Davies, *Caroline captivity*, pp. 54, 266; Milton, *Catholic and reformed*, p. 70. The inclusion of churchyards in this canon may also have been part

for the construction of new churches in the course of plantation. All three canons reflect a special emphasis on the eucharist and the church as a place set apart. Within the church, the altar was to be the focus of attention and in the hearts of the communicants absolution provided a way up to the altar – an altar at which the priest administered the sacramental wine in a precious cup. There might be no mandatory bowing, but Irish canon 18 extended the kneeling required of members of the universities (English canon 23) to all communicants.[207]

The new provisions were a plain assault on Irish practices. Bramhall was caustic about churches in Down and Connor where they had no altar 'but in place of it a table ten yards long, where they sit and receive the Sacrament like good fellows'.[208] In his own chapel, Ussher had no table[209] and in St Peter's, Drogheda, where he preached on Sundays, the communion table 'was placed lengthwise in the aisle'.[210] The campaign to remove Boyle's tomb from St Patrick's and the reordering of the Christchurch altar had been true heralds of things to come. Wentworth was quick to point out the canons on the altar and confession to Laud, who was sufficiently pleased to remark that the refusal to receive the English canons unchanged had advantages after all.[211] Again, Ireland had shown its potential as a place where the Church of England could be improved on.

Laud exhibited more enthusiasm for the canon on confession than that on the altar.[212] Why confession? If the provisions made in the Irish canons placed renewed emphasis on the sacraments, they also gave, in this canon above all, more attention to the role of the priest in the administration of the sacraments.[213] The more customary interpretation of resort to the minister as a form of spiritual consolation gave way at the end of the canon to a more sacerdotal and sacramental statement about the power of the keys. Bramhall, like Andrewes and Neile, acknowledged the usefulness and antiquity of confession but was always careful to castigate Roman

---

of a drive to halt the Irish practice of interment in the enclosures of medieval monasteries and churches by providing new burial grounds.

[207] Lori Anne Ferrell, 'Kneeling and the body politic' in Donna Hamilton and Richard Strier (eds.), *Religion, literature and politics in post-Reformation England, 1540–1688* (Cambridge, 1996) pp. 70–92.

[208] Bramhall to Laud, 20 December 1634, Shirley, p. 41.

[209] 'No bowing here I awarrant you!', Wentworth to Laud, 27 November 1638, Knowler II, p. 249.

[210] Brereton, *Travels*, p. 135.

[211] Laud to Wentworth, 12 May 1635, *WL* 7, p. 132: 'And one passing good thing we have got by it, besides the placing of the altar at the east end, and that is a passing good canon about confession.' See also Wentworth to Laud, 13 April 1635, Str P 6, p. 164; 14 July 1635, Str P 6, p. 201. See also *WL* 6, p. 7, 'Memorables of king James', no. 26: 'His regal censure of the moderate reformation of the Church of England, and particularly for the care of retaining of absolution, the comfort of distressed souls.'

[212] Laud to Bramhall, 11 May 1635, HA 15159.

[213] See Tyacke, *Anti-Calvinists*, pp. 221–2. Laymen have no power of absolution, *BW* III, p. 167.

abuses of it.[214] Since 'God absolves by the priest', the dignity of the clerical estate was a necessary adjunct to the dignity of the priest, which these canons emphasised.[215] Clericalism, resurgent in England during the 1630s, was capable, in Ireland, of expression not just through a vigorous temporalities campaign or visitations through sermons and enforcement of rubrics but also through the unsought task of compiling a new code of canons.[216]

Irish canon 71 made its own modest addition to new Irish clericalism by tacking a provision on to its English counterpart, canon 122, that those who exercised jurisdiction over ministers in causes criminal be themselves 'admitted into the holy orders of priesthood'. Irish canon 32, on examination of candidates for ordination, tightened up English canon 35 by requiring them to subscribe to the first four of the new Irish canons. Irish canon 4 stipulated the 1550 ordinal. What appears to have been happening here is that English canons 35 and 122, which required the bishop to work in concert with senior clergy, 'the pale reflections of the King's [James I's] instruction that episcopal jurisdiction "be somewhat limited"', were themselves 'ameliorated' by a more hierarchically clericalist sensibility.[217]

Not all the traffic went the one way. The canons relating to the ordination and quality of ministers also presented something of an admonition to any evocation of catholicity in defence of clericalism. Irish canons 29, 30 and 42 are based on English canons 31, 32, 33, 74 and 75. These English canons refer to 'the ancient fathers of the church, led by the examples of the apostles',[218] 'the practice of the primitive church'[219] and 'the true ancient and flourishing churches of Christ'.[220] All of these phrases were silently dropped from the

[214] *BW* V, pp. 160, 190–1, 223. A sermon on priestly absolution given by Lancelot Andrewes on 30 March 1601 at Whitehall caused a sensation: *XCVI sermons* (1629), 'Sermons upon several occasions', p. 49. In 1637, a similar sermon by Anthony Sparrow, a fellow of Queens' College, Cambridge, created a row: *A sermon concerning confession of sinnes and the power of absolution* (1637). The model of confession used in the Irish canon is similar to Andrewes's practice as canon of St Paul's of being available in the body of the church at certain hours: P. E. McCullough, 'Andrewes, Lancelot (1555–1626)', *ODNB*, http://www.oxforddnb.com/view/article/520, accessed 21 November 2004. Andrew Foster, 'Archbishop Richard Neile revisited', in Peter Lake and Michael Questier (eds.), *Conformity and orthodoxy in the English church, c. 1560–1660* (Woodbridge, 2000), pp. 159–68 at p. 167: 'He felt that confession "may be of great use in God's church" even though it was a practice abused by the Roman church'. See also Milton, *Catholic and reformed*, pp. 69–70, 72–6, 472–3.
[215] *BW* V, p. 213.
[216] Andrew Foster, 'The clerical estate revitalised' in Kenneth Fincham (ed.), *The early Stuart church 1603–42* (London, 1993), p. 139 and Tyacke, *Anti-Calvinists*, pp. 221–2.
[217] Patrick Collinson, 'The Jacobean religious settlement: the Hampton Court conference' in Howard Tomlinson (ed.), *Before the English Civil War: essays on early Stuart politics and government* (1983), pp. 27–52 at p. 47.
[218] EC 31.   [219] EC 32.   [220] EC 74.

Irish canons which are otherwise identical to their English original. Most likely this is the handiwork of Ussher who, although devoted to patristics, was part of a growing band of scholars pushing the point of 'corruption' further and further back. The collegiate suffrage of the British delegates at Dort (of whom Samuel Ward was one) was extremely selective in its use of the Fathers.[221]

By accident or by studied ambiguity, the book of canons left the relationship between the Church of England and the Church of Ireland variably defined. Three canons spoke of the '*churches* of England and Ireland' and another two of the '*church* of England and Ireland'.[222] Since four of these are direct references to articles of religion and Irish canon 1 speaks of 'the agreement of the church of England and Ireland in the profession of the same Christian religion', it may have been a little ploy to prevent the reopening of old wounds by having a book which could be quoted satisfactorily by either party. Yet Irish canon 32, in rewriting English canon 36 on ministerial subscription, shifted the balance considerably. It enjoined subscription to the first four Irish canons as opposed to the three articles contained in English canon 36. Irish canon 1 set up the English articles and is roughly equivalent to article 3 of English canon 36.[223] Irish canon 2 corresponds to article 2 of English canon 36 but is also an amalgam of English canons 1 and 2. In sum, an Irish minister subscribed not only to the king's supremacy but to a *duty* to declare it four times a year, while his English counterpart was merely *enjoined* to do so by canon. The real difference lies between Irish canons 3 and 4 as opposed to article 2 of English canon 36. English ministers were to subscribe that the ordinal and Prayer Book contained 'nothing contrary to the word of God, and that it may lawfully so be used'. The Irish canons went much further. They excommunicated those who preached or declared 'anything in the derogation or despising of the said book, or of anything therein contained' (even English canon 4 specified particular criticisms of the Prayer Book).[224] Irish ministers *subscribed* to Irish canon 4 (an amalgam of English canons 7 and 8 and article 2 of English canon 36), exposing themselves to excommunication for any attack on the church order and hierarchy. The Prayer Book was at the very centre of Irish subscription.

---

[221] I owe this last point to Seán Hughes with whom I have had many illuminating conversations. Bramhall did manage to slip a reference to the 'solemn ancient and laudable custom' in IC 17 (ECs 60 and 61) on confirmation: Milton, *Catholic and reformed*, pp. 32–3.

[222] ICs 4, 9, 39 and 1, 31.

[223] Unlike the Etcetera oath of 1640, ICs 1–4 are, even if highly elaborated, in a line of descent from Whitgift's Three Articles of 1583: Fincham, 'Clerical conformity', pp. 130–40.

[224] IC 3.

The Irish canons not only elevated the priest, but the priest holding the Prayer Book was regarded as the symbol and test of uniformity.[225]

Despite Bramhall's initial reluctance, the canons ended by making numerous allowances for Ireland. These are most obvious in the canons relating to the use of the Irish language, but also in those relating to ecclesiastical jurisdiction, recusants, schools, temporalities and a number of others such as the allowance in the canon on the visitation of the sick for those 'who have not formerly resorted to the church'.[226]

Three canons – Irish canons 8, 86 and 94 – cover the problem of language. Canon 94 is incidental, ordering 'that where all or the most part of the people are Irish', Prayer Books and a Bible are to be provided in the 'Irish tongue, so soon as they may be had'. This may reflect not only the difficulty in procuring Irish books but a slight lack of enthusiasm.[227] Irish canon 8, 'Of the ordering certain parts of the service', clearly shows that the use of Irish in worship was considered an interim stage along the road to the anglicisation of the populace: 'every beneficiary and curate shall endeavour, that the confession of sins and absolution, and all the second service . . . where the people all or most are Irish shall be used in English first and after in Irish'.

Some have argued that Bramhall opposed the inclusion of canons on use of Irish on the grounds that it contravened the 1536 Act for the English Order, Habit and Language which included an oath for ordinands in which they promised to learn English, use English and preach and teach in it.[228] Bramhall had little enthusiasm for Irish, but his opposition was probably intensified by the provision in Irish canon 86 for those parishes where the incumbent was English and 'many Irish in the parish'. In such cases the clerks might read 'those parts of the service, which shall be appointed to be read in Irish (if it may be)'. This was a lay intrusion into the realm of the minister; it can hardly have been countenanced by Bramhall and must be seen as one of his major defeats. Where did the push for Irish come from? The myth that Ussher opposed Bedell in the use of Irish has been well exploded and there is sufficient proof of his qualified favour for evangelisation through the language as well as his interest from a scholarly

---

[225] Note also the omission of EC 38, 'Revolters after subscription censured'. For enforcement of rubrics in England, see Fincham, 'Clerical conformity', pp. 147–8.

[226] IC 41.   [227] English Prayer Books and Bibles were to be provided within six months.

[228] 28 Henry VIII c. 15, article 9: 'to move, endoctrine and teach all other being under his order, rule and governance, to accomplish and perform the same' and moreover to 'bid the beades in the English tongue and preach the Word of God in English', W. E. Collins (ed.), *Typical English churchmen from Parker to Maurice* (1902), p. 94.

point of view.[229] William Bedell, who was famously committed to Irish, may have been behind the canons and may also have suggested the use of parish clerks for practical reasons in a manner akin to his own translation project.[230]

Each of the canons qualifies its provision for Irish in some way – the Prayer Books and Bibles are to be had 'as soon as possible', Irish canon 8 places the decision to use Irish in the hands of the ordinary, and Irish canon 86 qualifies the appointing of certain parts of the service to be read in Irish with the phrase 'if it may be'. These hesitations encapsulate the Church of Ireland's ambiguity about the language, and so fell far short of endorsing a concentrated missionary drive through that medium. This tendency is also apparent in the canons on catechesis. Irish canon 11 adds to English canon 59 with a special provision for Ireland and Irish canon 12 has no English counterpart.[231] While Irish canon 11 tacks on a stipulation that ministers should not marry anyone or permit anyone to be a godparent or receive communion unless 'they can say the articles of belief, the Lord's Prayer and the Commandments in such a language as they can understand', it makes no balancing provision for the use of Irish in the regular Sunday catechism. Irish canon 12 followed the spirit of the English royal instructions of 1629 and divided the catechism into as many parts as there are Sundays of the year; it also recommended preaching against superstitions, such as scapulars, and again made no allowance for preaching or teaching through Irish.[232]

Several of the Irish canons were concerned to keep a check on controversy in line with the 1626 and 1628 bans, and now in the wake of convocation. Irish canon 9 adds an admonitory note to English canon 45 on Sunday sermons:

therein he shall teach no vain opinions, no heresies, nor popish errors, disagreeing from the Articles of religion generally received in the churches of England and Ireland; nor anything at all, whereby the people may be stirred up to the desire of novelty or contention.

English canon 53 barring public disputation between preachers was repeated verbatim in Irish canon 10. Irish canon 12 enjoined ministers to moderation

[229] For the myth, see *UWW* I, p. 118; Hugh Trevor-Roper, *Catholics, Anglicans and Puritans: seventeenth-century essays* (1987), pp. 143–4. It is refuted in J. Th. Leersen, 'Archbishop Ussher and Gaelic Culture', *Studia Hibernica* 22–3 (1982–3), pp. 50–8; William O'Sullivan's review of Buick Knox, *Ussher* in *IHS* 16 (1968), pp. 215–19; See also Bernard, *Judgement* (1659), pp. 351–2; Bodl. Sancroft MS 18, p. 7; *Tanner letters*, p. 87, *UWW* XV, p. 483.

[230] Gaelic did less well in the Scottish canons of 1636 which provided for the catechism in Scots or Latin only, SC 10.2, Bray (ed.), *Anglican canons*, p. 544.

[231] IC 11 orders catechising on holy days as EC 59 does.

[232] Catechising was to replace afternoon sermons: Fincham, 'Clerical conformity', p. 150.

in discourse on the catechism so as not to run 'into curious questions, or unnecessary controversies'.[233]

Other canons dealt with Irish conditions in a more incidental way – Irish canon 91 adds dogs, hawks with bells and unruly small children to English canon 11 on behaviour in church. Irish canons 92 and 97 deal with Catholic practices – canon 92 specifies the feast of All Souls as among those abrogated by the Book of Common Prayer and bans tolling of bells on 'months and twelve months minds' and other remembrances of the dead. While English canon 88 leaves discretion on bell ringing to the local minister, Irish canon 92 allots it to the bishop. This is one of a number of Irish canons which place regulatory power in the hands of the ordinary where it is not so in the English canons. Irish canon 97 orders the abolition of 'all monuments of superstition' (with the approbation of the ordinary of the place), a mark of the absence in the previous century of popular iconoclasm and the spasmodic nature of official iconoclasm.

Irish canon 97 was based on canon 5 of 1571 and injunction XXIII of 1559. It did not, however, take up the requirement of the 1571 canon 'that the walls of the churches be new whited and decked with chosen sentences of the holy scripture'.[234] Three other canons – 12, 45 and 90 – are indebted to injunctions III, XV and XXXIV respectively. Bramhall maintained that canons based on the injunctions came from the 'faction' in convocation.[235] Canons 12 and 97 are an assault on superstition, canon 45 enjoins the payment of tithes and is probably aimed at recusant defaulting. Canon 90 outlines the 'Duty of churchwardens touching such persons as are out of the church in time of God's worship'. As in injunction XXXV, innholders and alehouse keepers are not to sell meat or drink during services, but Irish canon 90 goes back to the more rigorous tones of canon 5 of 1571 by bringing 'taverners' and victuallers into the net, going beyond the injunction in ordering that they should not receive anyone into their establishments at those times. While 'holydays' are duly mentioned along with Sundays, the thrust of the canon was sabbatarian and harked back to Irish article 56.[236]

Irish canon 49 re-established pre-reformation restrictions on marriage in Lent and on specific feast days, thus explicitly privileging season over

[233] For Laud's dislike of controversy, see Sears McGee, 'William Laud', pp. 323–5, and Anthony Milton, 'Laud, William (1573–1645)', *ODNB*, http://www.oxforddnb.com/view/article/16112, accessed 27 September 2004.

[234] EC. 1571 no. 5. 3, Bray (ed.), *Anglican canons*, p. 193.

[235] Bramhall to Laud, 20 December 1634, Shirley, p. 41.

[236] Four Irish canons appear to have been drawn in partly or wholly from the 1571 canons: IC 25 from 1571 no. 3; IC 34 from 1571 no. 10; IC 90 from 1571 no. 5 and IC 97 from 1571 no. 5 also. Again, I am grateful to Gerald Bray for drawing these connections with the 1571 canons to my attention.

Table 3.5 *Irish canons with no 1603 counterparts*

8. Of the ordering of certain parts of the divine service
12. The people to be informed in the body of Christian religion &c.
23. Of ordering ecclesiastical jurisdiction [1571/ 4.8]
24. Of ordering the revenues of ecclesiastical persons [1268/ 22; 1636/ 17]
25. Of archdeacons [1571/ 3.2]
34. Patrons of ecclesiastical benefices [1571/ 10.1]
43. Of consecrating of churches [1237/ 1; 1268/ 3]
45. Payment of tithes to be made [1559/ 15]
70. Maturity required in proceeding [1237/ 26; 1268/ 24]
80. The oath *de calumnia* not to be refused [1237/ 24]
90. The duty of churchwardens [1571/ 5.4; Irish article 1615, 56]
97. To abolish all monuments of superstition [1559/ 23; 1571/ 5.3]

Sabbath.[237] This kind of mixed message – sabbatarian on one hand and traditional on the other – was typical of a code which had been arrived at by negotiation and in which both sides strove to insert rulings they believed were of importance.

Nine Irish canons (almost one-tenth of the entire code) dealt with ecclesiastical revenues and residence.[238] Here Bramhall took the opportunity to complement the legislation passing through parliament. Of these, three – 24, 34 and 45 – were distinct Irish canons, not based on 1603, and most of the others had significant alterations.

Irish canon 24, 'Of ordering the revenues of ecclesiastical persons', addressed spoliation by ecclesiastical persons by condensing the main points of the recent Act for the Preservation of the Inheritance . . . of Land belonging to the Church and Persons Ecclesiastical. Mensal or demesne lands were not to be leased out except to curates actually discharging the cure. The curates, in turn, were not permitted to be absent for more than forty days a year, so reinforcing article 7 of the 1634 Act to Enable Restitution of Impropriations and Tithes, which imposed a residency requirement for the validity of incumbents' leases. This canon, then, completed the identification of residency with revenue. Bishops were required to preserve their churches, chancels and manse houses and to supervise other ecclesiastical persons in doing the same. Again here was canonical provision for an

---

[237] Martin Ingram, *Church courts, sex and marriage in England* (Cambridge, 1987), pp. 213–14; Keith Thomas, *Religion and the decline of magic* (London, 1973), pp. 741–2; Osborough, 'Ecclesiastical law', p. 243. Some English visitation articles upheld prohibited seasons but in Ireland we see them become *canonical* requirements. For the English articles, see Fincham (ed.), *Visitation articles*, vol. I, p. xvi.

[238] ICs 24, 26, 34, 35, 36, 37, 38, 44, 45.

earlier initiative.[239] Inclusion of manse houses was, naturally, connected to the campaign to ensure residency. A further clause of the canon, on the confirmation of leases and alienations, struck at collusive confirmations in a similar manner to the provision of a commission to determine the true values of church lands in the Act for the Preservation of the Inheritance.

Irish canon 26 harped on the theme of residency again by explaining that one purpose of ninety days' residence per annum was to stimulate purchase or the building of houses.[240] In this way cathedral chapters would not only be fully manned through residence but proper closes would develop in the cathedral towns and act as hubs for an expanding establishment.[241]

Irish canon 34 was inspired by a 1571 canon and, like the Act to Enable Restitutions, focused on the role of lay patrons. It was a codification of the sense of sacrilege which so suffused the temporalities campaign.[242] Here, perhaps reflecting Bramhall's sense of the importance of such measures, *ipso facto* excommunication was deployed for the only time in these canons and against the patron. Its 1571 progenitor thrust out the minister and required public penitence from the patron. The 1634 canon retained public penitence from the patron in order to expunge the excommunication but it was totally silent on the fate of the incumbent. It deployed the spiritual sword against the lay malefactor. Whether it was ever used is uncertain but the signal was unmistakeable.

Irish canon 35 took up the question of the clerk's fault. Here Bramhall sought to compensate for the failure of the simony bill in parliament.[243] He did so with a vengeance, 'improving' on English canon 40 by stipulating that if a clerk made a lease of any of the profits of his benefice to the patron:

or any belonging to him, or any other person, to his or their use, to continue during his incumbency, or for above three years, or with a notable diminution of rent under the true value he shall be holden convict of simony.

This was more than just another blow at collusion and undervaluation; it was enormous broadening of the concept of simony. This was very close to Bramhall's heart since he had been preaching on the story of Ananias around that time.[244] The canon had its own 'etcetera' moment when it

---

[239] See above chapter 2, p. 51.

[240] EC 42 specified ninety days' residence but offered no explanation.

[241] Cathaldus Giblin, 'The *Processus Datariae* and the appointment of Irish bishops in the seventeenth century' in Franciscan Fathers (eds.), *Father Luke Wadding* (Dublin, 1957), pp. 508–616.

[242] Patrons were 'to consider the necessaries of the churches, and to have before their eyes the last day of judgement and the tribunal seat of God'.

[243] See chapter 2, p. 52.   [244] Laud to Wentworth, 12 January 1635, *WL* 7, pp. 104–5.

warned culpable parties that they would be 'proceeded against according to the severity of the ancient canons in that behalf'.[245]

Irish canon 36 allowed the perpetual union of rectories and vicarages in line with a clause in the recent Impropriations Act, a reform perennially urged on the Church of Ireland.[246] It made allowance for the Irish situation in that the criterion of thirty miles for pluralities in English canon 41 was changed to a ban on holding more than one benefice of greater value than £40.[247] This was the practical response to Laud's desire for strict controls on pluralities. While English canon 41 commanded that the pluralist provide 'a preacher . . . to teach and instruct the people' in the benefice from which he was absent, Irish canon 36 altered this to 'a curate able to catechise and instruct the people, to have such maintenance as to the ordinary shall seem fit'. This is one of a host of small but significant changes made in the Irish canons. The emphasis on preaching is shifted to one of service. The preacher becomes a curate, the teacher a catechist. The ordinary rather than the licensed pluralist decides on the stipend.

Fusion of English canons 46 and 47 into a single Irish canon, 37, was glossed by a provision allowing the bishop of the diocese 'according to the laws of the church' to allot a maintenance out of the appropriations in parishes where both great and small tithes were taken by the appropriator.[248] Irish canon 38, on curates, was again realistic about pluralism, permitting them to serve two churches or chapels in one day.[249] While English canon 48 confined itself to specifying episcopal 'examination' of curates, its Irish counterpart spelled it out: 'trial first to be made of his sufficiency, sobriety and fitness every way for the ministration whereunto he is deputed'. Irish canon 45 was lifted from the 1559 injunctions but had a particular Irish resonance since it enjoined the payment of tithes even in default of ministerial duties.[250]

The inclusion of English canon 87 on terriers as Irish canon 44 sought to overcome the dearth of church records.[251] Bramhall's hand is very clear in the additions made to the original as the new version went far beyond matters of record. Bishops were specially directed in visitations to see the canon observed, and the terriers were to be renewed every ten years. Again,

---

[245] IC 35.   [246] 'Orders and directions', 1623 in Marsh MS Z3.1.3.

[247] That no dispensations be granted to hold more than one benefice of greater value than £40 English p.a.

[248] 'Orders and directions', 1623 in Marsh MS Z3.1.3 (30–8).

[249] EC 48 permitted service of only one church.

[250] Injunctions 1559/15, Bray (ed.), *Documents*, p. 339.

[251] Archbishop Abbot had enforced this canon very strictly in England: Kenneth Fincham, *Prelate as pastor* (Oxford, 1990), pp. 138–40.

leases of glebe lands or of benefices were not to be above a term of three years at the most. Bramhall's Irish terrier was capacious, going out beyond lands, orchards and other immoveables to '*all rights* whatsoever which are in possession or *of right* do belong to their several sees, or to any dignity . . .'.[252] The recovery of the *rights* of the church was at the very core of Bramhall's understanding of his mission in Ireland. This canon made his legalistic, historically charged approach to the temporal estate of the church mandatory for all bishops in Ireland. Irish canon 44 was his bid to ensure that his labours would not die with him.

Whatever may be said about Bramhall's personal ambitions, where did the 1634 convocation leave the Church of Ireland? Or, as some contemporaries asked themselves, what was the real status of the Irish articles after 1634? Ussher, as we know, insisted that the 1615 articles 'stand as they did before'.[253] During convocation, Wentworth, Bramhall and Laud had been at pains to prevent any debate on this matter, preferring to let Ussher believe what he would.[254] From the far safer distance of London in 1636 Wentworth told Wandesforde that he had reported:

The Church was improved in her patrimony, and become altogether conformable to this of England in doctrine and government, by the acceptance of the Articles and Canons of England, so as now they were become one, which properly they could not be said to have been before.[255]

This was a pleasing assertion for his royal audience but one that was far from being universally accepted. Contemporary accounts of convocation were fuelled, in the first instance, by the crisis of 1640–1 and, after 1656, by the battle for Ussher's posthumous reputation. Nicholas Bernard began with his *Life of Ussher* (1656), which became entangled with pamphlets by Hamon L'Estrange and Peter Heylyn.[256] Robert Baillie and William Prynne had originally provided much of the material for the contenders to work on. After the Restoration, John Vesey and Richard Parr inherited the contours of the debate in their biographies of Bramhall and Ussher respectively. Bernard and Heylyn were bitter in their opposition to each

---

[252] My italics.   [253] Ussher to Laud, 15 September 1635, *UWW* XVI, p. 9.
[254] See especially Laud to Wentworth, 20 October 1634, *WL* 6, pp. 386–7.
[255] Wentworth to Wandesforde, 25 July 1636, Knowler II, p. 16. In his report at Hampton Court on 21 June 1636, Wentworth had stated that 'the articles of the Church of England are there confirmed and those of Ireland silenced and passed by', PRO SP63/255/130.
[256] Hamon L'Estrange, *The reign of King Charles disposed into annals with at the end the observator's rejoinder* (1655); Bernard, *Life of Ussher*; Anon. [Heylyn], *Observations on the reign*; L'Estrange, *Observator observed*; Peter Heylyn, *Extraneus vapulans* (1656); Bernard, *Judgement*, 1st edn (1657); Heylyn, *Respondet Petrus*; Bernard, *Judgement*, 2nd edn (1659); Bramhall, 'Discourse of the Sabbath', c.1659 in *BW* V, pp. 3–86; Bernard, *Clavi trabales*; Heylyn, *Cyprianus Anglicus*.

other and the development of this complex debate has been tremendously influential on the way in which the history of the Church of Ireland in the seventeenth century has been written, particularly in its treatment of Ussher.

The earliest printed account of the convocation, by William Prynne, is the most sinister of all. For him, it was all an Arminian conspiracy and a brutal assault on the liberties of the Church of Ireland in which Laud exercised 'a kind of patriarchal jurisdiction'. There was no equivocation – the Irish articles had simply been called in and abolished.[257] Some of Prynne's information can be traced to the testimony of Joshua Hoyle at Laud's trial. Hoyle had been named by Bramhall as having voted against the English articles in convocation. He was bitterly opposed to Chappell as provost of Trinity and was deeply alienated after the imposition of the Laudian statutes in 1634.[258] He was bound to emphasise tyranny. Baillie shared in the notion of an Arminian conspiracy, was vitriolic about Bramhall and the treatment of Ussher, and painted a lurid picture of the lord deputy threatening to have the 'Antiarminian articles of Ireland' burnt by the hangman.[259] He shared Prynne's belief in a projected Laudian patriarchate extending over all three kingdoms.

Bernard's work is far more important as its effects were lasting. Bernard, who had been Ussher's chaplain, set out to mediate the primate's memory to the public and, in doing so, to mould it. He brought out his funeral sermon and biography of Ussher almost immediately after the obsequies and defended the primate's reputation in a series of pamphlets over the next five years. Furthermore, he sought to establish a 'canon' of Ussher's works.[260] He cast his net wider, publishing a brief account of Bedell's life.[261] Bernard was the first and most prolific historian of the Church of Ireland under Charles I.

Bernard's account of convocation in his 1657 *Judgement* eschews easy condemnation of Laudian intrusion. Instead, he built up his story carefully. First, he identified Ussher as the author of the Irish articles but added an extra twist by claiming that the future archbishop had also drawn up a code of canons for Ireland in 1615 drawn from 'the statutes, Queen Elizabeth's *Injunctions* and the Canons of England, 1571'.[262] He claimed to have found

[257] Prynne, *Canterbury's doom*, pp. 172, 177–8.
[258] See Brereton, *Travels*, p. 139, for a character of Hoyle.
[259] Robert Baillie, *Ladensium ΑΥΤΟΚΑΤΑΚΡΙΣΙΣ, the Canterburian's self-conviction* (Edinburgh, 1640), pp. 15, 39, Bodl. MS Rawlinson D 921, fol. 20.
[260] Bernard, *Life of Ussher*, pp. 111, 134.
[261] The life of Bedell is affixed to the 1659 edition of the *Judgement*.
[262] Bernard, *Life of Ussher*, pp. 49–50; *Judgement* (1657), pp. 67, 158.

two canons written in Ussher's hand among his papers. The first enjoined the use of the Prayer Book and the second decreed that 'no other form of ordination shall be used in this nation, but which is contained in the book of ordering bishops, priests and deacons'.[263] The omission of English article 36 was made up, then, by a putative Irish canon 2 of 1615 composed by an Ussher who used a set form of prayer before sermons (although English canon 55 is omitted from the Irish canons of 1634), who scrupulously observed holy days, and was enthusiastic about clerical habit, kneeling at communion and the consecration of churches.[264] According to Bernard, convocation decided that the Irish articles needed no further confirmation, Ussher 'readily consented' to the approval of the English articles, drew upon canon 1 and urged it upon convocation.[265] The Irish articles had not been abrogated and Ussher required subscription to both sets.[266] In Bernard's version, Ussher is a benign figure who already followed a number of the canonical practices before 1634 and who reacted with enthusiasm to the English articles on their own. There is no mention of the other canons of 1634, and Bramhall figures only as a marginal irritant. Changing political circumstances refined his narrative, and Ussher's approval of ritual grew in the second edition of the *Judgement* in 1659 and flourished in *Clavi trabales* in 1661.[267]

If Bernard was *parti pris*, so was Heylyn. In his narrative, the Irish articles had to go if there was to be peace because every time:

points were agitated here in England against the Sabbatarian and Calvinian rigours, the disputants were forthwith choked by the authority of these Articles, and the infallible judgment of King James who confirmed the same.[268]

[263] Bernard, *Judgement* (1657), p. 159.
[264] Bernard, *Judgement* (1657), pp. 159ff; consecration of churches is in *Clavi trabales*, p. 64, where Bernard claims he used the form devised by Andrewes.
[265] Bernard, *Judgement* (1657), pp. 116–19.
[266] Bernard, *Life and of Ussher*, p. 50; Bernard, *Judgement* (1657), p. 113.
[267] Bernard had become Oliver Cromwell's almoner after his time as Ussher's chaplain, a phase of his career which began sometime after his ordination by Ussher in 1626: Bernard, *Judgement* (1659), p. 57. He became rural dean of Kilmore, driving Bedell to complain of him as a bad pluralist and absentee who was endeavouring to have his Kilmore livings united with his rectory of St Peter's in Drogheda in the diocese of Armagh: Bedell to Laud, 2 September 1637, Shuckburgh, *Two lives*, p. 340. Bedell's repeated attempts to stop him from doing so over the years had turned Bernard into his implacable enemy – misrepresenting Bedell to Ussher and then spreading the word that Bedell had incurred a *praemunire* by his diocesan synod: Bedell to Ward, 14 November 1630, *Tanner letters*, pp. 97–8; Bedell to Laud, 24 May 1634, Shuckburgh, *Two lives*, p. 354; Patrick Little, 'Discord in Drogheda: a window on Irish Church–State relations in the sixteen-forties', *Historical Research*, 75 (2002), 355–62.
[268] Heylyn, *Cyprianus Anglicus*, p. 271. For his belief that the Irish articles were incompatible with the belief of the Church of England, see *Cyprianus Anglicus*, pp. 129–35.

For Heylyn, threatening to have the Irish articles burnt was a salutary action of Wentworth's in response to the manoeuvrings of certain members of convocation who prevailed on the hapless Ussher.[269] Heylyn repeats the story that convocation was won over by the argument that a confirmation of the Irish articles would only weaken their original authority. But he went further, contending that because of the incompatibility of the two sets of articles, the reception of 'the Articles of England was virtually and in effect an abrogation of the former Articles of the Church of Ireland'.[270] He also maintained that while Ussher tried to save appearances by writing specially to his 'friends in England' to tell them that the Irish articles still stood, the fact was they had been repealed by canon 1 of 1634.[271] Subsequent writers took their cue either from Bernard or Heylyn or mixed them together.

Only a single detail is common to all printed accounts – that Ussher and some other bishops required subscription to both articles.[272] All other points were disputed. In the late 1650s Bramhall chose to talk tough on double subscription:

> if any bishop had been known to have required any man to subscribe to the Irish Articles, after the English were received and authorised under the great seal of Ireland, he would have been called to account for it.[273]

This is not strictly true because only an overt refusal or denunciation of the English articles could have been proceeded against. Ultimately, double subscription, while much talked about during the 1650s and so *after* the Westminster confession, is never mentioned in the 1630s or early 1640s. The other certain fact is that after the Restoration the Irish articles did not re-emerge in the Church of Ireland. The petition of Dublin clergy in 1647 had defended the status of the 1615 articles and the autonomy of the church:

> the Articles of the Church of England were not held, or reputed, the Articles of the Church of Ireland, and when they were received, they were not received in any acknowledged subordination to the Church of England.[274]

---

[269] Heylyn, *Cyprianus Anglicus*, p. 273. In many ways, Heylyn's and Prynne's accounts mirror each other.

[270] Heylyn, *Respondet Petrus*, p. 271.

[271] Heylyn, *Respondet Petrus*, pp. 126ff; *Extraneus vapulans*, pp. 250ff; *Cyprianus Anglicus*, p. 273.

[272] Richard Parr, *Life of Ussher*, p. 42; Bernard, *Judgement* (1657), pp. 113, 120; Vesey, *Athanasius Hibernicus*, [p. 17]; Heylyn, *Cyprianus Anglicus*, p. 272; L'Estrange, *The reign of King Charles*, p. 137; Bernard, *Judgement* (1659), p. 352.

[273] *BW* V, p. 81. Robert Baillie, *Ladensium*, p. 15, attempts to create an air of conspiracy: 'whose invention are these privy articles which his [Laud's] creature my Lord of Derry presents to divers who take orders from his holy hands?'

[274] *A declaration of the Protestant clergy of the city of Dublin, showing the reasons why they cannot consent to the taking away of the Book of Common Prayer, and comply with the Directory* (1647), p. 4.

The petition, though, was a defensive document designed for very pressing times and the clergy needed to reject any hint of dependency to make an argument for retention of the Prayer Book for Ireland. The Irish convocation of 1661–2 made no mention of the 1615 articles. Their association with the Westminster assembly rendered them politically and theologically toxic.[275] In a Church of Ireland in which Bramhall had triumphantly carried out a mass consecration of bishops, there was no question of returning to, or defending, the 1615 articles. In his 1663 funeral sermon Jeremy Taylor launched Bramhall as an 'Anglican father'. John Vesey and Richard Parr offered deeply irenical accounts of the 1630s, and the old arguments gave way to defence of the judicious *via media*. The old battles of 1634–5 were irrelevant to the Anglican ascendancy of the eighteenth and early nineteenth centuries. It took the stresses of the Oxford movement, evangelical revival and, finally, disestablishment to breathe life into 1615 and 1634 once again.

Did the events of the years 1633–40 amount to a bid for a Canterburian primacy over all three churches, as Prynne and Baillie maintained? As far as Ireland was concerned, Laud's degree of involvement was certainly unprecedented. In July 1634, Laud joked with Wentworth about his deep engagement in both Scottish and Irish church affairs: 'I think you have a plot, to see whether I will be *universalis episcopus*, that you and your brethren may take occasion to call me Antichrist.'[276] In 1636, he deposited Wentworth's first report on Irish church improvements in the registry at Lambeth, so as to offer 'some encouragement to my successors to take some care of Ireland till all be settled there'.[277] He still conceived of his involvement in Ireland as aid. He accepted that temporal reconstruction was a necessary prelude to further reformation. On this level, his interest in the Church of Ireland was paternalistic rather than hegemonic. English doctrine and discipline were further means of repairing what was viewed as a rickety Irish establishment. Laud, as much as Ussher, would have regarded any revival of the twelfth-century claims of Canterbury to be *Brittanicarum Primas* or *Totius Britanniae Primas* as chimerical.[278] Laud wished to repair both Scotland

[275] Irish Presbyterian ministers declared their assent to the Irish articles in negotiations with Sir George Lane in 1660: Reid, *Presbyterian church*, vol. II, p. 284. The Solemn League and Covenant was duly censured and reproved and the 1662 Prayer Book enthusiastically accepted for Ireland on the grounds of the necessity of having agreement with England, although they duly went through the motions of appointing a committee to scrutinise it. TCD MS 1038, fols. 19–79, contains the journals of this convocation.

[276] Laud to Wentworth, 3 July 1634, *WL* 6, p. 385.

[277] Laud to Wentworth, 23 January 1636, *WL* 7, p. 230.

[278] Marie Therese Flanagan, *Irish society, Anglo-Norman settlers, Angevin kingship* (Oxford, 1989), pp. 7–55. See also Morrill, 'British patriarchy?', *passim*.

and Ireland and bring them into closer congruence with the Church of England. This did not mean that the Church of England was the standard. It, too, was in need of some restoration work. The opportunities to make settlements in Scotland and Ireland provided room for setting standards to which the Church of England could aspire. After 1636, the Scottish, Irish and English codes of canons had forty-one canons in common – notably those regulating the quality, discipline and behaviour of ministers, marriage regulations, the furniture and layout of churches, and conduct and gestures during services. Yet, the Scottish and Irish canons both allowed for sacramental confession and absolution, albeit in slightly different contexts.[279] Here was a sign of the beginnings of a new standard, to which all three churches might conform while still observing peculiarities of custom, discipline and organisation. After 1636, the churches of all three kingdoms had a Prayer Book, a set of canons and a High Commission. Each had a minimum of worship and discipline and each had, under the crown, a means of enforcing it.

The convocation of 1634, then, was not a victory of the Church of England over an autonomous Church of Ireland, but a realignment of the Church of Ireland within the three kingdoms. As it turned out, Ireland proved to be a deceptively easy exercise in realignment.

[279] IC 19 and Scottish canon 18.9, Bray (ed.), *Anglican canons*, p. 551.

CHAPTER 4

The bishops in the ascendant, 1635–1640

RAISING UP THE IRISH EPISCOPATE

An ecclesiology which held that bishops were a separate order had consequences across all three of the Stuart dominions throughout the 1630s. Their political, social and economic standing would have to match. This meant that in Ireland, once all the machinery of recovery had been put in place, they were the designated managers whether they wished it or not. At a practical political level, too, the established church in Ireland could not be reconstructed by the efforts of Laud, Bramhall and Wentworth alone. They would not remain in power forever and they could not guarantee the actions or attitudes of their successors, so it was vital to exercise great care in the appointment of new bishops and control of existing ones. In any event, emphasis on the dignity of the office precluded the possibility of a few salutary dismissals. Changes made to the Irish episcopate in the 1630s were no 'Arminian apocalypse' nor a roll call of churchmen sympathetic to Wentworth or Bramhall. Certainly, the revival of Cloyne as a separate diocese was a striking example of a reconstruction driven by the concept of the historical rights of the church. Yet at the same time, a three-year vacancy in Ardfert proved that smaller Irish dioceses continued poor and unattractive.[1] Bishops were now expected to be enthusiastic in the recovery of rights but also to take increased control of their clergy and their dioceses and, above all, their jurisdiction. Simultaneously, they themselves were expected to be more amenable to control and direction from the centre. The policy of enhancement coupled with chastisement was not an overwhelming success because, in 1640, the bishops became a centre of attention, but not by virtue of their popularity or brilliance. The bishop of Killala was before High Commission charged with making remarks favouring the Scottish National Covenant, the bishop of Waterford and Lismore was hanged for

[1] See Tadhg Ó hAnnracháin, *Catholic reformation in Ireland* (Oxford, 2002), pp. 63–4, for reports of robust diocesan organisation in the Catholic diocese of Ardfert.

sodomy and the bishop of Raphoe's officials were under physical attack in court by a local notable. This somewhat shambolic finale should not occlude the importance of the episcopate in the rebuilding programme of the 1630s.

The insistence of the Church of Ireland on making good its claim to be the national church and its consequent failure to organise itself along missionary lines severely damaged its prospects. Despite perpetual and personal unions, the number of bishoprics never fell below a total of twenty-five from 1541 to 1641 but the number of prelates in the latter half of the sixteenth century declined steadily.[2] Credit for placing the Church of Ireland episcopate on the footing on which it was to remain until the sweeping changes of the nineteenth century belongs to James I. He put an end to protracted vacancies and gave the Armagh province its first full complement of bishops since the reformation. Where James had inherited sixteen bishops from Elizabeth, Charles took over almost a full house of twenty-three. During his reign James appointed thirty-four new bishops and by 1641 his son had appointed twenty-six.[3]

By the time of his death James had thoroughly 'Briticised' the episcopate by slowly reducing the number of Irish incumbents.[4] There were now only four Irish incumbents as opposed to twelve English, five Scots and

[2] In 1558, there were 30 bishoprics and 28 bishops and no vacancies, but by 1603 there were 26 bishoprics, 16 bishops and 7 vacancies. For a fuller consideration of the Stuart episcopate, see John McCafferty, 'Protestant prelates or godly pastors? The dilemma of the early Stuart episcopate' in Alan Ford and John McCafferty (eds.), *The origins of sectarianism in early modern Ireland* (Cambridge, 2005), pp. 54–72.

[3] Much of the biographical information which follows for both bishops and deans is drawn from: Henry Cotton, *Fasti ecclesiae hibernicae*, 6 vols. (Dublin, 1848–78); J. B. Leslie, *Ardfert and Aghadoe clergy and parishes* (Dublin, 1940); *Armagh clergy and parishes* (Dundalk, 1911); *Clogher clergy and parishes* (Enniskillen, 1929); *Clergy of Connor* (Belfast, 1992); *Biographical succession lists of the clergy of the diocese of Down* (Dublin, 1937); *Succession lists of the diocese of Dromore* (Belfast, 1933); *Derry clergy and parishes* (Enniskillen, 1937); *Ferns clergy and parishes* (Dublin, 1936); *Ossory clergy and parishes* (Enniskillen, 1933); *Raphoe clergy and parishes* (Enniskillen, 1940). St John D. Seymour, *The diocese of Emly* (Dublin, 1913); E. A. Cooke, *The diocesan history of Killaloe, Kilfenora, Clonfert & Kilmacduagh, 639–1886* (Dublin, 1886); W. M. Brady, *Clerical and parochial records of Cork, Cloyne and Ross*, 3 vols. (Dublin, 1863–4); Philip Dwyer, *The diocese of Killaloe* (Dublin, 1878); John Begley, *The diocese of Limerick in the 16th & 17th centuries* (Dublin, 1927); Anthony Cogan, *The ecclesiastical history of the diocese of Meath*, 3 vols. (Dublin, 1867–74); John Healy, *History of the diocese of Meath*, 2 vols. (Dublin, 1908); W. H. Rennison, *Succession lists of the bishops, cathedral and parochial clergy of the dioceses of Waterford & Lismore* (1920); Walter Harris (ed.), *Whole works of Sir James Ware concerning Ireland*, 3 vols. (1739). John Leland, *Antiquarii de rebus Brittanicis collectanea*, 5 vols. (1774), vol. 5, pp. 261–8 has a Latin verse autobiography by William Chappell. For other sources, see the bibliography below and *ODNB* at http://www.oxforddnb.com.

[4] Analysis of the nationality and previous careers of appointees shows a real shift in the composition of the Irish bench under James. In 1603, James inherited ten Irish-born bishops, six English, no Scots and no Welsh: McCafferty, 'Protestant prelates', pp. 56–7.

one Welshman.[5] This shift away from Irish-born bishops nicely parallels the wider move away from Irish-reading ministers to English and Scottish graduates.[6] By the end of 1641 there were fourteen English, five Scots, three Irish and three Welsh bishops.[7]

Fourteen bishoprics were filled while Wentworth was chief governor. During his trial he laid the responsibility for the quality of the Irish episcopate at the door of the king which was, legally speaking, correct, just as Laud was to do in relation to England and Wales.[8] In reality, Laud had acceded to Wentworth's desire to control appointments.[9] Writing in August 1633 at a time when, with Bramhall's advice, the pair were formulating their Irish church policy, he promised he would 'not offer to engage his majesty for such bishoprics as may fall there till I have heard from you'.[10] He went on to express his trust in Wentworth's keeping to the highest standards but urged him to remember that 'his majesty is resolved to send some of his own chaplains thither as occasion shall be offered to him'.[11] On the whole, royal chaplains preferred to hold out for preferment in England because from 1633 to 1640 only three took Irish sees: John Leslie, Henry Leslie and George Webb.[12] Apart from these appointments, successful candidates were almost invariably proposed by Wentworth and recommended by Laud. So, as in England, the king appears to have been wholly dependent

[5] William Murray, Kilfenora 1622–7, might have been Welsh or English. On the basis of his translation to Llandaff in 1627, I have counted him as Welsh.

[6] Ford, *Protestant*, ch. 4.

[7] Two features stand out – the continued decline in Irishmen and the fact that Scots remained steady at five. Indeed, five Scots were appointed under Charles and two of those while Wentworth was chief governor. In terms of nationality, therefore, the reign of Charles saw no break with the pattern established by his father except in the fairly fortuitous increase in Welsh appointees. This suggests a distrust for the native products of the Dublin university and little commitment to the preferment of either Gaelic Irish or Old English Protestants. Indeed, of James I's Irish-born bishops only James Ussher had been educated at Trinity, three others had been educated at Cambridge and two of those at Emmanuel. The vast majority of bishops attended the English universities – thirteen of James's new men were at Cambridge and nine at Oxford, while the figures for Charles are five and nine respectively. Ussher was given Kildare in 1635. Chappell notoriously remained on as provost even after being promoted to Cork and Ross in 1638. John Richardson, Ardagh 1633–54, although English, was educated at Trinity (Cotton, *Fasti*, vol. III, pp. 49, 52, 183, 231, 257, 337); William Daniel, Tuam 1609–28 (Emmanuel); Anthony Martin, Meath 1625–50 (Emmanuel); Robert Draper, Kilmore 1604–12 (King's).

[8] Rushworth, pp. 122–3; for Laud, see Kenneth Fincham, 'William Laud and the exercise of Caroline ecclesiastical patronage', *JEH* 51 (2000), 69–93.

[9] Str P1, fol. 21.   [10] Laud to Wentworth, 16 August 1633, Str P 6, p. 16.

[11] This was the rule that Charles also followed in England: Fincham, 'William Laud', 87.

[12] Henry Leslie, who became bishop of Down and Connor in 1635, had already made his career in Ireland as a prebend of Connor from 1619 and dean of Down from 1627. He was one of Bramhall's early allies. John Leslie transferred from the Isles to Raphoe in 1633 so he was already a bishop. Webb became bishop of Limerick in 1634, having been Charles's chaplain while he was Prince of Wales: *WL* 7, p. 238.

on his archbishop's advice when candidates were not personally know to him.[13]

The lord deputy himself did not stick to his original lofty intention of enticing 'the ablest and the hopefullest' of English clergy over 'as probationers and upon their good, wise and orthodox government translated back into England in their elder years in . . . reward of their virtue'.[14] All but two of the new bishops had previous Irish careers of which the majority dated back to James I.[15] Bramhall was the only one who came close to fitting the description, though William Chappell of Cork (1638) and Henry Tilson of Elphin (1639) had been imported by Wentworth and made their careers under his protection. Despite his endless insistence on Ireland paying for itself, Wentworth still pushed for Dean Wandesforde of Limerick and John Atherton to be allowed to hold on to their livings on the other side of the Irish Sea.[16] Laud's reply was to stress that the king had 'publicly declared he will not suffer any Irish bishop to hold a commendam in England' and to offer his own opinion that 'if this once gets a footing in Ireland, we shall have it fall into practice in Scotland too, and the Church of England made a stale to both'.[17] Dynamic English clergy who were willing to commit wholly to Ireland were, in Laud's view, the only physicians qualified to cure the ills of the Church of Ireland.[18] As was often the case, Bramhall confirmed Laud's opinion from first-hand experience, telling him that those Irish clergy who had not been educated in England 'seldom know how to . . . manage the power of the keys'.[19] Yet English clerics were not just going to come over and radiate good example, propped up by the security of benefices at home. They were expected to commit themselves completely to the Church of Ireland. There might be an evolving congruence between the three national churches within Charles's dominions but the personnel remained distinct.

Laud and Wentworth did agree that Ireland should not be used as a dumping ground for aged worthies or the 'decrepit'. At the same time Laud was adamant that forty, not thirty-five, should be the minimum age.[20] Some months later, Wentworth had persuaded him to push for Bramhall for 'the

---

[13] Fincham, 'William Laud', 86.   [14] Wentworth to Laud, 9 September 1633, Str P 8, p. 17.

[15] John Leslie and George Webb were the only exceptions.

[16] Wentworth to Laud, 13 April 1635, Str P 6, p. 165; 14 July 1635 Str P 6, p. 201; Laud to Wentworth, 27 March 1635, WL 7, p. 119.

[17] Laud to Wentworth, 12 May 1635, WL 7, p. 131. This insistence was Laud's own: Fincham, 'William Laud', 87; Laud to Wentworth, 23 January 1636, WL 7, p. 238.

[18] Laud to Wentworth, 14 October 1633, WL 6, p. 321.

[19] Bramhall to Laud, 26 May 1634, HA 14043.

[20] Laud to Wentworth, 14 October 1633, WL 6, p. 322.

good of the church in that kingdom' and have the king 'dispense in this particular for the Doctor's being a little too young'.[21] This is interesting not only because it is a mark of the momentum Bramhall's Irish career had attained in less than a year but also as a sign of the degree to which Laud was willing to promote the lord deputy's nominees. Whenever Wentworth failed to secure a nomination during the 1630s it was only because a royal chaplain had popped up or his own man was not interested in the offer.

There were other times when it was difficult to find a suitable candidate. When Waterford and Lismore became vacant on the death of Michael Boyle late in 1635, Wentworth was determined to keep the Boyle family and its clients out.[22] The snag was finding someone both willing and capable of taking on this demanding see. John Atherton, 'for the soliciting part and recovering the rights of the bishopric were very fit. But I hold him not so fit to be the bishop.'[23] In that case, he believed it better to have someone sent over, such as 'Mr Marsh now one of the king's chaplains, well reported to be a quick stirring able man'. Marsh was not willing to stir, and so the only resort was 'Better Dr Atherton than a worse'.[24] Here, then, was another type of appointment – not a poor bishopric for a political opponent like Andrews or plum promotion for an agent like Bramhall but choice of an acknowledged inferior just because there was no one else to take it.[25] Like limited pluralism, it was a concession to the exigencies of the Irish scene, though in this case it turned into good propaganda for those who wished to prove the moral bankruptcy of episcopacy itself. Attracting English clerics was not the only problem Wentworth had to face – multiple moves were a tricky and time-consuming business. When Tuam became vacant, he proposed Edward King of Elphin and William Chappell for Elphin.[26] But King refused to move from Elphin where he had not only

---

[21] Laud to Wentworth, 14 May 1634, *WL* 6, p. 375. Bramhall was only about six months short of age forty at that time.

[22] There was a rumour, he wrote, that the earl of Cork would give '£100 to have Mr Lloyd his chaplain there'.

[23] Boyle died 27 December 1635: Cotton, *Fasti*, vol. I, p. 114. Wentworth to Laud, 3 January 1636, Str P 6, p. 299.

[24] Laud to Wentworth, 23 January 1636, *WL* 6, p. 238. Laud admitted that he shared Wentworth's apprehensions about Atherton and although this discussion took place about eleven months before Laud reported on the alleged ghostly appearance of Atherton's mother-in-law, Susannah Leakey, rumours of some sexual misdemeanour may have already been in circulation. For the most recent account, see Aidan Clarke, 'A woeful sinner: John Atherton' in Vincent P. Carey and Ute Lotz-Heumann (eds.), *Taking sides? Colonial and constitutional mentalités in early modern Ireland* (Dublin, 2003), pp. 138–49.

[25] For another view of the purpose of an Irish bishopric, see Laud to Wentworth, 22 June 1638, *WL* 7, p. 452, in which he proposes one for Williams of Lincoln as a form of exile.

[26] Wentworth to Laud, 28 February 1638, Str P 7, p. 66.

drastically improved the revenue but invested his own money. Accordingly, Wentworth proposed another set of changes: Richard Boyle of Cork for Tuam, Atherton to Cork, George Webb of Limerick to Waterford and Lismore and Chappell for Cork and Ross.[27] Then Webb refused to move so Atherton stayed put while Boyle's and Chappell's moves went ahead.[28] The lord deputy duly outlined each shuffle to Laud, who in turn reported the king's satisfaction with the proposal.[29] The clear impression is that he had established his as the preeminent, if not sole, voice in the apportioning of bishoprics. Unlike his English fellow primate, Ussher appears to have stayed out of episcopal appointments.[30] Bramhall, too, had no apparent role in selection.

Roughly half of the bishops sitting in the Irish House of Lords in 1640 were the product of pretty pragmatic appointments over the previous seven years. At one end of the spectrum there were vocal supporters of reconstruction such as Bramhall and Henry Leslie and at the other end the more ambiguous figures of Robert Ussher and George Andrews. Where mistakes had been made, as in the elevation of Atherton and the appointment of a serving provost to Cork, the damage was to be severe indeed. The episcopal bench did not have to be perfect because there were other ways to serve reconstruction.

Appointment of deans was in the gift of the lord deputy.[31] He chose to exercise it more programmatically so as to realise the potential for great impact on the running of the church. The fact that unions had not obliterated separate chapters along with Dublin's two cathedrals meant that there were thirty-three deaneries to play with.[32] Between 1633 and 1640, there were thirty-four appointments. Waterford alone got through

---

[27] Wentworth to Laud, 4 April 1638, Str P 7, p. 71; Terence Ranger, 'The career of Richard Boyle, 1st Earl of Cork, in Ireland 1588–1643', unpublished D.Phil. thesis, University of Oxford (1959), p. 322 on Wentworth's enthusiasm for Atherton.

[28] Wentworth to Laud, 26 May 1638, Str P 7, p. 102.

[29] See *inter alia* Laud to Wentworth, 27 March 1638, *WL* 7, p. 417; 11 November 1637, *WL* 6, p. 514; 30 July 1638, *WL* 7, p. 463.

[30] Ussher to Laud, 9 July 1638, *UWW* XVI, p. 36. The chancellor was George Synge.

[31] Formally it was in the hands of the crown, but this appears to be an instance of those regal powers exercised by the chief governor without reference. Edward Bullingbroke, *Ecclesiastical law; or, the statutes, constitutions, canons, rubricks, and articles, of the Church of Ireland*, 2 vols. (Dublin, 1770), vol. I, p. 239.

[32] There were ten in the Armagh province: Armagh, Down, Connor, Dromore, Derry, Clogher, Ardagh, Kilmore, Raphoe and Clonmacnoise. Meath had no dean and chapter. The Cashel province had eleven: Cashel, Emly, Lismore, Waterford, Cork, Ross, Cloyne, Ardfert, Limerick, Killaloe and Kilfenora. Tuam had six: Tuam, Killala, Achonry, Elphin, Clonfert, Kilmacduagh. Annaghdown appears to have been in abeyance. Dublin had six also: St Patrick's, Christchurch, Ossory, Ferns, Leighlin and Kildare.

five deans and only a scant nine of the thirty-three deaneries experienced no change.[33] There was much less concern at this level with sensitivities in the Irish church.[34] As early as December 1634, Christchurch had been wrested from the archbishop of Tuam and given to one of Wentworth's chaplains, Henry Tilson, whose main recommendation was that he had insisted his parishioners in Rochdale, Lancashire, kneel to receive communion.[35] In all, five of his own chaplains became deans.[36] At his trial, when defending his church policy, he made a particular point of naming deans Rhodes, Wentworth, Price, Forward, Gray, Thorpe, Cressy and Margetson as promising young clerics he had sent for out of England.[37] So it was at the decanal level rather than the episcopal that Wentworth realised his ambition of importing 'the ablest and hopefullest'.

Deaneries rather than palaces were where new or recent arrivals were deliberately inserted with a clear intention of transforming the senior administrative level of the church. A sample of five deans who were all associated with John Bramhall himself give a sense of the emergence of this new stratum in the clerical estate. Three successive deans of Derry – Michael Wandesforde, James Margetson and Godfrey Rhodes – were all Yorkshiremen who had been at Cambridge: an ecclesiastical cadre which mirrored the lord deputy's own group of Yorkshire *arrivistes*. Rhodes was at Sidney Sussex, Bramhall's own college. Michael Wandesforde was brother of Christopher, Derry's earliest patron. Rhodes was also brother-in-law to Wentworth, his sister Elizabeth being the latter's third wife. Margetson was both friend to and chaplain of Wentworth. Furthermore, Bramhall's sister Abigail married Robert Forward, dean of Dromore and chaplain of the lord deputy. Bramhall's old tutor from Sidney Sussex, Richard Howlett, was installed as dean of Cashel in March 1639 and married a Mrs Browne, kinswoman of Laud. Overlapping circles of birth, education, marriage and patrons opened up the possibility of a more reliable network just below the bishops. Such deans would be able to oversee the improvement of the cathedrals and keep an eye on less trustworthy bishops.[38] Laud's protégé William

---

[33] Raphoe, Clogher, Emly, St Patrick's, Kildare, Ferns, Ossory, Achonry, Kilmacduagh.

[34] In the Tuam province there was more reliance on local clergy because the western dioceses tended to be left to their own initiative until the Connacht plantation began.

[35] Wentworth to Laud, 18 May 1635, Str P 6, p. 180. See also Str P 20/129.

[36] Tilson in Christchurch who was succeeded by James Margetson. Hugh Cressy in Leighlin, Robert Forward in Dromore and Gervase Thorpe, who became dean of Waterford in April 1640. Wentworth's chaplains in Ireland were Bramhall, Tilson, Margetson, Cressy, Forward and Thorpe.

[37] Rushworth, pp. 123–4.

[38] They could also withhold consent from any potentially dubious land grants.

Chappell was in a position to report on the unreliable Archibald Hamilton of Cashel.[39] Dean Wentworth of Armagh was explicitly put under the supervision of Bramhall from whom he was to 'fetch his directions in all affairs concerning the government of the church not from some others who pretend what they please for certain sing their psalms something towards the tune of Geneva'.[40] Great care, too, was taken to settle the see lands in Armagh so that the dean would have a decent income.[41] A comfortable dean would not be too beholden to his bishop and, given Ussher's frequent absences and seclusions, the diocese could then be managed by a trusted figure reporting directly to Bramhall. Armagh was not the only diocese where this process can be discerned. In Ardfert, Thomas Gray offset the imprudent William Steere. Richard Boyle's elevation to Tuam was matched by the appointment of John King, prebend of Elphin, a relative of the favoured bishop Edward King. Margetson, Wentworth's chaplain, was in position when Atherton became bishop and passed the baton on to Edward Parry.[42] Robert Forward was paired off with the sharp-tongued Theophilus Buckworth in Dromore. George Andrews had to live with the very different, probably repugnant, churchmanship of his dean Hugh Cressy.[43] This informal means of control was matched by appointment of six deans to the 1636 High Commission.

Deans, of course, could not discipline their bishops but, as in the case of Peter Wentworth, they could report to the centre. The presence of a castle appointee in a diocese must have kept some of the more recalcitrant prelates on the alert. This was especially useful when steps were being taken to enhance the standing and powers of bishops but when it was not possible to remould the entire episcopate. The combination of a reliable, expanding decanal network, a near monopoly on episcopal appointments, along with victory in parliament and convocation, all topped off with vigorous action from Dublin Castle, meant that Wentworth and Bramhall enjoyed more than merely satisfactory control over the Church of Ireland they were seeking to reconstruct.[44]

---

[39] Laud to Wentworth, 2 December 1633, *WL* 7, p. 54.

[40] Wentworth to Laud, 10 July 1637, Str P 7, p. 36. This may well be a veiled reference to Ussher.

[41] Laud to Wentworth, 11 November 1637, *WL* 6, p. 516.

[42] At his trial, Strafford described Parry as one he had 'found in Ireland' and promoted. Parry was also a member of the 1636 High Commission. See also Ranger, 'Boyle', p. 327.

[43] Cressy had annoyed Ussher by 'some Arminian points touched . . . in his sermons before the state', Wentworth to Laud, 14 July 1635, Str P 6, p. 200. He was received into the Catholic church in 1646; see Patricia C. Brückmann, 'Cressy, Hugh Paulinus (1605–1674)', *ODNB*, http://www.oxforddnb.com/view/article/6676, accessed 11 July 2005.

[44] For changing expectations of the bishops, see Kenneth Fincham, 'Episcopal government, 1603–40' in Kenneth Fincham (ed.), *The early Stuart church, 1603–1642* (1993), pp. 71–98.

Church of Ireland bishops were given not only an improving temporal base but also a new canonical settlement to regulate their dioceses. The Irish canons paid much attention to the great 'disedification' of church courts, which William Bedell had depicted as 'amongst all the impediments to the work of God amongst us, there is not any one greater than the abuse of ecclesiastical jurisdiction'.[45] As with tithing, the temptation to exploit established status to the point of rank abuse was huge. Heavy fines and hasty excommunications in conjunction with commutations caused much tension with Catholics.[46] Outside the established system, an alternative, Roman, jurisdiction was taking root. The open corruption of the courts gave Protestant critics an added excuse to repudiate canon law and its enforcers. However, overhaul of the consistory courts was not only important for the internal reform of the Church of Ireland; it also had a place in the larger scheme. Fair and functioning tribunals would help validate the claim to be a national church and provide an important weapon in the coming fight against recusancy and dissent.

Wentworth and Bramhall saw jurisdiction as a serious problem from the very outset.[47] A document compiled by Dean Richard Jones of Waterford about 1633–4 offered a close-up view of an appalling racket. He listed twenty-two offences committed by Michael Boyle not through malice but through lack of judgement and 'a covetous desire of money'.[48] This catalogue of errors gives a good flavour of the malpractice Bedell thought so injurious: money taken never to question for recusancy, excessive fees for probate, admission of 'ignorant tradesmen' to holy orders for money, sale of 'dismisses with blanks', divorces and remarriages for purchase as well as financial considerations to overlook bigamy.[49] Here, at least, was a bishop abusing his own jurisdiction himself. The more usual pattern was to sell or license it out to laity who acquired the office as part of a lucrative portfolio.

---

[45] Bedell to Ussher, 15 February 1629, *UWW* XV, p. 467. For more on Bedell and the church courts, see Alan Ford, 'The Reformation in Kilmore before 1641' in Raymond Gillespie (ed.), *Cavan: essays on the history of an Irish county* (Dublin, 1995), pp. 73–98.

[46] The Connacht bishops used the hazard of living on jurisdiction as an argument for improved endowment in their petitions, *c.* July 1635, Str P 20/144 , 20/166. 'The truth is that the Catholics have reason to complain of the Protestant clergy by means of their extortions so that their officialities, or bishop's courts, be more chargeable to the land than would the maintenance of an army be. And, for example, this bishopric is almost worth nothing to the incumbent in demesne or lands, for they have dissipated all almost, yet his court is worth him a great deal. I am loath to say what a worshipful man of the diocese said to me, that it came to £1,000 what he profited by it in extortions on poor Catholics and notwithstanding the Catholic clergy must be thought the persons that are burdens to the realm.' John Roche, bishop of Ferns, Wexford 26 May 1630 to *Propaganda Fide* quoted in P. F. Moran, *History of the Catholic Archbishops of Dublin* (Dublin, 1864), p. 326.

[47] Wentworth to Laud, 31 January 1634, Knowler I, p. 189, Str P 20/149.

[48] Str P 20/152–3.   [49] Str P 20/153.

Bedell complained that his lay chancellor Allan Cook was also 'official to the Archdeaconry of Dublin, Judge of the Admiralty, Master of the Chancery, principal Advocate of the High Commission court, one of those of the Prerogative Court and Sovereign of the town of Cavan' as well as holding a selection of vicarages in Dublin, Clogher, Kilmore and Ardagh.⁵⁰

Irish canon 23, 'Of ordering ecclesiastical jurisdiction', was a blast of buckshot aimed at such abuses.⁵¹ As in English canon 127, chancellors, commissaries and officials were to be at least twenty-six years old, an MA or BL, learned in 'civil and ecclesiastical laws'. Then the canon got down to Irish business. Farming out of jurisdictions was forbidden and no grants or patents were to be given by bishops for longer than their incumbency. If the current patentee was unqualified under the terms of the canon, then the patent or grant was to be 'held and declared unacceptable'. Frequent and punitive visitation, much complained of, was to be regulated by archbishops and bishops. They were to ensure 'that the clergy and people be not burdened with unjust exactions by their servants and officers in their visitations', or excessive noctials and refections over and above 'ordinary procurations'. Finally, no prelate was to demand 'from executors or administrators of any of their clergy any heriots or mortuaries' – this being one of the very rare abolitions of customary duties in the 1630s. It was made plain that no bishop could expect to carry on as of old in any branch of their jurisdiction.

Irish canon 76 repeated the age and educational requirements for judges and surrogates, and sought to exclude recusants from administration of the church courts by requiring judges to take the Oath of Supremacy and subscribe to the first two canons. Registers were to take the oath and everyone exercising any ecclesiastical jurisdiction was to take the oath by Christmas 1635 on pain of suspension.⁵² As if these two canons were not comprehensive enough, Wentworth was told to issue an Act of State 'that no bishops appoint any chancellor but graduates in the civil and canon law'. Once again every effort was made to tie the hands of the bishops to make it impossible for them to misuse their power.⁵³

The canons sought to curb some other excesses in church courts. The unique Irish canon 70, 'Maturity required in proceeding', forbade

---

⁵⁰ Ford, 'The reformation in Kilmore', p. 91; Bedell to Laud, 29 December 1638, Shuckburgh, *Two lives*, p. 348.

⁵¹ It only incorporated a little of EC 127 since most of the canon was written with Irish conditions in mind.

⁵² There was no separate provision for registers in EC 127.

⁵³ Wentworth to Laud, 18 May 1635, Str P 6, p. 181; 14 July 1635, Str P 6, p. 205.

excommunication for 'the first absence'.[54] The practice condemned here was no less than vexatious excommunication and a notorious moneyspinner.[55] The Irish addition to English canon 120 aimed to stamp out an analogous abuse, 'when any person appears on a citation whatsoever that if the next day after there not be articles, or a libel put in against him, he shall then be dismissed with his costs'.[56] Irish canon 71 took another shot at lay judges by stipulating that only priests had jurisdiction over a minister 'in causes criminal'. Irish canon 85 capped the number of apparitors, allowing no more than a general apparitor in each diocese and only one additional one for each deanery. The cap meant that even if a bishop or judge was minded to profit from vexatious citations his ability to do so was restricted.[57] Laud allowed his passion for uniformity to win out over his admiration for historical rights by proposing to draw up fee tables for archbishops, bishops and archdeacons using English models, explaining that 'though in some dioceses we have different fees by ancient custom . . . yet I conceive where things are settled *de novo* it is best to keep them uniform'.[58]

The new canons aspired to reform of ecclesiastical jurisdiction in its head and members by curbing bishops in some ways and enhancing their powers in others. A fairly subtle readjustment of English canons tipped the balance. Irish canon 83, to take one example, ordered that a register was to display tables of fees after they 'have been delivered to him by the bishop of the diocese'. Its counterpart, English canon 136, made no mention of the bishop and so in Ireland this aspect of court reform was vested solely in the diocesan. Irish canon 56 ordered that probate of wills was to be in the first instance before the bishop of the diocese, so effectively bound bishops to sit personally in administration cases. Irish canon 37 gave the diocesan an extra power of allocation of the curate's salary in parishes where both great and small tithes were appropriate. Irish canon 38 placed the examination and admission of curates more firmly into the hands of the bishop than in English canon 48. Irish canon 44 on terriers not only stressed the rights

---

54 The absent persons were to be cited again. At the end of every court day 'the names of those that are decreed, shall be publicly read to the intent that they may avoid the danger of the fearful sentence of excommunication'.

55 Bedell said that excessive excommunication was 'an engine to open men's purses'. Shuckburgh, *Two lives*, pp. 36–7.

56 IC 69.

57 The Irish provision contrasts with EC 85 which ordered that there should be more apparitors than there had been in the last thirty years. Such a provision would have only legitimised the rapacity of the Irish courts.

58 Laud to Wentworth, 31 July and 3 August 1635, *WL* 7, p. 163. He did so at Wentworth's request: Wentworth to Laud, 18 May 1635, Str P 6, p. 208. As in the case of apparitors it was obvious that Irish custom was considered too corrupt to be used as a precedent.

of the church but also enshrined the particular role of bishops as overseers of ecclesiastical inheritance by stipulating that they themselves ensure that this canon be observed.[59]

Bishops were to have a greater supervisory role in the parishes as well. Whereas in English canon 91 the minister signifies his choice of parish clerk to the parishioners at Sunday service, in Irish canon 86 the incumbent is required to signify it to his bishop and if the minister fails to present someone within forty days, the bishop himself is given the power to nominate and appoint a clerk for a parish. This canon gave the diocesan a potential voice in the internal affairs of every single parish in a given diocese. Unprecedentedly intrusive episcopal control is further suggested by Irish canon 87, which added to English canon 89 by requiring churchwardens to take their oath before the 'bishop or his chancellor next consistory day after election' and further granted the ordinary power to appoint if the parish should fail to elect. These provisions made the arm of the Irish bishop a little longer and a little stronger.[60]

At the same time, more extravagant notions of episcopal authority were given short shrift. William Bedell's 'Borromean' moment, his diocesan synod and canons of September 1638, which was itself a part product of his dispute with his lay chancellor Cook, led Bramhall to propose hauling the errant bishop before High Commission.[61] Archibald Hamilton's order for a public fast in his province of Cashel drew a swift response. Laud urged the king's resolution 'to reduce that kingdom to order in all things' and the lord deputy agreed that Hamilton took 'himself to be a Pope of Munster'.[62] The hapless archbishop had to endure open chastisement at the council board.[63] Whatever had been permitted in the past either through lack of scrutiny or allowance of special circumstances was no longer on. In a reconstructed Church of Ireland where the bishops had been put back at the heart of the diocese to be responsive to the centre

---

[59] For Laud's concern with terriers see Andrew Foster, 'Church policies of the 1630s' in Richard Cust and Ann Hughes (eds.), *Conflict in early Stuart England* (1989), pp. 200–1; Kenneth Fincham, *Prelate as pastor: the episcopate of James I* (Oxford, 1990), pp. 138–40.

[60] The canon does not explicitly mention the bishop having a right of veto but the movement of oath-taking to the consistory court would tend in that direction.

[61] Bramhall to Laud, 22 January 1639, Shirley, p. 65. For a recent account of the dispute, see Ford, 'The reformation in Kilmore', pp. 92–3, especially for Bedell's denial of *praemunire* which was better founded than he knew since the Act for Submission of clergy (25 Henry 8 c. 19 (Eng.)) had never been passed in Ireland. Joseph Bergin, 'The Counter-Reformation church and its bishops', *P&P* 165 (1999), 30–73, gives a succinct account of the Borromean style.

[62] Laud to Wentworth, 20 November 1636, *WL* 7, p. 298; Wentworth to Laud, 3 December 1636, Str P 7, p. 1.

[63] Wentworth to Laud, 28 February 1637, Str P 7, p. 18.

and highly active in the localities, there was to be no deviation, no running off into peculiarities.

In 1631, Charles had written for the Church of England 'how necessary and fit it is, for the maintenance of the church that bishoprics dispossessed by violent usurpations and reduced to poverty should by all fit and lawful means be favoured and supported'.[64] In Scotland a politically dangerous late revocation was designed to boost the order as well. The task in Ireland was herculean but, at the same time, the 'lawful means' were at once greater and more elastic. From 1635 to 1640 the resumption campaign was prosecuted with great intensity and at every level from chapel up to cathedral. The bishops, as was clearly intended, stood to gain most. In return, they were expected to avail themselves of all of the opportunities which were now presented. Early days in Ireland, home to the largest episcopate in the Stuart dominions, had taught the new lord deputy not to confuse quantity and quality. He also quickly saw that dealing with the Irish bishops meant preserving the newly revived patrimony from the vagaries of personality:

I will have a care of all your bishops, some that they do themselves no harm as Kilmore [William Bedell] and Kilfenora [James Heygate]; some that do their sees no harm as Killaloe [Lewis Jones], Down [Robert Echlin], Downderry [*sic*, George Downham] and Cashel [Archibald Hamilton]; some that they take no harm as Clonfert [Robert Dawson], Raphoe [Andrew Knox] and the primate [James Ussher].[65]

A poor verdict, then, which dismissed the Irish bench, just as the army and the Irish landowners had been dismissed, as an assemblage of the unreliable, the rapacious and the naïve. As chief agent, John Bramhall was intended to be as much a supervisor as he was a negotiator and facilitator. Whatever Ussher's feelings might have been about the overall direction of ecclesiastical affairs, he was shrewd enough to recognise Derry's primacy in temporalities and promptly handed over management of that part of his affairs to his suffragan.[66] While Laud hoped that Spottiswood of Clogher could be lured elsewhere so as not to abuse the special new statute for the Ulster bishops, the unworthy incumbent enjoyed an augmentation of £720 per annum by 1639.[67] George Andrews, promoted to Ferns and Leighlin after acting as spokesman for the opposition in convocation, was dismissively portrayed as a sticky-fingered bully in correspondence between Laud

---

[64] PRO, SO 1/2 fol. 47v quoted in Kevin Sharpe, *The personal rule of Charles I* (New Haven, 1992), p. 316. For changing expectations of the bishops, see Fincham, 'Episcopal government', pp. 71–98.
[65] Wentworth to Laud, 7 March 1634 , Str P 6, p. 28.
[66] Ussher to Bramhall, 27 October 1635, HA 15950; 23 November 1635 HA 15951.
[67] Bramhall to Laud, January 1639, Shirley, p. 17.

and Wentworth. Yet when the new bishop wished to make recoveries from several prominent Wexford families in 1635 he enjoyed every assistance.[68] The business of the latter half of the 1630s was to build prosperity and make a counterweight to the Roman episcopate.[69]

Order and decency in cathedral liturgy were matched by a drive to put the dignity back into cathedral dignities. This process had started up fitfully in the 1620s and 1630s through reconstitution and attempted re-endowment of a number of chapters. Laud explained to Ussher in 1630 that he 'had no rule that only deans be bishops, but that bishops would not hold deaneries *in commendam*'.[70] This rule was generally adhered to under Wentworth. When Robert Ussher was given Kildare, Laud was loath to allow him to keep his archdeaconry in Meath as it gave such poor example: 'it makes laymen think that these dignities are of little use when they may be so held and executed by another'.[71] Yet poor bishoprics were still a staple on the Irish scene and so while Bramhall broke the link between archbishopric and deanery by prising Barlow of Tuam out of Christchurch, Dublin, he still had to put together a compensation package for the provincial.[72]

There were bishops who required no prompting at all to embark on reconstruction. King of Elphin found approbation as a model bishop who by skilful husbanding of his resources would ensure the eventual success of the reformation. During his progress into Connacht in 1635, Wentworth wrote to Laud from Elphin about this 'princely bishop' who had improved his see from 200 marks to £1,000 and 'in the town of Elphin where there was nothing but Irish cabins without a chimney, he has in his time built very prettily so as you would take it to be a handsome village in England'. King had also donated land of his own for the construction of a church and a small but 'strong' castle and so exhibited exemplary concern for his successors.[73] He was liked because he had realised plantation aspirations

---

[68] J. F. Ainsworth and Edward McLysaght (eds.), 'Survey of documents in private keeping, 2nd series – the Colclough Papers', *Analecta Hibernica* 20 (1958), 3–13.

[69] Wentworth to Laud, 3 January 1636, Str P 6, p. 292. Poor bishoprics were often turned down – Henry Leslie wouldn't touch Ferns and Leighlin and King of Elphin refused promotion because he believed that Tuam 'would be his *tumulum*', Wentworth to Laud, 1 March 1637, Str P 7, p. 71.

[70] Laud to Ussher, 5 July 1630, *UWW* XV, p. 527.

[71] Laud to Wentworth, 21 October 1635, *WL* 7, p. 199; Wentworth to Laud, 14 December 1635, Str P 6, p. 282.

[72] Laud to Wentworth, 12 April 1634, *WL* 7, p. 65 and 20 October 1634, *WL* 6, p. 398; Bramhall to Laud, 17 March 1634, HA 14048; Laud to Bramhall, 16 January 1635, HA 15157, see also Str P 20/129. When George Synge became bishop of Cloyne, he was persuaded to swap his deanery of Dromore with one of Wentworth's chaplains for the nearby rectory of Youghal: Wentworth to Laud, 8 June 1638, Str P 7, p. 10.

[73] Wentworth to Laud, 14 July 1635, Str P 6, p. 209. Laud considered it 'a greater miracle than the Jesuits have bragged upon', *WL* 7, p. 165.

through an ideal combination of good stewardship of his temporalities with settlement and anglicisation. Such a blend of Christianity, cultivation and civilisation was sought for in all the bishops, but found in few.

Three years later King wrote to Laud himself.[74] The letter is an excellent illustration of what a bishop could achieve in those years. In 1633 when revenue from see lands was £300 p.a. he began to refuse to renew leases without a fair increase in rent. The tenants appealed to the lord deputy in vain and income more than doubled to £700. King explained that Wentworth's tough line with those who had long leases or fee farms caused a further rise to £1,340. After that Bramhall was sent in to aid him in disposing of the *quarta pars episcopalis* to the parochial ministers, to make unions of the smaller parishes and to survey all benefices 'to the end that the ministers may not keep up variety of cures'.[75] If parishes were larger, the congregations would be bigger and funds could be found for church repairs. In addition, twelve benefices were prepared for twelve preachers. Everything would be in readiness when the new settlers arrived for the plantation of Connacht.

The bishop was initially encouraged by Laud. He then took a hard line with his tenants, sure of Wentworth's support. The lord deputy pressed home the advantage by forcing other lessees to come to favourable terms with the bishop. Finally, Bramhall was sent in to make the improvements effective and to prevail on the now indebted bishop to relinquish some of his own revenue for the general good of the parishes. Churches were to be built, proper records now existed and leases were made uniform and profitable. It was through this amalgam of encouragement, coercion, example, supervision and opportunism that the triangular relationship of Laud, Wentworth and Bramhall operated so effectively on the Church of Ireland.

King's improvements prefigured a new plantation while Bramhall's work in his own diocese was intended to perfect an old one. His 1639 report records a total improvement for Derry of £2,250, which incorporated an augmentation of the bishopric itself from £860 to £1,140 as well as recovery of termon lands, fisheries, erection of twenty new churches and a new

---

[74] King to Laud, 15 May 1638, Shirley, pp. 56–7.

[75] The *quarta pars* was a traditional arrangement by which clergy gave one quarter of their tithe income to the bishop. For a description of it, and other customs kept up after the reformation, see George Montgomery's report of 1611 in Shirley, pp. 25–38. In Ulster, the abolition of the *quarta pars* and the similar *tertia pars* had been part of the plantation reform of the church as Montgomery had recommended. What we have here then is some application of the plantation norms to a diocese in Connacht, ahead of the intended formal process. King also restored an impropriate rectory and vicarage which he had purchased to the church.

episcopal residence outside the walls.[76] Like King of Elphin, he started off by taking a tough line with the tenants by refusing their 'good fines' for confirmation of leases, instead compounding with them 'for improvements of rent of very near an hundred pounds a year'. He had no reservations about the efficacy of his methods: 'and [I] doubt not but that many more of them will take the same course'.[77] Bramhall believed he had broken the ice for the other Ulster bishops who could now exploit tenant anxiety over security of their tenure. This strategy appears to have worked because by December 1634, in the wake of his first trip north, he claimed to have doubled the fishings, brought in £14,000 and recovered a demesne. This exemplary success was given monumental effect in 1638 through provision of a new peal of bells for the recently completed St Columb's cathedral.[78] Swagger and viceregal support certainly rendered his early days effortlessly spectacular. The story of the years after 1635 is just as thorough but much more prosaic and painstaking. Like Montgomery before him, Bramhall was drawn into bickering with the Londoners and other assorted landowners. He gnawed bad-temperedly over old leases with Sir Thomas Staples right through 1634 to 1641. Even his more amicable negotiations with Viscount Chichester over lands and advowsons at Donally and Movill spread out over years.[79] While Termonomongan was the subject of a satisfying conciliar order as early as June 1635, a commission to investigate other termon lands started in 1636 moved far slower. Yet Bramhall's early labours, especially with those termon lands, had a deeper significance because they circumvented post-plantation leases by using interrogataries which aimed at establishing pre-plantation and, indeed, pre-reformation rights.[80]

In his letter of 29 January 1634, so saturated with the rhetoric of sacrilege, Wentworth singled out Sir Walter Raleigh's possession of Lismore for particular mention:

a woeful face of a church, God wot, reduced from one thousand to fifty pounds revenue by year, the dean and dignities impoverished, the fabric of the church ruined, the poor vicars choral beggared, the miserable lepers turned naked and

[76] Bramhall also planned to plant the area around Fawne [Fahan] and petitioned for a market and fairs in 1637, HA 14054.

[77] Bramhall to Laud, 21 August 1634, HA 14040.

[78] The bells were partially financed by High Commission fines: T. W. Moody and J. G. Simms (eds.), *Bishopric of Derry and the Irish Society 1602–1705*, 2 vols. (Dublin, 1968), vol. I, pp. 222–3.

[79] For Staples, see Moody and Simms, *Bishopric of Derry*, vol. I, pp. 178–80, 183–8, 190–3, 197–8, 212, 237–8, 244–5; for Chichester, pp. 193, 202–3, 206–7, 209–10, and Bramhall to Chichester, 28 October 1634, HA 14046.

[80] Lord deputy and council's order for possession of Termonomongan, 18 June 1635: Moody and Simms, *Bishopric of Derry*, vol. I, p. 200.

empty from those reliefs provided by the piety of former times, and that which might have been preserved a light of religion and charity, clouded under a palpable darkness of impiety and rapine

George Radcliffe proposed a smart but stark way of recovery. Waterford and Lismore, he argued, had been united in 1363 and so any leases granted by Bishop Wethred to Raleigh had been agreed by the Lismore chapter alone and were, as such, invalid.[81] Unsurprisingly this legalistic cleverness created unease. Despite pressing Laud repeatedly over months for approbation, no opinion was forthcoming and in August 1635, the archbishop admitted: 'I cannot yet get the lawyers whom I would have to lead to speak out.'[82] In October, all Laud had to offer the lord deputy was 'a little' as he found 'the lawyers here shy of Sir George Radcliffe's case'.[83]

While Bramhall worked on persuading Michael Boyle of Waterford and Lismore to complain, little could be done until the bishop died in December 1635. Once Atherton's reputation for business overcame the whiff of scandal, the earl of Cork found himself subject to a barrage of suits.[84] Weariness, wariness at the shakiness of Radcliffe's case and convenience prompted Cork and Wentworth to move to settlement outside court. A reference from council on 27 June 1637 produced a rapid report by Bramhall and Sir William Parsons who suggested a composition which was at once pragmatic and rhetorical. In real terms, as Bramhall told Laud, it meant £1,000 per annum recovered for the bishopric, a restored cathedral, fishing revenue from the great weirs at Lismore, five vicars choral endowed at Cork's expense and a grant of £500 towards a palace.[85] Cork got his titles to land at Lismore, Bewley and Kilmolash and a scattering of sixty-year leases confirmed by Atherton and both chapters.[86] The composition document made an explicit link between reconstruction and reformation by arguing that because the see was at such a low ebb, the bishop had been forced to 'live upon his jurisdictions to the great grievance and oppression of His Majesty's subjects' and that concomitant pluralism had depleted parishes of 'their lawful pastor'.

---

[81] Str P 6, pp. 8ff; 13. Kearney, *Strafford*, p. 126, mentions the attempt of Bishop Lancaster to recover his estate in the 1613 parliament; Ranger, 'Boyle', pp. 319–33, gives a detailed account of the Lismore affair.

[82] Laud to Wentworth, 31 July and 3 August 1635, *WL* 7, p. 160.

[83] Laud to Wentworth, 4 October 1635, *WL* 7, p. 183.

[84] Commission to investigate Lismore, Str P 20/169 (*c.* January 1637).

[85] Bramhall to Laud, 27 July 1637, SP 63/256/46,1.

[86] Act of 1640 confirming lands, *Commons jn. Ire.*, p. 158.

This message did not penetrate to Atherton who continued to push his jurisdiction to the hilt to yield still further revenue.[87] He also made recoveries and received surrenders on council orders of whole swathes of land in Waterford. In Lismore, again with Bramhall acting as arbitrator, he recovered the manor of Ardfinnan whose tangled tenurial history stretched back to Miler McGrath's time as commendator under Elizabeth.[88] By late 1639 he was mopping up the lazar house at Lismore and, as Joshua Boyle's post-Restoration account shows, projecting a whole series of other recoveries. Where the bishop led others followed. Archdeacon Gwyn (who popped up in Strafford's trial) made his own recoveries and the arrival of Dean Parry in 1640 triggered fresh suits in Lismore for deanery lands and vicars choral revenues.[89]

Waterford and Lismore was perhaps the most flamboyant of all recoveries. Accounts of it have naturally been highly personalised, focusing on Cork's chagrin, Wentworth's determination and Atherton's hubris. But when all of the grandees are set aside a much more familiar pattern emerges – a high-profile attack on a leading figure, invocation of historical rights and initiation of a campaign encompassing everything from individual ploughlands up to whole manors and townlands. Consequent prosperity was supposed to raise the whole clergy and provide a respectable parochial ministry. Finally in Lismore, just as in Elphin, Derry and elsewhere, a fully endowed, fully manned and newly refurbished cathedral church was to sit at the heart of the diocese.

While Scotland acquired a new bishop and diocese of Edinburgh in 1636, Ireland saw a revival of Cloyne as an independent diocese after a space of 211 years in 1638. Nicknamed 'five marks' because it had been farmed out to Sir John Fitz Edmond Fitzgerald at that annual rent, Cloyne first caught Bramhall's imagination on his maiden trip to Munster.[90] At that time the enticing prospect of re-erecting an entire diocese first sprang to mind.[91] A new bishop for Cloyne would be a spectacular validation of the historicity of the episcopal Church of Ireland. Charles reportedly liked the idea 'extremely well' and ordered Bramhall to proceed without delay to overthrow of the grant, but the project had to wait until Boyle's transfer to

[87] He even fined for eating meat in Lent: Ranger, 'Boyle', p. 345, University College Cork, Christchurch MS, fols. 1r–37v (July 1639).

[88] W. H. Rennison, 'Joshua Boyle's accompt of the temporalities of the bishopricks of Waterford', *Journal of the Cork Historical and Archaeological Society* 32 (1927), 42–9, 78–85; 33 (1928), 42–7, 83–92; 35 (1930), 26–33; 36 (1931), 20–5.

[89] Ranger, 'Boyle', pp. 325–9.   [90] Vesey, *Athanasius Hibernicus*, [p. 13].

[91] Bramhall to Laud, 20 December 1634, Shirley, p. 43; Wentworth to Laud, 12 April 1634, Str P 6, p. 47.

Tuam in May 1638.[92] On 11 November 1638 James Ussher consecrated his former chancellor George Synge at Drogheda, while William Chappell was consecrated to Cork and Ross in Dublin.[93] Synge might have been vehement in his criticism of Laud's protégé, James Croxton, but like George Andrews he was given assistance, through Bramhall's arbitration, in his recovery of the see lands. Aid was all the more important to Synge because he was actually consecrated before the Fitzgerald fee farm had been overthrown.[94] Wentworth's verdict on the whole affair, 'not only a bishopric but also a bishop restored to the church', turned out to have a particular resonance in those months after the signing of the National Covenant in Scotland.[95]

BRAMHALL IN AS CHIEF AGENT, 1634–8

Bramhall always presented himself as Wentworth's representative and claimed that his appearance as an emissary caused 'the poor oppressed clergy [to] begin to rouse themselves up in expectation of future hopes'.[96] He also encouraged clergy to address themselves to 'his Sacred Majesty and your Grace so their cause may come recommended to my Lord with more authority and a kind of necessitation'.[97] The message he wished to convey by this was that real powers were being mobilised to help the Irish church and he, Bramhall, was their agent.

Attending personally to the temporal well-being of the church was Bramhall's chief occupation of the latter half of the 1630s.[98] He characterised his work as 'troublesome, expensive, subjected to the envy of some and hatred of others'.[99] Officially, Bramhall's most frequent appointment was as arbitrator, a role which he carried out in every

---

[92] Laud to Bramhall, 16 January 1635, HA 15157.   [93] Dublin City Library, Gilbert MS 169, p. 218.

[94] Special provision was made for him to hold his deanery of Dromore *in commendam* until revenues began to flow, Wentworth to Laud, 26 May 1638, Str P 7, p. 102. Ranger, 'Boyle', pp. 341–3, 383; Brady, *Clerical and parochial records of Cork, Cloyne and Ross*, vol. III, pp. 4–6, 10–13, 24–5; *Cal. SP Ire.* 1611–14, pp. 367–8.

[95] Wentworth to Laud, 26 May 1638, Str P 7, p. 102.

[96] The feeling was mutual, Wentworth spoke of his daily recourse to Bramhall: Wentworth to Cottington, 15 September 1633, Str P3, p. 18.

[97] Bramhall to Laud, 19 February 19 1634, HA 15154.

[98] 'I lived sundry years a bishop in the Province of Ulster, whilst the political part of the care of the Church did lie heavily on my shoulders', *BW* V, p. 74; Bramhall to Laud, 21 August 1634, HA 14040; Laud to Wentworth, 10 July 1637, Str P 7, p. 37. See also Aidan Clarke, 'The Atherton file', *Decies: Journal of the Old Waterford History Society* 11 (1979), 45–55; Wentworth to Laud, 13 April 1635, Str P 6, p. 162 and 14 July 1635, Str P 6, p. 201.

[99] Bramhall to Laud, 13 September 1638, Shirley, p. 61.

ecclesiastical province.[100] The frequent references to Bramhall's improvement of see revenues were usually occasions where he acted as agent for the bishop concerned. At times, such as in his clash with Bedell in Kilmore in 1638–9, his views and those of the diocesan were at odds but generally individual bishops were more than happy to take his assistance. Most petitions sent to the lord deputy on ecclesiastical endowments would procure Derry's presence.[101]

He was also deployed in contentious matters involving individual bishops – such as a bitter dispute between Bedell and one of his clergy over a questionable presentation.[102] Accusations of simony against Spottiswood of Clogher were referred to Bramhall and Sir George Radcliffe. After the hearing, Spottiswood felt himself hard done by, and complained vociferously that he had been misjudged.[103] Wentworth was sceptical of claims of bias and remarked to Laud that 'fame noises him [Spottiswood] to be the worst bishop in Ireland'.[104] The degree of trust which Wentworth placed in Bramhall made it pointless to appeal against any of the bishop's actions. This solidarity made Bramhall more than just a plain representative; it made him a plenipotentiary.

George Radcliffe worked closely in conjunction with him from the outset, aiding him in the early round of treaties for impropriations.[105] Wentworth later explained that in the impropriations business he commended 'the soliciting part to my lord of Derry's, the legal part to Sir George Radcliffe's care'.[106] As with Laud and Neile in England, the cooperation of

---

[100] For typical deals, see his negotiations between Knox of Raphoe and his tenants and between Leslie of Down and some of his tenants, Bramhall to Wentworth, 16 May 1635, HA 14049; Wentworth to Bramhall, 11 May 1635, PRONI T415, p. 2.

[101] In a petition to the lord deputy and council of 1634, one clergyman did ask specifically that the matter be dealt with by the bishop of Derry: BL Harleian MS 4297, pp. 17–19.

[102] William Bayly was presented to a vicarage by the son-in-law of Bedell's predecessor, Thomas Moigne. Bayly was himself the son-in-law of Alan Cooke, Bedell's chancellor, with whom the bishop was locked in another protracted dispute. The dispute widened into questions over ordination without permission, false letters of induction and like almost every case in which Bedell became embroiled ended up as a matter of Byzantine complexity. For this reference, Bedell to Laud, 2 September 1637, see Shuckburgh, *Two lives*, p. 341.

[103] SP 63/254/104 *Cal. SP Ire.* 1633–47, p. 44. Laud to Wentworth, received 18 April 1634, WL 7, pp. 64–5, and 23 June 1634, WL 7, p. 78. See also Alexander Boswell (ed.), *James Spottiswood: a brief memorial* (Edinburgh, 1811), pp. 68–73, and Raymond Gillespie, 'The trials of Bishop Spottiswood, 1620–40', *Clogher Record* 12 (1987), 38–47.

[104] Wentworth to Laud, 30 June 1634, Str P 6, p. 74.

[105] Bramhall to Laud, 21 August 1634, HA 14040. He also drew up the fiant for the king's letter restoring the crown impropriations: Wentworth to Laud, 18 May 1635, Str P 6, p. 181.

[106] Wentworth to Laud, 2 November 1635, Str P 6, p. 265. Bramhall referred to his 'chapman for impropriations' in a letter to Laud of 26 May 1634, HA 14043; this may well be Radcliffe.

skilled lawyers was crucial for a strategy which was legalistic in conception and execution.

Like Laud's, Bramhall's churchmanship centred on the institutions of the church and he shared the view that the depletion of the church's patrimony had been bad in England but 'Ireland hath been worse'.[107] He also strongly believed ecclesiastical recoveries promoted broader prosperity in the commonwealth and so took pleasure in pointing out that a leading church tenant in Down and Connor who had improved his rents to the diocese by £20 had profited by £100 in a consequent composition with his undertenants. For him, a prosperous church meant a prosperous crown and a contented and peaceable people.[108]

Certainty of unfailing support from Wentworth coupled with a strong belief in his own rectitude lent Bramhall's pursuit of the rights of the church a tone which verged on the peremptory. This uncompromising attitude is apparent in the few letters that survive from him to landowners.[109] When dealing with inferiors, he could be blistering. The dean of Down, William Coote, had the temerity in 1639 to claim that he and not Bramhall would be responsible for the disposal of tithes bought in from the countess of Tyrconnell. This drew a crushing letter in which Coote was excoriated for his ingratitude and reminded who it was that knew the lord deputy's mind best.[110]

While Bramhall was short-tempered, his research skills were deeply impressive. Those scraps of evidence which survive show that any claim to ancient endowment was backed by an extensive trawl of all of the available sources. His report on a dispute between the vicars choral of Kilkenny cathedral and one Edward Comerford shows just this.[111] Having carefully sifted through evidence ranging from Henry IV to Elizabeth, he discovered that the vicars choral had conveyed land to Comerford's grandfather without reserving any rent, but he could find no fault in the conveyance. Despite this, he still managed to extract a commitment from Comerford to pay rent for the next ten years. Throughout the later 1630s, Bramhall was constantly honing and refining his tactics in order to extract maximum

---

[107] Laud to Bramhall, 4 March 1635, HA 15158.

[108] Bramhall to Laud, 1 April 1636, Shirley, p. 42.

[109] See Bramhall's letter to Sir Thomas Staples, 24 June 1634, Moody and Simms (eds.), *Bishopric of Derry*, vol. I, pp. 178–80. The only hint that Bramhall gives that he might be overstepping the mark was in an ambiguous apology for the 'boldness and tediousness' of his letter.

[110] Bramhall to Coote, 27 January 1639, *BW* I, p. lxxxvii. He was told he could no longer count on Bramhall's support: 'some other part of the church shall fare better for your disrespect'. The language of the letter allows perhaps a true interpretation of Jeremy Taylor's remark in his *Funeral sermon* that Bramhall's 'zeal broke out to warm his brethren', *BW* I, p. lix.

[111] The report survives in a nineteenth-century transcript, RCB MS C2/14/2/34.

benefit from the instruments given to him and to attempt to secure gains already made. He requested additional clauses in the king's letter for impropriations concealed from the crown.[112] He discovered that bishop's patents for Ulster had a clause which conflicted with the statute made on their behalf and found a remedy.[113] He was also able to give Laud a succinct description of how usurped crown appropriations were undervalued 'to pass for nothing in time of peace which was found to have been worth little or nothing in time of rebellion and war, and to take up appropriations as gentlemen do waifs in England'.[114]

Bramhall's pet project lay in developing a fund to buy in impropriations. His proposal was bound to find favour with Laud who himself hoped to use fines from High Commission (after St Paul's was completed) to buy in impropriations.[115] Laud's hopes were modest, to buy in 'two a year at least', but Bramhall was more ambitious. He was also optimistic about how the scheme would be financed: 'the clergy are forward here to give two subsidies towards this end. I rather think a present and free contribution of all, to which I conceive many will offer liberally.' But he was also realistic enough to suggest that the money could come from the fourth part set aside for the king in the grant to Porter and Murray for discovering hidden advowsons.[116] Wentworth was ordered to do this only if some other source of income could be found to compensate the crown.[117] As Bramhall was looking for £10,000 to broaden his scheme two years later, it seems that neither the voluntary contributions flowed in nor was money from the grant forthcoming.[118] Initially he named four clergymen who he thought

---

[112] Bramhall to Laud, 1 April 1636, Shirley, pp. 45–6. See also Laud to Bramhall, 11 May 1635 HA 15159; 20 April 1635, *WL* 7, pp. 119–22; Bramhall to Laud, 23 February 1638, Shirley, p. 52 and *Cal. SP Ire.* 1633–47, p. 135.

[113] Bramhall to Laud, 13 September 1638, Shirley, p. 61; Laud to Bramhall, October 1638, HA 15168.

[114] Bramhall to Laud, 23 February 1637, Shirley, p. 52.

[115] Bramhall proposed the scheme to Laud at the end of his account of his first successful series of negotiations with impropriators in his letter of 21 August 1634, HA 14040. For Laud, see *WL* 3, p. 255. John Vesey in his *Athanasius Hibernicus*, p. 15, claimed that 'the archbishop of Canterbury countenanced the work and lent him his hand and purse too, having designed £40,000 for it'. There is absolutely no evidence to support this statement and this story may have arisen as a result of the figures current on the scale of improvements, especially as Dudley Loftus gives a figure of £30,000 in his *Oratio funebris* (Dublin, 1663), p. 17.

[116] Bramhall to Laud, 20 December 1634, Shirley, p. 43; Laud to Wentworth, 20 October 1634, *WL* 6, p. 401.

[117] See *Cal. SP Ire.* 1633–47, pp. 7, 76. It is important to remember that the church campaign was carried out in a context in which the protection of crown revenue was of first and absolute importance. Accordingly, most petitions and schemes for the church stressed the degree to which they would enhance the receipts of the crown.

[118] Bramhall to Wentworth, 13 January 1637, Str P 8, p. 412.

would lend money to make up the stock.[119] The case of one of these, Henry Sutton, suggests that these loans were not entirely voluntary. Sutton, then dean of Derry, had been hauled up for simony in front of the lord deputy and council. Wentworth, as so often, was keen for a public trial at Castle Chamber: 'I trust by one sharp example to purge this leaven out of the church for many years hereafter.'[120] Some months later a money fine was now acceptable, 'least in some way his profession suffer in some measure as himself'.[121] Bramhall reached an arrangement with the dean for an expiatory donation to the scheme, remarking uncharacteristically that his misdeed had been 'the fault of the times'. As another of the clerical loans originated in a favour shown to the individual by Wentworth, there is good ground for speculating that these were really 'informal' fines in exchange for the stay of public proceedings.[122]

Bramhall gave a general account of his progress in January 1637.[123] The wave of contributions had not materialised and a scant £2,000 had been raised on two loans. With the funds Bramhall had purchased the impropriations of the priory of Lowth.[124] He then sold most of these back to incumbents or clerical investors, who would return the tithes to the churches in question after recovering a small profit. The modest surplus paid for a small parcel of tithes in Dromore. The only other substantial purchase was from the earl of Fingal and Lady Tyrconnell of 'sundry rectories and parcels in the diocese of Down' for £350. Again, most of these were sold to the incumbents, such sale being the major point of difference to the English feofees whose aim was to endow lectureships. Out of this surplus Dean William Coote got £100 to augment his deanery, £200 went towards the building of Down cathedral, and an unspecified sum (in conjunction with Lord Cromwell) was allocated to buy land for a palace for the bishop of Down and Connor. Finally, £1,300 went towards Christchurch, the Irish

---

[119] Bramhall to Laud, 20 December 1634, Shirley, p. 42.

[120] Wentworth to Laud, 29 January 1634, Str P 6, p. 23. Laud was equally keen on making a salutary example of Sutton; see his letter to Wentworth, 11 March 1634, *WL* 6, p. 353. For use of recusant funds for the buying in of impropriations, see chapter 5, pp. 174–5.

[121] Wentworth to Laud, 30 June 1634, Str P 6, p. 43. Ussher had been pleading for Sutton, but this is unlikely to have carried much weight with Wentworth who remarked peevishly: 'it is the genius of this country where, be the fault never so abominable, yet shall all men sue it may not be punished', Wentworth to Laud, 12 April 1634, Str P 6, p. 43.

[122] Bramhall to Laud, 21 August 1634, HA 14040. The lord deputy had freed this clergyman, Symons, from 'a litigious quarrel', Bramhall to Wentworth, 13 January 1637, Str P 8, p. 410. See a bond of 5 August 1634 for the terms agreed with Symons, HA 14041.

[123] The report is in Bramhall to Wentworth, 13 January 1637, Str P 8, pp. 409–12.

[124] Newport B. White, *Extents of Irish monastic possessions 1540–41* (Dublin, 1943), pp. 228–34. The impropriations were located in Co. Louth, the southern part of the diocese of Armagh.

St Paul's. Other money was earmarked for purchase of the remaining impropriations in Derry. Lastly, while anticipating profits of £500 in the first two years and £1,800 in the next two, Bramhall chose to emphasise his own altruism in deciding to 'make it a voluntary offering to God, towards a supply to the necessities of this church' rather than keep anything for himself.

The increases in the value of the livings in Bramhall's account ranged from 25 to 110 per cent p.a. Substantial leaps in rents as well as in tithe payments added to the general pressure on the Irish economy to yield up more for crown and for church. Vigorous enforcement meant there was little choice but to pay up for the time being.[125] Improving the standing of the clergy had another purpose: 'by this means three clergymen shall be enabled to serve His Majesty as Justices of the Peace in the diocese of Down, among the nonconformists and two others in the county of Louth . . . where for the want of resident clergy, there have been almost no Protestants heretofore'.[126] Just as in England and Scotland, clergymen were to play a more active role in local government.[127]

Bramhall's account ended, as his reports often did, in tones of absolute confidence about what great things could be done next. It was this confidence, along with his capacity to plan ahead, joined with his proven diligence and efficiency which won Bramhall great praise and, crucially, a reputation for being able to make prodigious improvements. Wentworth was rhapsodic: 'my judgement . . . is this – that if Dr Bramhall do not more service both in the church and state than any bishop of this kingdom has done this hundred years, I confess he answers not my expectation'.[128]

But was he really doing more than all the bishops of the past century had done? Was the campaign making any substantial difference to the church? Laud was certainly asking the second of these questions when he suggested

[125] Especially in Ulster where there were simmering discontents throughout the 1630s. See Raymond Gillespie, 'The end of an era: Ulster and the outbreak of the 1641 rising' in Ciaran Brady and Raymond Gillespie (eds.), *Natives and newcomers: the making of Irish colonial society 1534–1641* (Dublin, 1986), pp. 191–213; Aidan Clarke, 'The genesis of the Ulster rising of 1641' in Peter Roebuck (ed.), *From plantation to partition* (Belfast, 1981), pp. 21–45.

[126] Bramhall to Wentworth, 13 January 1637, Str P 8, p. 412.

[127] Andrew Foster, 'The clerical estate revitalised' in Kenneth Fincham (ed.), *The early Stuart church, 1603–1642* (1993), pp. 139–60; Allan Macinnes, *Charles I and the making of the Covenanting movement 1625–1641* (Edinburgh, 1991), pp. 95–6.

[128] Wentworth to Laud, 30 June 1634 , Str P 6, p. 76. See also his letter of 11 September 1637, Str P 7, p. 41, for equally extravagant claims. Wentworth who, as it has often been claimed, regarded personal profit as one of the legitimate prerequisites of office, was still extremely impressed by Bramhall's decision not to take any of the profits of the impropriations fund: Wentworth to Laud, 11 February 1637, Str P 7, p. 21.

to Wentworth that he send him 'a yearly calendar what livings you have that year recovered to the church'.[129] Instead, he received regular assurances from Bramhall and Wentworth that work was proceeding apace. Eventually, in January 1636, the lord deputy sent over an account for the church in Ulster and the diocese of Cork.[130]

It makes impressive reading.[131] Derry had been improved by £1,800 p.a., Raphoe £680, Down £1,984. Armagh, Clogher, Dromore, Kilmore and Ardagh came to no less than £3,000. Where values of individual livings or lands are given we can see that augmentations were anything from 40 to 1,200 per cent. Other substantial jumps were recorded for Derry where income from see land rose by £1,000 to £1,860, and for an individual benefice, the rectory of Racavan in Down where the income leaped from 30s to £40 a year. The overall improvement for the province of Armagh was £8,500. Increases in Cork brought the grand total to £10,600.

This document bears closer scrutiny. At the end, Wentworth had written: 'the whole improvement *will* amount to £10,600'. Bramhall would later admit that many of the livings 'were the flower of the appropriations in the North'.[132] Some of the figures which went into the total were the aggregate of what would accrue over four years. Other improvements were labelled 'at least' and the figure of £3,000 for the cluster of Ulster bishoprics was only an estimate as the work was still in progress. Taking these exceptions into account, the true figure of improvements *made* in the Armagh province by January 1635 was between £5,000 and £6,000. While later evidence does show that these projections were accurate, this desire to telescope a more gradual process into a report which gave more instant gratification shows that Wentworth really wished to push his ecclesiastical policy as a leading success story of his Irish tenure.

This impression of dynamism was carefully cultivated by Bramhall. In April 1636, he told Laud that now that the royal appropriations in Meath 'both the most and best' were passed, 'all the rest in Ulster will follow shortly, and those in Dublin after them, the troublesome past is passed, the rest is but a facsimile'.[133] At the same time, he told Wentworth that now 'all Ulster is in a manner settled . . . and so will Connacht be presently.

[129] Laud to Wentworth, 12 April 1634, *WL* 7, p. 69. This might be seen as an attempt to have a rough counterpart to the system of annual reports from bishops in England to which Laud attached great importance, *WL* 4, p. 274.
[130] Wentworth to Laud, 3 January 1636, Str P 6, p. 299.
[131] Wentworth's account, January 1636, Shirley, pp. 2–5.
[132] Bramhall to Wentworth, 5 April 1636, Moody and Simms (eds.), *Bishopric of Derry*, vol. I, pp. 207–8.
[133] Bramhall to Laud, 1 April 1636, Shirley, p. 45.

The other two (Munster and Leinster) are in a good forwardness.'[134] While Bramhall was able to provide Laud with a detailed report on the Armagh province in January 1639, he could only promise that accounts for the other three provinces would follow in time.[135] There is no evidence that these were ever compiled.[136]

He did, of course, make real gains for church and clergy and he was passionate about doing so. The greatest advances were made in Ulster, where it was easiest to do so because of the special statute and where a Protestant population which had anxieties about tenure had an incentive to negotiate. In other provinces recovery was taking longer. Bramhall's early deal with Sir Robert King for livings in Connacht was conditional on his father's death, so this took three years to come through.[137] Negotiations with Lord Cromwell dragged on for over three years until 1638.[138] A settlement he brokered between the bishop of Down and tenants was still not complete in 1639, four years after arbitration had begun.[139] Just as in his own diocese there were practical, personal and legal factors which caused delay. Early highs gave way to more measured progress.

Bramhall was also under constant pressure from Laud to act quickly. He rightly fretted about the enthusiasm of Irish landowners for reconstruction: 'the truth is, I trust none of their devotions but there is something else in it'. As the situation in Scotland deteriorated, Laud's innate pessimism welled up and he pressed harder, advising his Irish ally to follow his 'work the closer' and 'prevent as much future hurt as you can against the time shall come that the face of that state shall not look so favourably upon the Church as it now does'.[140] Bramhall frankly acknowledged that the business of the royal impropriations was a 'work of time and toil' but promised, probably to reassure Laud, that he would have it completed within a term.[141] After the National Covenant there was a shift away from lofty talk of laying a

---

[134] Bramhall to Wentworth, 5 April 1636, Moody and Simms (eds.), *Bishopric of Derry*, vol. I, pp. 207–8. Barlow of Tuam wrote to Wentworth on 26 June 1638 describing the chaotic state of his see lands, Str P 20/132.

[135] Bramhall to Laud, 12 January 1639, Shirley, p. 64.

[136] Bramhall also said he was anxious to go to work on Dublin in order to increase the archbishop's revenues so that he might 'do the state better service', Bramhall to Laud, 7 June 1637, Shirley, p. 48. See also Bramhall to Laud, 9 August 1637, Shirley, p. 51. A report written by Bramhall on 4–5 August 1637 shows that his initial round of compositions with the archbishop's tenants secured an increase of just over £204, SP 63/256/44, *Cal. SP Ire.* 1633–47, pp. 165–6. Yet in September 1639, he was still labouring at Dublin; see Shirley, p. 73.

[137] Bramhall to Laud, 7 June 1637, Shirley, p. 48.   [138] Laud to Bramhall, 28 March 1638, HA 15165.

[139] Bramhall to Laud, 7 August 1639, Shirley, p. 71.

[140] Laud to Bramhall, 28 March 1638, HA 15165; 20 June 1638, HA 15166.

[141] Bramhall to Laud, 23 February 1638 , Shirley, pp. 52–3.

secure foundation for the reformation to a more breathless talk of seizing opportunities while they continued to present themselves.

THE CHURCH OF IRELAND AND THE LAND OF IRELAND

In March 1633, Ussher urged William Laud to write to the lord treasurer, the earl of Cork, to thank him 'for his ancient care in standing for the maintenance of the church'.[142] Less than a year later Wentworth portrayed the earl as a master of chicanery, a forger and a man gorging on ecclesiastical revenues.[143] His proposed assault on Boyle had political purpose but used ecclesiastical means since a royal regrant of 1629 shielded so many of the earl's estates. Of the long lists of church lands and livings stretching in an arc from Waterford to Kerry, Youghal stands at a slight remove. The College of the Blessed Virgin provided a public platform for the lord deputy; it was another 'trouncing' opportunity but now the target was the wealthiest layman in the kingdom. This case was at heart a high political contest.[144] It was a fight over access to Charles worked out in the interstices of faction and marriage alliances. It was about the relationship between money and power, between an overt rhetoric of public reform and the whisperings of private interest.

Wentworth wanted a sentence but he got a composition. Ultimately the church was a beneficiary but only a collateral one, as Youghal yielded up only twelve impropriations worth £500 a year. This affair, unlike all other resumptions, was about just one person.[145] Pressure was brought to bear on Cork in various ways. While Wentworth argued that Lismore needed careful preparation, Youghal could run immediately because it centred on an alleged forgery and improper oath-taking.[146] Youghal was the last church case which Wentworth initiated and directed personally. After 1635 it was Bramhall and other bishops who made the running. Derry himself played only a minor part in this business by cajoling the Boyle bishops into

---

[142] Ussher to Laud, 24 March 1632, PRO SP 63/254/17, *Cal. SP Ire.* 1633–47, p. 6.

[143] Wentworth to Laud, 29 January 1634, Str P 6, pp. 10–16.

[144] For a summary of the case, see Kearney, *Strafford*, pp. 126–9; for a detailed account, see Ranger, 'Boyle', pp. 291–318; and for the aftermath, see Patrick Little, 'The earl of Cork and the fall of the earl of Strafford, 1638–41', *HJ* 39 (1996), 619–35. Wentworth's dossier of papers relating to the case is in Str P 24–25/437–442.

[145] The definitive work on Boyle's fortune is to be found in Terence Ranger, 'Richard Boyle and the making of an Irish fortune, 1588–1614', *IHS* 39 (1957), 257–97, and 'Strafford in Ireland: a Revaluation', *P&P* 19 (1961), 26–45.

[146] Str P6, pp. 9–16; *WL* 7, p. 67.

complaint and by making a few initial estimates and final arbitrations. The push to Castle Chamber was run *in tandem* with the successful bid to have the imposing Boyle family monument moved from the east end of St Patrick's cathedral.[147] Apart from being an Irish manifestation of altar policy, it injured Cork's prestige considerably and awoke a real animosity towards Wentworth in him.[148] Finally, Wentworth had already undermined Boyle's government as lord justice and outmanoeuvred him completely on the issue of recusancy fines.[149] Further action against Cork was designed to obliterate the prospect of any effective opposition forming around him.

Forcing the vicar Beresford to beg for a public hearing excited him because it was the first tiny blow struck: 'thus have I fixed the first link of that chain, which I assure myself will draw back after it a hundred livings with cure of souls into the bosom of the church, besides some thousands of acres of land for their glebes'.[150] Bramhall too attributed great weight to the prosecution, claiming this would embolden the clergy as nothing else 'when they see the great oak begin to shake'.[151] Public hearing was at the very heart of the Youghal case but behind the bravado lay constant anxiety, as shown by Wentworth's endless insistence on royal approval and his meticulous reiteration of each point at every stage.[152] As the affair wore on, Wentworth's repeated stress on the importance of making a conspicuous example of Boyle became ever more shrill. He rejected all deals or compromises: 'it ever had been my opinion that in all cases of this nature there was an example due to the public, and that such crimes as those once stirred could not without great scandal be folded up underhand'. He also professed himself fearful of the consequences of any scrapping or shelving of the suit: 'if this business is carried from us, it spoils our church work quite'.[153] There was truth in this even from a strictly Church of Ireland point of view, since so much depended on sustaining an atmosphere in which the greatest impropriators down to the humblest farmer of tithes

---

[147] Wentworth told Laud that since it was his custom to bow, he did not want the world to think he was making obeisance to the Boyle clan, letter of 18 March 1634, Str P 6, p. 35.

[148] He later added to his diary entry for 23 July 1633, the day of Wentworth's arrival in Ireland: 'A most cursed man to all Ireland, and to me in particular', *Lismore papers*, 1st series, III, p. 202.

[149] See Clarke, *Old English*, ch. 3 and Ford, *Protestant*, ch. 9: 'The Protestant church and the Protestant state'.

[150] Wentworth to Laud, December 1633, Str P 6, p. 4.

[151] Bramhall to Laud, 19 February 1634, HA 15154, and Laud to Wentworth, 14 May 1634, WL 6, pp. 374–5. For the petitions, see *Lismore papers*, 1st series, IV, p. 29.

[152] Str P 6, p. 216 for the longest example.

[153] Wentworth to Laud, 25 August 1635, Str P 6, p. 222; 12 September 1635, Str P 6, p. 242.

saw it as politic to come to terms. But there was greater truth in the fact that for Wentworth as viceroy this was a game played for the highest stakes. He was adamant that nothing less than the public appearance of Boyle in Castle Chamber would suffice. Nothing would stand in the way of this – he would have the earl's parliamentary privilege waived if necessary. He brushed aside Cork's protestations of innocence. He turned his back on all proposals of a settlement.[154]

Wentworth liked to pretend to himself there was no malice in his actions. This was not simply because he was aware of criticisms that he was 'over full of personal prosecutions', but because this affair was to represent the paradigm of public justice.[155] The image for public consumption was of honour and justice, of endeavouring to make 'this people live freer from oppression'. Yet behind the scenes, and in code, it was all gleeful banter about 'vomits' and 'purges' and of itching to fetch back the endowments of the church.[156]

The essence of the case was very simple. Boyle had allegedly made a compact with his namesake the warden (the bishop of Cork) without the privity of the fellows and twisted it so that the entire college passed on a fee farm to him.[157] Laud and Bramhall could be content with this tack because it reflected their wider concern to expose arrangements made between bishops and landowners. For good measure, and further proof of the personalised nature of this prosecution, Wentworth attacked Boyle's agent Dermot O Dingle who was supposed to have struck a deal with the bishop of Ardfert (or Ardfart as Laud called it, with predictably sorry puns) to saddle a clergyman with highly disadvantageous leases. Boyle had pushed the bishop into dealing with O Dingle by pressing him for a debt of £50.[158]

---

[154] Wentworth to Laud, 18 March 1634, Str P 6, p. 79; as it happened, Boyle himself waived his privilege, Str P 6, p. 103. Wentworth to Laud, 19 November 1634, Str P 6, p. 100; 14 July 1635, Str P 6, p. 208 and 20 July 1635, Str P 6, p. 223.

[155] Laud to Wentworth, 16 November 1635, *WL* 6, p. 441, for Boyle's view see *Lismore papers*, 1st series, IV, pp. 52–3.

[156] Wentworth to Charles I, 26 May 1634, Knowler I, p. 257; Wentworth to Laud, 20 July 1635, Str P 6, p. 218. For vomits, see Wentworth to Laud, 18 May 1635, Str P 6, p. 177; 14 July 1635, Str P 6, p. 204 *inter alia*.

[157] Boyle contracted to fill the fellowship up to its full complement of eight and to make a chest for storing the charter and seals of the college, which were then handed over to him. With the records in his possession, he went to Dublin and had all the endowments of the college passed in fee farm to Sir Laurence Parsons in trust for him. The rent was reserved at £13 6s 8d. All the while, the warden, who owed his appointment to Boyle, had been acting in collusion with him. Wentworth to Laud, 29 January 1634, Str P 6, p. 11; 'A collection of all the private preparations, public proceedings . . . against the Earl of Cork', Str P 6, p. 220; Laud to Wentworth, 23 June 1634, *WL* 7, p. 80.

[158] Wentworth to Laud, 7 March 1634, Str P 6, pp. 30–1; 23 April 1634, Str P 6, p. 53; 5 May 1634, Str P 6, p. 58; Laud to Wentworth, 12 April 1634, *WL* 7, p. 69; 23 June 1634, *WL* 7, p. 76.

Three charges were pressed in Castle Chamber – two relating to Youghal and the other to O Dingle and Ardfert.[159] There is no need to follow the suit as it dragged its way through 1635 and 1636, except to note that the real battle was being fought at Whitehall rather than Dublin Castle. After the failure of his initial efforts to come to terms, Boyle began a systematic campaign to push for trial in England or to have the proceedings suspended. He drew on the powerful support of the lord treasurer, the lord chamberlain and Lord Salisbury.[160] Laud was at pains to warn Wentworth that money and friends could go a long way.[161] At first, Wentworth was successful mainly because he had secured the king, but Boyle sent over emissary after emissary and made offer after offer thereby putting enormous strain on the lord deputy's credit.[162] In a dramatic encounter at Portumna on 16 August 1635, Cork produced a letter drafted by Windebank informing Wentworth that the king was now moved to accept the earl's surrender of the lands he held from Youghal along with a fine.[163] To the lord deputy's immense fury the letter proposed that he approve this course of action. It took months of desperate manoeuvring and much public embarrassment to avoid total humiliation. Wentworth himself was under increasing pressure to wrap the business up before returning to England to report on the state of his government. In the spring of 1636 he was forced to compromise after all.[164]

The last days of the affair were plain farce as both men sought to avoid loss of face. Wentworth tried to cloak his climb down by calling Boyle before him and blustering about 'war or peace'. Boyle, for his part, tried to brazen his way into a good bargain by insisting he wanted a public trial because he was so certain of acquittal. Wentworth attempted to hide his haste by insisting that he had only deigned to speak to Boyle at the earnest prompting of Ussher.[165] There were scenes in doorways and ships riding at the anchor. The outcome was a compromise fine of £15,000 (spread over

---

[159] Wentworth to Laud, 20 July 1635, Str P 6, pp. 220–2; Wentworth to Coke, 16 December 1634, Knowler I, p. 347 and *Lismore papers*, 1st series, IV, p. 206. See *Lismore papers*, 1st series, IV, pp. 61, 88, 93, 102, 106. See also Laud to Wentworth, 8 April 1636, WL 7, p. 247.

[160] *Lismore papers*, 2nd series, III, p. 248.   [161] Laud to Wentworth, 23 June 1634, WL 7, p. 77.

[162] Laud to Wentworth, 16 November 1635, WL 6, p. 440; 12 April 1634, WL 7, p. 67; 23 June 1634 WL 7, p. 77; 12 January 1635, WL 7, p. 103; 31 July and 3 August 1635, WL 7, p. 157; 4 October 1635, WL 7, p. 181: 'it is a wonder to see the king so constant'.

[163] Wentworth to Laud, 26 August 1635, Str P 6, pp. 311–15; Ranger, 'Boyle', pp. 308–10.

[164] Wentworth to Laud, 8 April 1636, WL 7, p. 250. Laud repeatedly reminded that there was no point in keeping personal records of the actions against Boyle since any prosecution ultimately depended on the will of the king. If Charles decided not to go ahead, then Wentworth could not very well start producing documents to show he had had promises from him to the contrary. This shows how brittle Wentworth's government really was in the event of the withdrawal of what had been almost unquestioning royal support.

[165] *Lismore papers*, 2nd series, III, pp. 248–9, 250ff.

three instalments), a fresh grant to Boyle of the lands of Youghal – but not of the livings, which Wentworth had made the *sine qua non* of any deal.[166]

Politically the outcome was a stalemate. Laud's attitude throughout is worth noting. He stood by Wentworth and mediated between him and the king, but his overall tones suggest that he was shrewd enough to realise the real benefits for the church lay in the secondary effects. He allowed the lord deputy his head but repeatedly warned against excessive personalisation. Youghal showed that Wentworth's great and unprecedented favour for the Church of Ireland was circumscribed by the support he enjoyed at court and the exigencies of his own political situation. Church and chief governor were bound up together and Youghal proved their contract to be a marital one – for better or for worse.

Wentworth and Cork were able to meet at Portumna in August 1635 because the lord deputy was there to hold a court of inquisition into title of lands in Co. Galway. Even before parliament had been dissolved, Wentworth was already hastening towards plantation by appointing a committee to look in Connacht.[167] Once again revenue and religion were bound up together. Finding the king's title to the western counties was intended as a prelude to a process that would culminate in conformity and prosperity.[168] Lying behind this vision of a 'perfected' Ulster scheme was an assumption that one way to get it right this time was to have an English rather than British plantation. Bramhall put considerable energy into making sure that the church would do very well out of any new arrangements and so consistently presented Connacht to Laud as a real upgrade to the Ulster scheme.[169]

Prospect of lands beyond the Shannon aroused even Laud's cupidity. Ussher fretted about his existing manors.[170] Wentworth hoped Connacht would be a triumphant moment of his viceroyalty. And, as with plantation under James, the crown saw the chance to slough off the burden of earlier grants by granting out chunks of wide-open space. During 1635–6 preliminary grants were made to both Trinity College Dublin and the dean and chapter of Christchurch. Bramhall's response to plantation was somewhat

---

166 The proceedings of the case were also to be removed from the file. 'The Earl of Cork's remembrances of the £15,000 imposed on him' in *Lismore papers*, 2nd series, III, pp. 250ff; Laud to Wentworth, 8 April 1636, *WL* 7, p. 250.

167 Clarke, *Old English*, p. 93; Nicholas Canny, *Making Ireland British* (Oxford, 2001), pp. 280–3.

168 Wentworth to Laud, 5 September 1636, Str P 6, p. 353; lord deputy and committee of the revenue to Coke, 9 July 1639, Knowler II, pp. 366–8.

169 Bramhall to Laud, 18 February 1635, HA 14048.

170 Laud to Bramhall, 11 May 1635, HA 15159; Ussher to Bramhall, 25 February 1636, HA 15954; Laud to Wentworth, 12 May 1635, *WL* 7, p. 133; Wentworth to Laud, 14 July 1635, Str P 6, pp. 206, 4 October 1635, Str P 6, p. 248.

less febrile. He was happy to use the grand rhetoric of a civilising plantation and to hail Charles as 'founder' of the church in Connacht, but he
also worked to ensure that potential ambiguities and conflicts stemming
from the pre-existing rights of the church in Connacht would be kept to a
minimum. So while Wentworth spoke expansively and vaguely of 'saving
everything for the church', Bramhall organised Tuam and his suffragans
into petitioning first the lord deputy and then the king.[171]

Both petitions start by praising Charles for continuing his father's mighty
work and then rapidly get down to the main business by outlining key issues
which Bramhall, with King of Elphin's assistance, had flagged as vital for
a proper settlement. An incumbent clergy could only be sustained if the
practice of *quarta pars episcopalis* was discontinued. By the same token
a resident episcopate was only feasible if the bishops were compensated
through recovery of rightful lands, renegotiation of existing leases and,
if necessary, new grants. To make it all happen the bishops asked for an
array of inquisitions with power to summon appropriators, tenants and
farmers of ecclesiastical lands.[172] They also called for conciliar examination
of farmers of lands which had been fraudulently passed off as parcels of
dissolved monasteries. Charles acceded to almost every single request by
vesting composition of all of the proposed commissions in Wentworth.[173]
Writing from Sligo on 20 July 1635, Bramhall moaned about the absence
of local bishops when he was trying to work out how lands would devolve
to the sees after the king's title had been found; but once word of the royal
answer had filtered back by winter of the same year both Barlow of Tuam
and King of Elphin began to press their suits expectantly.[174]

After trouncing the Galway jury in May 1636, Wentworth left for
England to give an account of his deputyship. Charles approved the plan
to continue with a new plantation. A new inquisition was in train a year
later when pressure of events in Scotland resulted in Clanricarde procuring
a regrant in February 1639 of all lands held by his father.[175] This spelled the
end of the entire project. On the ecclesiastical side loss of momentum gave
way to burgeoning disquiet. Edward King flatly refused to take Tuam in
spring 1638 and it had to be filled by whisking the disconsolate and compromised Richard Boyle away from Cork, Cloyne and Ross. By June 1639, the
new archbishop presented Wentworth with a doleful catalogue of dodgy
leases and alienations and begged for an emergency sequestration of tithes

---

[171] Managing the Connacht bishops proved difficult: Bramhall to Laud, 20 July 1635, HA 15159; Str P
20/144, 20/166, 20/167.
[172] Str P 20/166.   [173] Str P 20/144.
[174] Bramhall to Laud, 20 July 1635, HA 15159; Elphin and Tuam petitions, Str P 20/125, 20/126, 20/127.
[175] Clarke, *Old English*, p. 106.

in order to subsist.[176] King of Elphin, who died in March 1639, had worked hard on his diocese but it appears that throughout the rest of the province the ordinary work of recovery had been shelved from 1635 onwards as Clonfert's petition to the plantation commissioners in May 1639 shows. Despite his lucrative recovery of Portu Puro, Robert Dawson was still in financial straits and was growing most anxious about the consequences of resigning his *quarta pars*.[177] Bramhall glossed the petition heavily and proposed a set of solutions with a real weariness and an anxiety about accountability utterly absent from earlier correspondence. A bare month later Boyle of Tuam was again lamenting his difficulties and peevishly commenting on the dire consequences of having taken Bramhall's advice not to confer livings in advance of plantation.[178]

In the end, waiting on what had begun so promisingly turned into a liability for the western bishops. Boyle might praise Wentworth for his efforts, 'this church which has been relieved by you much more than by your foregoing predecessors these thirty-five years upon my knowledge', but ultimately the Connacht plantation itself stood on the shifting sands between Wentworth's personal credit and the king's necessities. In 1639 the latter won out. By June 1641, the archbishop of Tuam was petitioning again. This time he sounded the old note of recusancy rather than the new note of reconstruction: 'every church living throughout the diocese of Tuam and province of Connacht has a Romish priest as constantly as a Protestant minister entitled or assigned thereunto wherein they do duly officiate and receive the profit accruing'.[179]

REVENUE AND RECONSTRUCTION, 1638–41

In March 1638, a sombre and worried Laud began to put pressure on Bramhall to make a comprehensive report of all that had been done for the church in the past five years.[180] When he submitted his report in the following January he begged pardon for any inaccuracies since: 'at my Lord's first coming to the sword we dreamed not of such an harvest, much less of writing commentaries as finding the work itself a sufficient burden'.[181] Just

---

176 Richard Boyle to Wentworth, 26 June 1638, Str P 20/132.
177 Dawson to the commissioners for plantation, 3 May 1639, Shirley, pp. 69–70.
178 Richard Boyle to Wentworth, 27 June 1639, Str P 20/137.
179 Remonstrance of the diocese of Tuam, 12 June 1641, PRO SP 63/259/44/3; *Cal. SP Ire.* 1633–47, p. 308.
180 Laud to Bramhall, 28 March 1638, HA 15165.
181 Bramhall to Laud, 12 January 1639, Shirley, p. 64, is the covering letter for the report which Laud received on 22 January 1639, Shirley, pp. 5–24.

Table 4.1 *Armagh province reported improvements 1636 and 1639 (in £)*

	Improvement 1636	Improvement 1639
Armagh	–	+3,565
Derry	+1,800	+2,250
Down & Connor	+1,984	+3,338
Clogher	–	+1,470
Raphoe	+680	+0,753
Ardagh	–	+0,900
Kilmore	–	+0,724[a]
Dromore	–	+0,240[a]
Meath	–	+1,381[a]
	Others: 3,000	
	Lowth: 1,000	
Total	+8,464	+14,261

[a] Improvements not completed.

as in 1636, he was papering over the cracks by making a positive comment about the great extent of the whole endeavour.

Much of the preamble to the report, which dealt with matters like the salutary effects of suits at the council board, was a repeat of what had been said just over two years earlier. Two additional features are worth noting. The first is that Bramhall now listed only what had been gained to the church in perpetuity. The second is that, unlike 1636, rentals of varying detail were attached for a number of dioceses. Once again, though, the grand panorama gives way, on closer examination, to a grittier reality. Bramhall spoke of Armagh as being almost complete and drastic improvements in the other ecclesiastical provinces as imminent. Yet now, in 1639, Dromore still had to be resolved, Meath was 'only beginning', some leases in Armagh had been compounded but not perfected, and, given a dispute with Bedell, Kilmore was still in the balance.

Most effort had been put into dioceses covered by the statute for Ulster bishops and since 1636 the rate of improvement had flagged.[182] Raphoe, for example, increased by only £73. After the initial flush of success it would take much longer to wear away the rump of impropriations and leases as the emphasis shifted from gaining to waiting. Wentworth's partial loss of face over Boyle may also have had a braking effect on negotiations and compositions with other prominent gentry and nobility. Given that the dioceses

[182] Armagh, Derry, Raphoe, Clogher, Kilmore.

of Kilmore, Dromore and Meath were still incomplete after sustained effort over five years, Bramhall's breezy prediction of rapid improvement in the other provinces to the tune of £15,000 to £25,000 must be doubted. There is every reason to believe that Dublin, Cashel and Tuam (with or without plantation) would have taken a decade or more to complete.

The mean figure of Bramhall's estimate for these three provinces comes to £20,000. This means a projected improvement for Cashel, Dublin and Tuam, respectively, of £6,333 as opposed to nearly £15,000 for Armagh. Or, to put it another way, £1,250 for each of the sixteen remaining bishoprics as opposed to an average of £1,670 for each of the Armagh bishoprics. While it is frequently difficult to ascertain secure base figures against which improvements were calculated, in a few instances direct comparisons can be made between 1622 visitation returns and this 1639 report. Ardagh records spectacular improvements.[183] Thomas Moigne of Kilmore and Ardagh reported in 1622 that the rent on eleven cartrons of land in the area known as the Glynnes was £4 10s. He estimated its true value at £60. In Bramhall's report, the same land is down for £140. The overall return for the see lands in 1622 was £78, by 1639 the rental had leaped to £650. While there are some problems in interpreting the Down and Connor rental for 1639, it is plain that particular attention was paid to those lands which were claimed to belong to the diocese in 1622 but for which no rent was being paid, demonstrating once again that much attention was lavished on older endowments in bishoprics. Overall, rents of £350 in 1622 had risen to £960 by 1638.[184] By 1640 the agents of reconstruction, as table 4.2 shows, had accomplished an awful lot. They had fulfilled many of James I's fondest hopes, but the manner in which they had done so had consequences not just for Ireland but for the wider Stuart dominions.

On translation to Canterbury, Laud expressed his frustration at the limits of what could be attempted for church temporalities: 'it is so bound up in the forms of common law, that it is not possible for me, or for any man, to do that good which he would, or is bound to do'.[185] It quickly became apparent to Laud that Ireland, under Wentworth, might be a place where these disheartening limitations could be overcome as he showed in his wistful reaction to Wentworth's early decision to 'trounce' a bishop or two: 'Oh! that great deservers here might meet with such resolution.'[186]

In the case of the twenty-one-year leases, Ireland was not only conformed to England, but England as Laud wished it. This enthusiasm for moulding

[183] The figures for Ardagh in 1622 are taken from TCD MS 550.
[184] Again the 1622 figures are from TCD MS 550.
[185] Laud to Wentworth, 9 September 1633, *WL* 6, p. 310.
[186] Laud to Wentworth, 15 April 1634, *WL* 7, p. 71.

Table 4.2 *Episcopal revenues, 1629 and c.1640 (1655) (in £)*

Bishoprics[a]	1629[b]	1655[e]
Armagh	1800	3,500
Derry	800	2,000
Clogher	800	1,400
Raphoe	650	1,000
Down & Connor	300	1,000[f]
Kilmore	450[c]	700
Ardagh		600
Meath	700	1,000
Dromore	400	600
Dublin	450	1,200
Kildare	60	100
Ferns & Leighlin	170[d]	600
Ossory	–	500
Cashel & Emly	260	1,000
Ardfert	–[g]	150
Waterford & Lismore	100	1,000
Cloyne		600
Cork & Ross	200[h]	700
Limerick	126	700
Killaloe	–	400
Kilfenora	32[i]	60(0)
Tuam	144[j]	1,000
Elphin	300	1,500
Killala & Achonry	–[k]	800
Clonfert & Kilmacduagh	79[l]	600

[a] Unions of bishoprics are listed as in 1655.

[b] *Cal. SP Ire.* 1625–32, pp. 481–3.

[c] This figure is for Kilmore and Ardagh, which were united in 1629.

[d] This is the combined figure for the two bishoprics which were not united in 1629.

[e] BL Add. MS 15,856: 'A catalogue of the bishoprics of Ireland, with their respective values as they were upon improvements at the later end of my lord of Strafford's government'.

[f] This very low figure is probably a slip of the pen because in 1639 Bramhall had valued the rental at £3,338; see Shirley, pp. 14–15.

[g] Listed in 1629 as Ardfert and Kerry.

[h] This is the combined figure for Cork, Cloyne and Ross.

[i] The 1629 list places Kilfenora in the province of Tuam. This is extraordinary, especially as it is in a list sent by Ussher. The see was held with Tuam from 1661 to 1741, but in 1629 it was vacant despite the king's nomination of Dr Richard Betts in 1628. A letter of Ussher to Laud, 30 July 1629, mentions the dean of Cashel taking Kilfenora, with its sad revenue of £32, *Cal. SP Ire.* 1625–32, p. 471.

[j] This includes £13 for Annaghdown.

[k] These are listed separately in 1655 because the union was personal.

[l] This is the total of Clonfert at £54 and Kilmacduagh at £25.

the Church of Ireland in an improved image of the Church of England sometimes led him to overestimate the possibilities. This was apparent in his desire to place strict controls on pluralities, or his astounding inquiry as to whether all church preferments under bishoprics were in the gift of the lord deputy.[187] Bramhall and Wentworth saw themselves not only as availing themselves of greater freedom of action in Ireland but also as giving example to England – a reversal of the customary view of the Church of Ireland.[188] When making proposals for the improvement of tithes in Connacht, Bramhall remarked: 'I think such an exchange were not amiss in England if there were the like opportunity.' He also believed that the statute which limited leases and alienations left the Church of Ireland 'better provided in that respect than the Church of England'.[189] In the reports of improvements, in the Irish canons of 1634, in the use of the Irish High Commission, in the steps taken against nonconformity, in many of the appointments to the episcopate – all of which were personified in Bramhall – Laud saw, encouraged and helped to shape a church which, despite its originally unpromising aspect, fulfilled more of his wishes for the Church of England than the Church of England itself did.

The creation of this brave new Church of Ireland was not without its consequences. The note of uncertainty and anxiety which crept into the correspondence of Laud, Wentworth and Bramhall in the later 1630s was justified. Even when unveiling the great extent of his labour in the report of 1639, Bramhall was sounding a disquieting note: 'we are in a worse case looking no further than this kingdom than ever we were for friends at the Board'.[190]

In a letter to his master the earl of Cork, Thomas Walley summed up what must have been the view of many landowners:

like wolves, the churchmen now look and con about where to snatch and catch a prey, not regarding either right or wrong, but where they set on they must be served and no people so ravenous as they, for they grow insatiable . . . as they are now backed there will be no more questioning of titles or interests but present possession.[191]

The same sense of an arbitrary and intrusive government blindly favouring the church is found in *The humble petition of the Protestant inhabitants of Ulster* of 1641. The pamphlet declared:

---

187 Laud to Wentworth, 23 June 1634, *WL* 7, p. 80.
188 Wentworth to Laud, 18 May 1635, Str P 6, p. 183.
189 Bramhall to Laud, 18 February 1635, HA 14048; 13 September 1638, Shirley, p. 61.
190 Bramhall to Laud, 12 January 1639, Shirley, p. 64.
191 Walley to Cork quoted in Terence Ranger, 'Strafford in Ireland: a revaluation', *P&P* 19 (1961), 42.

the prelates with their faction have been injurious, not only to the spiritual, but also to the temporal estates of most men; for under colour of church lands they have injuriously seized into their hands, much of the best lands of every county, so that there is scarce a gentleman of any worth, whom they have not bereaved of some part of his inheritance, few daring to oppose their unjust demands; and if any did, yet none able to maintain their just titles against their power and oppression.[192]

The simple lesson of 1640–1 was that reconstruction was so bound up with Wentworth's thorough style that his removal, when combined with a volatile political scene across the three kingdoms, spelled not only the end of recoveries but also their reversal.

Was Bramhall's work merely a paper settlement and so incapable of enduring even if Wentworth had not returned to England? There was still a great deal to be done before the process could be completed. Appointment of a less enthusiastic lord deputy or a change in Wentworth's priorities could have halted the process. The statutes were on the books but the Ulster one had expired in 1639 and the most that can be claimed for the others is that, in themselves, they only ensured that bishops had an improved bargaining position. Amelioration on the scale achieved by Bramhall was only possible when prerogative action, or the shadow of it, lent added strength to the statutes. The way was open to a future lord deputy and council, if they chose, to license any number of sixty-year leases. The Act to enable restitution of impropriations had no intrinsic effect other than making conveyance easier. Waiting around for landowners (who exhibited no qualms in 1640–1 about resuming possession of church lands and livings) to make donations would have left Irish bishops in no better position than Laud was in England. Taken on its own, the legislation of 1634–5 offered scant succour.

Did Bramhall's work actually endure? Cloyne was one prominent victim. The overthrow of the fee farm was abortive due to the outbreak of war and Cloyne was reunited with Cork in 1661.[193] The traumatic events of the 1640s and 1650s make it virtually impossible to judge his legacy. The fact that Bramhall attempted without great success to resume his programme in almost every detail after the Restoration shows that he himself believed there was a need to start from scratch. John Vesey's contention in 1676 that many clergy had reason to be grateful to the erstwhile bishop

---

[192] *The humble petition of the Protestant inhabitants . . . of Ulster* (London, 1641), article 30, p. 11.
[193] See Russell and Prendergast's extended note on Bodl. Carte MS 62 and the Cloyne fee farm in *Cal. SP Ire.* 1611–14, pp. 367–8. The issue flared up again in the mid 1660s. Brady, *Clerical and parochial records of Cork, Cloyne and Ross*, vol. III, pp. 1–32, prints a manuscript history of the property written by Bishop Bennet in 1813.

of Derry hardly constitutes hard evidence. Griffith Williams's account of his diocese of Ossory suggests that the restitution of impropriations in the Act of Settlement was not very meaningful without assiduous support from Ormonde. Church temporalities were only one small part of a much greater land question in the early 1660s.[194]

Reconstruction of the Church of Ireland in the 1630s can only really be judged in the context of that decade. The grand aim had been to further the reformation through mending the broken fortunes of the church. The recovery and enhancement of revenue was to be effected by further 'anglicising' the Church of Ireland, which in turn would restore the dignity of the clerical estate and so make the clergy more dependent on the crown. Yet, the desire to improve the income of the clergy as a necessary bulwark of social standing and ecclesiastical influence, which also allowed them to act as more effective and more visible servants of the state, was part of a programme for the Churches of England and Scotland as well. Overt favour was shown to the church by government and in lawsuits to a more limited degree in England. In Ireland, the superficial similarity of the problems of both churches was used to do all these things in a more extreme and more marked manner. This had serious consequences: much of what had happened in Ireland in the past – confiscation, plantation, surrender and regrant – had little relevance for what was going on in England itself. But an Ireland which was largely at peace, where the barbarian was no longer at the gate, could now be perceived as a testing ground or a laboratory for policies which would eventually be applied in England or even Scotland. This worried some when it was happening and was made to worry many more when personal rule came to a close in England.

Despite what the pamphleteers and speechmakers of 1640 and 1641 claimed, the genuine aim of Bramhall, Wentworth and Laud was universal conformity to the Church of Ireland. Their message was drowned out because the bulk of their work in the 1630s was on the established church. Their immediate focus was introspective. The combination of internal reconstruction among the Protestants with the *de facto* toleration of the Catholic church allowed its hierarchy to draw off considerable revenue in their own right and to construct a Tridentine church in those same years.[195]

---

[194] Griffith Williams, *The persecution and oppression of . . . Right reverend bishops of Derry* (1664).

[195] Ó hAnnracháin, *Catholic reformation*, ch. 2, 'Development and reform in the Irish church, 1618–1645'; P. J. Corish, 'The reorganization of the Irish Church, 1603–1641', *Proceedings of the Irish Catholic Committee* (1957), 9–14; Donal Cregan, 'The social and cultural background of a counter-reformation episcopate 1618–60' in Art Cosgrove and Donal MacCartney (eds.), *Studies in Irish history presented to R. Dudley Edwards* (Dublin, 1979), pp. 85–117.

The temporalities campaign bequeathed little to Bramhall's episcopal posterity in Ireland. And, in the short term, it supplied one of the many ingredients for the brew of discontent that simmered during Wentworth's viceroyalty. Yet, despite its incompleteness and its subsequent obliteration, this programme still has an importance for the history of the Protestant reformation in Ireland because it was based on a simple realisation that in order to vindicate the claim to be a national church there must first be a proper structure for that church on the ground. By 1640, much financial work had been done, but there was little point in ordered terriers and newly roofed churches if the clergy who were to officiate in them and the congregations who were to worship in them were themselves left unreconstructed.

CHAPTER 5

Enforcing the new order, 1635–1640

CONFORMITY TO THE NEW CANONS, 1635–40

Nicholas Bernard's *Penitent death of a woeful sinner* (Dublin, 1642) transforms the penitence of the most embarrassing contemporary figure in the Church of Ireland into a critique of its government from 1633 onwards. Atherton finally comes to true contrition when he repudiates not only his carnal sins but also his ecclesiastical sins.[1] What are those sins? Prosecuting 'too bitterly in the High Commission court', attending too much to 'law business', too much 'over-reaching of men' (criticisms of Atherton's part in the temporalities campaign) and his neglect of public preaching.[2] At the root of it was 'his too much zeal, and forwardness, both in introducing and pressing some church innovations, and in dividing himself from the House of Convocation, Anno 1634 in opposition to the Articles of Ireland'.[3] Atherton had been motivated in order to 'please some mens persons'. Bernard understood the imposition of the English articles as the work of a few powerful people. He went still further and equated corruption and sexual immorality with the 1634 settlement, High Commission and the means by which church property had been restored. Wentworth and Bramhall were not only misguided, they were also immoral.

The *Penitent death* was, above all, a work of sensational edification but it also tapped into a current of resentment flowing through the Church of Ireland during the 1630s.[4] There was a real awkwardness for many clergy in relishing the temporal fruits of reconstruction when they were served up

---

[1] *Penitent death of a woeful sinner* (Dublin, 1642), p. 30; Aidan Clarke, 'A woeful sinner: John Atherton' in Vincent P. Carey and Ute Lotz-Heumann (eds.), *Taking sides? Colonial and constitutional mentalités in early modern Ireland* (Dublin, 2003), pp. 138–49.

[2] *Penitent death*, pp. 16, 28, 27.

[3] *Penitent death*, p. 15. Bernard went on to claim, unsurprisingly, that Atherton was deeply consoled by reading Downham's *Covenant of Grace* and Foxe's *Martyrs*; see *Penitent death*, p. 17.

[4] See *BW* V, p. 76 for Bramhall's awareness of Bernard's slant from having read *Clavi trabales* for himself.

alongside a more bitter fare of canonical conformity. The 1634 code was a qualified triumph for Bramhall and Wentworth, though they liked to present it to Laud as a signal victory. The reality of the following years was that awkwardness. In November 1636, Laud wrote to Ussher in the king's name commanding bishops to wear episcopal attire, especially rochets. In a postscript, he also sought that 'all priests and ministers throughout that kingdom read public prayers and administer the Sacraments duly in their surplices', an indication, perhaps, that Irish canon 7 was not being complied with.

According to one of his biographers, Bedell placed the communion table in the body of the church, an infringement of Irish canon 94 (as Ussher's practice was, if he continued it), he preferred to use psalms directly from the Bible rather than the Prayer Book (a possible violation of Irish canon 3) and 'he came often to church in his episcopal habiliments, but oftener without'.[5] Again, in late 1636, Laud found occasion to complain of the 'general neglect of the keeping of all holydays' (contravening Irish canon 6), a sign that the reductionist attitude to holy days found in Daniel's Prayer Book was still alive and well in the Church of Ireland. Wentworth praised the reliability of the clergy he had imported in contrast to the others who 'are more affected with the service of Mr Calvin than with our English liturgy'.[6] One of his imports, James Croxton, drew criticism in Ossory by hearing the confessions of some of his congregation to prepare them for the sacrament. Croxton appealed to Laud, justifying himself on the basis of Irish canon 19.[7] So while auricular confession was allowed by the canons, it was not possible to act upon it without causing controversy. The change of penalty from *ipso facto* excommunication to 'let him be excommunicated' in several canons blunted the edge of the Irish canons in print, but non-compliance blunted them, ambitious as they were, in practice.[8] Some bishops were prepared to turn a blind eye to the activities of their clergy. High Commission could not prosecute every recalcitrant clergyman. In the book of canons, Irish churchmen had preserved a little autonomy, and in the parishes they

---

[5] Shuckburgh, *Two Lives*, pp. 152–3. Ussher's practice is described in William Brereton, *Travels in the United provinces . . . Ireland, 1634–1635*, ed. Edward Hawkins (1844), p. 135: 'in the great church (Drogheda) my Lord primate preaches every Sunday. In the body of the church, over against the pulpit, the communion table is placed lengthwise in the aisle.' Brereton also noted Ussher's attitude to the Book of Sports, p. 139: 'he used this expression: that there was no clause therein commanding the ministers to read the book, but if it were published in the church by the clerk of churchwardens, the king's command is performed; this was his sense and opinion.'

[6] Wentworth to Laud, 23 April 1638, Str P 7, p. 92.

[7] Croxton to Laud, 18 April 1638, SP 63/256/84; *Cal. SP Ire. 1633–47*, p. 84.

[8] ICs 1, 2, 3, 4, 5, 22. For contemporary criticisms of *ipso facto* excommunication, see Gerald Bray (ed.), *The Anglican canons 1529–1947* (Woodbridge, 1998), p. 825.

preserved something of more austere customs and Jacobean flavour. Two printed sets of visitation articles survive from after convocation. These are George Synge's of 1639 and a 1640 set for 'The Lord Primate's Visitation Metropolitical'.⁹ These are considerably larger than the 1626 and 1628 sets. Both were printed in Dublin and are identical in design and layout, the only difference being that the primatial set has extra sections on cathedrals, cathedral clergy and ecclesiastical jurisdiction. They were clearly intended to secure conformity to the new code. Article 7 checked that all churches and chapels had 'the Book of Canons agreed upon in the Convocation begun at Dublin Anno 1634'.¹⁰ Many of the particular features of the Irish canons were included in the articles. Article 34 asked about parishioners bringing hawks with bells to services. Articles 54 and 55 addressed the canons dealing with the specific flaws of the Irish church court system. Article 11 enquired about the 'abolition' of 'all monuments of superstition and idolatry'.¹¹ These articles were a domestic production whose author is unknown. As an experienced chancellor, George Synge may have written his own after which his patron Ussher might have tacked on the cathedral and court sections. There are some clues which suggest that the framer of these articles was not entirely happy with aspects of the 1634 settlement. While article 16 gives pride of place to an 'Ussherian' canon by asking after the division of 'the heads' of Christian religion into the Sundays of the year, some of the victories of the other party are absent. There is nothing on Irish canon 19 on confession. Article 6 does call for the silver cup mentioned in Irish canon 94, but there is total silence on the accompanying 'fair table to be placed at the east end of the church'. What Laud and Bramhall celebrated most, these articles omit. They also skip the provision of Irish canon 94 that 'where all, or most part of the people are Irish, they shall provide also the said books in the Irish tongue'. This absence is more than just a reflection of the difficulties of procuring the relevant Irish texts; it is indicative of a reflexively aspirational attitude to evangelisation through the native language.

It may be that the particularly pressing circumstances of 1639–40 made Bramhall and Wentworth unwilling or, indeed, unable to press for a more complete set of articles.¹² Laud's main concern in the row over James

⁹ *Articles to be inquired of by the churchwardens and questmen of every parish in the ordinary visitation of the Right Reverend Father in God George by divine providence Lord Bishop of Cloyne* (Dublin, 1639); *Articles to be inquired of by the churchwardens and questmen of every parish in the Lord Primate's visitation metropoliticall* (Dublin, 1640).
¹⁰ Article numbers are drawn from the 1640 set.   ¹¹ ICs 94, 91, 69, 72 respectively.
¹² Though Wentworth was furious about northern churchwardens who were refusing visitation articles, Wentworth to Laud, 22 October 1638, Str P 7, p. 133: 'I have adventured to send for the churchwardens

Croxton's implementation of Irish canon 19 was to allow it to fizzle out, 'the times indeed being ill-disposed for the stirring of any questions'.[13] The other possibility is that, as in the use of the blurry formula of 'the articles generally received in the churches of England and Ireland' in article 19, they were prepared to bide their time and not press too hard on individual bishops until the new practices took hold. These articles are the product of a church recently regulated by a full code of canons but also a church not entirely at ease with itself.

THE IRISH COURT OF HIGH COMMISSION, 1636–40

The Irish Commission for Causes Ecclesiastical has been characterised as essentially anti-Presbyterian and a Laudian reversal of the previous policy of using it as a weapon against recusancy.[14] Little has been written about the Irish court and the tiny literature on Irish canon law has not much to offer: 'the extent and exercise of that authority are now matters of mere speculation and curiosity'.[15] The first commission to cover the whole country was granted in 1564 and another in 1594.[16] The 1564 commission, dominated by Archbishop Adam Loftus, was primarily dedicated to advancing the Protestant reformation through the coercion of Catholics. Yet the Elizabethan commissions were not wholly occupied with recusancy. Their powers were extensive: to 'enquire and search out all masterless men, quarrellers, vagrant and suspected persons', to deal with heresy, schism, ecclesiastical crimes, marriage, simony and so on.[17] A significant Irish addition in 1594 commanded the commissioners to put into execution the clauses of the 1537 Act for the English order, habit and language: 'the lack of the due execution whereof has engendered a great forwardness, perverseness and dangerous diversity amongst our people in Ireland and specially in the clergy'.[18] This

that will not submit to the articles prescribed for them by their ordinary and upon their appearance will lay them in prison, till they enter me good bond to submit to the bishop, and present upon the articles as is most meet.' There is no evidence that he pursued this course.

[13] Laud to Wentworth, 29 December 1638, *WL* 6, p. 552.

[14] Nial Osborough, 'Ecclesiastical law and the reformation in Ireland' in R. H. Helmholz (ed.), *Canon law in Protestant lands* (Berlin, 1992), p. 234; Kearney, *Strafford*, pp. 116–17.

[15] Edward Bullingbroke, *Ecclesiastical law, or the statutes, constitutions, canons, rubrics and articles of the Church of Ireland*, 2 vols. (Dublin, 1770), vol. 1, pp. 48–9. *UWW* I, pp. 187–90 describes the 1636 commission *en passant*.

[16] Jon Crawford, *Anglicizing the government of Ireland* (Dublin, 1993), pp. 155–8.

[17] James Morrin (ed.), *Calendar of the patent and close rolls of chancery in Ireland of the reigns of Henry VIII, Edward VI, Mary and Elizabeth* (Dublin, 1861), pp. 489–90.

[18] James Morrin (ed.), *Calendar of the patent and close rolls of chancery in Ireland from the 18th to the 45th of Queen Elizabeth* (Dublin, 1862), pp. 292–3, G. I. R. McMahon, 'The Scottish courts of High Commission, 1610–38', *Records of the Scottish Church History Society* 15 (1966), 193–210, esp. 197.

may be interpreted as an additional power to bring the many Irish-reading ministers into line. Although High Commission was concerned with discipline within the Church of Ireland, there is no doubt that contemporaries understood it to be a special weapon against recusancy. For instance, in a list of 'Grievances' of about 1626, Malcolm Hamilton, archbishop of Cashel, requested a High Commission 'for the better taking order with papists of great note'.[19] Hugh Kearney points out that lord deputy Falkland pressed for a High Commission in 1629 'to be used primarily to enforce the collection of recusancy fines'. He also argues that Ussher opposed a commission in 1632 because this time 'it was clearly with the Puritans not the Catholics in mind'.[20] However, a look at Ussher's letter to Laud of 24 March 1632 shows the primate's opposition was grounded on the politic consideration of not making the recusants 'whom we shall find discontented enough with the sole persecution of the state made by their own forefathers' even more exasperated.[21] There is nothing to indicate that the Irish commission of 1636 was conceived of *at the outset* as a mechanism for an assault on puritans.

Before any separate Irish court was erected, a patent directed to Laud of 17 December 1633 extended the powers of the London commissioners in every clause to 'this realm of England and Ireland and the dominion of Wales'.[22] In April 1633 Laud requested Wentworth to have one Christopher Sands, a Jew working as a schoolmaster in Derry, sent over to face High Commission in England.[23]

Apart from the inconveniences of distance, why establish a new High Commission in Ireland? A position paper dated 24 January 1634 offered ten reasons.[24] The first, very typical of the new style, was 'it will countenance the despised state of the clergy'. After this, the paper got down to specifics – supporting and reinforcing the ecclesiastical courts in the light of both internal corruptions and the threat posed by foreign jurisdiction. It would also have a moral dimension, punishing 'shameful polygamies, incests, adulteries'. For the clergy it would enforce residence, provide for the maintenance of curates, assist in the repair of churches and clergy houses and make orders for hospitals, for tithes, and for 'moneys given to

---

[19] TCD MS 1188 fol. 11v; for the context and an edition see Alan Ford, 'Criticising the godly prince: Malcolm Hamilton's *Passages and consultations*' in Vincent P. Carey and Ute Lotz-Heumann (eds.), *Taking sides? Colonial and confessional mentalités in early modern Ireland* (Dublin, 2003), pp. 116–37.

[20] Kearney, *Strafford*, pp. 116–17.   [21] SP 63/254/17, *Cal. SP Ire.* 1625–32, p. 653.

[22] Thomas Rymer, *Foedera, conventiones, literæ, et cujuscunque generis acta publica, inter reges Angliæ, et alios quosuis imperatores, reges,* . . . 20 vols. (1704–35), vol. XIX, p. 487.

[23] Laud to Wentworth, 30 April 1633, *WL* 6, pp. 308–9.

[24] 'Considerations concerning the present state of the Church of Ireland', Str P20/149. Much of this was repeated in Wentworth to Laud, 31 January 1634, Knowler II, p. 188.

pious uses' and set down rules for schools. Finally, there was the familiar clinching argument: 'it will bring in large funds yearly to his majesty'.
The original purpose of the Irish High Commission was twofold. First,
to overhaul and direct ecclesiastical jurisdiction, clerical behaviour and the
fabric and condition of church properties. Second, to curb the growth of
'foreign jurisdiction' and bring recusants into line with the official church
courts. So even though it was eventually used against nonconformity, its
promoters were wholly focused on repair of the legal and material fabric
of the church.[25] High Commission and the council board, operating in
tandem and under the careful supervision of the lord deputy, were to be
twin engines working for the reconstruction of the Church of Ireland.

The initial wording of the proposal deserves a little attention in passing:
'That a High Commission be settled in Dublin *and at such other places as
shall be thought convenient*'. In the letter to Laud only Dublin was mentioned.[26] If Ireland had followed the English pattern there might have been
four courts, one for each province. That this did not happen illustrates still
further the point that the existence of four archbishops meant very little in
the Church of Ireland and was coming to mean even less during the 1630s.

Knowing the spectres a High Commission would raise, Wentworth suggested it would not be established until after the outcome of parliament was
known.[27] Laud approved this caution, stressing the importance of careful
choice of commissioners.[28] Wentworth heeded this advice. More impor-
tantly, Laud moved to ensure that the jurisdiction of the English court
would not be nullified.[29] Wentworth was happy to accept the English
court as 'higher', but emphasised the need for clear procedure in order to
forestall the longstanding tendency to use appeals into England to wear
down opponents.[30] In fact, by the 1560 Supremacy Act, the lord deputy

---

[25] They were also impatient of any potential objections on the grounds of 'the abuses of the times or of
some eminent persons'. These could be 'prevented by the choice of fit commissioners, officers and
places for execution', Str P20/149.

[26] Wentworth to Laud, 31 January 1634, Knowler I, p. 188.

[27] Wentworth to Laud, 31 January 1634, Knowler I, p. 188.

[28] Laud to Wentworth, 12 April 1634, WL 7, p. 67. He noted that inclusion of 'all the council . . . and
all the judges and all the bishops' in England tended towards 'the making of parties'.

[29] Laud to Wentworth, 12 April 1634, WL 7, p. 67: 'leave power to the commission here to call over such
causes as may appear too strong for that court, or in any great respect be fit to be heard here'. The
arrangement also ensured that those who might want to use Ireland as a safe bolthole could still be
hauled back to England. W. N. Osborough, 'Ecclesiastical law and the Reformation in Ireland' in R.
H. Helmholz (ed.), *Canon law in Protestant lands* (Berlin, 1992), pp. 234–5, discusses the problem of
appeals into England. See also Marsh MS Z3.2.5 (80) for an undated Irish episcopal petition against
the appeals system and HMC *Report on various collections*, vol. III (1904), p. 182, Lord deputy and
council to Coventry, 30 June 1638, for proposed names of delegates in Ireland to handle appeals from
Irish ecclesiastical courts to the court of chancery in England.

[30] Wentworth to Laud, 15 May 1634, Str P 6, p. 56; see also Laud's reply, 23 June 1634, WL 7, p. 75.

had his own power of granting an ecclesiastical commission but, as with the canons, he preferred direct royal mandate.[31]

Once parliament had been dissolved on 18 April 1635, the way was clear. In June, while urging Wentworth to get on with it, Laud stressed again its potential 'to rectify the exorbitancies which are too big for the diocesan and his ordinary jurisdiction'.[32] Raising up and supporting the church courts was one part of the strategy of reconstruction which generated widespread enthusiasm amongst clergy not least because of the message it sent to recusants. Not only was High Commission an ecclesiastical supreme court which gave backbone to the entire system, it was also one amongst the array of prerogative instruments at the disposal of the church. The Act of State for the prevention of simony, for example, stipulated that offenders be proceeded against in Castle Chamber until such time as High Commission was established.[33]

The new court was still not in place in October when Ussher wrote to Bramhall requesting that the patent should be drawn up so his presence might not be mandatory.[34] He even made a rare suggestion: 'I should advise that the Commission should be in every way as large as those which have been erected heretofore. However the execution go forward in such branches as only my lord deputy in his wisdom shall think fit.' This typical sample of Ussher's studied ambiguity in business matters has nestled within it a fond hope that at some future date action on recusants might once more 'go forward' as it had in the past.[35]

The patent was finally issued on 11 February 1636 and the court met for the first time sixteen days later.[36] Why it took ten months to get started is unclear. Only a nineteenth-century précis of the patent survives which gives a list of officers and an enacting clause.[37] It was certainly as capacious as Ussher had hoped:

---

[31] 2 Eliz. c. 1, art. vi. Arthur Browne, *A compendious view of the ecclesiastical law of Ireland*, 2nd edn (Dublin, 1803), pp. 219–20, has a very brief discussion of this point.

[32] Laud to Wentworth, 12 June 1635, *WL* 7, p. 142. For the importance of High Commission in Scotland as a prop to episcopacy there, see McMahon, 'The Scottish courts of High Commission', 194–5. R. H. Helmholz, *Roman canon law in Reformation England* (Cambridge, 1990), p. 48, points out that High Commission 'stiffened the effect of the sanctions available to the ordinary diocesan courts'.

[33] The draft version of the Act of State is in Str P20/124. The king's letter, 8 June 1635, is in SP 63/255/39, *Cal. SP Ire.* 1633–47, p. 104.

[34] Ussher to Bramhall, 27 October 1635, HA 15950. It was another sign of his retirement from public life.

[35] Ussher excused himself from the first meeting on grounds of ill health, Ussher to Bramhall, 25 February 1636, HA 15954: 'it would be much prejudicial to my health to travel or stir my body much as yet'.

[36] Dublin City Library, Gilbert MS 169, p. 216, 27 February 1636.

[37] *Lib. mun. Hib.*, vol. I, pp. 181–2.

We minding to have the two several acts (before mentioned in Queen Elizabeth's commissions) to be put in due execution and such persons shall hereafter offend in anything contrary to the tenor, effect and true meaning of the same . . . do authorise, appoint and assign you . . . to be our commissioners to inquire *&c* as in Queen Elizabeth's commissions.

Here was a re-enactment of the 1564 and 1594 commissions to enforce the 1560 supremacy and uniformity statutes along with a slew of auxiliary powers over everything from 'seditious books' and 'evil education' to fornication and simony.[38] A letter of June 1636 from the lord deputy to the commissioners reveals a little more about the powers of the court. They were directed to investigate the neglect of freeschools and proceed, if necessary, to deprive them of any Catholic stipendaries.[39] But, as always, Wentworth went on to direct the churchmen to look to their own house:

we cannot but take notice of the general non-residence of clergymen, to the dishonour of God, the disservice of their cures, the vain expense of their means in cities and corporate towns and to the great scandal of the church.

He went on to call for both speed and severity and warned he would be monitoring their progress. High Commission might have been created at his own request, and staffed with many of his allies, but it was not to go unsupervised. In April 1635 Laud had signalled a royal desire for summoning corrupt or inefficient chancellors before High Commission, thus making up a third sharp prong, along with canons and Act of State, against these officials. So true to the spirit of its first proposal, High Commission was designated for control and repair of the church and its personnel.[40] Even the very financial sanctions of the court were made to fit the exemplary fashion of reconstruction when, with ponderous symbolism and to Bramhall's glee, the first £500 in fines was earmarked to pay for a peal of bells of the new cathedral of St Columb in Derry.[41] Just as Bramhall reinvested the profits from his fund for buying in impropriations for the purchase of more, the revenue of the supreme ecclesiastical court made up

---

[38] But the mention of only two statutes hints that the powers connected with the Act for English Order of the 1594 commission were not part of the 1636 tribunal. This sits well with the (aspirational) provisions for Irish in the canons – otherwise High Commission and the 1634 settlement might have conflicted with each other

[39] 2 June 1636, Knowler II, p. 7. Freeschools attracted attention as the future seedbeds of the reformation.

[40] Laud to Wentworth, 20 April 1635, *WL* 7, p. 121.

[41] Order for Derry bells, T. W. Moody and J. G. Simms (eds.), *The Bishopric of Derry and the Irish Society, 1602–1705*, 2 vols. (Dublin, 1968), p. 90, 20 July 1638. Possibly emboldened by this largesse Leslie of Down and Connor begged for part of the revenue from fines to be spent on a cathedral church for his diocese: Wentworth to Laud, 8 June 1635, Str P 7, p. 105; 7 July 1638, Knowler II, p. 194; Henry Leslie to Laud, 24 July 1637, SP 63/255/41, *Cal. SP Ire.* 1633–47, p. 164.

an extraordinary purse for church projects. Expectation of a decent revenue was realistic since, as the Irish Commons complained in November 1640, prohibitions against High Commission were not entertained. Ultimately, as in England, association with 'arbitrary' rule was to make the court especially odious.[42]

Not only is the patent lost but there are no surviving Act books, precedents or registers. A slender twenty folios of notes on proceedings between 25 January 1639 and 14 February 1640 in the distinctive (and difficult) slanting hand of Thomas Howel, clerk of the court, are extant.[43] These are quite bare – usually giving the date, names of the commissioners present, names of parties and the briefest of notes on the outcome of the day's business: 'to answer', 'to refer', 'ad informandum' and so on. There are also fragments of orders and articles on eight other cases ranging from 4 February 1637 to 15 May 1639. Beyond that, references to nine other cases in High Commission are scattered through various sources.[44]

The Dublin court sat in St Patrick's cathedral.[45] Like its London counterpart it kept legal terms.[46] It also used the same procedure – the unpopular *ex officio* oath was bitterly complained of in the Ulster Petition of 1641.[47]

---

[42] *Commons' jn. Ire.*, p. 163. On prohibitions and High Commission, see Helmholz, *Roman canon law*, pp. 50–1.

[43] MS Z4.2.1. N. J. D. White, *Catalogue of the manuscripts remaining in Marsh's Library, Dublin* (Dublin, 1913) mistakenly identifies him as the register. He is also described as a 'menial servant of the Archbishop of Dublin' in *Commons' jn. Ire.*, p. 317; Raymond Gillespie, *Thomas Howell and his friends: serving Christ Church Cathedral, Dublin 1570–1700* (Dublin, 1997).

[44] Isabella and Abraham Pont for support of the covenant in Wentworth to Laud, 2 January 1639, Knowler II, p. 270. Archibald Adair for favouring the covenanters in George Radcliffe to Strafford, 3 March 1640, SP 63/258/16 *Cal. SP Ire. 1633–47*, p. 237: this case will be dealt with at the end of this section on High Commission. William Stoute and Richard Pountaine, case promoted by Richard Holt, priest; nature of the case unknown, 17 June 1640, *Commons' jn. Ire.*, p. 148. Robert Rosse, David Kennedy, Robert Wilson all deprived for nonconformity, 4 August 1641, *Commons' jn. Ire.*, p. 282. Lewis Bayly's case against Murtagh King who was a member of Bedell's translation team, December 1638, Shuckburgh, *Two lives*, pp. 344 ff; Bramhall to Laud, 20 April 1639, Shirley, p. 66; articles against King, SP 63/256/126. Robert Cunningham for nonconformity in Thomas McCrie (ed.), *The life of Mr Robert Blair, containing his autobiography from 1593 to 1636* (Edinburgh, 1848), pp. 148–9. Dudley Boswell, prebendary of St Audoen's, against Robert Cusack of Rathgar for erecting buildings which obstructed a lane leading to the church, 27 April 1638, *The Irish Builder*, 1 March 1886 (I wish to thank Professor Nial Osborough for drawing this case to my attention). George Cloyne against Sir William Power 1639 over presentation to Kilbolane, Terence Ranger, 'The career of Richard Boyle, 1st Earl of Cork, in Ireland 1588–1643', unpublished Oxford D. Phil. (1959), pp. 335–6. Marsh MS Z4.2.1 (4b), edited by Brendan Jennings, 'The indictment of Fr. John Preston, Franciscan', *Archivium Hibernicum* 26 (1963), 50–5. In a letter to Wentworth of 25 April 1638, Francis Fuller says she intends to use High Commission against her husband for beating and otherwise maltreating her unless it can be privately settled, Str P18, p. 24.

[45] Marsh MS Z4.2.1 (21), fol. 8r.

[46] R. G. Usher, *The rise and fall of the High Commission* (repr. Oxford, 1968), pp. 258–9.

[47] *The humble petition of the Protestant inhabitants of the counties of Antrim, Down, Tyrone &c* (1641), p. 10: 'They proceed in the said court by way of most cruel and lawless inquisition, not only into

Cases were generally brought *ex officio promoto*. Dublin also followed the practice of setting aside the morning of court days for 'informations', or preliminary work on briefs and articles.[48] Given that three members of the Irish commission – Wentworth, Bramhall and Christopher Wandesforde – had been named in the York commission of 1630, they most likely ensured English procedure would be followed.[49]

There were thirty-five names on the patent, making it the largest Irish commission ever.[50] There were twenty-three clerics and only twelve laymen.[51] The Irish court, as Laud had advised, was a select grouping encompassing neither all bishops, nor all privy councillors, nor all judges. Whereas Wentworth worked in Castle Chamber to establish complete control by excluding almost all of those not of his party, this ecclesiastical tribunal was, especially in its clerical members, more of a mixed bag.[52] This was possible for a number of reasons. Attendance at the court tended to be low, and when low it was clerical and of the clerics Bramhall and Henry Leslie were the most consistent attenders. The lay commissioners were also mixed, but again the balance tipped heavily in favour of Wentworth. There was little likelihood that even in a very divisive matter the commission would fail to reflect the outlook of Dublin Castle.

Perhaps the striking thing about the clerical membership is the absence of Archibald Hamilton, archbishop of Cashel. His exclusion may well have been a deliberate snub. There were reasons to punish him, given Bramhall's difficulties in getting him to 'vomit up' commendams, and there was distrust of a Scottish bishop who was not terribly amenable to central control. The commission was weighed heavily towards the provinces of Armagh and Dublin.[53] There were no bishops from Cashel at all and Tuam was

---

men's actions and words, but reaching even to their very thoughts, in imposing that most unlawful oath *ex officio*, to force to accuse, not only others, but likewise their own selves, contrary to law and the very maxims of nature.'

[48] Just as in England: Usher, *High Commission*, pp. 259, 261–2; Marsh MS Z4.2.1 (6, 8, 10, 11, 12).

[49] W. H. Longstaffe (ed.), *Acts of the High Commission within the diocese of Durham*, Surtees Society 34 (1857), pp. 258–9. Bramhall's involvement got him entangled in a Star Chamber case: Bramhall to Laud, 7 June 1637, Shirley, pp. 48–9.

[50] There were fifteen in 1564 and twenty-one in 1594. This increase in size and proportion of clergy was in line with the English commission of 1633.

[51] 1564: four clerics, eleven laity. 1594: three clerics, eighteen laity. The York commission of 1630 had fifty-nine clergy and thirty-five laity. The 1633 Canterbury commission had forty-six clergy and sixty-two laity (one of whom was Wentworth). The Irish quorum is unknown, except that Ussher was not of it.

[52] Kearney, *Strafford*, pp. 70–2. In order for it to be quorate, the Scottish High Commission had to have a bishop in attendance: Allan Macinnes, *Charles I and the making of the Covenanting movement* (Edinburgh, 1991), p. 143.

[53] Spottiswood of Clogher and Buckworth of Dromore were the only Armagh bishops excluded.

Table 5.1 *The 1636 commissioners*

Clergy
Archbishops
Armagh*   James Ussher pc
Dublin*   Lancelot Bulkeley pc
Tuam   Randolph Barlow

Bishops
Meath*   Anthony Martin pc
Raphoe   John Leslie
Clonfert   Robert Dawson
Kilmore   William Bedell
Ardagh   John Richardson
Derry   John Bramhall c
Down & Connor   Henry Leslie

Deans
Christchurch*   Henry Tilson c
St Patrick's*   Benjamin Culme
Cashel* (also Provost TCD)   William Chappell
Clogher   Robert Barkeley
Waterford   James Margetson c
Dromore   George Synge

Other clergy
Archdeacon Cashel   Edmund Donnellan DD
Chancellor Christchurch   John Atherton DD
Archdeacon Dublin*   John Heynes
Treasurer Christchurch*   Edward Parry
Treasurer Killaloe, prebend St Patrick's   Robert Sibthorpe BD
Prebend, St Patrick's   Ambrose Aungier BD
Chancellor St Patrick's   William Bulkeley

Laity
Lord deputy*   Wentworth
Lord chancellor*   Adam Loftus pc
Lord treasurer*   Richard Boyle pc
Vice-treasurer*   Francis Annesley pc
Privy councillor   Robert, Lord Dillon pc
Chief justice of king's bench*   George Shurley pc
Master of wards*   William Parsons pc
Chief justice of common pleas*   Gerard Lowther pc
Chief baron of exchequer*   Richard Bolton pc
Master of rolls*   Christopher Wandesforde pc
Privy councillor   Sir George Radcliffe pc
Judge of prerogative court*   William Hilton

* = ex officio   pc = privy councillor   c = chaplain of Wentworth

represented only by its archbishop and Dawson of Clonfert. At decanal level, there were three deans from the Dublin province, two from Armagh and one from Cashel.[54] Of the seven lower clergy, six were attached to the two Dublin cathedrals and Edmund Donnellan represented Cashel. In total, Cashel and Tuam had two representatives each compared to ten from Dublin and nine from Armagh.[55]

The court was a resort for the fast track clergy of the 1630s. By August 1639, five of the clergy named in the original patent had become bishops.[56] Atherton, Sibthorpe and Synge continued to sit and since Chappell was in the original commission as provost he would have continued to be entitled. This meant that there were now fourteen bishops out of thirty-five members.[57] Three of the other clergy went up in the world as well – William Bulkeley became archdeacon of Dublin, Aungier chancellor of St Patrick's and Edward Parry dean of Waterford.[58]

A faint impression of the court's seal survives in Marsh MS Z2.4.1, which also gives an equally faint indication of the other officials of the court. The register was Michael Stanhope, a notary public.[59] There were at least three messengers – George Bewley, George Blacker and John Mottershed.[60] Thomas Howel and George Ryves appear as clerks.[61] Two lawyers are in evidence. Bedell spoke of Allan Cooke as 'principal advocate of the High Commission court', most likely a position similar to that of king's advocate in London, responsible for the prosecution of all cases.[62] His successor

[54] Barkeley of Clogher and Synge of Dromore seemed to be compensating for their untrustworthy bishops.

[55] Armagh was also the only province which had a commissioner from every single diocese.

[56] Tilson to Elphin, Chappell to Cork and Ross, Atherton to Waterford and Lismore, Sibthorpe to Kilfenora, Synge to Cloyne.

[57] To put it another way, five of the thirteen non-prelates of 1635 were now bishops. Margetson went on to be archbishop of Dublin from 1661 to 1663, then Armagh from 1663 to 1678. Parry became bishop of Killaloe in 1647. Aungier, Culme and Parry were all signatories of the 1647 Dublin clerical petition for retention of the Prayer Book.

[58] Because some of these promotions moved named clerics into positions which made them *ex officio* members there must have been a slight fall in the clergy total – from twenty-three to twenty-one. There is no evidence of the naming of new commissioners. In any case, the small reduction was offset by the more episcopal complexion of the tribunal.

[59] Marsh MS Z4.2.1 (7).

[60] Marsh MS Z4.2.1 (7, 13). The last name makes it tempting to connect him with Thomas and Edward Mottershed who were named as receivers in the 1633 commission, especially as Edward was advocate-general in the north of England: Rymer, *Foedera*, vol. 19, p. 487; PRO SO 3/11, February 1634; R. A. Marchant, *The Puritans and the church courts in the diocese of York, 1560–1642* (1960), pp. 53–4. Andrew Foster, 'Neile, Richard (1562–1640)', *ODNB*, http://www.oxforddnb.com/view/article/19861, accessed 29 September 2005, mentions that Neile employed a Mottershed as an ecclesiastical lawyer.

[61] Marsh MS Z4.2.1 (9). George Ryves was also a master in chancery, Marsh MS Z3.2.6 (103).

[62] Marsh MS Z4.2.1 (6) is a set of articles drawn up by him: Usher, *High Commission*, pp. 263–4.

was Edward Lake, doctor of civil law and MP for Co. Cavan in 1640.[63] Lake helped draft the clerical subsidies bill in 1640 and may have been developing a practice as a useful canon lawyer in Dublin.[64] The Dublin court was quite a compact operation and had no need of a large number of auxiliary officials.

The nature of the twenty-one cases spread between 4 February 1637 and 14 February 1640 can be determined.[65] They can be broken down into rough categories. Clerical income and property lead the field with eight cases in all. Six of these concern curate's salaries and benefices and two relate to leases on ecclesiastical properties.[66] This is followed by nonconformity, four cases in all.[67] There are two marriage cases, two usury, and two defamation cases. One of these was a remark made in the consistory court of George Webb of Limerick: 'your lordship has neither law, honesty nor conscience'.[68] Beyond that, there are miscellaneous cases such as that of the man who caused malicious damage to Kilcullen church, breaking the windows, setting fire to the communion table and 'did ease himself most beastly in the chancel'.[69] There was also the prosecution of Murtagh King, Bedell's Irish translator, for his continuing recusancy even while beneficed in Kilmore. The articles against him are an amazing cocktail of drunkenness and blatant recusancy, including one sad manifestation of a troubled conscience: 'that when his son demanded moneys of him he made answer "poor slave woe is me that am going to hell to get you maintenance"'.[70] At the other end of the spectrum were the words allegedly spoken by Bishop Adair of Killala in favour of the National Covenant. So, of twenty-one identifiable suits only four involved nonconformity and just one the Covenant, even when the bulk of the

---

[63] Laud to Wentworth, 17 May 1639, *WL* 7, p. 574, where Laud recommends him as 'long . . . an instrument for the bishop of Lincoln, and expert in all their feats, very serviceable for you. And as exquisite a K[nave?] as need be found anywhere.' He had also been co-defendant in Bishop Williams's case in Star Chamber and chancellor of Lincoln. See also Michael Perceval-Maxwell, *The outbreak of the Irish rebellion of 1641* (Dublin, 1994), p. 75.

[64] Ussher to Bramhall, 7 May 1640, HA 15958, mentions Lake and the subsidies. His ascent came to an abrupt halt in November 1640 when he was expelled from the Commons for 'misconduct' on a committee appointed to investigate the privileges claimed by Stanhope, the register: *Commons' jn. Ire.*, p. 164, 9 November 1640. For Bramhall's account of this, see Bramhall to Laud, 4 November 1640, HA 14061.

[65] All except seven of these date from 1638 onwards.

[66] Marsh MS Z4.2.1 (21), fols. 9r, 10v, 3r (6, 7, 9) are curates, Marsh MS Z4.2.1 (21), fols. 4v, 7r properties.

[67] Marsh MS Z4.2.1 (21) fol. 12r – John and Maria Clotworthy, Robert Cunningham, the Ponts (who were accused of holding a conventicle as well as urging the Covenant) and the ministers Rosse, Kennedy and Wilson.

[68] Marsh MS Z4.2.1 (11), Marsh MS Z4.2.1 (21), fol. 12v.   [69] Marsh MS Z4.2.1 (21), fol. 9v.

[70] SP 63/256/16. See Shuckburgh, *Two lives*, pp. 143, 344, and Bramhall to Laud, 26 April 1639, Shirley, p. 66.

evidence dates from 1638 onwards.[71] Temporalities and salaries remained the commissioners' prime concern. Only as events unfolded were other applications of this executive tribunal considered. It was not until January 1639 that Bramhall remarked to Laud:

I hope His Majesty and your Grace will find now the benefit of an High Commission in Ireland that we shall speedily purge the kingdom of all our separatists, the greatest part of them by conformity, the more factious by running over to their own mates and better in their proper *ubi* than dispersed abroad among the purer parts.[72]

Even in this case the emphasis was on the salutary effect of a few prosecutions rather than on systematic use of the court to stamp out the problem.

The set of proceedings from 25 January 1639 to 14 February 1640 show just how much clergy dominated the tribunal.[73] Only two of the twelve lay members attended at all.[74] No archbishops sat, but all but two of the bishops were present over that year.[75] Of the deans, only William Chappell failed to turn up. The most consistent attenders were deans Benjamin Culme of St Patrick's and Edward Parry of Waterford. Bramhall was by far the most frequent of the bishops, with Synge of Cloyne and Bedell trailing behind him.[76] The heart of the court was the two viceregal clients Bramhall and Parry along with a rising Benjamin Culme.[77]

The number of suits ranged from nine to twenty-nine per day, making an average of twelve to thirteen per sitting. Business picked up from late November 1639. This is nowhere near the eighty to a hundred suits a day calculated by R. G. Usher for London, but given relative scales and the recusancy of much of the Irish population, the Dublin court was a busy one.[78] It functioned on a national scale, naturally attracting litigants from Dublin and nearby – Swords, Dunboyne, St Audoen's – but also the wider Leinster area, Kilmacanogue, Kilcullen and far beyond, Limerick, Monaghan and Tuam.[79] Costs are hazy, though 40s is common, fines of

---

[71] The Scottish High Commission was restrained in its actions against nonconformity too: Macinnes, *Charles I*, p. 143.
[72] Bramhall to Laud, 12 January 1639, Shirley, p. 64.   [73] Marsh MS Z4.2.1 (21).
[74] These two were William Hilton and George Radcliffe. Each came only once each out of the sixteen of the twenty-four court days where attendance was recorded.
[75] This does not mean that archbishops never attended, because Bulkeley of Dublin was present on 11 March 1636, Marsh MS Z4.2.1 (7).
[76] Culme (14 times); Parry (12 times); Margetson (6 times); Bramhall (12 times), Synge (5 times), Bedell (4 times).
[77] There were usually anything from three to six commissioners present and there was no day when any fewer than two deans sat.
[78] Usher, *High Commission*, p. 260.   [79] Marsh MS Z4.2.1 (21) fols. 13r, 3v, 13r, 14r, 9r, 10r, 2r, 6v.

from £50 to £300 are recorded. Howel's laconic notes show the imposition of penances in conjunction with fines in two sentences.[80]

The picture emerging from the manuscript survivals is of a compact and busy court exercising a national jurisdiction from Dublin, using English procedure and precedent, and concentrating above all on those who obstructed the recovery of the church and its clergy. It was dominated by deans and managed by Bramhall. It ran alongside the other prerogative tribunals as part of an interlocking system at the centre of which lay a chief governor ostensibly pursuing a coordinated programme for church and state. In many respects the court of High Commission was a perfect miniature of the workings and assumptions of Wentworth's viceroyalty.

The first episcopal *cause célèbre* of 1640 highlighted the court as just such a microcosm. The case centred on remarks allegedly made by Archibald Adair, bishop of Killala, in July 1639 to John Corbet, author of the inflammatory anti-covenanter pamphlet *The epistle congratulatory of Lysimachus Nicanor.*[81] Corbet fled from Scotland for Ireland where he received the favour of Bramhall and Wentworth and a benefice in Killala. About four miles from Killala, he deposed, he met some other clergy who told him that Adair had publicly called him 'an impure corbie thrust out of God's ark and that dares not return hither again'.[82] When they finally met, the bishop and the exile had a spat over the bishop's *quarta pars* at which the former made the fatal remark: 'he had rather subscribed the Covenant than to have left wife and children'. To which Corbet's cool response was that he would shortly return to his home and offered to 'remember his [Adair's] love to the bishops of Scotland'. This caused Adair to fly completely off the handle: 'I do not regard the bishops of Scotland. I wish they had been all in hell when they did raise the troubles in Scotland.'[83]

This incident involving a Scottish bishop, coming as it did when Wentworth was out of the country and with a parliament in prospect, called

---

80 Marsh MS Z4.2.1 (21) fols. 12r, 13r. These were a marriage and a defamation case which tended to carry restitutive penances.

81 John Corbet, *The epistle congratulatory of Lysimachus Nicanor of the Society of Jesu to the covenanters in Scotland* (1640), the conceit of the 'epistle' was that the covenanters were in league with the Jesuits. Robert Baillie's reply is in the postscript of his *Ladensium ΑΥΤΟΚΑΤΑΚΡΙΣΙΣ, the Canterburian's self-conviction* (Edinburgh, 1640) and also D. Laing (ed.), *The letters and journals of Robert Baillie, Principal of the University of Glasgow, 1637–1662*, 3 vols. (Edinburgh, 1841–2), vol. I, pp. 89, 243. For Corbet's other writings and views, see David Mullan, *Scottish Puritanism 1590–1638* (Oxford, 2000), pp. 266, 315–17.

82 Corbet's deposition, 10 August 1639, SP 63/257/28; *Cal. SP Ire.* 1633–47, p. 221.

83 When a bystander deplored the bishop's words, Adair retorted 'Hell in scriptures is taken for the grave.' Corbet further testified that the bishop's intense displeasure with his book was common knowledge around Killala.

for prompt and exemplary action.[84] Once Wentworth signified royal willingness to proceed, Adair answered the charges on 11 October.[85] Then, on 20 February 1640, he faced no less than twenty of the commissioners.[86] As it was less than forty days to parliament he tried to claim privilege in the hope of benefiting from the forthcoming general pardon. In fact the Irish privy council had already decided to retransmit the pardon specifically exempting Adair and to stop his writ of summons. The commissioners more cautiously indicated they would proceed to a conditional hearing and sentencing subject to a final decision from the House of Lords, when they met, on denial of the writ. Despite Bedell's plea that there was no spiritual or doctrinal offence at issue, Adair was sentenced to degradation by his metropolitan, a £2,000 fine and imprisonment.[87] On 31 March the Lords unanimously found him unfit to have any summons to parliament. He was formally deposed *ab officio et beneficio* by Richard Boyle, archbishop of Tuam, in St Patrick's cathedral on 18 June. The overall message was quite clear: even bishops were not immune from the sanctions of High Commission. On 3 March 1640, George Radcliffe wrote to Strafford describing what had been done.[88] Adair also suffered the further indignity of seeing his bishopric granted away to John Maxwell of Ross.[89]

In January 1640 William Bedell told Samuel Ward 'I am a commissioner, an honour whereof I am not proud, as I was never ambitious of it. We are daily fuel to the fire.'[90] In November 1640 Bramhall was in typically ebullient form as the Irish Commons geared up to attack the court: 'the other business concerns the High Commission, which I have ever expected. How could it be otherwise, it being the present scourge of the puritan and the future fear of the papist?'[91] Both Bedell's embarrassed pessimism and Bramhall's defiance were a consequence of the way in which the Adair business along with actions against Lady Clotworthy and the godly Ponts pushed High Commission into the limelight. Adair's sentence, compounded by the Atherton scandal, fused the attack on nonconformity

---

[84] Even if it meant taking the pretty drastic step of depriving Adair: Laud to Bramhall, 18 January 1640, HA 15173.

[85] Bramhall to Laud, 10 October 1639, Shirley, pp. 74–5.

[86] Twenty of the commissioners (all who were in Dublin at the time) were present at the hearing: the lords justices, six bishops, the lord chancellor, four judges, five deans, the vice-treasurer and master of the wards. Radcliffe to Wentworth, 3 March 1640, SP 63/258/16 *Cal. SP Ire.* 1633–47, p. 237.

[87] Bedell to Samuel Ward, 23 April 1640, *Tanner letters*, pp. 141–2. Radcliffe commented: 'the bishop of Kilmore exercised his wit (as boys do in school declamations endeavouring to maintain a paradox) for he commended or excused him in all the particular charges laid against the defendant'.

[88] SP 63/258/16, *Cal. SP. Ire.* 1633–47, p. 237.   [89] See chapter 6, p. 194 below.

[90] Bedell to Ward, 31 January 1640, *Tanner letters*, p. 122.

[91] Bramhall to Laud, 4 November 1640, HA 14061.

and the issue of the Covenant with the notion of arbitrary and even immoral government.[92] So, belatedly, the Irish High Commission joined its English and Scottish counterparts as a prime symbol of the government's unpopularity and a focus for opposition by puritan and papist alike. Even for many loyal to the established church, High Commission could be said to prove that the means of reconstruction were not justified by the ends.[93]

RECUSANCY AND RECONSTRUCTION

Catholic recusants are virtually absent from John Bramhall's correspondence in the 1630s. In the letters moving between Laud and Wentworth they are almost entirely a political and factional proposition. Where there was a tacit and strategic halt to recusancy proceedings, relations between the Catholic church and the Church of Ireland were going to turn on points where that toleration impinged on or interfered with the process of rebuilding and preparation for the great Protestant leap forward.[94]

Always very sensitive to taunts about fragmentation amongst reformed churches, Bramhall made a rare and rueful reference to the Catholic side in his first report from Ireland: 'It is some comfort to see the Romish ecclesiastics cannot laugh at us, who come behind none in the point of disunion and scandal.'[95] Although Catholic bishops were themselves engaged in a similar programme of reconstruction during the 1630s their clergy were far from tranquil. Bitter dissension between seculars and regulars (also a feature of contemporary English recusant life) sprang from the efforts of the Irish hierarchy to institute functioning parochial systems.[96] This was essentially a problem with the Tridentine notion that 'within his diocese all pastoral mission derived from the bishop'.[97] David Rothe, bishop of Ossory, and

---

[92] According to Alexander Clogie, Atherton was especially harsh on Adair in High Commission: Shuckburgh, *Two lives*, p. 149.

[93] Radcliffe, Bolton and Bramhall, three of the four impeached in 1640, were also members of High Commission. For Scotland, see McMahon, 'Scottish courts of High Commission', 209.

[94] As was certainly intended; see Wentworth to Coke, 28 November 1636, Knowler II, p. 39: 'It will ever be far forth of my heart to conceive that a conformity in religion is not above all other things principally to be intended. For, undoubtedly till we be brought all under one form of divine service, the crown is never safe on this side, but yet the time and circumstances may very well be discoursed, and since I do not hold this a fit season to disquiet or sting them in this kind and my reasons are divers . . . the great work of reformation, ought not, in my opinion to be fallen upon, till all the incidents be fully provided for, the army rightly furnished, the forts repaired, money in the coffers.'

[95] Bramhall to Laud, 10 August 1633, *BW* I, p. lxxxii.

[96] Patrick Corish, *The Catholic community in the seventeenth and eighteenth centuries* (Dublin, 1981), pp. 26–9; Brendan Jennings (ed.), *Wadding papers 1614–38* (Dublin, 1953), pp. 69, 104, 256; Ó hAnnracháin, *Catholic reformation*, pp. 41–56.

[97] Corish, *Catholic Community*, p. 27.

first member of the new counter-reformation episcopate being established
in Ireland from 1618, was alleged to hold the view that members of religious orders had forfeited their rights to the old monastic impropriations
and even speculated that members of religious orders were not, in the strict
sense, members of the ecclesiastical hierarchy.[98] Rothe's regular opponents
even dubbed him *un Segundo Richardo Armachano* after Richard FitzRalph
the anti-mendicant fourteenth-century archbishop.[99] As bishops and secular clergy re-emerged, the regulars found themselves being displaced from
the parishes where they had ministered by virtue of extensive delegate powers in more difficult times. Much of the conflict came to centre on alms,
on whether or not the religious were exempt from a new form of division
designed for the needs of the reinvigorated Tridentine diocesan system.[100]
This dispute might have rumbled on quietly enough if the intervention of
Peter Caddell, a Meath priest, and Paul Harris, an English secular working in Ireland, had not escalated the whole conflict to the point where it
threatened to split the Irish Catholic church.[101] Caddell and Harris, in turn,
helped Luke Rochfort and more notoriously Patrick Cahil, a Dublin secular, in their war with Franciscan archbishop Thomas Fleming of Dublin.
Their dispute was over the benefice of St Michael's in the city. Cahil had
secured a bull confirming his entitlement in the teeth of Fleming's attempt
to impose his own man, Patrick Brangan, a native Dubliner.[102] In the end
the Irish hierarchy, which was deeply troubled by this rivalry, triumphed
because in 1636 Urban VIII made each archbishop an apostolic delegate for
an initial period of two years. Before Rome had spoken, though, recusant
laity witnessed an internal feud of marked bitterness.

In 1629, Cahil published a list of eleven propositions he maintained
were held by all the Irish regulars. It was inflammatory stuff: 'Ecclesiasticae
Hierarchiae pars prudentior selectiorque sunt Regulares', 'Superiores Regularium digniores sunt Episcopis' and the very clumsy and obvious 'Privilegia
Regularium non potest Papa revocare'.[103] The propositions were wild

---

[98] Jennings (ed.), *Wadding papers*, p. 554; P. F. Moran, *History of the Catholic archbishops of Dublin*
(Dublin 1864), pp. 369–80; Gerard Rice, 'Thomas Dease of Meath and some questions concerned
with the rights to ecclesiastical property alienated at the Reformation', *Ríocht na Midhe* 6 (1975),
69–89. W. D. O'Connell, 'The Cahil Propositions of 1629', *Irish Ecclesiastical Record*, 5th series, 62
(1943), 118–23.

[99] Thomas Strange to Luke Wadding, Jennings (ed.), *Wadding papers*, p. 320.

[100] Alison Forrestal, *Catholic synods in Ireland 1600–1690* (Dublin, 1998), p. 6.

[101] For Comerford's fear that it would cause a new schism, see Jennings (ed.), *Wadding papers*, p. 468.

[102] Jennings (ed.), *Wadding papers*, pp. 309, 516 *inter alia*.

[103] Declan Gaffney, 'The practice of religious controversy in Dublin 1600–1641' in W. J. Sheils and
D. Wood (eds.), *The churches, Ireland and the Irish*, Studies in Church History 25 (Oxford, 1989),
pp. 150–2; Ó hAnnracháin, *Catholic reformation*, pp. 43–5; Moran, *Archbishops*, pp. 373–5.

distortions of an insistence by some regulars, especially Thomas Strange OFM, on the rights of the orders to operate outside of episcopal control.[104] Cahil journeyed to Paris to have the propositions condemned at the university and then to Rome where he was detained by the inquisition.[105] In the meantime, the Irish regulars – Jesuits, Franciscans, Dominicans, Capuchins and other orders – met to protest their innocence in letters to the Holy See.[106] A pamphlet war began in Dublin which caused Archbishop Fleming to suspend Harris and Caddell in March 1631.[107] The papacy ordered an investigation by two secular and two regular bishops in May 1631. Caddell and Harris continued to pour out tracts. The regular broadsides, such as Thomas Strange's 'Philalethes' series, were in manuscript or published abroad like Francis Matthews's *Examen juridicum*, while Harris's contributions were printed by the Society of Stationers. This row, an internal Catholic matter, became public and acrimonious enough for Bramhall to hear of it within weeks of arriving in Ireland. Thomas Fleming was particularly worried that Harris would invoke the secular arm.[108] Here was an alluring prospect for the castle – that some Catholic clergy would voluntarily open themselves up to legal sanctions.

By the time of Wentworth's arrival the row was still current in Dublin but tapering off elsewhere in the country. A position paper entitled 'The state of the difference between the seculars and regulars', dated 14 September 1633, aimed to stoke it up all over again.[109] It outlines the turn the dispute had taken in Dublin and offers a set of 'considerations to be proposed', which is most revealing of the official conception of toleration. The very exposition of differences was *parti pris*: 'the present controversy is between the titular archbishop and the regulars generally and some of the meaner sort of parish priests who have been preferred by him on the one part and the better sort of the clergy on the other side'. It then moved on to a rehearsal of the standing grievance that, as a friar, Fleming had sought to drain away much of the income of the seculars to his own side. Interdiction of Harris and Cahil was presented as malicious exercise of an illegal and excessive jurisdiction

---

104 Jennings (ed.), *Wadding papers*, pp. 516, 595–6; O'Connell, 'Cahil', p. 121; see also Jennings (ed.), *Wadding papers*, p. 557, where Fleming writes about his sermon.

105 Jennings (ed.), *Wadding papers*, pp. 350, 456, 568. He had, by then, distributed 3,000 copies of a treatise against the regulars throughout France and Germany.

106 Jennings (ed.), *Wadding papers*, pp. 326, 350.

107 Paul Harris, *The excommunication published by the lord archbishop of Dublin* (Dublin, 1632); *Fratres sobrii estote* (Dublin, 1634); *Exile exiled* (Dublin, 1635). Ussher sent some of them over to Laud to read: Laud to Wentworth, 9 September 1633, WL 6, p. 311; Moran, *Archbishops*, p. 373.

108 Archbishop Thomas Fleming to Thomas Fleming OFM, 12 October 1631, Jennings (ed.), *Wadding papers*, p. 604: 'he abuses me calling me to my face, neither good Catholic, nor good subject'.

109 Str P 20/175. This appears to have been written by Bramhall in his fair hand.

which would not have even been tolerated 'under a Roman Catholic prince before the reformation'.[110] The document also tried to imply that Fleming's actions were prompted above all by Harris's resort to 'the civil magistrate' against another Catholic cleric.[111] The disgruntled seculars might pave the way for a far superior attack on Roman jurisdiction than the usual proscriptions. At the very least, rehearsal of the possibility reinforced the message of a rejuvenated, reformed jurisdiction of the statuory church. An accompanying set of seven considerations toyed with three scenarios. The first, 'that this contention be fomented', was attractive for its sheer simplicity. The second was the inverse: suspension of all proceedings in this matter as in everything else in order to secure Catholic support for 'acts beneficial for the church' in teeth of 'puritanical' opposition in the forthcoming parliament. The third option was *ad hominem*: to use the whole affair as a lever against Thomas Fleming.

The next four 'considerations' addressed the issues at hand. In exchange for official restraint, the titular archbishop would 'be commanded to restrain the exorbitant begging of his friars and their numerous increase' as provided for by a papal bull of 1628. So, the odious exercise of 'titular' archiepiscopal jurisdiction in the case of Harris and Cahil might be allowable if directed towards an end desired by the authorities. Nonetheless Fleming should still renounce his 'usurped power' of exiling and refrain from blocking resort of any person to the civil magistrate and declare his former censures to be void.[112] Finally, there was to be a reminder of whose ecclesiastical writ ran in Dublin. Harris was prosecuting the regular, Doyle, for 'scandalous libels' in the consistory court at St Patrick's. The recommendation was 'that it be commended to the cure of the lord archbishop of Dublin to see that the said cause be not ended without a public hearing and censure'.[113] The Catholic archbishop of Dublin, then, was to forbear from interfering with secular and ecclesiastical jurisdiction and his clergy were to be publicly dealt with in the official church courts.

The government's problem was with the open exercise of jurisdiction which cut across the official church courts in the imposition of sentences

[110] He had exiled 'sundry of the best secular clergy as Dr Cahil, Fr Harris without alleging any crime against them, without legal proceedings . . . and has excommunicated or suspended them for disobeying his sentence . . . all which is repugnant both to the canons of this church and the customs of this kingdom', Str P 20/175.

[111] 'he does not only legally determine civil causes wherein ecclesiastical persons are interested after a legal manner but has declared Paul Harris to be excommunicated *a iure* for bringing another priest before the civil magistrate for detaining his books', Str P 20/175.

[112] 'Or otherwise revoke them', Str P 20/175, a small sweetener at the end if the titular archbishop proved unwilling to deny his authority over his own clergy.

[113] This is an nice example of Catholics using the official church courts.

of excommunication. Fleming's ruling was a violation of the rights of the established church and a violation of a statute. Furthermore he had meddled in the exercise of the common law. The lord deputy might harness prerogative powers and muzzle the secular courts for the sake of the state church but this was not to be permitted in a titular archbishop. Toleration did not confer the liberty to pretend to the same status as the Church of Ireland. Wentworth had already made this clear to Fleming when he summoned him in August 1633 on receipt of petitions from the seculars who claimed to be nearly overcome by 'the infinite swarms of friars that are here'.[114] Wentworth impressed on Fleming that he as lord deputy: 'must not endure an authority [that] should make it criminal in any subject of my master to pursue his particular rights . . . to set a wall of separation between the king and his people'. Wentworth drove his point home by threatening to haul the archbishop 'and his associates' into Castle Chamber, though he admitted privately that it would be a hard task to persuade the archbishop to revoke his excommunication.[115] What the 'considerations' show is that the policy of toleration was not one of non-interference. Catholics were to be treated gingerly for political advantage but at the same time their leaders were to be left in no doubt that there were limits, especially where Catholic activities impinged on the workings of the state and on the state church. Penal action might be in abeyance but there was no harm in fanning the flames of Catholic controversy. This was the line which Wentworth chose to take in the end, reporting to Laud that he was mounting the pressure on the archbishop to take off the excommunications while 'underhand hearten Harris and the rest of the priests to stand yet a while to their tackling'.[116]

Appended to the 'State of the difference' there is reference to an attempt by Luke Plunkett, a merchant with interests in Dublin and Meath, to create a charitable trust for the maintenance of students in continental seminaries.[117] Plunkett endowed it with £1,000 and a priest added another £107 to the total. Wentworth proposed to make the trustees surrender the funds and, very pointedly, apply them for the purchase of impropriations.[118]

---

[114] Wentworth to Laud, 28 August 1633, Str P 8, p. 13.
[115] For Laud's strong approval of this course, see his letter to Wentworth of 9 September 1633, *WL* 6, pp. 311–12.
[116] Wentworth to Laud, 22 October 1633, Str P 8, p. 43. Wentworth proceeded to 'dealing with them gently till the revenues of the Crown be settled' in parliament. By the end of October, the excommunication had been called in 'and the two priests preserved, of whom I assure I trust to make very good use of hereafter', Wentworth to Laud, 31 October 1633, Str P 8, p. 43.
[117] Str P 20/174.
[118] Wentworth to Laud, 31 October 1633, Str P 8, p. 45.

Wentworth eventually recovered the money publicly and made the example he wished to as well.[119]

In Limerick, the Church of Ireland bishop, Francis Gough, had been locked in litigation with a member of the aldermanic Stritch or Streatch family for years: 'the matter concerned £80 a year, given by one Lofthouse [Loftus] (whose daughter and heir this Streatch since married) to the Catholic bishop of Limerick, intending sure the Roman; but we hold ours the Catholic bishop'.[120] Streatch initially resisted this ploy and threatened to appeal; he then backed down, at which point Wentworth mischievously offered a settlement based on the original sum of £80. In the end, though, Streatch was ordered to release 'all his interest to the church, and take back a lease of twenty-one years from the bishop, paying £40 rent and £40 fine'.[121] In 1635, a commission issued under the great seal began an overhaul of St Anne's guild, which led to an order in council in July 1638 for the recovery of guild revenues for use by St Audoen's parish.[122] Wentworth and his associates began by cutting through old litigation and old collusions for the recovery of Church of Ireland land. He did the exact same with Catholic sources of funding. The message here was straightforward: any effort by Catholics to husband their own resources for use by their own institutions would not be tolerated. Any money found to be so allocated would be diverted to the benefit of the established church. There was room for the reconstruction of only one church in Ireland.

Short-term cooperation with the Old English did not, of course, alter Wentworth's fundamental analysis: 'I see plainly that so long as the kingdom continues popish, they are not a people for the Crown of England to be

[119] This was all at the same time as he was setting up a commission to investigate abuse of commutation moneys in the Church of Ireland: Laud to Wentworth, 2 December 1633, *WL* 7, p. 53; Laud to Wentworth, 13 January 1634, *WL* 7, p. 58; Wentworth to Laud, 31 January 1634, Knowler I, p. 188; Wentworth to Laud, 12 April 1634, Str P 6, p. 46.

[120] Wentworth to Laud, December 1633, Knowler I, pp. 171–2; Laud to Wentworth, 13 January 1634, *WL* 7, p. 58: 'I read likewise to his Majesty your passage concerning the bishop of Limerick, where you so excellently stretched the donor's meaning into a right sense. The king laughed at it heartily, and said it was as good as might be'; see also Wentworth to Laud, 7 March 1634, Str P 6, p. 28; Laud to Wentworth, 12 April 1634, *WL* 7, p. 68; Wentworth to Laud, 5 May 1634, Str P 6, pp. 57–8; Laud to Wentworth, 23 June 1634, *WL* 7, p. 76, Wentworth to Laud, 23 August 1634, Knowler I, p. 298; Laud to Wentworth, 20 October 1634, *WL* 6, p. 397.

[121] I am grateful to Colm Lennon for attempting to identify this particular individual. See his *The urban patriciates of early modern Ireland: a case-study of Limerick, the 28th O'Donnell Lecture* (Dublin, 1999) and John Begley, *The diocese of Limerick in the 16th and 17th centuries* (Dublin, 1927), pp. 164, 168, 189, 282, 324–6, 337, 472.

[122] Colm Lennon, 'The chantries in the Irish reformation: the case of St Anne's guild, Dublin, 1550–1630' in R. V. Comerford, Mary Cullen, Jacqueline R. Hill and Colm Lennon (eds.), *Religion, conflict and coexistence in Ireland* (Dublin, 1990), pp. 6–25.

confident of.'[123] During the first year of his deputyship steps were taken to do some preparatory monitoring and trimming of Catholic activities. He announced to Laud that as part of his campaign to revive freeschools he would 'be sure to turn out all [masters] such as are popish'.[124] Irish canon 99 obliged schoolmasters to subscribe to the first two canons of 1634 and commanded ordinaries to compel non-subscribers to desist from teaching.[125] An Act of State 'to restrain the sending over children to be bred in foreign parts' – a familiar weapon from the penal armoury – aimed to bring recusant children into a rejuvenated freeschool system. Catholic minors continued to be placed in the care of Protestant guardians through the court of wards. In short, steps were taken prevent the further growth of popery.

In his large letter on ecclesiastical policy of 31 January 1634, the lord deputy drew attention to the problem of clergy whose wives and children were recusants. He considered them latter-day Miler McGraths prone to disastrous alienations who should be deprived. Laud reported that Charles thought this approach too harsh and instead they opted to compile a list of the clergy concerned.[126] Two lists of 'secular and regular clergy' apparently supplied by recusant priests accompanied the 'state of the difference' position paper.[127] The regulars claimed that Dublin contained a dozen seculars and thirty-four of themselves, while the bilious counter-list supplied by the seculars fixed their own numbers at ten and those of their 'ignorami' and 'malitiossimi' rivals at eighty-one. Despite the particular rancour in this case the general strategy of compiling information for programmatic use is familiar from the temporalities campaign. The lists could be dusted off when the time was right.

George Radcliffe reported to Bramhall that Catholics were fearful at the publication of the new book of canons.[128] They had particular reason to be worried. The requirement to subscribe would compel even the most elastic

---

[123] Wentworth to Coke, 16 December 1634, Knowler I, p. 351.

[124] Wentworth to Laud, 12 April 1634, Str P 6, p. 45.

[125] 'Gravamina Regni Hiberniae 1640' in Moran, *Archbishops*, pp. 387–8: 'By public proclamation, Catholic teachers are prohibited to teach Catholic youth, so that a nation, otherwise most eager for knowledge, must be enveloped in the darkness of ignorance, or otherwise its children, in their tender years, must be subjected to Lutheran teachers and thus corrupted with the errors of heretical depravity.'

[126] Knowler I, p. 188; Laud to Wentworth, 12 April 1634, *WL* 7, p. 66. Charles was particularly interested in prominent clergymen. However, if the articles against Murtagh King are anything to go by (and they might have been exaggerated by malice), there may have been still a contingent of mostly ageing clergy who remained somewhat ambiguous in their commitment to the established church.

[127] Str P 20/175. Wentworth to Laud, 15 May 1634, Str P 6, p. 56; Laud to Wentworth, 12 June 1634, *WL* 7, p. 75.

[128] Radcliffe to Bramhall, 22 September 1635, *Rawdon*, pp. 22–3.

consciences to decide. Application of the canons would force Catholics out of many legal positions within the church court system and out of teaching in schools. In a more general way, a Church of Ireland cleaned up by application of the code could well be a more effective partner to the civil government if any fresh persecution should begin.

All of these actions against recusant clergy, against their funding and against the blurred edges of the Church of Ireland took place within the first year of Wentworth's government in Ireland. This suggests that the thrust of official strategy within an overall framework of pragmatic toleration was towards spelling out to Catholics that whatever they did, they were not permitted to hamper the recovery of the Church of Ireland or encroach on its prerogatives. Whenever Catholic actions or pretensions seemed to do so, swift action was taken. Finally, agitation of Catholic differences and the collection of information on the rival church showed that this time of toleration was an intermission, not a reprieve.

PROTESTANT NONCONFORMITY AND THE NATIONAL COVENANT

'In the great united dioceses of Down and Connor I found almost the whole resident clergy absolute irregulars, the very ebullition of Scotland, but conformists very rare, and those in judgement rather than practice.'[129] On his journey to Ulster in winter 1634 Bramhall made two unwavering readings of Protestant nonconformity. The first was that Scots were the root of the problem. The second was that, if properly supported, conformity would emerge and gradually triumph.[130] In his view, nonconformity was an error bred out of bad conditions and bad leadership – remove these and a *natural* and proper tendency to conformity would blossom.

Plantation was no more successful in its spiritual form than it had been in its temporal: 'it would trouble a man to find twelve Common Prayer Books in all their churches, and those not only cast behind the altar because they have none, but in place of it a table ten yards long, where they sit and receive the sacrament together like good fellows'. Defiant disregard for liturgy undermined a clerical estate whose members, he believed, eschewed tithing and ingratiated themselves with cynical landowners.[131] The church

---

[129] Bramhall to Laud, 20 December 1634, Shirley, p. 41.

[130] 'My lord [has] a notable opportunity to reform them whilst their benefices lie bleeding at the stake . . . his pleasure is that none shall have a patent without conformity which I see strictly observed. Sundry of them are come in already, and all the rest will follow shortly', Shirley, p. 41.

[131] 'they never use tithing for fear of scandal; I think rather superstition; which is the reason that a great part of their presentative livings were almost turned appropriations; and this ingratiates them with the laity'.

in the northeast was the acme of an institution dominated by the laity, rotten at its temporal core and a breeding ground for nonconformity as lay grandees strove to keep the clerical estate from reasserting itself.[132] Bramhall's response to the northern dioceses was a reflex of both his nationality and his churchmanship. The policy his response helped shape had both contemporary and posthumous effect. It opened up, during 1637 and 1638, an apparent vista of relentless persecution of the godly in Ulster and gave birth, in the 1660s, to an enduring origin myth for Irish Presbyterians.[133]

Plantation Ulster was peculiar. It formed a part of the Stuart dominions where very large numbers of Scots and English came into close contact. It was also a most complicated kaleidoscope of birth, language and religious affiliation.[134] Gaelic Ulster itself had withered away or, rather, shrivelled up in the wake of the flight of its leaders and a further rebellion in 1609. In its place was a British plantation that was hobbled by its own internal contradictions of exploitation and reform, and common law and holy writ overlaid the region. In 1641 Ulster exploded again and proved to be a catalyst for all three kingdoms.

When interpreting religious affairs in Ulster in particular, a lot of attention has been paid to a small team of godly ministers who have left autobiographies and other accounts of their pastoral endeavours.[135] At the invitation of 'virtuous and religious' landowners such as James Hamilton, Viscount Clandeboye, and the English Clotworthys, father and son, Scottish dissenters such as John Livingstone and Robert Blair crossed the water. They found a church with no settled canons and a set of articles that were not only doctrinally palatable but also in no way binding. The supreme governor of the Church of Ireland and his bishops asked for no subscription. These powerful and independent gentry were making a silk purse out of the sow's ear of impropriations by lavishing their encouragement and their presentations on the incomers so they could exercise an 'official'

---

[132] 'They declaim in their pulpits (which, with the long table, is all the implements they require to set up with) against kneeling at the sacrament as the sin of Jeroboam, and run away from a priest's coat with high sleeves, as the devil from the sign of the cross.'

[133] John McCafferty, 'When reformations collide', in Allan Macinnes and Jane Ohlmeyer (eds.), *The Stuart kingdoms in the seventeenth century: awkward neighbours* (Dublin, 2002), pp. 186–203.

[134] On the religious composition of Ulster, see Michael Perceval-Maxwell, *The Scottish migration to Ulster in the reign of James I* (1973, repr. Belfast, 1990), ch. 10. All page numbers given below are to the 1990 edition; Ford, *Protestant*, ch. 7.

[135] W. K. Tweedie (ed.), 'The life of Mr John Livingstone' in *Select Biographies I* (Edinburgh, 1845). This is, in fact, an autobiography with attached reminiscences of his fellow clergy by Livingstone; McCrie (ed.), *Blair*; Patrick Adair, *A true narrative of the rise and progress of the Presbyterian Church in Ireland 1623 to 1670*, ed. W. D. Killen (Belfast, 1866). Adair died in 1694. Much of his work is composed of chunks lifted from Blair's autobiography.

ministry. Clandeboye even went so far, apparently, as to arrange matters so that Livingstone might receive an agreeable ordination from the Scottish bishop Andrew Knox of Raphoe.[136] This former bishop of the Isles, Livingstone claimed, gave him permission to alter the printed ordinal after his own scruples. The candidate found, as he put it himself, 'that the book had been so marked by some others before me that I needed not mark anything'.[137] For the equally scrupulous and apprehensive Robert Blair, another episcopal compatriot, Robert Echlin of Down and Connor, consented to 'come in among' the generality of ministers, 'in no more relation than a presbyter'.[138] In both of these edifying accounts and in a scattering of other stories about James Ussher of Armagh and his son-in-law Theophilus Buckworth of Dromore the bishops of Ireland are respectful of the scruples of the new men and keen to ensure the maintenance of a broad Protestant preaching ministry above all. Blair was particularly gratified after a private conversation with Ussher, which he interpreted as a guarantee that the primate would never be provoked into an assault on the more painful group of ministers in Down and Connor on the sticky matter of ceremonies.[139]

From the godly accounts it appears that Blair and his associates were not only free of the fear of attack but that they also enjoyed liberty to pursue their own style of liturgical (or perhaps anti-liturgical) worship and even their own church order and discipline. Both Blair and Livingstone speak of having public worship 'free of any inventions of men' and a 'tolerable discipline' of elders and deacons and the machinery for public rebuke and public repentance. Blair's own parish contrived to remain outside regular ecclesiastical jurisdiction until one of his congregation, a rich young man (who else?), came to dislike communal discipline and appealed to the bishop. Their parishes of Bangor and Killinchy were not the only two to be overhauled because by the middle of the 1620s a busy network of evangelical ministers had come into being. Their monthly exercises or godly conferences bloomed into a monthly lecture, at the suggestion of John Ridge, an English minister. In turn these discourses, which drew large crowds from across the nine parishes of the main participants and even beyond,

---

[136] McCrie (ed.), *Blair*, p. 58. Andrew Knox held the Isles and Raphoe together and was thus the first bishop to be preferred to dioceses in two Stuart kingdoms simultaneously. He took a chief part in negotiating the 1609 Statutes of Iona (or Icolmkill) and his career as a 'civilising' cleric deserves serious study: Julian Goodare, 'The Statutes of Iona in context', *Scottish Historical Review* 77 (1998), 31–57.

[137] Tweedie (ed.), 'Livingstone', pp. 140–1.

[138] McCrie (ed.), *Blair*, p. 59; Perceval-Maxwell, *Scottish migration*, pp. 268–70.

[139] McCrie (ed.), *Blair*, pp. 79–80.

burgeoned into the mass communions and preachings of the original 'holy fairs'.[140] This mass demonstration of a reformed piety (later known as the Sixmilewater revival) spelled the beginning of the end for the combination of preachers.

Enthusiasm gave way to eye-catching excesses. Participants fell down in convulsions and spoke in tongues. Dean Henry Leslie is said to have waspishly remarked that it was as if congregations felt 'the necessity of a new birth by bodily pangs and throes'.[141] The frenzied preaching and other antics of James Freeman, who was, allegedly, a fasting and ranting Arminian ascetic, led Bishop Echlin to take action. Moving in tandem with Dean Leslie and, interestingly, Bishop Maxwell of Ross, the diocesan suspended four of the ministers.[142] This set in motion a long series of suspensions and restorations which might have gone on indefinitely without any settled resolution had not the convocation and canons of 1634 brought in a new standard of conformity for Ireland.[143] Now Bramhall of Derry and Henry Leslie moved in to smash the evangelical circle, after a disastrous public disputation on kneeling in August 1636, the leading ministers threw in the towel and set sail for the certain godly frontier of New England.[144] Blair and his associates were driven back by appalling weather and found themselves once again in Scotland.[145] According to Blair and Livingstone, their followers in Ireland went underground.[146] Meanwhile events hurtled along towards the National Covenant and all the momentous consequences of that bond. Lord Deputy Wentworth's response in Ireland was to impose

---

[140] Leigh Eric Schmidt, *Holy fairs: Scottish communions and American revivals in the early modern period* (Princeton, 1989), ch. 1; W. D. Baillie, *The Six Mile Water revival of 1625* (Belfast, 1976, repr. 1993).

[141] McCrie (ed.), *Blair*, pp. 89–90; Tweedie (ed.), 'Livingstone', p. 146.

[142] Some indiscreet preaching by Blair and Livingstone at a communion while on a trip to Scotland initially brought the pair to the attention of John Maxwell then 'one of the ministers of Scotland who was gaping for a bishopric', McCrie (ed.), *Blair*, p. 90; Tweedie (ed.), 'Livingstone', p. 145. This is a nice example of conformist cooperation across the two churches of Scotland and Ireland. See also David Stevenson, 'Conventicles in the Kirk, 1619–1637', *Records of the Scottish Church Historical Society* 18 (1974), pp. 98–114.

[143] McCrie (ed.), *Blair*, pp. 94–9; Tweedie (ed.), 'Livingstone', pp. 46–9; Adair, *True narrative*, pp. 32–9.

[144] McCrie (ed.), *Blair*, p. 101: 'that violent man, bishop Bramhall of Derry, with all importunity extorting from me a dispute about kneeling in receiving the Lord's Supper (wherein he succumbed in the judgement of the conform clergy, denying the papists were idolaters in adoring the host in the Mass), procured from the lord deputy the recalling of his second letter; and so all hopes of longer liberty were cut off '. For recent discussion of the polemics of kneeling, see Lori Anne Ferrell, 'Kneeling and the body politic' in Donna Hamilton and Richard Strier (eds.), *Religion, literature and politics in post-Reformation England, 1540–1688* (Cambridge, 1996), pp. 70–92, and Dougal Shaw, 'St Giles' church and Charles I's coronation visit to Scotland', *Historical Research* 77 (2004), 481–502, esp. 489–91.

[145] See Perceval-Maxwell, *Irish rebellion*, pp. 96–7 and his 'Strafford, the Ulster Scots and the Covenanters', *IHS* 18 (1973) pp. 524–51.

[146] McCrie (ed.), *Blair*, pp. 146–8; Tweedie (ed.), 'Livingstone', p. 152.

the Black Oath abjuring the covenant on all Scottish settlers. This, in time, sparked off attacks on conformist clergy, the partial exodus of the Scottish population and calls for Root and Branch elimination of episcopacy.[147] In short, earlier broad tolerance had been strangled by the 1634 convocation and then utterly asphyxiated by the Black Oath.

This broad interpretation has had important effects on the writing of Irish history in the nineteenth century when the great confessional narratives were published. Presbyterian historians, especially Reid in the 1840s and Killen in the 1860s, painted a riveting and much enduring portrait of the apostles of liberty in Ulster who were humiliated and then exiled.[148] *Ardentes sed virentes*, the preachers of Sixmilewater became the seed of the burning bush that was to be the Presbyterian church in Ireland. They also became the angels of vengeance who ministered to the covenant whose winnowing fan exposed prelatical Antichristianity for what it was. Thus when Monro and his troops arrived they were an army of liberation and the consequent founding of the Carrickfergus presbytery was the first sweet fruit of new liberty.

This general narrative rests mainly on avowedly Presbyterian accounts found in Robert Blair's *Life*, John Livingstone's *Life* and Patrick Adair's *True narrative*. Although they have often been treated as such, these are not directly contemporary works. Blair was reflecting back on his career from the vantage point of 1662–3, the same for Livingstone in 1666, and Adair was only born about 1625 and wrote his history sometime in the 1690s.[149] Thus this most influential narrative of blissful evangelical liberty followed by cruel persecution and then exile was fashioned after the civil wars. The only truly contemporary account emanates from John Ridge the English minister.[150] His account cuts across the neat pilgrim's progress of his erstwhile associates.

---

[147] Perceval-Maxwell, 'Strafford, the Ulster Scots', pp. 524–51; *The humble petition of the Protestant inhabitants of the counties of Antrim, Downe, Tyrone &c.* (London, 1641).

[148] James Seaton Reid, *History of the Presbyterian Church in Ireland*, 3 vols. (Belfast, 1867). Reid's interpretation has been followed by subsequent historians of Irish Presbyterianism; see, amongst others, Thomas Hamilton, *History of Presbyterianism in Ireland* (Edinburgh, 1886); Peter Brooke, *Ulster Presbyterianism: the historical perspective, 1610–1970* (Belfast, 1986); Finlay Holmes, *The Presbyterian Church in Ireland: a popular history* (Dublin, 2000). In his study of Ussher, R. Buick Knox offers a nuanced account of the Blair and Livingstone ordinations but resorts to the familiar explanation of an Ussher distracted and engrossed by his studies, *James Ussher, Archbishop of Armagh* (Cardiff, 1967), ch. II.

[149] Finlay Holmes, 'Adair, Patrick (1624?–1693/4)', *ODNB*, http://www.oxforddnb.com/view/article/83/accessed 14 November 2004.

[150] Ridge's account is in NLI, MS 8014/i. Despite the impression given in Reid, *Presbyterian Church in Ireland*, vol. I, p. 100, that Ridge was only a deacon, it is clear from the 1634 visitation record, TCD, MS 1067, p. 96, that he had been ordained priest in 1612.

The key player in the Presbyterian accounts is the godly Ulster landowner who shelters the godly exile. English bishops had problems with puritan gentlemen during their subscription campaign, so how did things stand in Ulster? Take James Hamilton, Viscount Clandeboye. He was powerful in a diocese where bishops had few presentations in their gift. Hamilton certainly invited Blair (who by his own account was called in a dream rather like St Patrick) and Livingstone, but then he was patron of other livings where the incumbents were never suspect afterwards or who are known to have conformed without much fuss.[151] Hamilton himself was one of those Scots trusted by Wentworth's Dublin Castle; he took the Black Oath promptly in 1638 and assisted, like other leading Scottish planters, in its administration. When Blair arrived in the fresh Ulster air and went to celebrate communion, his patron, to his great dismay, knelt to receive.[152] If Hamilton was not *ad idem* with his new man on this matter why then bring in these fugitives from Scotland? On this point Bramhall, who was cynical about everything to do with Blair and his associates, may well have divined the truth.[153] Here were ministers who were painful in their preaching and in their exercises, but who were not active when it came to campaigning for the recovery of ecclesiastical lands nor in challenging lay appropriations. From the patron's point of view, the ministers worked hard and asked little of them. This was not a bad arrangement.

In the Presbyterian accounts much play is made of the efforts of individual landowners and the connivance or sympathy of individual bishops. This consistent emphasis on *individual* sympathisers is striking because it shows that no one was prepared to claim that the Church of Ireland as a whole was accommodating or that the particular state of the Irish church was helpful. Also if there are questions to be asked about the motivation and the degree of support offered by the planters, what questions can be raised about the bishops? Bishops Knox and Echlin are alleged to have participated in the modified ordinations. Kenneth Fincham has pointed out that in England: 'claims for non-subscription were usually made many years after the event . . . and since they enhanced the integrity of the Puritan we should treat them with caution'.[154] This comment fits in very well with the case of Livingstone and Blair. Instead of looking back with both men

[151] Bramhall's list of ministers in Down and Connor Str P20/179; the 1634 visitation of Down and Connor, TCD, MS 1067, pp. 77–105; Perceval-Maxwell, *Scottish migration*, p. 269; McCrie (ed.), *Blair*, pp. 51–2; Tweedie (ed.), 'Livingstone', p. 13.

[152] McCrie (ed.), *Blair*, p. 61.

[153] Str P 20/179; see also Henry Leslie, *Treatise on the authority of the church . . . a sermon given Belfast, 10 August 1636* (Dublin, 1637), pp. 154, 159.

[154] Kenneth Fincham, *Prelate as pastor: the episcopate of James I* (Oxford, 1990), p. 221.

from the distance of the 1660s, it is worth glancing at the 1634 visitation records and a letter written by Echlin at the time of the first round of suspensions. The 1634 lists record Blair, Livingstone and others of their set as validly ordained by the bishop. The majority of Down and Connor clergy at the time of that visitation had been ordained by Echlin himself.[155] In most cases it appears that he abided by English canons 31 and 32 of 1603 by confining ordinations to the Ember days and not conferring the diaconate and priesthood at once. In Blair's own account Bishop Echlin listened to his scruples and then replied: 'only I must ordain you else neither you nor I can answer *the law*'.[156] If other presbyters laid hands on the candidate this was neither an innovation nor a sop since it is one of the oldest traditions in western Christendom and canon 35 of 1603 enjoined it.[157] Blair was validly ordained and Echlin made no overt concession. Had this taken place even after 1634 not only would the bishop have granted no special privilege but it would have been in accordance with Irish canon 32. In April 1632 the bishop wrote to the lords justices 'about' as he put it 'the charges of nonconformity brought against the clergy of my diocese'. Nowhere in this letter is there any reference to allegations of irregular or compromise ordinations. Echlin insisted that Blair had shown no signs of dissent at the time of the ceremony. Whether the bishop is to be believed is an open question, but the fact that the mode of ordination is not at issue is striking. What was at issue, though, was conformity and Echlin's statement that he had issued 'an oath of conformity' which Blair and his associates refused.[158] But conformity to what? Did the Irish church have an informal or *de facto* minimal requirement after all?

Ussher, as mentioned before, was the churchman that Blair, Livingstone and others were at pains to associate themselves with. The great archbishop is enveloped in a haze of myths one of which is of the deeply tolerant Calvinist saint and scholar. High-church historians have sighed at his leniency and other-worldliness and Presbyterian writers have exalted his graciousness and delicacy before he was usurped by the twin ogres Bramhall and Leslie.[159] In the Blair account of his audience with Ussher the primate

---

[155] TCD, MS 1067, pp. 77–105.   [156] McCrie (ed.), *Blair*, p. 81.

[157] On the imposition of hands in Scotland and on ordinations there in general, see W. R. Foster, *The church before the covenants* (Edinburgh, 1975), pp. 139–55, and Duncan Shaw, 'The inauguration of ministers in Scotland: 1560–1620', *Records of the Scottish Church Historical Society* 16 (1968), 35–62.

[158] Echlin to the lords justices, April 1632, SP 63/253/2116, *Cal. SP Ire.*, 1625–32, pp. 661–2. Echlin also downplayed the raptures by arguing that they mainly affected women, a strategy later employed by John Corbet in connection with the Prayer Book riots in his *Epistle congratulatory*, pp. 74–5.

[159] J. S. Reid, *Seven letters to the Rev. C. R. Elrington occasioned by animadversions in his life of Ussher on certain passages in the history of the Presbyterian church in Ireland* (Glasgow, 1849).

gave assurances that there would be no punitive actions.[160] But how did he make that promise? Did he, in fact, give any real undertaking? What he did, according to Blair's own account, was to warn against 'too explicit dissatisfaction against ceremonies'. It would break his heart, he is supposed to have said, if their 'successful ministry in the north should be interrupted or marred'. He appreciated their scruples but went on to say: 'I confess all these things you except against might . . . be removed but that cannot happen here.'[161] This can easily be interpreted as something quite familiar – an attempt to embark on negotiations about conformity by an admission that the settlement was not ideal. This yoking together of minimal conformity and godly acquiescence is well known for the Church of England. Ussher was not a puritan saint or even an especially Irish product; he was a Jacobean churchman of a well-known variety. If Ussher emerges as more of a churchman and the Church of Ireland as more conformist then why was there not a crackdown on the Down and Connor ministers a lot sooner? Here the archbishop of Armagh might have been making a political judgement. James Hamilton had been his tutor in Trinity College and he was now a major landowner in Ussher's own province. Affection and calculation would have suggested that it might be wiser to leave Hamilton and the local ordinary to sort it out between them. Therefore instead of Ussher tenderly winking at Blair it seems a good deal more plausible to see him marking his cards and espousing a minimal conformity.

In the Presbyterian histories, Sixmilewater is advanced as a proof of divine approbation and noted also as the beginning of the time of tribulation. Here John Ridge's account comes to the fore as the only contemporary description. He talked of large crowds (anything from 100 to over 1,000), the mass communions and the holy fairs, and is in all these things at one with Blair, Livingstone and Adair.[162] There are, however, differences. The Scots emphasise the total unity and the common purpose of all the ministers. Ridge expressed his own anxieties to his anonymous correspondent about the Scottish habit of topping up the bread and wine at large gatherings, causing unconsecrated species to be consumed as communion. He also hinted broadly about tensions between Scottish and English participants.

---

[160] McCrie (ed.), *Blair*, pp. 79–81. The whole encounter is best described as private admonition, a procedure that even the hard-line Leslie recommended in his *Treatise*, pp. 9–10. In April 1634 Wentworth ordered Echlin to attempt a personal conference as well: Wentworth to Echlin, 10 April 1634, Str P 8/102.

[161] McCrie (ed.), *Blair*, p. 80. See also Adair, *True narrative*, pp. 24–5; Tweedie (ed.), 'Livingstone', pp. 145–6; Robert Wodrow, *Analecta or materials for a history of remarkable providences*, 4 vols. (1842–3), vol. 2, p. 364; vol. 3, pp. 132–4.

[162] NLI, MS 8014/i, p. 3.

The Scottish version has it that persecution began because a 'counterfeiting spirit' crept into the revival.[163] Ridge indicates more earthly forces at play by pointing out that the blank refusal of the Scottish preachers to read, on occasion, a token excerpt from the Prayer Book service was the cause of the subsequent attacks upon them. Ridge also noted that on Bishop Echlin's diocesan visitation an especial 'stir was made about observing the Common Prayer Book'.[164] By September 1631 Echlin had already suspended Blair and Livingstone and by May 1632 he had deposed them and two others.[165] Again this strongly suggests that all along the Prayer Book was the test of conformity in Ireland and that the bishops, whether Old English or Scottish or English, were not prepared to tolerate preaching against their church's English constitution or its book.

Blair's next move was to go to London to petition the king 'that for simple unconformity we might, in respect of our Scottish breeding be forborne in such a barren place as the north parts of Ireland'.[166] This was hardly the sort of request designed to appeal to Charles, but after various tribulations Blair secured permission for a new trial.[167] The royal letter was supposedly addressed to Wentworth, who was less than impressed with Blair: 'he reviled the Church of Scotland and menaced me to come to my right wits'.[168] Only in May 1634 did Sir Andrew Stewart, a sympathiser, persuade the lord deputy to grant the ministers six months' reprieve.[169] At this point Bramhall 'that violent man' entered, convincing Wentworth to revoke a further half year's allowance.[170]

Wentworth's correspondence gives a somewhat different picture. In a letter to Echlin of 10 April 1634, he did indeed instruct the bishop on the

---

[163] Tweedie (ed.), 'Livingstone', p. 146, Adair, *True narrative*, pp. 32–3, McCrie (ed.), *Blair*, p. 90.

[164] NLI, MS 8014/i, p. 5. This emphasis on the Prayer Book was continued by Leslie, *Treatise*, p. 178, and Bramhall, Str P 20/149.

[165] Tweedie (ed.), 'Livingstone', p. 145; McCrie (ed.), *Blair*, p. 90; SP 63/253/2116, *Cal. SP Ire.*, *1625–32*, pp. 661–2.

[166] Tweedie, *Livingstone*, p. 146.

[167] With a clause in the letter that 'if the information made to him proved false, the informers should be punished', McCrie, *Blair*, pp. 94–5; Tweedie, *Livingstone*, pp. 146–7; Adair, *True narrative*, pp. 32–9.

[168] McCrie, *Blair*, p. 99: 'Primate Ussher, who, when he heard how that lofty man had answered the King's letter and abused me, his eyes watered for sorrow.'

[169] McCrie, *Blair*, p. 100. Livingstone maintained that there was a sort of tacit toleration for political reasons: 'at that time there being some little difference between Strafford and some of the English nobles in Ireland and Strafford speaking occasionally with my Lord Castlestewart (then Sir Andrew Stewart) a good and wise man, he took occasion to show him he might gain the hearts of all the Scots in Ireland, if he would restore the deposed minister; for which he had also had some warrant from the king. Hereupon he wrote that we should be restored.'

[170] McCrie, *Blair*, p. 101.

action to be taken against the 'inconformable ministers'.[171] The bishop was not to cast them out but arrange for a personal conference 'better to inform them of the vanity and lightness of their fantastic doctrine'. If they conformed, all would be forgotten 'and a particular care will be had of their preferment'. But if they still refused by the feast of All Saints next 'the orders, constitutions and ceremonies of this church', they were to be deprived.[172] Here was the ultimatum: a choice between full conformity to the new canons or deprivation. Not only was there no longer any room for the old minimal conformity, but the new set of canons would raise the level of conformity to far beyond the point Blair, Livingstone and the other ministers would be willing to go to remain within the Church of Ireland.

Conformity was not just an abstraction, a virtue in itself, as a report compiled for Wentworth on 'the State of the diocese of Down before the last visitation in October 1634' shows.[173] It listed twenty-five preaching ringleaders who had allegedly led their peers into 'neglect of all order'. Once again, and this report is likely to have been composed by Bramhall, Scots are the core problem. If Robert Blair and George Dunbar could be silenced then a general conformity would follow. The bulk of the report consists of a survey of advowsons and appropriations, especially those under Clandeboye's patronage. Marginal notes show that the policy iterated in Bramhall's letter of 20 December had been initiated because after five 'conformed' there is the stark comment: 'Five young preaching schoolmasters. Desperate nonconformists'.

This report on Down and Connor also attempted a more profound analysis of nonconformity which explicitly linked dilapidation with dissent. The manner of proceeding in the northeast shared characteristics with the general programme of reconstruction in that it sought to destroy what were deemed to be collusive networks.[174] As with the recusants, revenue streams were to follow into the established church. In turn, sound ministers would rescue the local landowners from their errors and along with them would

---

[171] Wentworth to Echlin, 10 April 1634, Str P 8/102: 'Mr Blair, Mr Welsh, Mr Lewiston [Livingstone], Mr Dunbar, Mr Calvert and others'.

[172] Str P 8/102: 'and cast out as incorrigible without hope to be admitted again unto the exercise of the ministry within this kingdom'.

[173] Str P 20/179.

[174] Str P 20/179 noted that appropriations would be restored to the incumbents upon their conformity. This was, in effect, reconstructing the diocese from the ground up. Thus episcopal control over the clergy was re-established, the church was in charge of its own fortunes once more and the die-hards would be pushed out.

come the poorer and more impressionable bulk of the flock.[175] Puritan practices and nonconformity were rendered down, in this analysis, from principled beliefs to venal excuses.[176]

Blair and his associates may have been at the receiving end of policies which had already targeted establishment figures and recusant merchants alike, but their sins were compounded by their allegedly rapacious and subversive bent. They were, in themselves, a threat to good ecclesiastical order and he railed against 'the natural propensity of that nation against order . . . their sacrilegious desire to hold what they have from the church'.[177] These particular British planters were impious spoliators, anarchic and greedy, and as far as the two prelates and the viceroy were concerned they threatened the well-being of the plantation and of the church and thus the security of the crown.[178] What the very few good Scots really wanted, the bishop of Derry insisted, were English bishops and clergy.[179] Presbyterian tendencies were just the ugly fruit of the cankered tree that was the Scottish nation itself. This sort of anti-Scottishness oozes out of the official correspondence right through the 1630s and from well before the Bishops' Wars. Even Henry Leslie as a good and faithful servant of new regime shared in much of the disparagement of his compatriots, though he did always prefer even when reviling 'the stench of the Scottish Reformation' to talk in terms of a curable disease rather than a rotten root stock.[180]

---

[175] Similar ideas, though cast in a more polemical form, are found in Leslie's *Treatise*, when he links the 'presbyterial dictators', sig. 3v, and those who 'devour all manner of holy things', sig. **1 – the one justifying, absolving and supporting the other in a symbiosis of error and rapine.

[176] Leslie, *Treatise*, sig. 2v, pp. 153–4. Their ultimate plan, in Leslie's opinion, was (sig. **1): 'to prey upon bishoprics and cathedral churches as they had done before upon the abbeys'. Another proof of the bogus credentials and meaningless scrupulosity of nonconformist reservations about kneeling, ecclesiastical jurisdiction and all the rest was to be found in the appeal it all had for women. Leslie fulminated: 'it is natural unto the daughters of Eve to desire knowledge and those men puff them up with an opinion of science, enabling them to prattle of matters of divinity'. He went on to describe opposition to the church's power of excommunication as a 'feminine heresy' and to deplore those who 'seduced' the simple, 'especially of the opposite sex' into a refusal of kneeling, *Treatise*, sig. **2, pp. 86, 113. Wentworth also considered women to be particularly prone to the 'contagion' of nonconformity, as did Bramhall who was somewhat stunned by the 'gadding up and down' of 'anabaptistical prophetesses' in his own diocese: Wentworth to Laud, 26 April 1638, Str P 7, p. 95; Bramhall to Laud, 23 February 1638, Shirley, p. 54.

[177] Bramhall to Laud, 7 August 1639, Shirley, p. 71.

[178] *WL* 7, p. 420; Jane Ohlmeyer, 'Strafford, the "Londonderry business" and the "New British history"' in J. F. Merritt (ed.), *The political world of Thomas Wentworth, earl of Strafford* (Cambridge, 1996), pp. 187–208; see also Leslie, *Treatise*, sig. **1, **2.

[179] Shirley, p. 72.

[180] Leslie, *Treatise*, pp. 154, 159. Writing to Laud about a successor for Echlin, Wentworth was insistent on Dean Leslie who had established his conformist credentials as opposed to a candidate proposed by Viscount Montgomery and the earl of Stirling: 'I little hope to bring them to a conformity . . . by any Scottishman but Leslie. So little friendly or indulgent have I ever observed that nation to

This perception of nonconformity as a compound of bad leadership, greed and a bad national trait was not lost on the nonconformists themselves. On 10 or 11 August 1636, a 'conference' took place in Belfast between Bishop Leslie and the remainder of the godly network: George Brice, John Ridge, Robert Cunningham, Henry Colwart and James Hamilton.[181] This spawned two accounts. The first, in manuscript form, circulated among Scots. The second is Leslie's version, found in his *Treatise on the authority of the church*, and is mostly a denial of the nonconformist account.[182] Leslie was at pains to reject the bullying, hectoring image of Bramhall projected in the manuscript account. Derry came in by accident, he said, and spoke little and only to him. In any case, he had trounced these 'pygmies' in debate during the 1634 visitation.[183] The manuscript version has Bramhall as an episcopal ogre, baying for blood: 'it were more reason and more fit this fellow were whipped than reasoned with'.[184] Whoever wrote the account was implying that Bramhall just could not see that the issue of kneeling at communion was a matter of conscience.[185]

This inability to accept Protestant rigorism as being in any way principled or as having real roots in the hearts of adherents led Bramhall into false confidence during in the summer of 1637:

the ringleaders of our nonconformists were all embarked for New England but their faith was not answerable to their zeal, they returned back and are now in Scotland. This church will quickly purge herself from such peccant humours if there not be a supply from thence.[186]

A familiar vocabulary of disease and 'contagion' when deployed in these instances created the same conceptual trap as it did in the case of temporalities. Wentworth, Bramhall and Laud too easily assumed deep gratitude

---

church government or the church's patrimony', Wentworth to Laud, 20 July 1635, Str P 6, 209–11. He continued, 'Therefore I beseech your lordship to have an eye upon it, or prevent it by any means, if you hope that ever a tippet or surplice shall under a curse come within that diocese.'

[181] Reid, *Presbyterian Church in Ireland*, vol. I, pp. 435–54, prints a defective manuscript account. Leslie dates it 10 August, while the manuscript account in Edinburgh University Library MS Laing III, p. 536, gives 11 August.

[182] Leslie's *Treatise* is written very much in what Peter Lake has described as the Laudian style. See his 'The Laudian style: order, uniformity and the pursuit of the Beauty of Holiness in the 1630s' in Kenneth Fincham (ed.), *The early Stuart Church, 1603–1642* (1993), 161–86, esp. 179–80, and 'The Laudians and the argument from authority' in B. Y. Kunze and D. D. Brautigam (eds.), *Court, country and culture: essays on early modern British history in honour of Perez Zagorin* (Rochester, 1992), pp. 149–75.

[183] Leslie, *Treatise*, pp. 111–12.

[184] Edinburgh University Library, MS Laing III, p. 536; Reid, *Presbyterian Church in Ireland*, p. 445.

[185] Laud disapproved strongly of Leslie's holding the conference in the first place: Laud to Bramhall, 5 April 1637, HA 15162. Leslie's defence of his actions is in the *Treatise*, sig. 3*v, pp. 113–14.

[186] Bramhall to Laud, 7 June 1637, Shirley, pp. 47–8; Adair, *True narrative*, pp. 42–3.

on the part of their 'patients' when, in fact, they had left a bitter residue. Holding the problem 'solved' in Ireland, Laud wished that Scotland could be physicked as well.[187] The two bishops were more right than they knew when they wished that the refugee Ulster Scots had successfully reached New England because these new exiles 'were specially instrumental', as Patrick Adair put it, 'in the beginnings of reformation' in Scotland from 1637 onwards.[188] Up to the spring of 1637, when the deposed ministers fled the country, their movement had gone underground, meeting and praying in private houses.[189] In the wake of enforcement a new narrative of Charles I's reign became possible in which communion seasons, ministerial deprivations and the broad Scottish experience in Ulster could all be read as precursors of more momentous events.

The Scottish National Covenant looked like just such an event.[190] It lifted nonconformity and the religious tensions generated by Ulster's unique environment out of its immediate context and made it part of a cluster of problems which also included the relationship of the king to his Scottish subjects, the balance of military power within the three kingdoms and the disintegration of the plan for greater ecclesiastical congruence. On the Irish scene, one 'local' component of the impending crisis of the multiple monarchy was the question of the future of the Londonderry plantation and its relationship to the reconstruction programme. There were now multiple dimensions to controlling Ulster. So many dimensions, in fact, that no one could have managed all of them effectively. Bramhall's own reaction, even as late in the day as December 1638, was a complacent resort to his much loved image of the therapeutic ague coupled with a sense of vindication that this was a particularly Scottish hiatus.[191] Less than a week before events at Greyfriars kirk he offered Laud his analysis of Hamilton's Londonderry bid in his dual character of bishop and sequestrator.[192] Unsurprisingly, he predicted disaster. In doing so, he made a series of important linkages.

---

[187] Laud to Bramhall, 27 June 1637, HA 15163: 'I heartily wish they were as able and had as good means to purge out these humours, as (God be thanked) you in Ireland have.'

[188] Adair, *True narrative*, p. 57. See Perceval-Maxwell, *Outbreak of the Irish*, pp. 96–7, and 'Strafford, the Ulster Scots and the Covenanters', 524–51; Mullan, *Scottish puritanism*, p. 303.

[189] McCrie, *Blair*, pp. 146–8; Tweedie, *Livingstone*, p. 152; this development became important later on in establishing the reputation of the Ulster ministers. See Robert Armstrong, 'Ireland's puritan revolution? The emergence of Ulster Presbyterianism reconsidered', unpublished paper forthcoming in *English Historical Review*; Stevenson, 'Conventicles in the kirk'. I am grateful to Dr Armstrong for allowing me see his paper in advance of publication.

[190] Perceval-Maxwell, 'Strafford, the Ulster Scots', pp. 524–51.

[191] See Bramhall to David Mitchell, 19 December 1638, HA 14057.

[192] Bramhall to Laud, 23 February 1638, Shirley, pp. 53–5; Ohlmeyer, 'Strafford, the "Londonderry business" and the "New British History"', pp. 209–29.

The expected weakening of the church – bishop and dean losing their manse houses, confiscation of glebes – would 'raise up the sleeping ghosts of monstrous and dangerous opinions'. Already, the contagion of nonconformity had flared up again in Down and Connor and spread even to his own diocese, manifested by 'anabaptistical prophetesses' and defiance of all ecclesiastical jurisdiction. Hamilton's own agent, George Barr, was 'known to have been a maintainer of secret conventicles' who had only just escaped High Commission in the past.[193] It was critical, Bramhall pleaded, 'that a well begun and settled reformation be not thus destroyed. Save me and my chancellor from the insolent madness of these lay elders.' Next, he put on his secular hat and prophesied a mass exodus of English settlers with consequent desolation of plantation and trade. Here was the old familiar association of ideas – Scottishness, dilapidation and consequent nonconformity.

The metaphor of disease was applied to the new disturbances in the wake of the covenant as it had been for nonconformity alone. In his letters to Laud, Wentworth put a lot of emphasis on halting the march of infection and, as he said of the covenant (more than once – he had a depressing habit of working all his conceits to death), 'crush that cockatrice in the egg'.[194] This Scottish virus was a new strain and while the lord deputy sought to rob it of any religious charge by treating it as a matter of loyalty, a matter of state,[195] it was too late. The covenant linked Scottishness and ecclesiology. Wentworth's oath fused Scottishness to treason. A very simple syllogism was all it took to leave the reconstructed Church of Ireland performing a holding operation.[196]

---

[193] This is only one of a number of jibes at Barr. Wentworth called him an 'arrant covenanter', 'half an anabaptist' and an 'arrant anabaptist', Str P 7, pp. 95, 114, 134.

[194] Wentworth to Laud, 26 April 1638, Str P 7, p. 95; 3 July 1638, Str P 7, p. 113; 17 September 1638, Str P 7, fol. 132v.

[195] Though he reassured Laud: 'it is true we decline the ecclesiastical part, which howbeit not mentioned in the oath yet shall never go out of our thoughts, till we bring them therein to an equal conformity to the superiors and government of the church, as here to the king in the temporal. But this is to be done in the familiar way by High Commission and by the ordinary of the diocese, nor shall we sit down or let them alone till we have thoroughly bowed them to the ordinance of Holy Church in all kinds', Wentworth to Laud, 10 April 1639, Str P 7, p. 179.

[196] Samuel Rutherford considered taking the Black Oath as detrimental to salvation: Armstrong, 'Ireland's puritan revolution?' Wentworth's view was that an unambiguous declaration of allegiance was essential for security, hence his proposal to extend the Black Oath to England. 'It will extremely hearten the well affected English [*lege* Scots?] when they shall not only see (I trust) considerable party declare itself for the king in Scotland but the two ancient kingdoms belonging to the crown of England, thus at unity.' Laud accepted Wentworth's reasoning on the omission of any ecclesiastical matters from the oath: Laud to Wentworth, 5 April 1639, WL 7, p. 551; 11 May 1639, WL 7, pp. 562–8.

Bishops like Henry Leslie and Bramhall saw the optimism of the summer of 1637 evaporate.[197] Advances in outward conformity vanished with increasing rapidity during 1638.[198] In his *Confutation of the Covenant*, Leslie lambasted those who loitered outside during service and then rushed into church as 'into a play-house' to hear the sermon, but Bramhall found church doors barred up.[199] In Down, many of the churchwardens refused the bishop's jurisdiction and his officers were beaten up in open court. Leslie begged Wentworth unavailingly to make some examples to 'strike a terror in the rest of that faction'.[200] Emergence of covenanting sympathies in Raphoe (the westernmost diocese of the Armagh province) was a new and worrying phenomenon as previous difficulties had all been encountered on the east coast from which Scotland was a short journey. There Abraham Pont 'made a most pestilent and virulent sermon against bishops their jurisdiction' which climaxed with his wife Isabella urging the congregation to enter the covenant.[201] Pont later fled and his wife was arrested and hauled into High Commission with others such as Lady Clotworthy.[202] Wentworth declared, perhaps for political reasons, his readiness to take firm measures to uphold ecclesiastical jurisdiction and bring all 'the Scottish to a conformity in our church government'.[203] Bramhall, for his part, was right to point to a lack of leadership amongst the covenanters: 'they have neither lords to encourage them, nor ministers to incite them'.[204] But the rash of actions against ecclesiastical jurisdiction over such a wide geographical area indicates the dangers that were inherent in making being a Scot itself suspect.

Laud, too, took comfort in construing national character when he declared 'the natural propension of that nation' against episcopacy to derive 'from their sacrilegious humour'.[205] The recent troubles in Scotland

---

[197] They had secured some outward conformity – Wentworth presented Laud with a list compiled by Leslie of 1,000 people who had communicated kneeling: Wentworth to Laud, 12 January 1639, Knowler II, p. 27.

[198] Wentworth to Laud, 26 April 1638, Str P 7, p. 96: he reported he had spoken to Leslie who complained that over 1,000 who had knelt had not done so this year and that 'women of all qualities are stark mad'.

[199] Henry Leslie, *A full confutation of the covenant lately sworn and subscribed by many in Scotland* (1639), p. 4; Bramhall to Laud, 23 February 1638, Shirley, p. 54.

[200] Henry Leslie to Wentworth, 18 October 1638, Str P20/138.

[201] Wentworth to Laud, 30 October 1638, Str P 7, p. 133. See also 17 September 1638, Str P 7, p. 132; 22 September 1638, Knowler I, p. 219, and Laud to Wentworth, 8 October 1638, WL 7, p. 489; 13 November 1638, WL 7, p. 501.

[202] Wentworth to Laud, 12 January 1639, Knowler II, p. 270. Lady Clotworthy was Margaret, daughter of Roger Jones, first Viscount Ranelagh, and one of Wentworth's leading New English opponents.

[203] Wentworth to Laud, 12 January 1639, Knowler II, p. 273.

[204] Bramhall to Laud, 13 November 1638, Shirley, p. 61.

[205] Laud to Bramhall, 2 September 1639, HA 15172.

were a consequence of the efforts of bishops to recover their rights.[206] Recovery of rights was at the heart of the reconstruction of the Church of Ireland. Reconstruction was at once a road to securing conformity as well as a springboard for further reformation. Dissent, whether Protestant or Catholic, disturbed the process of reconstruction and was to be dealt with accordingly.[207] Conformity meant adherence to a Church of Ireland under episcopal government. Bishops, buttressed by royal prerogative and statute law, were considered by Wentworth and his allies, as they had been by James VI & I, one of the very best means of reforming Ireland. Reconstruction had aimed to rejuvenate the entire clerical estate. By 1639 the experiment was coming to an end as the new conformity began to be spoken of as a manifestation of arbitrary rule.

---

[206] K. Fincham and P. Lake, 'The ecclesiastical policies of James I and Charles I' in Kenneth Fincham (ed.), *The early Stuart Church* (1993), p. 41: 'the eventual resistance from the covenanters was described by Charles as a conspiracy of factions and grasping lay interests, alienated by the king's concern for his clergy'.

[207] Leslie, *Treatise*, p. 104; Wentworth to Laud, 8 June 1638: 'doubt you not but the Jesuits will gather and conserve it dexterously and carefully'; Corbet, *Epistle congratulatory*, p. 23.

CHAPTER 6

The downfall of reconstruction, 1640–1641

LEGISLATION AND COMPLAINT: MARCH–JUNE 1640

The Irish parliament of 1640–1 has attracted considerable attention both for the abrupt and dramatic downfall of Strafford's administration and as a prelude to the violence of 1641. More recently, it has regained its place in a wider three kingdoms narrative.[1] In this large literature it is easy to lose sight of the Church of Ireland and of Bramhall himself because they are so enmeshed with other events. Bramhall's own impeachment was, in many ways, ancillary to the demise of the lord lieutenant. There was no Irish trumpet blast equivalent to Root and Branch. The Irish High Commission fell victim not to rioters but rather to the Irish House of Commons. In Strafford's trial the Church of Ireland made only a few appearances and in Laud's trial it figured only to further corroborate charges of ritualism and lust for clerical wealth.[2] If episcopacy were abolished in England, it would be abolished in Ireland as well. Irish bishops were merely a secondary branch to be lopped off.[3]

The gradual breakdown of authority in Ireland during 1640 and 1641 raised some large constitutional questions and ushered in two decades of

---

[1] Kearney, *Strafford*, chs. 13–15, Aidan Clarke, *The Old English in Ireland* (1966); 'The policies of the Old English in parliament, 1640–41', *Historical Studies* 5 (1965), 85–102; 'The breakdown of authority, 1640–41' in *NHI* III, pp. 270–87; Michael Perceval-Maxwell, *The outbreak of the Irish rebellion of 1641* (Dublin, 1994); Conrad Russell, 'The British background to the Irish Rebellion of 1641', *Historical Research* 61 (1988), 166–82; *The causes of the English civil war* (Oxford, 1990); *The fall of the British monarchies, 1637–42* (Oxford, 1991); Nicholas P. Canny, 'Irish, Scottish and Welsh responses to centralisation, c.1530–c.1640: a comparative perspective' in Alexander Grant and Keith Stringer (eds.), *Uniting the kingdom? The making of British history* (1995), pp. 147–69; Jane Ohlmeyer, 'The Irish peers, political power and parliament, 1640–41' in Ciaran Brady and Jane Ohlmeyer (eds.), *British interventions in early modern Ireland* (Cambridge, 2005), pp. 161–85; D. Alan Orr, *Treason and the state: law, politics, and ideology in the English civil war* (Cambridge, 2002), pp. 70–93.

[2] *WL* 4, pp. 176–7, 288–9.

[3] Robert Armstrong notes that the Ulster petitioners were quick to spot this connection, 'Ireland's puritan revolution? The emergence of Ulster Presbyterianism reconsidered', unpublished paper forthcoming in *English Historical Review*.

violence. Yet even before 23 October 1641 the reconstruction work of the 1630s had already been comprehensively dismantled. Book of canons apart, almost every aspect of Bramhall's work was obliterated or undermined to the point of collapse over five sessions from 16 March 1640 to 17 November 1641. During those eighteen months he himself was imprisoned, impeached and tried, Wentworth was tried and executed and Laud was interned.

For the Church of Ireland as for the lord lieutenant, parliament got off to an excellent start. On 30 March the clergy assembled in convocation led the way by voting six subsidies; they were then prorogued until 10 June for their second session, when the upper house agreed on Bramhall's motion to petition the lord deputy for a public fast in support of the king and for a new taxation of benefices.[4] Gratifyingly, arrangements were made for the solemn reconciliation of John Matthews to the Church of Ireland in Christchurch by Bramhall and George Synge.[5] Overall this was a busy time for Bramhall, the late summer of his influence, when he was prominent and active in convocation and in the House of Lords.[6] He pushed hard for the much resented preamble to the subsidy bill which eulogised Strafford's administration.[7] He was vicious in his condemnation of Adair of Killala: 'Fit to be thrown into the sea in a sack, not to see the sun, nor enjoy the air'.[8] Bramhall was determined to ensure that issue of a writ would not overturn the sentence of the High Commission against this episcopal 'favourer of the Covenant of Scotland'.[9]

---

[4] TCD, MS 1038, fols. 96v–98v.

[5] TCD, MS 1038, fol. 98r. Matthews had deserted 'the communion of the holy church of England' to become a Jesuit. His return was attributed to the teaching of Ussher and Bramhall who had assisted him in his doubts about the doctrine of transubstantiation and 'many other papal errors'. See also Ussher to Bramhall, 7 May 1640, HA 15958; 29 July 1640, HA 15959.

[6] HA 15958. The same kind of impression comes across in a letter from Ussher to Bramhall of 7 May, showing the latter at the zenith of his power and influence. Ussher discussed the Act for clerical subsidies, the first fruits of Armagh and reconciliation of Matthews in the cordial tones of a good working relationship. That relations were good was probably a result of Bramhall's endeavours to raise the revenue of Ussher's see, something which kept communications open even in the tense days of the 1634 convocation. Ussher also mentioned Derry's ability to secure ecclesiastical preferment for Matthews and his knowledge of the temporalities of Armagh ('better than myself'). In a letter of July, Ussher spoke of 'the power you have with my Lord Lieutenant', 29 July 1640, HA 15959.

[7] It also thanked the king for 'tender care' in 'the deputing and supporting so good a governor', *Lords' jn. Ire.*, pp. 110–11.

[8] *Lords' jn. Ire.*, p. 112.

[9] *Lords' jn. Ire.*, p. 112. The Lords agreed that it was 'not fit that any writ of summons issue to the bishop of Killala because of his crime'. So the authority of High Commission went unchallenged for the time being. Even in the more secular sphere Bramhall was successful, being deputed by the house to present a petition to the lord deputy for the removal of an Act of State concerning tracts (cattle rustling, not pamphlets) drawn up by himself and Viscount Gormanstown: *Lords' jn. Ire.*, pp. 120–1; W. N. Osborough, 'The Irish custom of tracts', *Irish Jurist* n.s. 32 (1997), 439–58.

Five bills, originating in the House of Commons and beneficial to the church, received royal assent on 17 June. Four of these were private bills, intended to formalise agreements made between clergy (mostly bishops) and laymen about church lands.[10] They represented the maturing and settlement of the compositions made by Bramhall or by other churchmen with his encouragement since the last parliament. When inscribed in public acts the rights and duties of the parties were clear and open. If events had not taken a different turn a plethora of these may well have been passed.[11] Many of the fruits of the 'leading examples' of the earlier years were now taking on a settled legal form, but the maturing programme of reconstruction was not confined to private treaties alone, for a fifth bill – an Act for Endowing Churches with Glebe Lands – encouraged residence of clergy.[12] This attributed much non-residence to the widespread loss of records of ancient glebes. In such cases recovery could not, naturally, be made on the basis of historical rights, so provision was made for 'any devout person without licence of mortmain' to endow glebeless churches with land.

Bramhall's attempts to drown out other voices and the castle's efforts to convey the impression that the legislative programme was advancing smoothly could not prevent pressure of events across all kingdoms manifesting itself in Ireland. On 17 June, the last day of the second session, the Church of Ireland was an attractive first target for a Commons who drew up a petition of remonstrance addressed to lord deputy Wandesforde listing forty-four grievances about the 'many grievous exactions, pressures and vexatious proceedings of some of the clergy of this kingdom and their officers and ministers against the laity . . . to the great impoverishing and general detriment of the whole kingdom'. The move served several purposes. It was a clear declaration of opposition. It introduced the useful theme of persistent and corrosive abuse of privilege. It was a signal to the discontented and dissolved English MPs. It was also as much a riposte to the perceived hubris of the clerical estate as it was a set of genuine

---

[10] These were: 'For securing Church lands in Co. Wexford from Nicholas Loftus to George Lord Bishop of Ferns & Leighlin and vice versa'; 'For settlement of divers lands and rents in the Lord Archbishop of Dublin, Lord Bishop of Elphin and Nicholas Barnewall'; 'For confirmation of certain estates made by the Lord Archbishop of Dublin to Sir William Usher, knight'; 'To secure &c several estates to William Bulkeley, priest, in Counties Dublin, Wicklow and Wexford'. Only the titles survive.

[11] In a report by Bramhall and Sir William Parsons of August 1637 on the 'treaty between the lord treasurer of Ireland [Cork] and the bishop of Waterford and Lismore', SP 63/256/46,1, they propose a bill in the next parliament. It received royal assent on 12 November 1640.

[12] 15 Charles I c. 11.

complaints.[13] The grievances can be broken down into three rough categories. The first was antipathy to the continuation of Gaelic and medieval customary dues: 'In Connacht, a *mescan*, or dish of butter, once per annum in summer of every parishioner' along with other exotica such as 'muttue' and 'Mary-gallons'. The second class of grievance picked at the old sore of abuse of ecclesiastical jurisdiction: 'married couples that live together are brought into the courts to prove their marriages and when they prove it, pay 7s for a dismiss'. Excessive charges made up a third, related, class of complaint: '3s for marriages in some places more, let the parties be never so poor' or 'breaking ground in the chancel for £14'.[14]

The grievances were no sudden eruption. They were, rather, a sign of the gradual disintegration of the government party over the second session.[15] Wandesforde lost control of the Commons to a widespread opposition based upon 'a shared hostility' to Strafford's administration for its abuse of nearly all of the interest groups in Irish society.[16] Given the lord lieutenant's very partisan support of the church, it made a natural target. Significantly, the Commons took the first steps towards indictment of Atherton of Waterford by admitting the petition of John Child against him on the same day as the grievances.[17] High Commission was also directed to absolve William Stoute and Richard Pountaine of sentence and excommunication in a case promoted by a clergyman on the grounds that it had exceeded its jurisdiction and so jeopardised the liberties of the subject.[18] On a single day, then, a group of related targets had been selected all of which were summed up in Atherton: an immoral bishop who was also a member of the High Commission, and notorious both for his recovery of lands and heavy use of his jurisdiction. Nowhere as dramatic as Root and Branch, but nonetheless a challenge to some of the most grating aspects of seven years of church reconstruction.[19]

These grievances did highlight some key deficiencies of the policies of the 1630s. The continuing tensions caused by medieval peculiarities (such as *mescan*) are striking because here the objection was not only to the burden of these customs but a feeling that these pre-reformation relics had no

---

[13] *Commons' jn. Ire.*, pp. 150–1. While the English canons were not published until 16 June, word or rumour of their content is likely to have reached Ireland sometime earlier.

[14] Reporting from London in the early summer of 1641, Ussher mentioned that he had 'prevailed since in the matter of those customs which they term barbarous', *Rawdon*, pp. 82–3, PRONI T415, pp. 22–3.

[15] Clarke, 'The breakdown', pp. 276–7; Perceval-Maxwell, *Outbreak*, pp. 77–8.

[16] Clarke, 'The breakdown', p. 277.   [17] *Lords' jn. Ire.*, p. 148.   [18] *Lords' jn. Ire.*, p. 149.

[19] It does share, in its modest way, the concern of the Root and Branch petition that the relics of the old Roman system were an oppression. S. R. Gardiner, *The constitutional documents of the puritan revolution 1625–1660*, 3rd edn (Oxford, 1906), pp. 141–3; articles 19–20, 22–8.

proper place in the Church of Ireland. The renovations of the 1630s left old dues untouched because all energy had gone into the retrieval of *rights*. Thus, the temporalities campaign was concerned with enforcement first and reform and replacement of tithing customs as a poor second, leaving its promoters wide open to the criticism that they were more interested in exaction than reform.[20] Bramhall did not realise his vulnerability and opted for exasperation and dismissiveness. He argued that most complaints arose from the actions of 'very few' clergy.[21] Ever the clericalist, he insisted that 'on the other [lay] side there were other customs as prejudicial to the church'. His solution was the old one, based on an old assumption. Disputed customs should be considered by the king or lord deputy and council. So, in the face of a substantial complaint, all Bramhall could do was offer the 1630s remedy – 'arbitration' at what he knew and expected to be a favourable tribunal. And, as with nonconformity, he failed to appreciate that opposition could be something other than covetousness or petulance.

The last eight grievances in the parliamentary list also bore on particulars of the church settlement. The Commons decried excessive numbers of apparitors, overactive consistory courts, extortionate citations and absence of fee tables. These were violations of Irish canons 85, 74, 70 and 83, which suggests that the high plan to reform ecclesiastical jurisdiction had been a flop. Other allegations – that bishops failed to administer the oath to schoolmasters to teach in English, the continuing lack of freeschools in every diocese, persistent siphoning off of commutation moneys and use of blank processes by apparitors – all point in the same direction. Moreover Wentworth had publicly promised a commission for commutations and to look into freeschools. So the grievances neatly blamed the government for failing to deliver on planned reforms and simultaneously hinted that it had permitted abuse to flourish. It would only take a very small step now to begin to argue that all of the recent reforms were really abuses and that reconstruction had tended to tyranny.

UNRAVELLING IN IRELAND AND ENGLAND:
OCTOBER–NOVEMBER 1640

The winter session saw the programme for the church grind to a halt and immediately start to unravel. James Ussher had departed for England

---

[20] They do not appear to have considered extending the 1624 tithing table for the escheated counties of Ulster to the rest of the kingdom.

[21] Bramhall to Laud, 4 November 1640, HA 14061. Very few clergy or indeed 'none at all are concerned' in a number of cases.

sometime in May and, as it happened, would never return to Ireland again. Politically, church affairs were caught up in an Irish drive to dismantle the works of Strafford's viceroyalty and a concurrent bid by the new English parliament to topple the man himself.[22] The fate of ecclesiastical bills during this short session sums up the change in atmosphere. Six church measures received royal assent on 12 November. Four were private and originated in the House of Lords.[23] Convocation's six subsidies went through (even as the Commons secured a reduction in their own liability) along with a bill relating to twentieth parts which altered the penalty for non-payment from deprivation to a fine.[24] This last reform, which had the effect of strengthening the rights of patrons, was an uncontentious minor matter.

All other ecclesiastical legislation intended to aid recovery died a death. These bills started in the upper chamber, where as late as 4 November Bramhall could claim, 'we do well enough'.[25] When transmitted to the Commons they either vanished after the first reading or were deemed unfit to pass. Bills for 'the real union and division of parishes and for exchanges' and for 'churches and freeschools' both disappeared after a first reading on 26 October, as did a private bill for the archbishop of Dublin and the earl of Meath on 29 October.[26] The Act for 'union and division' was most likely designed to rationalise the medieval parochial system by merging tiny parishes into viable units.[27] Doing so would have strengthened the Church of Ireland by further bolstering residence of a well-maintained clergy with

---

[22] Clarke, 'The breakdown', pp. 279–80; Perceval-Maxwell, *Outbreak*, pp. 83–6; Patrick Little, 'The English parliament and the Irish constitution, 1641–9' in Micheál Ó Siochrú (ed.), *Kingdoms in crisis: Ireland in the 1640s: essays in honour of Donal Cregan* (Dublin, 2001), pp. 106–21.

[23] These were compositions and agreements between the earl of Cork and the bishop of Waterford and Lismore, Viscount Ranelagh and the bishop of Elphin, the archbishop of Armagh and Sir Philip Mainwaring and the archbishop of Dublin and Richard Bealing.

[24] Clarke, 'The breakdown', p. 279. Bramhall was worried about the cost of the clerical subsidies and proposed to Laud that he would oversee a new taxation of benefices which would end up raising more revenue but without causing hardship or discontent. Bramhall to Laud, 4 November 1640, HA 14061.

[25] Bramhall to Laud, 4 November 1640, HA 14061.

[26] The first two of these bills were clearly descended from a single failed bill in the 1634–5 parliament.

[27] The 1662 Act for Real Union and Division of Parishes, 14 & 15 Charles II, sess. 4, c. 10 begins: 'whereas parishes are in some parts of this kingdom so little, that five or six lie within a mile or two'. It allowed a twenty-year period for exchanges and amalgamations on the authority of the chief governor and council with the advice and approbation of the bishops. On the problem of parochial structure in Ireland, see K. W. Nicholls, 'Rectory, vicarage and parish in the western Irish dioceses', *Journal of the Royal Society of Antiquaries of Ireland* 101 (1971), 53–84; B. J. Graham, 'The high middle ages c. 1110–1350' in B. J. Graham and L. J. Proudfoot (eds.), *An historical geography of Ireland* (1993), pp. 58–91; K. Simms, 'Frontiers in the Irish church – regional and cultural' in Terence Barry, Robin Frame and Katherine Simms (eds.), *Colony and frontier in medieval Ireland* (1995), pp. 177–200. The relationship between both the diocesan and parochial structure of the medieval church and the effect this had upon the Protestant reformation has been little examined.

a genuine national presence. The brief record of debate in the Lords' committee for Acts shows that Bramhall's bill for churches and freeschools was designed to complement its mate by providing means for 'building the church in the centre of the parish' and for moving the freeschools 'to more convenient places'.[28] This was an important acknowledgement of changing settlement patterns, especially in plantation areas, where new urban networks did not correspond to the inherited ecclesiastical divisions. While policy makers always drew back from interfering with the diocesan system, it is clear that Bramhall was happy to contemplate reorganisation at a lower level. Had these measures passed into law and been thoroughly implemented they would have been the most practical step towards an island-wide establishment since the 1560 Act. Systematic, well-financed local restructuring might not have won the battle for souls, but it would have made the Church of Ireland a much more serious combatant.

Two other bills never made it out of their respective houses of origin. The bill for the 'improvement of the revenue of the church and securing of estates derived from ecclesiastical persons' was swallowed up by a Commons' committee, never to re-emerge.[29] The Lords debated a bill 'concerning tithings, oblations and mortuaries' on 19 October.[30] Lord Chief Justice Lowther's speech on that occasion indicates that it was an attempt to recast some of the forty-four grievances into statute form.[31] On 20 October, the house ordered that the bill stand committed and it did not resurface. Another bill which aimed to make statutory provision for fees in courts temporal and spiritual also sputtered out.[32] Apart from assent given to the bills on 12 November, all legislative initiative had ceased by the end of October. Statutory reconstruction was over.

On 7 November, the Commons entered a Petition of Remonstrance which was the antithesis to the fawning preamble to the Subsidy Act.[33] It was a detailed indictment of Strafford's government, designed for export, in the name of the 'loyal and dutiful people of this land of Ireland, being now for the most part derived of British ancestors'. It was fuel for the burning of the lord lieutenant.[34] On 11 November (the day Strafford was

---

[28] *Lords' jn. Ire.*, p. 132. Bramhall told the committee that he had penned the bill and was responsible for it.

[29] *Commons' jn. Ire.*, pp. 157–9.   [30] *Lords' jn. Ire.*, p. 129.

[31] *Lords' jn. Ire.*, p. 129. He suggested that the Act stipulate that both clerical and lay opinion should be heard by the lord deputy and council.

[32] *Commons' jn. Ire.*, pp. 158–60.

[33] *Commons' jn. Ire.*, pp. 162–3; Clarke, 'The breakdown', p. 280, points out that it was never debated by the Commons, springing out full-formed. See also Clarke, 'Policies of the Old English in parliament, 1640–41', 85–102, esp. 89–90.

[34] Perceval-Maxwell, *Outbreak*, pp. 84–5; Kearney, *Strafford*, p. 202.

arrested in London), the Irish Commons named a committee to travel to England to act as agents for the house in redress of grievances. With the Irish Remonstrance in hand, Pym was able to launch a detailed attack.[35] The inclusion of the Church of Ireland in the Remonstrance furnished extra colour to the general picture of subversion, unconstitutionality and arrogance. Ecclesiastical affairs appeared in five of the instances of destruction of the commonwealth: the court of High Commission, 'the exorbitant and barbarous fees and pretended customs exacted by the clergy against the law' and 'fees in ecclesiastical and civil courts'. Church lands were high up on the petition where it denounced excessive and 'illegal' use of paper petitions and of the council board.[36]

On 12 November, Wandesforde prorogued parliament and forbade the Commons' committee to leave the country. Less than a month later, Strafford's influence over Irish affairs was utterly obliterated when news reached Dublin of his impeachment alongside a warrant for George Radcliffe's arrest. On 3 December Wandesforde died.[37] Following a trial that had dragged out over the summer, Bishop John Atherton was hanged for sodomy on 5 December.[38] In London, the English Commons took the unprecedented step of establishing an Irish committee of the whole house at which the gadfly of the three kingdoms, Sir John Clotworthy, spoke on the state of the Irish church.[39] Strafford was committed to the Tower on 11 November. Exactly one month later came the launch of the Root and Branch petition. On 21 November Laud was arrested and on 18 December he was accused of high treason.

Strafford was the target of Clotworthy's speech which was delivered on the same day, 7 November, as the Irish Remonstrance. It was also one of

---

[35] The Remonstrance was read to the English Commons on 21 November: Russell, 'British background to the Irish rebellion of 1641', 166–82. See also Little, 'The English parliament', pp. 106–21; Orr, *Treason and the state*, pp. 61–100, Aidan Clarke, 'Patrick Darcy and the constitutional relationship between Ireland and Britain' in Jane Ohlmeyer (ed.), *Political thought in seventeenth-century Ireland* (Cambridge, 2000) pp. 35–55; Russell, *Fall of the British monarchies*, pp. 281–3.

[36] *Commons' jn. Ire.*, pp. 162–3.

[37] The succession of John Borlase and William Parsons as lords justices rather than Ormond and Dillon put an end to any hope of continuity in government. Bramhall attended Wandesforde on his deathbed: Alice Thornton, *Autobiography*, Surtees Society 72 (York, 1875), p. 24.

[38] For the trial in king's bench, see Aidan Clarke, 'A woeful sinner: John Atherton' in Vincent P. Carey and Ute Lotz Heumann (eds.), *Taking sides? Colonial and constitutional mentalités in early modern Ireland* (Dublin, 2003), pp. 138–49. Considerable, often salacious, interest was aroused by the case: Anon., *The case of John Atherton, bishop of Waterford in Ireland who was convicted of the sin of uncleanness with a cow* (1641); *The life and death of John Atherton, lord bishop of Waterford & Lismore . . . who for incest, buggery and many enormous crimes . . .* (1641).

[39] Russell, *Fall of the British monarchies*, p. 214.

the few depictions in England of the state of the Irish church by someone who might claim firsthand knowledge. It came, too, after John Pym's two-hour offering in which he had identified papistry as the root of England's troubles.[40] The Ulster planter concentrated heavily on the apparent moral emptiness, indeed rottenness, of the Church of Ireland: 'rake hell and you cannot find worse . . . clergy bad both in life and government, drunkenness. One bishop was indicted of whoredom and sodomy. Many of these so. Active against the good and scandalous in life is the way to get preferment.'[41] Atherton had become the very symbol of the corruption of the Church of Ireland. All of which was the product of blind arbitrary government whose High Commission was the root of 'unlimited oppressions'. Worse still, there was toleration of popery and its alarming regeneration 'in one town . . . five or six monasteries, priories and nunneries'.[42] To round off his denunciation, Clotworthy returned to the most graphic point: 'the question is who commended this whorish incestuous bishop who lay with his sister in England? His sister suffered and he escaped. Dr Atherton, bishop of Waterford in Ireland.' What the Church of Ireland proved, the speech implied, was that episcopacy and arbitrary government were as one and their fruit was moral and spiritual bankruptcy. Moreover, toleration of Catholicism transformed bad government into tyranny, especially when a papist army of 8,000 stood in the wings.[43] A church where Atherton and his ilk were preferred was a telling example of misgovernment and a dire warning to England. This analysis was compelling for many of the English Commons and much suited to the high moral tone of the long parliament.[44] In Ireland, the first trumpet of the apocalypse had been sounded, even though October 1641 would be the shrillest blast of them all. So, although the Church of Ireland furnished none of the articles against Strafford, its purported condition clinched the argument that the Laodiceans were in charge.[45]

---

[40] Russell, *Fall of the British monarchies*, p. 216.

[41] Maija Jansson (ed.), *Proceedings in the opening session of the long parliament: House of Commons, 3 November–19 December 1640* (Woodbridge, 2000), p. 37; Wallace Notestein (ed.), *The journal of Sir Simonds D'Ewes* (New Haven, 1923), p. 13.

[42] Jansson, *Proceedings*, p. 44; Notestein, *D'Ewes*, p. 13.

[43] Jansson, *Proceedings*, p. 37: 'the civil government is corrupted. All hearings are in chambers and at council table and by referees, and those are named by the parties whom they please and matters dispatched without jury, without trial'; Notestein, *D'Ewes*, p. 14.

[44] J. S. Morrill, 'The attack on the Church of England in the Long Parliament' in J. S. Morrill (ed.), *The nature of the English revolution* (1993), pp. 69–90.

[45] Caroline Hibbard, *Charles I and the Popish Plot* (Chapel Hill, NC, 1983) pp. 82–3.

In the fourth session the swing from submissive legislating to militant action was complete. Bramhall bore the brunt of hostility both as chief agent of ecclesiastical policy and as a confidant of the viceroy. Even though the Commons were most voluble on the large issue of constitutional relationships, individual cases such as the arrest of William Calthropp, former register of Waterford, kept up pressure on ecclesiastical jurisdiction.[46] On 16 February the Irish judges were presented with a set of twenty-one queries designed to establish the illegality of Wentworth's administrative practices and to provide suitable material to the managers of his trial. Beginning grandiloquently with a large question, 'whether the subjects of this kingdom be a free people and to be governed only by the common laws of England and statutes of force in this kingdom', the Commons moved on to every segment of the governing apparatus.[47]

The fourteenth query, on the status of deans, made the judges, who already felt cornered, even more nervous and they begged not to be pressed further on a matter which 'may concern many men's estates which may come judicially in question before them'.[48] Patrick Darcy's gloss on both question and answer reveals the importance of what looks at first glance to be a fairly innocuous question: 'Many have lost great estates and possessions by orders of the council board, although the actual deans elected, or actual deans confirmed their estates, when no donation from the crown was found upon record to a confirming dean.'[49] Darcy's contention was that decanal confirmations of leases were not only sound in law but especially vital in Ireland where earlier records of bishoprics and deaneries were scant. This query raised again the recent spectre of Radcliffe's device in the Lismore case as the quintessence of the resumption drive of the 1630s.[50] If overturned, as the judicial reply indicated it could be, the way was clear for wholesale reversal of many gains tabulated by Bramhall in his reports.

The mood in the Lords changed too. On 11 February they set up a committee of grievances and a week later they had drawn up a slightly

[46] *Commons' jn. Ire.*, p. 167.

[47] Clarke, 'The breakdown', p. 282; 'Patrick Darcy', pp. 38–9. Perceval-Maxwell, *Outbreak*, pp. 172 ff. considers them a 'bill of rights' for Ireland.

[48] *Commons' Jn. Ire.*, p. 179: 'Whether deans or other dignitaries of cathedral churches be properly, and *de mero jure* donative by the king, and not elective or collative? If so, why, and by what law, and whether the confirmation of a dean *de facto* of the bishop's grant be good and valid in law or no? If not, by what law?' The judges' answer is in *An argument delivered by Patrick Darcy esq.* (Waterford, 1643), p. 33.

[49] *An argument*, p. 51.   [50] *An argument*, pp. 108–9.

amplified version of the Remonstrance to be sent to their own committee in England.[51] They said nothing new on the church, but there was still enough in the Remonstrance for Anthony Martin of Meath to take the unusual, and possibly tactical, step of requesting that the lords spiritual should not be named. Legal opinion held that any matter decided by 'plurality of voices' should be in the names of both temporal and spiritual lords.[52]

On 17 February the lower house drew up a 'protestation concerning the Earl of Strafford and his manner of government' which was a trailer for the 27 February decision to appoint a select committee to draw up charges against Lord Chancellor Bolton, Lord Chief Justice Lowther, Sir George Radcliffe and Bishop John Bramhall himself.[53] This simple ploy was designed to prevent Strafford calling his allies as witnesses. The plain tactic, though, instantly gave birth to a complicated constitutional issue which turned a vague and half-hearted trial into a row over the judicature of the Irish parliament. In the end, neither Bramhall nor his church business stood trial but the kingdom of Ireland itself. The ability of the Irish parliament to proceed in this matter lay entirely in analogy with England. Such an argument gave rise to the question of whether the Irish parliament under the Irish crown ran parallel to the English parliament under the English crown or whether it was subordinate. This was a question which mesmerised Irish members, bored or irritated Westminster members and gave Charles some little room for manoeuvre.

Choice of the four impeached was not dictated by their office (since Bolton's position caused manifold technical difficulties and Bramhall was not even a privy councillor) but was intended as a blow to all of the most unpopular limbs of the previous administration. Bolton and Lowther were the two most prominent members of the commission for defective titles.[54] Radcliffe was not only Strafford's chief legal adviser but also his representative on the customs farm.[55] Bramhall represented church policy in his work as chief retriever of church lands and revenues, as the leading member of High Commission and as an arch-conformist. As a Londonderry commissioner he represented a widely disliked plantation policy.

Between formation of the committee and reading of the articles on 4 March, there was vigorous debate on the confinement of the accused, which

[51] *Lords' jn. Ire.*, pp. 150–2. This was a copy of the Commons' remonstrance, with a few special concerns of the peers tacked on such as objection to those with seats in the house by virtue of their titles even though they had no Irish estates: *Lords' jn. Ire.*, p. 152.

[52] *Lords' jn. Ire.*, p. 150.

[53] Captain Audley Mervyn was sent directly to the Lords to ask for their arrest and sequestration from the upper house and all other judicature, *Commons' jn. Ire.*, pp. 165–6.

[54] Kearney, *Strafford*, p. 81.   [55] Kearney, *Strafford*, p. 163.

ran alongside a campaign to have the queries transmitted to England.[56] Imprisonment of Lord Chancellor Bolton was a sticky issue since he was Speaker and Keeper of the Great Seal. In his case, after a row between Ormond and Lord Lambart, who urged instant committal on grounds of recent English precedent, the debate shifted to bail terms.[57] Bramhall, by contrast, sparked no debate and the sergeant-at-arms was ordered to arrest him.[58] On 1 March, Bolton and Lowther entered recognisances of £20,000, at which the latter made a short speech protesting his innocence while hinting strongly that he expected little to come of the procedure.[59] On 4 March, under continuing pressure from below, the Lords decided to vote, and after an unsuccessful bid to exclude the bishops the majority of the house resolved on committal.[60] A delegation to the lords justices to request a new speaker returned with a brusque reply that as there was 'more than ordinary use of' Bolton and Lowther 'at present at the Council board', they should be bailed.[61] It was in this sort of proceeding that all the disadvantage of the informality of Bramhall's position under Strafford was revealed. Once the power and protection of the chief governor were taken away, the bishop was exposed in his person. Simultaneously, the prerogative cement which had held the whole church settlement together was to crumble.

Lambart's jittery insistence that Ireland follow 'the late precedents of England' has duly attracted the attention of historians. Audley Mervyn's dramatic speeches and Patrick Darcy's *Argument* have kept eyes on the constitution. Behind the oratory a trickle of petitions commenced. It quickly went into full spate and, by acting upon it, the Irish parliament expanded its judicature in a real sense, something which the better-noticed campaign failed to do. On 26 February the commissioners admitted a petition of the tenants to the dean and chapter of Christchurch against Bramhall.[62] On 2 March a petition by Dean William Coote of Down, also against Derry, was considered by the Lords' committee for privileges and grievances. These were the harbingers of a great flood of petitions to come against Bramhall and other ecclesiastics in the fifth session. Now that he was exposed through the severing of the Strafford connection, all of the deals made during the 1630s and all of the cases referred to him during that time were liable to be

---

[56] Clarke, 'The breakdown', 282; *Commons' jn. Ire.*, pp. 189–90; *Lords' jn. Ire.*, pp. 165–8.

[57] *Lords' jn. Ire.*, pp. 176–8.   [58] *Lords' jn. Ire.*, p. 168.   [59] *Lords' jn. Ire.*, p. 170.

[60] *Lords' jn. Ire.*, p. 177.   [61] *Lords' jn. Ire.*, p. 178.

[62] *Commons' jn. Ire.*, p. 184. This petition was brought to the Lords for answer by the same committee which was appointed to draw up the articles against Bramhall and the others. See RCB, MS 6. 26. 13 (8), fols. 1r–4r, for Bramhall's notes on the leases of the tenants made over 18 March 1640–3 July 1640.

questioned. Given the absence on 4 March of anything but the most general articles of impeachment, this surge of petitions substituted for particular charges and explains why he was the first arrested, longest confined, and the only one to have the proceedings against him suspended rather than dropped.

Four articles of impeachment were written into the record of the lower house on 4 March 1641:[63]

First that they, the said Sir Richard Bolton, Knight, Lord Chancellor of Ireland, John Lord Bishop of Derry, Sir Gerard Lowther, Knight, Lord Chief Justice of the Common Place and Sir George Radcliffe, Knight, intending the destruction of the Commonwealth of this realm have traitorously contrived, introduced and exercised an arbitrary and tyrannical government against law throughout this Kingdom, by the countenance and assistance of Thomas Earl of Strafford, then Chief Governor of this Kingdom.

Secondly that they and every of them . . . have traitorously assumed to themselves and every of them regal power over the goods, persons, lands and liberties of His Majesty's subjects of this Realm; and likewise maliciously, perfidiously, and traitorously given, declared, pronounced and published many false, unjust, and erroneous opinions, judgements, sentences and decrees in extrajudicial manner against law; and have perpetrated, practised and done many other traitorous and unlawful acts and things; whereby, as well divers mutinies, seditions and rebellions have been raised, as also many thousands of His Majesty's liege people of this Kingdom have been ruined in their goods, lands, liberties and lives; many of them being of good quality and reputation, have been utterly defamed by pillory, mutilation of members and other infamous punishments; by means whereof His Majesty and the Kingdom have been deprived of their service in juries and other public employments, and the general trade and traffic of this Island for the most part destroyed, and His Majesty highly damnified in his customs and other revenues.

Thirdly, that they . . . the better to preserve themselves and the said Earl of Strafford in these and other traitorous courses have laboured to subvert the rights of Parliament and the ancient courses of Parliamentary proceedings: and all which offences were contrived, committed, perpetrated and done at such times, as the said Sir Richard Bolton, Sir Gerard Lowther, Sir George Radcliffe, Knights, were Privy Councillors of State within this Kingdom, and Sir Gerard Lowther, Knight, was Lord Chief Justice of the Common Place, and against their oaths of the same: and at such time, as the said John Lord Bishop of Derry was actually Bishop of Derry within this Kingdom; and were done and perpetrated contrary to their, and every of their Allegiance, and several and respective oaths taken in that behalf.

[63] *Commons' jn. Ire.*, pp. 198–9.

Fourthly, for which, the said Knights, Citizens and Burgesses, do impeach the said Sir Richard Bolton, Knight, Lord Chancellor of Ireland, John Lord Bishop of Derry, Sir Gerard Lowther, Knight, Lord Chief Justice of the Common Place and Sir George Radcliffe, Knight and every of them, of High Treason against Our Sovereign Lord the King, His Crown and Dignity.

Here were general articles which reproduced the pith of the June grievances, remonstrances, queries and protestation. As Richard Bolton pointed out immediately, the charges were 'too general' and, as such, unworthy of any response.[64] He went on to point out that they were unprecedented and they impinged on the royal prerogative.[65] His rebuttal undoubtedly irritated as it exposed the nakedly tactical impulse behind impeachment and so lent further impetus to insistence on judicature even after Strafford's execution on 12 May. Audley Mervyn's later printed bombast – the accused had left Magna Carta 'besmeared and grovelling in her own gore' – could not conceal the brittleness of the Commons' position.[66] His insistence that impeachment was the essential prelude to restoration of proper legal government was joined to a passing reference to 'supply from our neighbouring nations' in a bid to evoke a spectre of tyranny and subversion stalking all three kingdoms.[67]

On 5 March 1641, the last day of the session, Bramhall made his first response to the charges against him in a petition to the lords justices for bail on the same terms as Lowther. Attached to it was an 'Apology . . . to all those petitions which are exhibited against him in both houses of parliament'.[68] This was a careful defence of his actions in church causes and, indeed, his whole career in Ireland. He began by stressing that he came to Ireland not in search of profit but because he was:

> moved (it was not my seeking) to come here into Ireland for the good and settlement of this church which I have endeavoured faithfully, diligently . . . zealously with infinite toil to myself with great expense of mine own means which grieves me to write for very unthankful men.

For all of the dignities or benefices which had been at his disposal he protested he had not received one farthing, nor even the loan of a farthing, 'except a pair of gloves or some such small acknowledgement'. Having denied profit as his motive, Bramhall moved on to what he described as

---

[64] *Lords' jn. Ire.*, p. 176.

[65] John McCafferty, '"To follow the late precedents of England": the Irish impeachment proceedings of 1641' in D. S. Greer and N. M. Dawson (eds.), *Mysteries and solutions in Irish legal history* (Dublin, 2001), pp. 51–73, esp. 62–3.

[66] Audley Mervyn, *A speech before the Lords in the Upper House in Ireland* (1641), 2, 4.

[67] Mervyn, *A speech*, p. 9.   [68] 6 March 1641, HA 14064.

the 'main charge', determining cases on reference from the council board on foot of petitions.[69] He pointed out that if it really was treason to act upon paper petitions then not only himself but every judge and sheriff in the kingdom would be equally guilty. Bramhall's defence shows that he saw a link between impeachment and the other petitions to parliament. He knew that he stood accused as an agent of the recent regime.[70] Prospective petitioners were themselves emboldened by an atmosphere where not only the personalities involved were on trial but where the very legality of decisions and judgements made and given was under siege. A combination of personality, power and prerogative in a sealed system had made many of the gains of the 1630s feasible. Once the seal was cracked, everything stood to be destroyed in the explosion.

Bramhall moved on to an eight-point defence of actions he had taken upon references from the board. When addressing 'some further abuses charged upon me', the new vulnerability of his tactic of securing private treaty with a hint of some public example lurking behind became apparent. His accusers claimed, he said, that: 'I certify mutual consent where there was none', 'I threatened them that I would turn them out of their possessions and so compelled them to consent', 'I directed references to myself'. Such were the charges levelled by the recipients of the 'purges' and 'vomits' of the early years. In every instance, Bramhall had a precise riposte but the very accusations themselves do give a flavour of his past methods. At the zenith of his power, he had believed both law and right to be on his side, and he also had the lord deputy. He had always been meticulous in detail, well aware he had opposition. Yet again he ascribed resistance to jealousy and covetousness, never really conceiving there might be any sense of injustice.

On 23 March Bramhall entered into a bond of £20,000, which permitted him to live in custody in his own house in St Patrick's close and go out into the city or suburbs under supervision.[71] Earlier in the month he had written to his wife protesting his innocence and expressing his hope that it would all be over by the time she came to Dublin: 'I send you a copy of the charge; my lord chancellor and the chief justice believe not to be

---

[69] 'Which is objected against me almost in every particular and the ground of my impeachment is the hearing and determining of causes upon references from the council table, the lord lieutenant and lord deputy made upon paper petitions in an extrajudicial way which is said to be contrary to his majesty's printed book of instructions, against the laws of this kingdom and against the great charter', HA 14064; G. J. Hand and V. W. Treadwell (eds.), 'His Majesty's directions for the ordering and settling of the courts and the course of justice within his kingdom of Ireland', *Analecta Hibernica* 26 (1970), 179–212.

[70] For a similar two-pronged approach in the attempted impeachment of Buckingham case, see McCafferty, '"To follow"', p. 68.

[71] HA 14065.

of any great moment.'[72] Naturally he was being brave in order to reassure his spouse, but it is also true to say that just like Bolton and Lowther he interpreted the whole affair as a straightforward attempt to keep them from Strafford's trial. Writing to Ussher on 26 April, Bramhall returned to the themes of his 'apology': 'my force was only force of reason and law; the scale must needs yield when weight is put into it'.[73] He then reminded the primate of the improvements he had secured for bishops in a long litany, ending: 'I not know wherein I ever in all those passages deviated from the rule of justice.' Apart from his own troubles, Bramhall identified a new and disturbing threat from the petition against episcopacy circulating in Ulster addressed to the English parliament. He proposed a counter-petition of '5,000 . . . of better rank' as opposed to these 1,500 'rabble'.[74] This combination of self-justification about temporalities and alarm about anti-episcopal movements was probably intended to spur the primate into a defence of the Irish church in England.[75] By now Bramhall was completely on the defensive – for himself, for the revitalised clerical estate in Ireland and for episcopacy itself.

While Bramhall worked on his defence during the Irish recess, Strafford came to trial in England. Once the English Commons decided upon attainder, the Irish charges evaporated. As it was, the Church of Ireland had made no separate appearance in the articles but it did weave its way into several of the alleged abuses of power. Article 4, on paper petitions, was illustrated by the case of a rectory and tithes in Co. Tipperary and Strafford's presentation of a clergyman, Arthur Gwyn (supposedly Cork's coachman's groom).[76] Article 4 also reopened the question of the Youghal lands and Strafford's initial replies caused Cork huge anxiety.[77] The emphasis was, however, on Strafford's 'threats' to Cork rather than the resumption campaign itself. Article 9 concerned a warrant granted by the lord deputy to Leslie of Down and Connor to attach those who ignored citations to his consistory court or who failed to perform sentences imposed by the court.[78] Here Strafford was easily able to prove that his predecessors had issued such warrants. When questioned on 28 March, Ussher defended the

---

[72] *Rawdon*, pp. 74–6.　　[73] *BW* I, pp. lxxxi–xci.

[74] Bramhall believed that half of these 1,500 could be brought to sign his petition. He alleged that the solicitor had got £300 for circulating the anti-episcopal petition and that people were duped into believing that it was for 'purity of religion' and the 'honour of that [Scottish] nation'. Here still were all his old readings of nonconformity.

[75] See Ussher to Bramhall, *Rawdon*, pp. 81–3; dated in PRONI T415 (22–3) as 19 June 1641.

[76] Rushworth, p. 175.

[77] Patrick Little, 'The earl of Cork and the fall of the earl of Strafford 1638–41', *HJ* 39 (1996), 619–35.

[78] Rushworth, p. 65.

legality of this action as well as use of paper petitions.[79] In article 19 on the usurpation of regal power in framing the Black Oath, Whitelock pushed very hard to maintain that reference was made to ecclesiastical discipline in it: 'my lord interpreted it to extend to the observation of the ceremonies and government of the church established and to be established'.[80]

Just as in Laud's trial and in the long parliament in general, the church appeared as part of a general argument about misrule and usurpation rather than as a discrete issue. Rhetorically and emotionally, though, invocation of ecclesiastical affairs and fears of the exaltation of the clerical estate had particular effect. In his opening statement on 23 March 1641, Pym decried, above all else, the moral depravity of ecclesiastical imperialism:

For religion we say, and we shall prove, that he has been diligent indeed to favour innovations, to favour superstitions, to favour the encroachments and usurpations of the clergy: but for religion it never received any advantage by him, nay, a great deal of hurt.[81]

So the stage was set to maintain, despite Ussher's counter-testimony, that Strafford's policy had been hollow, self-seeking and tending to the ruin of the established church. Recovery of lands was in reality the taking away of men's inheritances and a bid to curry favour with Laud.[82] Strafford had neither built a single new church nor provided 'spiritual edification' in Ireland. Finally, and predictably, there were the clergy promoted by him – 'Dr Atherton, he is not to be found above ground', 'Dr Bramhall . . . preferred to a great bishopric; but he is a man that now stands charged with high treason . . . but a few years in Ireland and yet has laid out at least £30,000 in purchases.' This was both ironic and ingenious. Ironic because Bramhall's impeachment was a direct consequence of Strafford's and ingenious because the large sums handled in impropriation purchase funds were made to look like personal profit. The speech introduced Canterbury as puppet master, overseeing ecclesiastical innovation supported by a treacherous, ignorant and morally flawed *corps* of clergy. Yet of all these only Gwyn actually appeared in the charges. Though Strafford defended himself in detail, even confessing that he had recommended Atherton in ignorance of his 'secret fault', Pym's general depiction of a Church of Ireland subverted and corrupted by a chief governor who grovelled to Canterbury stuck fast,

---

[79] Rushworth, pp. 236–9. Ussher's answers to the interrogatory, BL Add. MS 34,253. Orr, *Treason and the state*, p. 90: 'This seemingly insignificant article summed the case against the Earl most concisely: that he had unlawfully assumed the sovereign law-giving power and exercised it tyrannically without customary restraint over the king's subjects.'

[80] Rushworth, pp. 489–500, 510.   [81] Rushworth, p. 104.   [82] Rushworth, p. 107.

contributing greatly to an atmosphere in which the conviction of Strafford became a political *sine qua non*.

Before his execution, Strafford left two instructions, one moral and one personal, which make up an epitaph on his Irish church policy.[83] The first urged his son to forbear from profiting from sequestered church revenues 'for the curse of God will follow all them that meddle with such a thing, that tends to the destruction of the most apostolical church on earth'. The other was a request to James Ussher to impress Bramhall's plight on the king.[84] As Bramhall turned to face the Irish parliament's demolition of his works and to make his own response to impeachment, his patron, attended by the Irish primate, was executed on Tower Hill on 12 May 1641.

THE UNDOING OF HIGH COMMISSION:
JUNE 1640–AUGUST 1641

The Dublin parliament reconvened on the eve of Strafford's execution. In the short time before 23 October 1641 there was opportunity to focus on domestic issues, especially as Charles was engrossed with Scotland. The Irish members moved against the instruments, the chief agent and the outcomes of reconstruction. By August 1641 all three had been eliminated or neutralised. The downfall of the Irish High Commission encapsulates many aspects of parliamentary assault on Wentworth's regime during 1640–1. The court had a three kingdoms dimension, it was an issue on which Catholic and Protestant MPs could make common cause and criticism of its workings rapidly turned into scrutiny of its very legality.[85]

The attack on the court went in tandem with the push against Atherton and ecclesiastical jurisdiction in general on 17 June 1640. On the foot of a petition by Richard Stoute and William Pountaine, the Commons requested the commissioners to absolve the pair on the grounds that the case taken *ex officio promoto* was temporal and not within its jurisdiction.[86] Portentously, especially as it came just before the general grievances against courts spiritual, they maintained that it was 'a matter much concerning the liberty of the subjects of this kingdom in their persons and estates'. On 22 October the register, Michael Stanhope, was summoned to the committee of grievances.[87] On 27 October the house dissolved itself into a grand committee 'to consider of the privileges claimed' by Stanhope.[88] At his

---

[83] Rushworth, p. 763.   [84] Ussher to Bramhall, n.d. [May/June 1641], *Rawdon*, pp. 84–5.
[85] Bramhall to Laud, 4 November 1640, HA 14061.
[86] *Commons' jn. Ire.*, p. 148.   [87] 22 October 1640, *Commons' jn. Ire.*, p. 158.
[88] *Commons' jn. Ire.*, p. 161.

first summons, he had been asked to show the table of fees, a catalogue of fines and the patent itself. On Bramhall's advice he presented the fees but told the committee that all of the other information they desired was to be found in the exchequer and on the patent rolls.[89] Stanhope managed to escape charge by claiming privilege as a domestic servant of the lord lieutenant. This accident hugely irritated Bramhall because he felt it gave the lower house a hook against the viceroy.[90] On the whole though, he was optimistic because he felt any ploy to discover 'exorbitancy' in fines would not succeed and that their questions about estreatment were grounded in a misunderstanding. What Bramhall failed to see, or could not bring himself to see, was that the very right of High Commission to fine or have mitigations was itself going to be questioned.

On 7 November the Irish tribunal featured as the ninth grievance in the Remonstrance. Since High Commission existed on both islands it was easily presented as a stinging tentacle of an evil church policy in every kingdom. The phrasing of the article managed to blend a whiff of innovation with violation of proper legal procedure, financial burden and usurpation of jurisdiction.[91] On 9 November Dr Edward Lake was expelled from the house for 'misconduct' on the grand committee and committed for 'contemptuous words' as he 'did not', the journal recorded, 'perform the trust so reposed in him, but shifted and put off the said committee'.[92] By the end of the third session, then, High Commission had been identified as a major oppression and both its register and leading civil lawyer had incurred parliamentary censure. Impeachment kept the Commons busy during the short spring session of 1641, but the fifth session brought the edifice down completely. On 11 May the committees of the Irish parliament in London informed the Irish committee of the English privy council that mere suspension of the tribunal would not suffice to 'answer their expectation of great redress'.[93] On 10 June the Irish Commons formed a committee 'for drawing up the abuses and charge against the High Commission court

[89] Bramhall to Laud, 4 November 1640, HA 14061.

[90] Bramhall to Laud, 4 November 1640, HA 14061.

[91] *Commons' jn. Ire.*, p. 163: 'The late erection of the court of High Commission for causes ecclesiastical in those necessitous times; the proceedings of the said court in many causes, without legal warrant; and yet so supported, as prohibitions have not been obtained, though legally fought for; and the excessive fees exacted by the ministers thereof; and the encroaching of the same upon the jurisdiction of other ecclesiastical courts of this kingdom.'

[92] *Commons' jn. Ire.*, p. 164. Bramhall to Laud, 4 November 1640, HA 14061: 'your grace has now heard how Dr Lake was brought upon his knees for the church at the bar. His crime was saying at a committee, "it is not so, it is not so".'

[93] SP 63/259/6, *Cal. SP Ire., 1633–47*, p. 254.

and for all clergy exactions'.[94] This determination rendered the king's offer of suspension at pleasure in his answer to the Remonstrance on 16 July not only inadequate but confrontational.[95] By the end of the month, the Commons had ordered a copy of the patent and arranged for a debate on the commission in general and Stoute and Pountaine in particular.[96] On 3 August, after the house sat as a grand committee, the proceedings promoted by the clergyman Richard Holt against Stoute and Pountaine were declared null and void and the pair were free to recover their costs.[97] The next day, the house voted to nullify the High Commission in its entirety.[98] Two further cases were declared void and the fines reduced to nominal sums. The excommunications against the Down ministers Robert Rosse, James Hamilton, David Kennedy and Robert Wilson were cancelled and struck out. Zachary Travers, former register of Cork, Cloyne and Ross, was restored to office.[99] So not only was the court itself abolished but two highly disliked aspects of its working – imposition of conformity and reform of the church courts – were ritually and publicly erased. After four days' debate, on 7 August 1641, the house claimed twelve points of illegality in the commission of February 1636 which tended to 'the subversion of the fundamental laws'.[100] While most of the points concentrate on alleged violations of the 1560 Supremacy Act, the last on the list is a nice snapshot of the running of Strafford's ecclesiastical policy:

Whereas by the said statute . . . the warrant for naming commissioners or drawing the commission ought to be under the great seal, the fiat of the said commission

---

94 *Commons' jn. Ire.*, p. 230. In mid June, *The humble petition of the Protestant inhabitants of the counties of Antrim, Down, Tyrone &c part of the province of Ulster in the kingdom of Ireland concerning bishops* (1641), pp. 9–10 complained: 'The prelates and their faction, as they inherit then superstition of the Papacy, so of late they exact with all severity the absolute customs of St Mary-gallons, mortuaries, portions, &c which as they were given by superstition and used to idolatry, so now they are taken by oppression and applied to riotousness. They have also constantly practised and suffered, the buying and selling of the sacraments, which is a heavy burden; and where the poor have to pay the minister and clerk's fees, they will not marry them, nor suffer their dead to be buried. In the High Commission court against all law and equity, they sit as judges in their own cause and take cognizance of the highest and smallest matters, going therein without control.'

95 SP 63/260/1, *Cal. SP Ire., 1633–47*, p. 319. The Irish committee suggested to the king sometime in July that the petition concerning High Commission should be complied with, *Cal. SP Ire., 1647–60*, p. 251: 'High Commission shall be suspended until his majesty sees cause to have the same put again in execution, and then no retrospection to be had upon offences formerly passed.'

96 *Commons' jn. Ire.*, pp. 273, 276.   97 *Commons' jn. Ire.*, pp. 280–1.

98 *Commons' jn. Ire.*, p. 281: 'It is ordered upon question *nullo contradicente* that the High Commission court in that commission where it is grounded, and all several parts thereof is voted by this House to be void.'

99 *Commons' jn. Ire.*, p. 282. The overturned sentences were to be posted publicly: Armstrong, 'Ireland's puritan revolution?'

100 *Commons' jn. Ire.*, pp. 288–9.

as appears by the docquet thereof was drawn by the verbal direction of the late lord lieutenant, signified by the lord bishop of Derry to his majesty's then attorney general contrary to the said statute.

Charles's rather grudging offer of suspension coupled with his refusal to modify Poynings's law proved to be insufficient for an Irish House of Commons which was shrilly insisting on its judicature. While the push against the court had begun as part of a broad assault against the church in June 1640, it is likely that repeated demands by the English privy council for precedents in the impeachment cases spurred Irish MPs into defiant negation of the 1636 commission. They brought that same defiance and same insistence on judicature to bear on John Bramhall as chief ecclesiastical agent.

THE REVERSAL OF RECONSTRUCTION AND PURSUIT OF JOHN BRAMHALL: MAY 1641–SPRING 1642

Strafford's attainder turned the Irish treason trial into a political relic animated only by the constitutional issues attendant on the impeachment process. On 13 May Bramhall and his co-accused made their formal answers to the articles.[101] Bramhall's defence was a straightforward combination of insistence on the weakness of the case against him and of rejection of the general allegations. He pointed out, at length, the absence of precise charges and then proceeded to reproduce each article in the form of a denial.[102] Bolton and Lowther took the same line.[103] The real business of 13 May was a summons by the lords justices to inform both houses of a royal letter of 28 April in which the king had questioned the Irish parliament's right to impeach and requested precedents.[104] From this point on Bramhall's affairs were eclipsed by a debate which culminated in the production of the 'instruments' on 24 May.

In the meantime, parliament was concerned with the bishop only as a security issue. On 18 May the lords justices reported to Vane that he had still not been bailed but continued under the custody of the gentleman usher

---

[101] HA 14072, draft version HA 14073 but there is no substantive difference between the draft and the fair copy: 'that the said articles and every of them by the laws of this kingdom ought to be certain and particular'. The date of his reply is given in lords justices to Vane, 18 May 1641, SP 63/259/15, *Cal. SP Ire.*, 1633–47, p. 288. See also DOC bound MS 'political tracts', pp. 12–20.

[102] The only personal note came at the end of his rejection of the first article, where Bramhall added 'he has ever prayed and yet does pray from his heart for the happiness and prosperity of this kingdom. And has sold his fortunes in another kingdom to place them here.'

[103] DOC bound MS 'political tracts', pp. 12–20; Perceval-Maxwell, *Outbreak*, pp. 167–8.

[104] Lords justices to Vane, 18 May 1641, SP 63/259/15, *Cal. SP Ire.*, 1633–47, p. 288.

'from the last session to this'.[105] All the justices could do was ensure he was still permitted to go out under escort but no more because 'the dislike taken against him seemed then to us to be so general, and the desires of proceeding against him . . . much more vehement than against the other two'. The opprobrium reserved for Bramhall was a mark of his close personal, rather than official, association with Strafford, which generated its own political momentum separate from that of the constitutional. On 19 May he was permitted counsel.[106] The following day a Commons delegation, twenty strong, was sent up to the Lords to request that he be moved to more secure lodgings because his house in St Patrick's close was deemed too near the water.

On 24 May, in a series of 'instruments', the Commons insisted on their right to try and punish traitors, and rejected the need to furnish precedents as it tended to draw into question not only the judicature of parliament 'but all other courts'.[107] Furthermore, even though English precedents easily sufficed for Ireland, by analogy, 'intestine wars and troubles' had destroyed many of the records of parliament and many others had been 'embezzled and destroyed'. Almost immediately the ground shifted again. On the one hand, the judges' answer to the queries on 28 May led to Patrick Darcy's *Argument* of 9 June 1641. On the other hand, arguments about the relationship between the royal prerogative and the Irish executive were overshadowed by a row triggered by the willingness of the English Lords to entertain petitions relating to Ireland. By 5 August the Lords had given Charles the chance 'to pass the buck with distinction' and suspend passage of the 'Graces' while the matter of Ireland's dependency on England was resolved.[108] The 'instruments', along with Patrick Darcy's *Argument*, offered a constitutional framework within which they believed government in Ireland should be conducted. But whatever the future of this nascent constitutional tradition, the actual outcome, as Aidan Clarke has shown, was a stalemate.[109] By the summer of 1641, both the personnel and procedure of the Strafford administration were set aside, the crown prepared some concessions and withheld others and all the Irish parliament could do was strike attitudes.

---

[105] Lords justices to Vane, 18 May 1641, SP 63/259/15, *Cal. SP Ire.*, 1633–47, p. 288.

[106] *Commons' jn. Ire.*, p. 209.

[107] Perceval-Maxwell, *Outbreak*, p. 147; *Commons' jn. Ire.*, p. 213: 'the court of parliament of this kingdom has always had and ought to have full power and authority to hear and determine all treasons . . . within this realm and likewise to inflict condign punishment upon all offenders'.

[108] Russell, 'British background', 176. John Clotworthy also proposed in June that the Root and Branch bill should apply to Ireland: Clarke, 'The breakdown', pp. 285–7.

[109] Clarke, 'The breakdown', p. 286.

The Commons chose to act tough even as the community of interest between Old English and New English slowly dissolved. On 19 June they set up a committee to draw up particular charges, conferred with the Lords about procedure, and asked for sight of all privy council records from 1633 onwards while making the necessary arrangements for keeping any interrogatories and depositions secret.[110] Outwardly at least the lower house remained defiant, so when on 10 July the lords justices requested they forebear further proceedings against Bolton and Lowther they reacted by formally sending evidence concerning use of threats at the council board to the charges committee.[111] The castle omitted to mention Bramhall. The Commons, for their part, pressed on with petitions against him all through July. On 20 July eight members were sent up to ask the Lords not to 'admit of any bail to be taken for the bishop of Derry'. The chief business still remained the question of judicature. On 26 July the Commons produced a 'declaration' to the queries which began with the resounding words: 'the subjects of this his majesty's kingdom are a free people'. Parliament adjourned on 7 August. It reconvened on 9 November in the wake of the Ulster violence and so in a new political universe in Ireland in which the rebels claimed to have risen to defend the crown against the pretension of the English parliament. Effectively, the rising marked the end of action against Bramhall.[112] In June 1642 Bolton and Lowther's petition to the Commons for an end to proceedings against them was granted and they were restored to their offices. The Commons committee insisted they were still preparing particular charges against John Bramhall and George Radcliffe.[113] Even when Bramhall petitioned again in April 1644 and February 1645 the house was unmoved.[114] The Lords acquitted Radcliffe on 20 April 1644 and, finally, Bramhall on petition on 20 January 1645.[115] On 3 February 1645 the Commons curtly agreed to the suspension of further proceedings.[116]

Bramhall was fortunate that in both its origin and outcome impeachment had been affected by wider politics, because both his close association with

---

[110] *Commons' jn. Ire.*, p. 236, 19 June 1641, p. 238, 22 June 1641, p. 249, 7 July 1641.

[111] *Commons' jn. Ire.*, p. 254.

[112] The case of Henry Stewart, who had been imprisoned for refusing to take the Black Oath, blew up when the Scots required punishment of those who had gaoled him: Russell, 'British background', 176; Perceval-Maxwell, *Outbreak*, p. 153. This, in turn, caused the English House of Lords to summon the Irish privy council, bringing up the whole issue of whether the Westminster parliament had jurisdiction over Ireland. On 30 July 1641, Charles I wrote to Bramhall, PRONI T415 no. 26, to thank him for his efforts on behalf of Scottish refugees. In a letter to the Speakers of the Irish houses of parliament on 10 August 1641, *Cal. SP Ire.* 1633–47, p. 332, Charles suggested that if they were tender in their dealings with Bramhall and the two others it would help their case with him.

[113] *Commons' jn. Ire.*, p. 297.   [114] *Commons' jn. Ire.*, pp. 321, 337.

[115] *Lords' jn. Ire.*, pp. 203–4, 217.   [116] *Commons' jn. Ire.*, p. 337.

Strafford and the thoroughness and extent of his dealings during the 1630s left him utterly exposed. Furthermore, for Charles, who was juggling three kingdoms and so striving to reach a settlement with the Dublin parliament, the bishop was politically expendable. For the Irish parliament here was a living embodiment of their grievances. But although Bramhall's person was safe his projects were not.

Just like their English counterparts in the Buckingham case of 1626, the Irish Commons based their accusations upon 'common fame' and 'notoriety'. They also accepted and proceeded on particular petitions. In England the Lords experienced a sharp rise in demand for their judgement and by November 1640 individual cases threatened to choke parliament. In Ireland both the Commons (who had restricted themselves to matters of privilege in previous Stuart parliaments) and the Lords began to record petitions and carry out investigations via select committees. While the Christchurch petition against Bramhall had heralded his impeachment, there were only two petitions in the entire fourth session but between 20 May and 24 July 1641 forty-seven more were referred to the Derry committee.[117] A torrent commenced, and not just against him but also against the archbishop of Tuam and the bishops of Ardagh, Cloyne, Cork, Down and Connor, Elphin, Kildare, Meath and Raphoe as well as High Commission and the provost of Trinity College and assorted lower clergy who were not members of parliament. The great bulk of these were directed against Bramhall and most likely intended as material for the specific charges.[118] Since only the names of the complainants and complainee are listed it is hard to determine the nature of these cases. An order on a petition of Sir Robert Piggott and Sir John Piggott against Jonathan Hoyle, clerk, does survive.[119] The Commons overturned a decision made at the council board on two rectories in Queen's county on the grounds that a deed made by Sir Robert had been procured from him, 'partly by promises of compensation' and 'partly by the menaces of the late lord lieutenant'. This was not a very benign reading of the temporalities campaign, but it was not

---

[117] Forty before it became 'the earl of Kildare and bishop of Derry' committee on 15 July, *Commons' jn. Ire.*, p. 258. Not all of the petitions would have been aimed at Bramhall in person, but the fact that a separate committee for ecclesiastical causes did exist (*Commons' jn. Ire.*, p. 237) and that a lot of other petitions against bishops were not referred to the Derry committee suggests that what ended up in that committee was either directed at him in name or that he was concerned in a large way with it.

[118] On 4 June 1641, the Commons ordered that the bishop of Derry should have no copies of the petitions against him, *Commons' jn. Ire.*, p. 221. A list of members of the 'lord of Derry's committee' in the Commons journal for 10 June shows it was a fairly balanced affair, being composed of sixteen Protestants and ten Catholics, *Commons' jn. Ire.*, p. 230.

[119] *Commons' jn. Ire.*, p. 251, 10 July 1641.

a wholly inaccurate one. Another petition by Thomas Davells, referred to the Derry committee on 6 July 1641, for which Samuel Mosley, clerk, was summoned to appear, is probably related to a case which came before the lord deputy and council on 17 September 1634 when Mosley complained that Davells had usurped the tithes of his rectory of Clonmulske in the diocese of Leighlin. Upon reference from the board, Bramhall found for the rector.[120] These two cases are a hint that many, maybe the majority, of petitions in the summer of 1641 aimed to overturn decisions made at the council board.

By the middle of July the pressure on Bramhall was mounting. The clerk of the Commons was ordered on 16 July to make a schedule of the petitions exhibited against Derry to be presented to the house and transmitted to the Lords.[121] On 29 July, sixteen days after the Commons requested them to do so, the Lords ordered Bramhall to begin answering.[122] The flow of petitions, then, wholly occupied the Commons in the ten days that followed their declaration of 26 July. Even after the grand constitutional strategy peaked, the far less lofty business of pulling Bramhall's works apart piece by piece continued unabated.

Reconstruction was reversed over May, June and July 1641 as petitioning pressure coupled with the crown's need to make concessions opened up the way for legal overturn of nearly all lands resumed since 1634. There was not even a whisper against the 1634–5 legislation because it was in parliament's interest to insist on what it defined as correct use of statute rather than push for erasure of previous acts. During May, the Irish committees in London plugged away at the forty-four grievances. As they bargained, they opened up a possibility of a more decisive strike against the church temporalities than that afforded by petitioning. In a reply to the Irish committee of the English privy council, the Irish parliamentary committees in London went so far as to depict resolutions on paper petitions as tending towards a revival of Gaelic practices. They pushed for blanket restoration of those who had lost lands by this means since 8 Charles I, 'leaving the church the ordinary legal remedy'.[123] Naturally this bid to set almost all of Bramhall's labours aside at once was a bargaining position predicated on particular antipathy to the temporalities programme as well as a desire to attack the

---

[120] *Commons' jn. Ire.*, p. 248; BL Harl. MS 4297, p. 97.

[121] *Commons' jn. Ire.*, pp. 246, 259.

[122] While the Lords were both wary and tardy in compelling the bishops of Cork and Down and Connor to answer, they did order Derry to start responding to the 'foulest' of them on 29 July 1641, *Commons' jn. Ire.*, p. 276.

[123] SP 63/259/6, *Cal. SP Ire. 1633–47*, p. 284.

chief governor's prerogative.[124] On 17 May the Irish committees offered a suitably modified resolution to the English council. Those aggrieved 'by the extra-judicial proceedings of the church in Ireland may prosecute their suits against the church in any court of justice or equity there'. Charles duly incorporated the resolution in his formal answer to the Irish parliament on 16 July though wisely left 'extrajudicial' undefined.[125]

Throughout June and July other acts of Strafford's ecclesiastical administration came under scrutiny or were reversed. The king wrote to the lords justices revoking the deposition of Archibald Adair and appointing him to Waterford and Lismore.[126] The Commons voted all acts of William Chappell since he became provost of Trinity 'great grievances, and fit to receive redress' and formed a committee, as we have seen, to draw up a charge against High Commission.[127] Henry Stewart and his family were released from Dublin Castle and the Commons signified to the Lords that they believed Leslie of Raphoe 'had run into praemunire' for arresting Isabella Pont.[128] Around mid June, the Ulster petition against episcopacy in thirty-one heads was presented to the English Commons, decrying 'manifold evils and heavy pressures caused and occasioned by prelacy and their dependants'.[129] As Robert Armstrong has remarked, the pamphlet combined 'puritan and pecuniary' strands of complaint and overlapped with the grievances presented by parliament. It devoted considerable attention to the 1634 canons as the chief means by which godly preaching had been suppressed and overtaken by 'many corruptions in the worship of God and government of the church, which exceedingly retarded the work of reformation to true Protestant religion, animated papists, and made way for divers superstitions'.[130] This line of complaint, coming as it did in the wake of the 1640 canons, joined powerfully with English concerns. More locally, but equally resonantly, the resumption campaign was presented both as rapine by arrogant clerics and as deeply damaging to English and Scottish planters.[131]

---

[124] See also threat to the church in a further reply of the Irish committees, SP 63/259/9, *Cal. SP Ire. 1633–47*, p. 286: 'Freeholds should be set up in Ulster on the bishops' lands, in order that there be resident persons of quality there, and strong buildings for defence.'

[125] Draft is in SP 63/259/13, *Cal. SP Ire. 1633–47*, p. 287. The king's answer is in SP 63/260/1, *Cal. SP Ire. 1633–47*, p. 318.

[126] 7 June 1641, *Cal. SP Ire. 1633–47*, p. 300; Gilbert MS 169, 224; SO 3/12.

[127] *Commons' jn. Ire.*, p. 228, 8 June 1641.   [128] *Commons' jn. Ire.*, p. 246, 3 July 1641.

[129] *Humble petition*, p. 3; Perceval-Maxwell, *Outbreak*, pp. 114–15; Clarke, 'The breakdown', pp. 284–5.

[130] *Humble petition*, p. 3; Armstrong, 'Ireland's puritan revolution?'

[131] The repair of the 'material' church was dismissed as rapine: 'under colour of church lands they have impiously seized into their hands much of the best lands in every county, so that there is scarce a gentleman of any worth, whom they have not bereaved of some part of his inheritance', *Humble*

On 30 June the Commons voted a decree of the Irish council against the earl of Kildare at the suit of Leslie of Down and Connor for some townlands in Co. Down to have been 'extrajudicial and contrary to the Great Charter and void in law and vacated'.[132] They ordered Kildare to be restored and compensated immediately and awarded damages. This action effectively ensured that there would be strong pressure to interpret the king's concession of recourse grounded on 'extrajudicial' proceedings in one direction.

Sensing danger on all sides, convocation petitioned the lords justices in mid June.[133] While they started off by complaining about the spate of prosecutions against clergyman for collecting tithes, they rapidly moved on to express their anxiety at parliament's apparent desire to annul all orders for church lands on the basis of paper petitions. They vigorously defended the legality of such determinations on grounds of the 1622 instructions and claimed that there had been many orderly and amicable arbitrations despite claims to the contrary. Furthermore, there had been many compositions and many orders had been 'pursuant to an Act of parliament'. The archbishops of Dublin, Tuam, as well as Clogher, Clonfert, Raphoe, Kilmore, Killala, Down and Connor, Kilfenora and Cloyne and Dean Edward Parry of Waterford all signed the petition.[134] These were no Bramhallian 'rump' but took in the whole spectrum stretching from a protégé like Henry Leslie to a maverick such as Bedell across to an 'old-style' Church of Ireland bishop like Spottiswood. The clerical estate sought to defend the temporal gains made since 1633 despite the fact that some of them would have regarded the past eight years as otherwise quite black ones.

Episcopal solidarity against parliament did not extend as far as a defence of the temporising treatment of Catholics. Drawing on the same vocabulary as Clotworthy and the Ulster petitioners, the bishops prefaced their defence of reconstruction by cataloguing the apparent failure of a phased approach to recusancy. They deplored the temerity of the 'swarms of popish priests and friars no longer contented with his majesty's gracious connivance' in their exercise of a 'foreign jurisdiction'. 'The truth', they warned was 'now

---

petition, p. 11. They also turned the campaign against simony on its head: 'they have frequently made simonical pactions and bargains in the conferring of benefices, and ordinarily permit ministers to exchange their livings, thereby to nullify leases of tithes, which the former incumbent ministers have let at certain terms', *Humble petition*, p. 7.

[132] *Commons' jn. Ire.*, p. 241.

[133] SP 63/274/ 44 and 45, *Cal. SP Ire.* 1647–60, pp. 254–8. Dated sometime before 30 June, lords justices and council to secretary Vane, SP 63/259/44, *Cal. SP Ire.* 1633–47, p. 307.

[134] Bulkeley, Richard Boyle, Spottiswood, Dawson, John Leslie, Bedell, Maxwell, Henry Leslie, Sibthorpe and Synge respectively.

in great danger'. Here were voices that had been muted for almost a decade taking the opportunity to raise themselves again in the hope of returning to the *status quo ante* of an anti-Catholic consensus.[135] The mixture of concerns in the petition – anxiety for the new temporal settlement and alarm at the fruits of toleration – reflected the quandary in which the Irish episcopate found itself. They were trying to prop up an ecclesiastical land settlement of which the chief agent was impeached and which most members of parliament had marked out as the prime product of Strafford's misrule. In addition, like their English and Scottish counterparts, they found themselves denounced as Rome roaders and persecutors of the reformed.[136] In summer 1641 the Irish hierarchy had no political influence to offer and it had no allies. The resumption campaign of the 1630s cut the cords that had bound churchmen to the Protestant gentry. The bishops and clergy had watched Bramhall and his assistants tear up the 'social contract' of Irish settler Protestantism.[137]

On 16 July negotiations in London culminated in a set of royal concessions which were dispatched to Dublin at the close of the month along with the bills of grace transmitted the previous April. This caused the lords justices to move for prorogation on 7 August for fear that concessionary legislation would be passed before parliament compensated the king for loss of revenue in the form of two additional subsidies.[138] The response to the church grievances was a mixture of stalling and concession. Conciliar decisions on church lands might be brought into the ambit of the ordinary courts, especially given the earl of Kildare case of 30 June. High Commission was suspended. 'The exorbitant and barbarous customs' of the clergy would be subject to a bill after appropriate evidence had been gathered by

---

[135] In that context, two printings of the *Protestation of the archbishops and bishops of Ireland* of 1626 in 1641 was especially apt. One of these (BL Thomason tracts E.171[11]) carried a note to the reader explaining that the protestation proved that bishops were no Laodiceans and, far from endlessly complying with bad law, had laboured 'against the stream'. Indeed the omission of those twelve names in the 1626 original (*UWW* I, pp. 73–4) made it look like a new statement from the entire Irish episcopate. In a supporting set of 'declarations', Andrews of Ferns and Leighlin, Dawson of Clonfert and Sibthorpe of Kilfenora catalogued the spread of Catholic jurisdiction, schools, the re-establishment of religious houses and all the consequent drain of revenue, SP 63/274/47-9, *Cal. SP Ire.* 1647–60, pp. 257–8.

[136] *Humble petition*, p. 7: 'The most learned and seemingly moderate and pious of the prelates, publicly in sermons at Dublin, exclaimed against, and condemned the Scottish Covenant and religion professed in that kingdom with most invective terms.'

[137] This is not to claim that there were no disputes between clergy and laity before 1633 over church lands because of course there were. It was the methods, and the assumptions lying behind those methods about the role of the clergy in society, and the thoroughness of the resumption programme that really divided the clergy and laity.

[138] Perceval-Maxwell, *Outbreak*, pp. 153–4; Clarke, 'The breakdown', p. 287.

the castle from the Irish parliament on condition that clergy would not lose any legitimate income as a consequence.[139] This looks like an attempt to shield the Irish church from parliamentary enthusiasm for lightening the tithe burden under the guise of weeding out old abuses. While the English Commons moved in spring 1641 to expand a clerical disabilities bill out to exclude bishops from parliament, the Irish assembly contented itself with a ban on clerks serving as justices of the peace.[140]

Signs from Ulster in July and early August indicate that there would have been sustained pressure from that quarter to push harder on ecclesiastical grievances. On 20 July the Commons professed themselves scandalised at non-payment of tithes in the wake of 'proceedings in this house against certain barbarous customs used in some parts of this realm'.[141] On 4 August they ordered duties payable to parish clerks and ministers in Ulster not voted as grievances to be duly paid.[142] This 'tithe strike' can partly be explained as a response to economic hardship, but when taken with the anti-episcopal petitions and the rancour aroused by the Black Oath it is reasonable to speculate that Protestant opinion there would not have been assuaged by the July concessions.[143] On 7 August the Commons entered their list of a dozen reasons why High Commission tended 'to the subversion of the fundamental laws and statutes of the kingdom'.[144]

Twelve days later, Thomas Tempest, the Irish attorney general, wrote to Lord Keeper Littleton about affairs in Dublin, mentioning petitions about episcopal possessions which had been entertained in the Lords.[145] He explained that James I's printed directions of 1622 were now being 'conceived' to be illegal.[146] For Tempest this was just one part of a great spate of litigation and constitutional uncertainty that threatened to choke up the legal system entirely. For the church, though, a near total collapse of revenues by legal challenge and non-payment of tithes and dues loomed very

---

[139] SP 63/260/1, *Cal. SP Ire.* 1633–47, pp. 318–22.

[140] Russell, *Fall of the British monarchies*, pp. 277, 342. A proposal that freeholds might be permitted on episcopal lands in the Ulster plantation was not granted, SP 63/260/1, *Cal. SP Ire.* 1633–47, p. 322.

[141] *Commons' jn. Ire.*, p. 263.   [142] *Commons' jn. Ire.*, p. 281.

[143] Bramhall to Wandesforde on the bad harvest, 16 April 1640, HA 14059; Raymond Gillespie, 'The end of an era: Ulster and the outbreak of the 1641 rising' in Ciaran Brady and Raymond Gillespie (eds.), *Natives and newcomers* (Dublin 1986), pp. 204–48.

[144] *Commons' jn. Ire.*, p. 286.

[145] SP 63/260/6 *Cal. SP Ire.* 1633–47, pp. 332–3.

[146] G. J. Hand and V. W. Treadwell (eds.), 'His Majesty's directions for the ordering and settling of the courts and the course of justice within his kingdom of Ireland', *Analecta Hibernica* 26 (1970), 190: 'And that neither the Lord deputy, Governors nor Council table, do hereafter intermeddle or trouble themselves with common business that is within the cognizance of the ordinary courts . . . causes recommended from the Council table of England, and special causes concerning the Church, excepted.' Tempest was, in fact, pretty certain that a crisis could be averted by good legal argument.

large. So by summer 1641 reconstruction was not just halted but actually in reverse. As it turned out, the outbreak of violence three months later set in motion a chain of events which led to an entirely different kind of collapse.

Early in 1642, according to Vesey, Bramhall was quietly released without acquittal.[147] He returned to Derry but, encountering hostility there, left for England and Yorkshire where he attached himself to the marquis of Newcastle.[148] After Marston Moor he went into exile on the continent. After Laud's execution in 1645 he was the sole survivor of the triumvirate who had controlled Irish church policy during the 1630s. Reconstruction was utterly bound up with the relationship between the archbishop of Canterbury, the lord deputy and the bishop of Derry. This arrangement worked well as long as they were able to reinforce each other, but once influence was lost all of their achievements were unshielded. The Irish parliament of 1640–1 did not, indeed could not, strike at the statutory and canonical heart of their programme. Instead it sought to blunt and then break the instruments which had made that programme so effective – personality, prerogative and private composition. Political interaction across both islands, especially the initial cooperation between Dublin and Westminster, made this endeavour successful. Simultaneously, the Irish application of a plan for enhanced religious conformity to an established church served by a resurgent clergy in all the Stuart realms was paraded as evidence of a popishly induced religious tyranny. Old fears and new anxieties combined to dismantle the recent Irish church settlement and made it part of the transformation of the religious settlement in the three kingdoms.

[147] Vesey, *Athanasius Hibernicus*, [p. 26].
[148] He preached at York minster on 28 January 1644, *BW* V, pp. 87–110.

CHAPTER 7

Conclusion: reconstruction as reformation

For my care of this church, the reducing of it into order, the upholding
of the external worship of God in it, and the settling of it to the rules
of its first reformation[1]

William Laud, *Speech at committal of Prynne, Burton and Bastwick*

I make not the least doubt in the world but that the Church of
England before the reformation and the Church of England after
the reformation are as much the same church as a garden before it is
weeded and after it is weeded is the same garden.[2]

John Bramhall, *A just vindication of the Church of England*

The English reformation failed to make Ireland Protestant. The reconstruction of the Church of Ireland failed because it was a variant of a
reconstruction of the Church of England. Once again in the 1630s, Ireland's
failure to be or to become England was at the heart of the matter.

The programme of reconstruction carried out from 1633 to 1640 came
close to being a refoundation of the established church in Ireland. It was
ambitious and it was vigorous and the lord deputy, the lord archbishop
of Canterbury and the lord bishop of Derry worked on it with energy
and determination. Everything they did concerned itself with the visible
church. There were the new canons, acts of state, statutes, and even another
formulary. Dublin's Christchurch cathedral was reordered to begin with,
and then there was a viceregal visitation which was intended to stimulate
improvement in ecclesiastical revenues that would eventually lead to the
repair and restoration of the entire network of cathedral and parochial
churches. A new corps of conformist ministers was scheduled to serve
inside the newly refurbished buildings. The new Irish canons would require
these clerics to subscribe to the proposition that reformation was full and
complete. For both Laud and Bramhall, repair of the 'material' encompassed

---

[1] *WL* 6, p. 42.   [2] *BW* I, p. 113.

the concomitant repair of the 'spiritual' church. For his part, Wentworth was happy to support an enhanced conformity which was explicitly intended to stimulate and enhance the authority of the crown. As the chief governor first wished to make Ireland pay for itself and then proceed to generate a surplus, he was keen to endorse a plan for the established church which ran along exactly parallel lines. First the Church of Ireland would be made capable of maintaining a resident and socially respected clergy in every single diocese and then it would be able to bring in the extra souls.

Several chapters of this book have shown that financial overhaul and outward forms of worship were given relentless scrutiny from 1633 up to the end of the decade. It is clear from their correspondence that the three main promoters of reconstruction genuinely relished their task. The degree to which that enjoyment sprang from self-interest or political pride or the degree to which they showed a vision of a new ecclesiastical order varied from one to another and fluctuated over time. In a sense, whether they were spurred on by 'thorough' or 'Laudianism' or any ideology or strategy is less important than the fact that the headiness of the first three or four years allowed Laud, Bramhall and Wentworth consciously to suppress any sense of the resentment or anxiety their very vigour was causing. Three interest groups were very explicitly dismissed by the three men during the 1630s. They are important because even if events had not unfolded as they did in 1640–1 these constituencies would have had a considerable impact on the reconstruction scheme over the longer term no matter who was at the helm.

The first group consisted of the bishops and clergy of the Church of Ireland itself. They found themselves faced with a perplexing combination of an alluring temporalities programme with a disquieting practical theology. Opposition to the Laudian ecclesiology promoted by Dublin Castle and to the new embryonic clerical clique manifested itself quite openly during convocation. Ussher's disgruntlement was quite marked and his high reputation across all three kingdoms was certainly instrumental in ensuring that Ireland developed a new code of canons rather than importing Bancroft's 1603 code wholesale. In the end, though, while there were some consolations for the primate and his supporters in the new book, Ireland was given a settlement of a kind that in England could only find expression in some visitation articles and some individual actions of ordinaries. What was a tendency in the Church of England was the national code in the Church of Ireland. While later claims for double subscription to the Irish articles and the Thirty-Nine articles may have been a self-consolatory myth of writers during the 1650s, it is true that there was some leeway during the 1630s in regard to some of the more ceremonialist flourishes in the new code. Nonetheless the 1634 book was there to be built upon. Simultaneously the incumbent ministers discovered they were being given every encouragement to pursue recovery of lands and revenues on the basis of a historically driven concept of their rights. This economic counterpart to belief in continuous visible succession in the church did not spring primarily from an impulse to promote conformity amongst Irish recusants. It was easy to argue that it was so, and this Wentworth and Bramhall did with gusto, but at its Laudian root it was of a piece with contemporaneous schemes for revocation and resumption in England, Wales and Scotland. Irish clergy of all hues supported the temporalities scheme for its outcomes despite many misgivings about the manner in which Laudian writers and preachers appeared to have abandoned traditional lines of attack and defence against the Roman Antichrist.

The temporalities campaign was not supported by the landowners of Ireland. While their opposition was easily dismissed by Wentworth and Bramhall as the chagrin of people whose peculation was being exposed, they were, nonetheless, a grouping with infinitely more political clout than the established clergy. Wentworth knew this and experienced it firsthand in his dealings with Richard Boyle and in the Connacht plantation. Historians have long recognised that the chief governor's land policy was one of the things which eventually precipitated a temporary alliance between Catholic and Protestant interests. His pronounced insistence on the primacy of the crown's interests led him into zesty prosecution of many wealthy figures. His enemies, in turn, were able to insist that he had actually usurped the authority of the crown. Aggressive re-endowment of the church was backed by a use of prerogative instruments similar to those deployed in his plantation and in other land schemes. It also drew on the theological trope of sacrilege. This particular notion of sacrilege, again found elsewhere in the three kingdoms, was closely tied to notions of the visibility and continuity of the church along with its first cousin *jure divino*, episcopacy. Members of the Dublin and Westminster parliaments countered sacrilege with a charge of arbitrary government which easily allowed Old English, Gaelic Irish, Scots and New English men of property to suppress their differences in the winter of 1640.

John Bramhall's Christchurch sermon of August 1633 declared Rome 'merely' schismatical and the pope a patriarch. However shocking this may have been to his Dublin auditory, his words were part of a wider process of displacement of the Roman Antichrist. George Abbott and James Ussher's godly remnants – Waldensians, Cathars and Lollards – were giving way to

John Bramhall and William Laud's mitred apostolic succession lists in a significant switch from eschatology to institutional history. This lowering of the theological temperature should have been good news to the third Irish grouping, the Old English Catholics. It was certainly intended to be so. In England Richard Neile, amongst others, placed renewed emphasis on recusancy and it is fair to say there is a sense in which the renewed emphasis on liturgical order and hierarchy was intended to catch Catholic attention and even gain affection. In Ireland conditions were quite different. Recusants were no minority who could be assessed as ripe for comprehension within a vigorously episcopal church. An emergent Anglican vision of judicious tradition certainly informed the Irish reconstruction, but the message instantly succumbed to circumstances. Events in convocation in 1634–5, followed by a new High Commission in 1636, along with the castle's tinkering in the feud between seculars and regulars, only served to deepen Old English resentment at the shelving of the Graces. Catholics were looking for toleration rather than an invitation to conformity. Crisp administration of ecclesiastical justice turned inwards on the Church of Ireland itself which, in turn, stimulated a fresh Scottish Protestant recusancy in the period following the National Covenant. The imported style of the 1630s allowed many Church of Ireland clergy themselves to recast the years between 1615 and 1633 as a minor 'golden age'. This was the kind of sentiment reflected in Theophilus Buckworth's outburst against Laud and in Ussher's trenchant reference after convocation to standing by 'the purity of our ancient truth'. It is also found in a swift return to comforting anti-popery in Irish episcopal petitions of 1640. The idea of good old days in the Church of Ireland under the government of godly bishops, which Nicholas Bernard promoted so vigorously in his pamphlets of the 1640s and 1650s, found early printed expression in an anonymous annotation to a 1641 reprint of the 1626 Irish declaration against toleration:

This declaration of the bishops of Ireland against popery, howsoever fifteen years ago, is now thought fit to be further published. If thou shalt hear the whole order taxed with a continual complying with the times, here thou shalt find them labouring against the stream . . . if Laodicean like, of lukewarmness in religion; here thou findest their zeal burning.[3]

Bramhall, Wentworth and Laud scoffed at or ignored the reactions of all three groupings – incumbent Church of Ireland clergy, landowners and the Old English interest – in their pursuit of reconstruction. Behind the brittle rhetoric there was a reality of compromise, incompleteness and limits. This

---

[3] BL Thomason E171 [11].

is inevitable in any political endeavour but their inability to admit, even to themselves, that their quest for this variety of more and better anglicisation was fraught with difficulty and productive of unintended consequences is of some significance. Thomas Wentworth is well known as a highly self-conscious correspondent whose distance from court made him more than usually jealous of his reputation. He was touchy and controlling. William Laud was touchy and insecure. They needed each other and were careful to present Charles with a unified account of Church of Ireland affairs. Bramhall's relation to the other two was as client and enforcer. Whenever he was critical it was always of the approved butts – Catholic clergy, unconforming Protestants, covetous landlords, corrupt bishops and deans – but never of either of his patrons to the other or of reconstruction itself. The nature of relations between the three men is important because between them they conceived of, shaped, promoted and enforced the entire process of reconstruction. This had two main consequences. First, their attitudes were mutually reinforcing. For instance, Wentworth wished to please and flatter Laud so he accepted the archbishop's ecclesiology and its attendant strategy in its entirety. Whether he was sincere in all of this is less important than knowing he made almost no attempt to instruct Laud on the particulars of the Irish situation. Any information he gave tended to confirm Canterbury's analysis. John Bramhall, whose main work was ecclesiastical affairs, did give somewhat more detail in his letters to Lambeth Palace but he supported a Laudian overhaul of the establishment without waiver or demur. It took all the pressure of the crisis in Scotland for the two bishops to have their first strategic disagreement over the suitability of Ireland as a venue for Scottish Episcopalian refugees. Compromise or modification could never be explicitly mentioned. The second consequence was that their authority was mutually reinforcing. Naturally the formal powers of the archbishop and lord deputy were quite considerable. Bramhall, though, was a youthful bishop of Derry, a recent appointee, who carried out his tasks on commission and who never became a privy councillor. Reconstruction worked so well because it was so personalised. Bishops, estate owners, corporations and tithe farmers alike knew that Derry had not only the ear of the castle but also the viceroy's total support. The bishop's reputation as an Irish Canterbury rested not just on the similarity of his churchmanship to Laud's but also on his status as a valued protégé. Once the newly created earl of Strafford ran foul of parliament, and before any explicit push in Ireland against recent settlements, the entire project was in deep trouble.

All three men were arraigned for treason but only John Bramhall died in his bed. His posthumous reputation has rested on his pamphlet war with Hobbes. Jeremy Taylor's reworking of him as an Anglican 'father' linking Lancelot Andrewes to the Restoration divines has been highly effective. It, too, rests on his writings while in continental exile. His first Irish career, whether recalled by post-Restoration writers or by nineteenth-century Anglo-Catholics, has either been presented as a prelude to the indignities and struggles of the exile years or suitably sanitised for a self-consciously Anglican readership. John Vesey was the first to do this in his 1676 biography in which Wentworth and Bramhall are the Castor and Pollux of Charles I's Ireland and where Armagh and Derry are the Peter and Paul of the Church of Ireland. The man himself took a different view and regarded the 1630s as one of the most dynamic periods of his life. His rather brief primacy during 1660–3 was marked by strenuous efforts to turn the clock back three decades. Just one month before his death from a stroke, Bramhall finally received a long-solicited mandate for a royal visitation which was intended to assist the composition of a definitive book of taxations of ecclesiastical livings in Ireland. His career ended, then, with a proposed return to his earliest Irish activity.

Bramhall's first journey into Ulster during the winter of 1634 was echoed by what he dubbed his 'northern visitation' of August 1661. Where he had found the 'ebullition of Scotland' twenty-seven years earlier, he now found Ulster Scots Presbyterians.[4] These same Presbyterians had in the mean-time come to a historical understanding of the 1630s which provided their nascent church with a suitable foundation narrative. While the accuracy of that tradition has been challenged here, it does reflect very well one key impact of the reconstruction programme: the deep fears it aroused. One of the themes of this book has been the ambitious manner in which a resurgent clericalism, whether economically or canonically expressed, was implemented in Ireland. William Laud loved it and John Bramhall loved delivering it. Much was actually done in Ireland that could only be contemplated in England and Scotland. Paradoxically, Ireland, the most Catholic of the Stuart realms, was for seven years the place where many of the most radical aspects of the Laudian vision were introduced. For Laud's opponents the Church of Ireland became a shocking inverse of what it had been for some English MPs in 1626 and 1628. Then it had been a hefty stick composed of 101 articles to beat alleged Arminians and Romanisers, but as the 1630s wore on the Irish church took on a far more sinister aspect. It appeared to bear two hallmarks of popish plotting. First, the 1634 convocation could

---

[4] Bramhall to Laud, 20 December 1634, Shirley, p. 41; Bramhall to Sir Edward Nicholas, 16 September 1661, *Cal. SP Ire.* 1660–2, p. 425.

be interpreted as a coup against the clear identification of Antichrist in the 1615 articles. Second, the canons that enjoined the replacing of all altars and the encouragement of auricular confession were alarming in themselves and still more so when followed up by the Scottish canons and Prayer Book in quick succession. Accordingly, the Ulster anti-episcopacy petition of June 1641 was able to make a perfect equation of conformity and corruption. Ireland, bright hope of Laudianism in the 1630s, became instead a stormy petrel for godly British subjects.

BIBLIOGRAPHY

MANUSCRIPTS

DUBLIN

Trinity College

545 Ussher to John Spelman, Sept 1639
550 1622 visitation
551 Table of procurations for Meath, seventeenth century
580 Letters concerning the church, 1620–3
582 Instructions for the church, 1620; Ussher's notes on the primacy dispute
672 Various papers – Ireland seventeenth century
806 Report on the church, 1648
808 1622 commission
842 Speech by Ussher at Dublin Castle, 1627
853 Various documents, reign of James I
865 A brief narration concerning the primacy dispute
1038 Convocation journals, Dean Andrews on the canons
1040 Valuations, ministers, schoolmasters late 1640s; fragment of Derry visitation
1062 Bishop Reeves's notes on convocation
1066 The college of Youghal 1615
1067 1634 visitation
1073 Bishop Reeves's annotated Elrington *UWW*
1120 Bishop Reeves's interleaved copy of Ware's 'Bishops'
1188 Archbishop Hamilton on state of religion, 1626
1697 Bishop Reeves's notes on Shirley, *Documents*
2158 1634 visitation (eighteenth-century transcript)
3659 Ussher to Spelman 4 Sept 1639 (copy from Pierpoint Morgan Library, New York)

Marsh's Library

Z3.1.3 1622 visitation; orders and directions for the Church of Ireland, 1623
Z3.2.5 Extracts from parliamentary journals, 1640–1

Z3.2.6	Bramhall to Charles Vaughan, 12 Dec 1639
Z4.2.1	High Commission proceedings and fragments
Z4.2.6	Royal grants in Ireland, 1604–31

Representative Church Body Library

61.4	Derry (?1622)
61.4.1	J. B. Leslie's biographical index of clergy
92	Armagh and Dromore 1622
150	R. B. Phair, notes on seventeenth-century visitations
C2.14.2.34	Bramhall's report on Ossory lands, 1638
C6.26.13	Bramhall report on Christchurch lands, ?1637
Gs2.7.3.8	Calendar of Armagh Registry
Gs2.7.3.20	St John Seymour's notes on church in 1640s and 1650s
Gs2.7.3.24	Endowments of Meath bishopric; Ossory 1622
Gs2.7.3.25	Clogher 1622 and 1634
Gs2.7.3.27	Down, Connor and Dromore 1616
Gs2.7.3.31	'The diocese of Derry as of old', copied 1666
Gs2.7.3.33	Armagh see leases

National Archives of Ireland

2/444/33	Index of patents, Charles I
2/446/19	Calendar of Inquisitions, James I and Charles I
2/446/20	Chancery pleadings, Charles I
2/446/22	Calendar of presentations, Charles I
2/446/34	Calendar patents, 1634–5
2/448/12	Christchurch deeds MS calendar
2/448/13	Christchurch deeds, misc.
2/448/16	Lodge records of the rolls, 1634–8
2/448/22	Acta Regia Hibernica

Gilbert Library, Pearse St

| 169 | Sir James Ware's 'Diary of occurrences' |

BELFAST
Public Record Office of Northern Ireland

| Dio 4/5/1–8 | Archive of material relating to Armagh diocese assembled by Primate Robinson and John Lodge |
| T415 | Typescript copy of letters presented by Miss E. Berwick |

EDINBURGH
University archives

D c 4 16	Concerning certaine incendiaries of the Scottish nation in Ireland
Laing III 536	A conference between Dr Leslie Bishop of Downe and Dr Bramhall Bishop of Derrie . . . and the Revd Mr James Hamilton . . . held August 11th 1636

LONDON
British Library
Additional

4756	Entry book of 1622 commissioners
15,856	Catalogue of bishoprics in Ireland . . . 1655
19,831	Documents relating to Richard Boyle
19,832	Earl of Cork correspondence, 1633–44
34,253	Ussher's evidence to the House of Lords, 1641
38,492	Treatise on toleration of ceremonies (?Bedell)

Harleian

4297	Council order book, 1634

Sloane

1012	Extracts from Bramhall on liberty and necessity
1015	List of privy councillors under Wentworth (fol. 21r)
1449	The church history of Ireland
2681	Petition of Sir Maurice Williams (p. 268)
3827	Correspondence of Falkland on Irish affairs, 1604–32
3838	A short view of the state of Ireland from 1640

Duchy of Cornwall Office, Buckingham Gate

Bound MS	Political tracts and treatises: subsidies and the Irish grievances, 1640–1

Public Record Office

SP63	State Papers, Ireland
SO1/2	Signet Office

SHEFFIELD

Sheffield City Libraries

Str P

I	Letterbook of Wentworth's correspondence as lord deputy prior to arrival in Ireland, Jan 1632–Dec 1632
3	Correspondence with Charles I, Cottington and Weston, June 1633–Apr 1640
4	Royal letters under signet, Feb 1632–Aug 1638
5	Letterbook of correspondence with royal secretaries
6	Wentworth–Laud correspondence, Nov 1633–Nov 1636
7	Wentworth–Laud correspondence, Nov 1636–May 1639
8	Misc correspondence, May 1633–Mar 1636
10–19	Guard books of letters and papers, 1630–40
20	Church affairs
24–25	Miscellaneous state papers

CAMBRIDGE

Cambridge University Library

Add 4344	Disputation between Bishop Leslie and the presbyterians, 1636

OXFORD

Bodleian Library

Additional

C286	Letters of Wandesforde to Wentworth, 1636–40
	Carte 1, 64, 65, 66, 67, 176

Rawlinson

B479	Collectanea varii Jacobi Waraei
C439	Council petition book, 1636
D320	Bramhall's conference at North Allerton
Letters, 57	Life of Henry Leslie

Sancroft

18	Ussher letters

USA

Henry E. Huntington Library, San Marino, California

Hastings

Irish papers   Boxes 5–8, unsorted material, 1623–41
HA 14037–80   Bramhall correspondence and papers, 1633–62
HA 15153–73   Laud–Bramhall correspondence, Aug 1633–Jan 1641
HA 15948–60   Ussher–Bramhall correpondence, Jan 1634–Mar 1645

CONTEMPORARY BOOKS AND PAMPHLETS, MODERN EDITIONS AND PRINTED PRIMARY SOURCES

Adair, Patrick, *A true narrative of the rise and progress of the Presbyterian Church in Ireland 1623 to 1670*, ed. W. D. Killen (Belfast, 1866).

Ainsworth, J. F. and McLysaght, Edward (eds.), 'Survey of documents in private keeping, 2nd series – the Colclough Papers', *Analecta Hibernica* 20 (1958), 3–13.

Alexander, A. F., 'The O' Kane papers', *Analecta Hibernica* 26 (1970), 67–127.

Andrewes, Lancelot, *XCVI sermons* (1629).

Anon., *The case of John Atherton, bishop of Waterford in Ireland, who was convicted of the sin of uncleanness with a cow* (1641).

The life and death of John Atherton, lord bishop of Waterford & Lismore . . . who for incest, buggery and many enormous crimes . . . (1641).

Anon. (ed.), 'After the death of Queen Elizabeth', *Duffy's Irish Catholic Magazine* (Nov. 1848), 270–5; (Dec. 1848), 296–302.

Articles given in charge to be inquired upon and presented to, by the church wardens (Dublin, 1626).

Articles to be inquired of church wardens in the Lord Primates Visitation Metropoliticall, 1629 (Dublin, 1629).

Articles of religion agreed upon by the Archbishops and Bishops and the rest of the clergie of Ireland (Dublin, 1615).

Articles given in charge to be inquired upon and presented to, by church wardens. . . . Christopher [Hampton] (Dublin, 1623).

Articles to be inquired of by the church wardens . . . George, lord bishop of Cloyne (Dublin, 1639).

Articles to be inquired of by the church wardens . . . Lord Primate's visistation metropolitical (Dublin, 1640).

Baillie, Robert, *Ladensium ΑΥΤΟΚΑΤΑΚΡΙΣΙΣ, the Canterburian's self-conviction* (Edinburgh, 1640).

Letters and journals, 1637–1662, ed. D. Laing, 3 vols. (Edinburgh, 1841).

Barksdale, Clement, *Remembrance of excellent men* (1670).

Barlow, William, *Sum and substance of the conference . . . at Hampton Court* (1638)

Barnard, John, *Theologo-Historicus or The true life of . . . Peter Heylyn D.D.*, 3rd edn (1683).

B. B. [Robert Rochford], *The life of the glorious S. Patricke apostle and primate together with the lives of the holy virgin S. Bridgit and of the glorious abbot Saint Columbe, Patrons of Ireland* (St Omer, 1625).

B. E., *Curse of Sacrilege* (Oxford, 1630).

Bernard, Nicholas, *The penitent death of a woeful sinner* (1642).

The life and death of the most reverend and learned father of our church Dr James Ussher (1656).

The judgement of the late Archbishop of Armagh (1657).

The judgement of the late Archbishop of Armagh . . . unto which is added a character of Bishop Bedell (1659).

Clavi trabales or, nails fastened (1661).

Berwick, Edward, *The Rawdon papers* (1819).

Bolton, Richard, *A justice of the peace for Ireland* (Dublin, 1638).

Borlase, Edmund, *The reduction of Ireland to the crown of England* (1675).

The history of the execrable Irish rebellion (1680).

Boswell, A. (ed.), *James Spottiswood: a brief memorial* (Edinburgh, 1811).

Bramhall, John, *The works of the most reverend father in God, John Bramhall*, ed. A. W. Haddan, 5 vols. (Oxford, 1842–5).

Bray, Gerald (ed.), *Documents of the English reformation* (Cambridge, 1994).

The Anglican canons 1529–1947 (Woodbridge, 1998).

The York convocation book 1545–1640, unpublished edn (Birmingham, AL, 2000).

Records of Irish convocations, unpublished edn (Birmingham, AL, 2000).

Records of the Irish councils, synods and convocations 1101–1704, unpublished edn (Birmingham, AL, 2001).

Convocation facts and figures, unpublished edn (Birmingham, AL, 2004).

Brereton, William, *Travels in the United Provinces, England, Scotland and Ireland*, ed. Edward Hawkins (1844).

Brewer, J. S. and William Bullen (eds.), *Calendar of the Carew manuscripts preserved in the archiepiscopal library at Lambeth, 1515–1624* 6 vols. (1867–73).

Burke, W. P., 'The diocese of Derry in 1631', *Archivium Hibernicum* 22 (1959), 163–73.

Burnet, Gilbert, *The life of William Bedell D.D., bishop of Kilmore in Ireland* (1685).

Caldicott, C. J. C. (ed.), *Patrick Darcy: an argument*, Camden Society 4th series, 44 (1992), pp. 191–320.

Calendar of the state papers relating to Ireland, in the reign of James I, preserved in Her Majesty's Public Record Office and elsewhere, 5 vols. (1872–80).

Calendar of the state papers relating to Ireland, in the reign of Charles I, preserved in the Public Record Office and elsewhere, 3 vols. (1900–3).

Clarke, Samuel, *A caution against sacrilege or sundry queries concerning the lives of thirty-two English divines*, 3rd edn (1677).

Comber, Thomas (ed.), *A book of instructions written by Sir Christopher Wandesforde to his son and heir*, 2 vols. (Cambridge, 1777).

Constitutions and canons ecclesiastical (Dublin, 1635).

Cooper, John Phillips (ed.), *Wentworth papers, 1597–1628*, Camden Society 4th series, 12 (1973).

Corbet, John, *Epistle congratulatory of Lysimachus Nicanor of the Society of Jesu to the Covenanters in Scotland* (Dublin, 1640).

Crant, Thomas, *The plot and progress . . . Irish rebellion . . .* (1644).

Cressy, Hugh, *Exomologesis, or, A faithful narration of the occasion and motives of the conversion unto Catholique unity of Hugh-Paulin de Cressy* (Paris, 1647).

Daniel, William, *Leabhar na nUrnaightheadh gComhchoidchiond* (Dublin, 1608).

Darcy, Patrick, *An argument delivered by Patrick Darcy esq.* (Waterford, 1643).

Davies, Sir John, *Le premier report des cases & matters en ley* (Dublin, 1615).

Ford, Alan (ed.), 'Correspondence between Archbishops Ussher and Laud', *Archivium Hibernicum* 46 (1991–2), 5–21.

Fuller, Thomas, *Church history of Great Britain; from the birth of Jesus Christ until the year 1648*, 3 vols. (1655).

Fulwar, Thomas, *Sermon preached at Graye's Inn, 2 October 1642* (1642).

Gilbert, J. T. (ed.), *A contemporary history of affairs in Ireland from 1641 to 1652*, 3 vols. (Dublin, 1879).

  Calendar of the ancient records of Dublin, 5 vols. (Dublin, 1889–95).

Gillespie, Raymond (ed.), *The first Chapter Act Book of Christ Church cathedral, Dublin, 1574–1634* (Dublin, 1997).

Grosart, A. B. (ed.), *Lismore papers*, 10 vols. (1886–8).

Hall, Joseph, *Episcopacy by divine right asserted* (1640).

Hand, G. J. and Treadwell, V. W. (eds.), 'His Majesty's directions for the ordering and settling of the courts and the course of justice within his kingdom of Ireland', *Analecta Hibernica* 26 (1970), 179–235.

Harris, Paul, *The excommunication published by the lord archbishop of Dublin, T. Flemming* (Dublin, 1632).

  Fratres sobrii estotes (Dublin, 1634).

  Exile exiled (Dublin, 1635).

Harris, Walter (ed.), *Whole works of Sir James Ware concerning Ireland*, 3 vols. (1739).

  Hibernica, 4 vols. (Dublin, 1747).

Heylyn, Peter, *History of the Sabbath* (1636).

  Extraneus vapulans or the Observator rescued (1656).

  Pespondet Petrus (1658).

  Cyprianus Anglicus (1668).

[Heylyn, Peter], *Observation on the history of the reign of King Charles published by H. L. esq.* (1656).

  Humble and just remonstrance of the knights, citizens and burgesses, in parliament assembled in Ireland (1641).

  The humble petition of the Protestant inhabitants of the counties of Antrim, Downe, Tyrone &c (1641).

Hickson, Mary (ed.), *Ireland in the seventeenth century or the Irish massacres of 1641–2*, 2 vols. (1884).

Historical Manuscripts Commission:

Report on the manuscripts of the Earl Cowper, 2 vols. (1884).

Report on the Ormond manuscripts, n.s., vols. 1–2 (1902–3).

Report on manuscripts in various collections, vol. 3 (1904).

Report on the manuscripts of the Earl of Egmont, vol. 1 (1905).

Report on the Pepys manuscripts (1911).

Report on manuscripts in various collections, vol. 8 (1913).

Report on the manuscripts of the late Reginald Rawdon Hastings esq., 4 vols. (1928–47).

Hogan, Edmund (ed.), *Ibernia Ignatiana* (Dublin, 1880).

I. C. [John Copinger], *The theatre of Catholique and Protestant religion divided into twelve bookes* (St Omer, 1620).

Jansson, Maija (ed.), *Proceedings in the opening session of the long parliament: House of Commons, 3 November–19 December 1640* (Woodbridge, 2000).

Inquisitionum in officio rotulorum cancellariae Hiberniae asservatarum, reportorium, 2 vols. (Dublin, 1826–9).

Jennings, Brendan (ed.), *Wadding papers 1614–38* (Dublin, 1953).

'The indictment of Fr John Preston, Franciscan', *Archivium Hibernicum* 26 (1963), 50–5.

Jones, Henry, *A remonstrance of divers remarkable passages concerning the Church and Kingdom of Ireland* (1642).

St Patrick's Purgatory: containing the description, original, progress and demolition of that superstitious place (1647).

Jones, T. W. (ed.), *The life and death of William Bedell* (1872).

Journals of the house of commons of the kingdom of Ireland, vol. 1, 1613–66 (Dublin, 1796).

Journals of the house of lords of the kingdom of Ireland, vol. 1, 1634–99 (Dublin, 1779).

Knowler, William (ed.), *The earl of Strafford's letters and dispatches*, 2 vols. (1799).

Laing, David (ed.), *The letters and journals of Robert Baillie, Principal of the University of Glasgow, 1637–1662*, 3 vols. (Edinburgh, 1841–2).

Lascelles, R. (ed.), *Liber munerum publicorum Hiberniae*, 2 vols. (1824–30).

Laud, William, *The works of the most reverend father in God, William Laud*, ed. W. Scott and J. Bliss, 7 vols. (Oxford, 1847–60).

Leland, John, *Antiquarii de rebus Brittanicis Collectanea*, 5 vols. (1774).

Leslie, Henry, *A treatise of the authority of the church . . . a sermon given Belfast, 10 August 1636* (Dublin, 1637).

A full confutation of the covenant lately sworn and subscribed by many in Scotland: delivered in a speech at the visitation of Downe and Conner. Held in Lisnegarvy the 26th September 1638 (1639).

A sermon preached at the publique fast (Oxford, 1643).

The blessing of Iudah (Oxford, 1644).

The martyrdome of King Charles (Hague, 1649).

L'Estrange, Hamon, *The reign of King Charles disposed into annals with at the end the observator's rejoinder* (1655).

The observator observed or animadversions upon the observations on the history of King Charles (1659).

Lodge, John (ed.), *Desiderata curiosa Hibernica*, 2 vols. (Dublin, 1772).

Loftus, Dudley, *Oratio funebris habita post Exuvias Iohannis Archiepiscopi Armachani* (Dublin, 1663).

Longstaffe, W. H. (ed.), *Acts of the High Commission within the diocese of Durham*, Surtees Society 34 (1857).

McCrie, Thomas (ed.), *The life of Mr Robert Blair, containing his autobiography from 1593 to 1636* (Edinburgh, 1848).

McDonnell, Randal, *A continuation of the diurnall passages in Ireland* (1641).

McEnery, M. J. and Raymond Refaussé (eds.), *Christ Church deeds* (Dublin, 2001).

McNeill, Charles (ed.), *The Tanner letters* (Dublin, 1943).

Mahaffy, J. P. (ed.), *The particular book of Trinity College* (Dublin, 1904).

Marron, Lawrence, 'Documents from the state papers concerning Miler McGrath', *Archivium Hibernicum* 21 (1958), 73–189.

Meehan, C. P. (ed.), *The portrait of a pious bishop; or the life and death of the Most Reverend Francis Kirwan, bishop of Killala. Translated from the Latin of John Lynch, archdeacon of Tuam* (Dublin, 1864).

Mervyn, Audley, *A speech made before the Lords in the Upper House of Parliament in Ireland, 4 March 1640* (1641).

Ireland's complaint (1641).

Mhágh Craith, Cuthbert (ed.), *Dán na mBráthar Mionúr*, 2 vols. (Dublin, 1967).

Moody, T. W. and Simms, J. G. (eds.), *The bishopric of Derry and the Irish society, 1602–1705*, 2 vols. (Dublin, 1968).

Morrin, James (ed.), *Calendar of the patent and close rolls of chancery in Ireland of the reigns of Henry VIII, Edward VI, Mary and Elizabeth* (Dublin, 1861).

Calendar of the patent and close rolls of chancery in Ireland from the 18th to the 45th of Queen Elizabeth (Dublin, 1862).

Murray, L. P. (ed.), 'A rent-roll of all the houses and lands belonging to the see of Armagh', *Archivium Hibernicum* 8 (1941), 99–120.

Notestein, Wallace (ed.), *The journal of Sir Simonds D'Ewes* (New Haven, 1923).

O'Brien, George (ed.), *Advertisements for Ireland*, Royal Society of Antiquaries of Ireland, unnumbered extra volume (Dublin, 1923).

O'Connell, W. D., 'The Cahil Propositions of 1629', *Irish Ecclesiastical Record*, 5th series, 62 (1943), 118–23.

O'Donovan John (ed. and trans.), *Annála ríoghachta Éireann: Annals of the kingdom of Ireland by the Four Masters from the earliest times to the year 1616*, 7 vols. (Dublin, 1851).

Osborough, W. N., *Irish Statutes: 3 Edward II to the Union, 1310–1800* (Dublin, 1995).

Parr, Richard, *The life of the most reverend father in God, James Ussher* (1686).

A protestation of the archbishops and bishops of Ireland (1641).

Plummer, Charles, *Bethada náem na nÉrenn: Lives of Irish saints*, 2 vols. (Oxford, 1922).

Prynne, William, *Canterbury's doom* (1646).

Rennison, W. H., 'Joshua Boyle's accompt of the temporalities of the bishopricks of Waterford', *Journal of the Cork Historical and Archaeological Society* 32 (1927), 42–9, 78–85; 33 (1928), 42–7, 83–92; 35 (1930), 26–33; 36 (1931), 20–5.

Report of the Deputy Keeper of the public records of Ireland, XV–XVI (1884–5).

Report of Her Majesty's commissioners on the revenues and condition of the established Church of Ireland (Dublin, 1868).

Reynell, Thomas (ed.), 'The estate of the diocese of Derry', *Ulster Journal of Archaeology*, n.s. 1 (1894–5), 167–77, 243–53; 2 (1895–6), 127–31, 146–55, 253–61; 3 (1896–7), 55–7, 187–92.

Ronan, M. V. (ed.), 'The visitation of Dublin, 1615', *Archivium Hibernicum* 8 (1941), 1–55.

'Archbishop Bulkeley's visitation of Dublin, 1630', *Archivium Hibernicum* 8 (1941), 56–98.

Rothes, John earl of, *A relation of proceedings concerning the Kirk of Scotland from August 1637 to July 1638*, ed. Laing, Bannatyne Club (Edinburgh, 1830).

Rushworth, John (ed.), *The trial of Thomas, Earl of Strafford* (1680).

Historical collections of private passages of state, 1618–48, 6 vols. (1682–1701).

Rymer, Thomas, *Foedera, conventiones, literæ, et cujuscunque generis acta publica, inter reges Angliæ, et alios quosuis imperatores, reges*, 20 vols. (1704–35).

Scrinia sacra; secrets of empire in lives of illustrious persons (1654).

Rvyes, Thomas, *The poor vicar's plea* (1620).

Regiminis Anglicani in Hibernia defensio (1624).

Selden, John, *The history of tithes* (1618).

Shelford, Robert, *Five pious and learned discourses* (Cambridge, 1635).

Shirley, E. P. (ed.), *Papers relating to the Church of Ireland, 1631–9* (1874).

Shuckburgh, E. S. (ed.), *Two lives of William Bedell* (Cambridge, 1902).

Sparrow, Anthony, *A sermon concerning confession of sins and the power of absolution* (1637).

Spelman, Sir Henry, *De non temerandis ecclesis* (1616).

The larger treatise concerning tithes (1647).

The history and fate of sacrilege (1698).

Spenser, Edmund, *A view of the present state of Ireland* (Dublin, 1633).

Stephens, A. J., *The Book of Common Prayer . . . according to use of the united Church of England and Ireland*, 3 vols. (1849).

Thomson, T. (ed.), *Acts and proceedings of the Kirk of Scotland from the year 1560 collected from the most authentic manuscripts, part third, 1593–1618* (Edinburgh, 1845).

Thornton, Alice, *Autobiography*, Surtees Society 72 (York, 1875).

Tweedie, W. K. (ed.), 'The life of Mr John Livingstone' in *Select Biographies I* (Edinburgh, 1845).

Udall, Ephraim, *Noli me tangere* (1642).

Ussher, James, *A discourse of the religion anciently professed by the Irish and British* (1631).

A speech delivered in Castle Chamber the 22nd of November, anno 1622 (1622).

An answer made to a challenge made by a Jesuit in Ireland (1625).

The whole works of . . . James Ussher, ed. C. E. Elrington and J. H. Todd, 17 vols. (Dublin, 1847–64).

Valor beneficiorum ecclesiasticorum in Hibernia (Dublin, 1741).

Vesey, John, *Athanasius Hibernicus or the life of the Most Reverend Father in God, John Lord Primate of Armagh* (1676).

Ware, James, *The history of Ireland, collected by three learned authors viz. Meredith Hanmer Doctor in Divinity: Edmund Campion sometime fellow of St Johns College in Oxford: and Edmund Spenser Esq.* (Dublin, 1633).

Whitaker, T. D. (ed.), *The life and original correspondence of Sir George Radcliffe* (1810).

Wilkins, John, *Concilia Magnae Britanniae et Hiberniae*, 5 vols. (1737).

Williams, Griffith, *The persecution and oppression of . . . John Bale . . . and of Gruffuth Williams . . . two learned men, and Right Reverend Bishops of Ossory* (1664).

Wodrow, Robert, *Analecta: or, materials for a history of remarkable providences mostly relating to Scotch ministers and Christians*, 4 vols. (Edinburgh, 1842–3).

Wood, Anthony, *Athenae Oxoniensis*, ed. P. Bliss, 4 vols. (1815–20).

SECONDARY SOURCES

Anon., *The case of John Atherton, bishop of Waterford in Ireland fairly represented* (1710).

Armstrong, Robert, 'Ireland's puritan revolution? The emergence of Ulster Presbyterianism reconsidered,' unpublished paper forthcoming in *English Historical Review*.

Atherton, Ian, 'Viscount Scudamore's "Laudianism": the religious practices of the 1st Viscount Scudamore', *HJ* 34 (1991), 567–96.

Bagwell, Richard, *Ireland under the Stuarts and during the Interregnum*, 3 vols. (1909).

Baillie, W. D., *The Six Mile Water revival of 1625* (Belfast, 1976, repr. 1993).

Presbyterian worship in Ulster prior to the introduction of the Westminster directory (Belfast, 1987).

Baker, J. H., 'United and knit to the imperial crown' in D. S. Greer and N. M. Dawson (eds.), *Mysteries and solutions in Irish legal history* (Dublin, 2001), pp. 51–72.

Ball, J. T., *The reformed Church of Ireland, 1537–1886* (1886).

Barnard, T. C., *Cromwellian Ireland* (Oxford, 1975).

'The uses of 23 October and Irish Protestant celebration', *English Historical Review* 106 (1991), 889–920.

'1641: A bibliographical essay' in Brian Mac Cuarta (ed.), *Ulster 1641* (Belfast, 1993), pp. 173–86.

Begley, John, *The diocese of Limerick in the 16th and 17th centuries* (Dublin, 1927).

Bell, W. and Emerson, N. D., *The Church of Ireland AD 432–1932: the report of the Church of Ireland conference held in Dublin, 11–14 October 1932* (Dublin, 1932)

Bergin, Joseph, 'The Counter-Reformation church and its bishops', *P&P* 165 (1999), 30–73.

Bernard, G. W., 'The Church of England c.1529–c.1642', *History* 75 (1990), 183–206.

Bolton, F. R., *The Caroline tradition of the Church of Ireland* (1958).

Bossy, John, 'The Counter-Reformation and the people of Ireland', *Historical Studies* 7 (1971), 155–69.

Bottigheimer, K., 'Kingdom and colony: Ireland in the westward enterprise, 1536–1660' in K. R. Andrews, N. P. Canny and P. E. H. Hair (eds.), *The westward enterprise: English activities in Ireland, the Atlantic and America* (Liverpool, 1978), pp. 45–65.

'The failure of the Reformation in Ireland: *une question bien posée*', *JEH* 36 (1985), 196–207.

Bottigheimer, K. and Lotz-Heumann, Ute, 'The Irish Reformation in European perspective', *Archiv für Reformationsgeschichte* 89 (1998), 268–309.

Boydell, Barra, *Music at Christ Church before 1800* (Dublin, 1999).

Bradshaw, Brendan, 'The opposition to the ecclesiastical legislation in the Irish reformation parliament', *IHS* 16 (1969), 285–303.

'George Browne, first reformation Archbishop of Dublin', *JEH* 21 (1970), 301–26.

'The beginnings of modern Ireland' in Brian Farrell (ed.), *The Irish parliamentary tradition* (Dublin 1973), pp. 68–87.

'The Edwardian reformation in Ireland', *Archivium Hibernicum* 26 (1976–7), 83–99.

'Sword, word and strategy', *HJ* 21 (1978), 475–502.

The dissolution of the religious orders in Ireland under Henry VIII (Cambridge, 1974).

'The Elizabethans and the Irish: a muddled model', *Studies* 70 (1981), 233–43.

'The reformation in the cities: Cork, Limerick and Galway, 1534–1603' in John Bradley (ed.), *Settlement and society in medieval Ireland* (Kilkenny, 1988), 445–76.

'Geoffrey Keating: apologist of Irish Ireland' in B. Bradshaw, A. Hadfield and W. Malley (eds.), *Representing Ireland: literature and the origins of conflict 1534–1660* (Cambridge, 1993), pp. 166–87.

'The English reformation and identity formation in Ireland and Wales' in Brendan Bradshaw and Peter Roberts (ed.), *British consciousness and identity: the making of Britain 1533–1707* (Cambridge, 1998), pp. 43–111.

Brady, Ciaran, 'Court, castle and country: the framework of government in Tudor Ireland' in Ciaran Brady and Raymond Gillespie (eds.), *Natives and newcomers* (Dublin, 1986), pp. 22–49.

'"Constructive and Instrumental": the dilemma of Ireland's first "New Historians"' in Ciaran Brady (ed.), *Interpreting Irish history* (Dublin, 1994), pp. 3–31.

The chief governors (Cambridge, 1995).

'Comparable histories?: Tudor reform in Wales and Ireland' in Steven G. Ellis and Sarah Barber (eds.), *Conquest and union: fashioning a British state, 1485–1725* (1995), pp. 64–86.

'England's defence and Ireland's reform: the dilemma of Irish viceroys, 1541–1641' in Brendan Bradshaw and John Morrill (eds.), *The British problem c. 1534–1707* (1996), pp. 89–117.

'The attainder of Shane O'Neill, Sir Henry Sidney and the problems of Tudor state-building in Ireland' in Ciaran Brady and Jane Ohlmeyer (eds.), *British interventions in early modern Ireland* (Cambridge, 2005), pp. 28–48.

Brady, W. M., *Clerical and parochial records of Cork, Cloyne and Ross*, 3 vols. (Dublin, 1863–4).

State papers concerning the Irish church in the time of Queen Elizabeth (1868).

Brooke, Peter, *Ulster Presbyterianism: the historical perspective, 1610–1970* (Belfast, 1986).

Brown, Keith, 'British history: a sceptical comment' in R. G. Asch (ed.), *Three nations – a common history* (Bochum, 1993), pp. 117–27.

Browne, Arthur, *A compendious view of the ecclesiastical law of Ireland*, 2nd edn (Dublin, 1803).

Bullingbroke, Edward, *Ecclesiastical law; or, the statutes, constitutions, canons, rubricks, and articles, of the Church of Ireland*, 2 vols. (Dublin, 1770).

Burtchaell, G. D. and Sadleir, T. U. (eds), *Alumni Dublinenses* (Dublin, 1935).

Caball, Marc, *Poets and poetry: continuity and reaction in Irish poetry, 1558–1625* (Cork, 1998).

'Faith, culture and society: Irish nationality and its development 1558–1625' in Brendan Bradshaw and Peter Roberts (eds.), *British consciousness and identity: the making of Britain 1533–1707* (Cambridge, 1998), pp. 112–39.

'Innovation and tradition: Irish Gaelic responses to early modern conquest and colonization' in Hiram Morgan (ed.), *Political ideology in Ireland, 1541–1641* (Dublin, 1999), pp. 62–82.

Canny, Nicholas, 'Why the Reformation failed in Ireland: *une question mal posée*', *JEH* 30 (1979), 423–50.

The upstart earl: a study of the social and mental world of Richard Boyle, first earl of Cork (Cambridge, 1982).

'Protestants, planters and apartheid in Early Modern Ireland', *IHS* 25 (1986), 105–15.

From Reformation to Restoration: Ireland 1534–1660 (Dublin, 1987).

Kingdom and colony: Ireland in the Atlantic world (Baltimore, MD, 1988).

'Irish, Scottish and Welsh responses to centralisation, *c.*1530–*c.*1640: a comparative perspective' in A. Grant and K. J. Stringer (eds.), *Uniting the kingdom? The making of British History* (1995), pp. 147–69.

'The attempted anglicisation of Ireland in the seventeenth century' in J. F. Merritt (ed.), *The political world of Thomas Wentworth, Earl of Strafford 1621–1641* (Cambridge, 1996), pp. 157–86.

Making Ireland British 1580–1650 (Oxford, 2001).

'Writing early modern history: Ireland, Britain and the wider world', *HJ* 46 (2003), 723–47.

Capern, Amanda, '"Slipperye times and dangerous dayes": James Ussher and the Calvinist Reformation of Britain 1560–1660', unpublished PhD thesis, University of New South Wales (1991).

'The Caroline church: James Ussher and the Irish dimension', *HJ* 39 (1996), 57–85.

Carlton, Charles, *Archbishop Laud* (1987).

Carroll, Clare, *Circe's cup: cultural transformations in early modern writing about Ireland* (Cork, 2001).

Carte, James, *The life of James Duke of Ormond*, 3 vols. (1736).

Clarke, Aidan, *The Old English in Ireland, 1625–42* (1966).

The graces 1625–41 (Dundalk, 1968).

'The policies of the Old English in parliament, 1640–41', *Historical Studies* 5 (1965), 85–102.

'Colonial identity in early seventeenth century Ireland', *Historical Studies* 11 (1978), 57–71.

'Pacification, plantation and the Catholic question, 1603–23', *NHI* III, pp. 187–231.

'The government of Wentworth, 1632–40', *NHI* III, pp. 243–69.

'The breakdown of authority, 1640–41', *NHI* III, pp. 270–88.

'The history of Poynings' Law, 1615–41', *IHS* 18 (1972), 207–22.

'The Atherton file', *Decies: Journal of the Old Waterford History Society* 11 (1979), 45–55.

'The genesis of the Ulster rising of 1641' in Peter Roebuck (ed.), *From plantation to partition* (Belfast, 1981), pp. 21–45.

'Varieties of uniformity – the first century of the Church of Ireland' in W. J. Sheils and Diana Wood (eds.), *The churches, Ireland and the Irish* Studies in Church History 25 (Oxford, 1989), pp. 105–22.

'Bishop William Bedell (1571–1642) and the Irish reformation' in Ciaran Brady (ed.), *Worsted in the game: losers in Irish history* (Dublin, 1989), pp. 61–72.

'Colonial constitutional attitudes in Ireland, 1640–60', *Proceedings of the Royal Irish Academy* 90 (1990), 357–75.

'The 1641 rebellion and anti-popery in Ireland' in Brian Mac Cuarta, (ed.) *Ulster 1641* (Belfast, 1993), pp. 139–57.

'Patrick Darcy and the constitutional relationship between Ireland and Britain' in Jane Ohlmeyer (ed.), *Political thought in seventeenth-century Ireland* (Cambridge, 2000), pp. 35–55.

'A woeful sinner: John Atherton' in Vincent P. Carey and Ute Lotz-Heumann (eds.), *Taking sides? Colonial and constitutional mentalités in early modern Ireland* (Dublin, 2003), pp. 138–49.

Cogan, Anthony, *The ecclesiastical history of the diocese of Meath*, 3 vols. (Dublin, 1867–74).

Collins, W. E., 'John Bramhall' in W. E. Collins (ed.), *Typical English churchmen from Parker to Maurice* (1902), pp. 81–119.

(ed.) *Lectures on Archbishop Laud* (1895).

Collinson, Patrick, *The religion of the Protestants* (Oxford, 1982).

'The Jacobean religious settlement: the Hampton Court conference' in Howard Tomlinson (ed.), *Before the English Civil War: essays on early Stuart politics and government* (1983), pp. 27–52.

'Shepherds, sheepdogs and hirelings: the pastoral ministry in post-Reformation England' in W. J. Sheils and Diana Wood (eds.), *The ministry: clerical and lay*, Studies in Church History 26 (Oxford, 1989), pp. 185–220.

The birthpangs of protestant England (1988).

Connolly, S. J., 'Religion and History', *Irish Economical and Social History* 10 (1983), 66–80.

Conway, Dominic, 'The Anglican world: problems of co-existence, during the pontificates of Urban VIII and Innocent X, 1623–1655', *Sacra Congregationis de Propaganda Fide Memoria Rerum* 1 (Rome, 1972), pp. 149–76.

Cooke, E. A., *The diocesan history of Killaloe, Kilfenora, Clonfert & Kilmacduagh, 639–1886* (Dublin, 1886).

Cooper, J. P., 'Strafford and the Byrnes' country', *IHS* 15 (1966), 1–20.

'The fortune of Thomas Wentworth, earl of Strafford', *Economic History Review*, 2nd series, 11 (1958), 227–48.

Corish, Patrick J., 'Two reports on the Catholic church in Ireland in the early 17th century', *Archivium Hibernicum* 22 (1959), 140–62.

'The reorganization of the Irish Church, 1603–41', *Proceedings of the Irish Catholic Historical Committee* (1957), 9–14.

The Catholic community in the seventeenth and eighteenth centuries (Dublin, 1981).

The Irish Catholic experience (Dublin 1985).

Cosgrove, Art, 'The writing of Irish medieval history', *IHS* 27 (1990), 97–111.

Cotton, Henry, *Fasti ecclesiae hibernicae*, 6 vols. (Dublin, 1848–78).

Crawford, J. G., *Anglicizing the government of Ireland* (Dublin, 1993).

Cregan, Donal, 'The social and cultural background of a counter-reformation episcopate, 1618–60' in Art Cosgrove and Donal McCartney (eds.), *Studies in Irish history presented to R. Dudley Edwards* (Dublin, 1979), pp. 85–117.

Cunningham, Bernadette, 'Seventeenth-century interpretations of the past: the case of Geoffrey Keating', *IHS* 25 (1986), 116–28.

'Native culture and political change in Ireland, 1580–1640', Ciaran Brady and Raymond Gillespie (eds.), *Natives and newcomers* (Dublin, 1986), pp. 148–70.

'The culture and identity of Irish Franciscan historians at Louvain 1607–1650' in Ciaran Brady (ed.), *Ideology and the historians* (Dublin, 1991), pp. 11–30.

The world of Geoffrey Keating (Dublin, 2000).

Cunningham, B. and Gillespie, R., '"The most adaptable of saints": the cult of St Patrick in the seventeenth century', *Archivium Hibernicum* 49 (1995), 82–104.

Davies, Julian, *The Caroline captivity of the Church* (Oxford, 1992).

Davies, R. R., 'In praise of British history' in R. R. Davies (ed.), *The British Isles 1100–1500* (Edinburgh, 1988), pp. 9–26.

Dawson, J. E. A., 'Two kingdoms or three? Ireland in Anglo-Scottish relations in the middle of the 16th century' in R. A. Mason (ed.), *Scotland and England, 1286–1815* (Edinburgh, 1987), pp. 113–38.

'William Cecil and the British dimension of early Elizabethan foreign policy', *History* 74 (1989), 196–216.

Dickens, A. G., *The English reformation*, 2nd edn (1989).

Donagan, Barbara, 'The York House conference revisited: laymen, Calvinism and Arminianism', *Historical Research* 64 (1991), 312–30.

Donald, Peter, *An uncounselled king: Charles I and the Scottish troubles, 1637–1641* (Cambridge, 1990).

Donaldson, Gordon, 'The attitude of Whitgift and Bancroft to the Scottish church', *Transactions of the Royal Historical Society*, 4th series, 24 (1942), 95–115.

Duffy, Eamon, *The stripping of the altars* (1992).

Duffy, Seán, 'The problem of degeneracy' in James Lydon (ed.), *Law and disorder in thirteenth-century Ireland: the Dublin parliament of 1297* (Dublin, 1997), pp. 87–106.

Dwyer, P., *The diocese of Killaloe* (Dublin, 1878).

Edwards, R. D., *Church and state in Tudor Ireland: a history of the penal laws against Irish Catholics, 1534–1603* (Dublin, 1935).

'Irish Catholics and the Puritan revolution' in Franciscan Fathers (eds.), *Fr. Luke Wadding commemorative volume* (Dublin, 1957), pp. 93–118.

Edwards, R. D. and O'Dowd, M., *Sources for early modern Irish history 1534–1641* (Cambridge, 1985).

Eliot, T. S., *Selected essays* (1951).

Elliott, J. H., 'A Europe of composite monarchies', *P&P* 137 (1992), 48–71.

Ellis, Steven, 'John Bale, bishop of Ossory, 1552–3', *Journal of the Butler Society* 2 (1984), 283–93.

Tudor Ireland (1985).

The Pale and the far north (Galway, 1988).

'Nationalist historiography and the English and Gaelic worlds in the late Middle Ages', *IHS* 25 (1986), 1–18.

'Crown, community and government in English territories, 1450–1575', *History* 71 (1986), 187–204.

'England in the Tudor state', *HJ* 26 (1983), 201–12.

'Economic problems of the church: why the Reformation failed in Ireland', *JEH* 41 (1990), 239–65.

Erck, J. C., *An account of the ecclesiastical establishment in Ireland, as also, and ecclesiastical register* (Dublin, 1830).

Ferrell, Lori Anne, 'Kneeling and the body politic' in Donna Hamilton and Richard Strier (eds.), *Religion, literature and politics in post-Reformation England, 1540–1688* (Cambridge, 1996), pp. 70–92.

Fincham, Kenneth, *Prelate as pastor: the episcopate of James I* (Oxford, 1990).
　'Episcopal government, 1603–1640' in Kenneth Fincham (ed.), *The early Stuart church, 1603–1642* (1993), pp. 71–91.
　Visitation articles and injunctions of the early Stuart church, vols. I and II, Church of England Record Society (Woodbridge, 1994, 1998).
　'Clerical conformity from Whitgift to Laud' in Peter Lake and Michael Questier (eds.), *Conformity and orthodoxy in the English church c.1560–1660* (Woodbridge, 2000), pp. 125–58.
　'William Laud and the exercise of Caroline ecclesiastical patronage', *JEH* 51 (2000), 69–93.
　'Restoration of altars in the 1630s', *HJ* 44 (2001), 919–40.
Fincham, K. and Lake, P., 'The ecclesiastical policy of James I', *Journal of British Studies* 24 (1985), 169–207.
　'The ecclesiastical policies of James I and Charles I' in Kenneth, Fincham (ed.), *The early Stuart church* (1993), pp. 23–49.
Flanagan, Marie T., *Irish society, Anglo-Norman settlers, Angevin kingship* (Oxford, 1989).
Fletcher, Alan, *Drama, performance and polity in pre-Cromwellian Ireland* (Cork, 2000).
Ford, Alan, *The Protestant reformation in Ireland, 1590–1641* (Frankfurt, 1985).
　'The Protestant reformation in Ireland' in Ciaran Brady and Raymond Gillespie (eds.), *Natives and newcomers* (Dublin, 1986), pp. 50–74.
　'The Church of Ireland: a critical bibliography, 1603–41', *IHS* 27 (1993), 352–8.
　'"Standing one's ground": religion, polemic and Irish history since the Reformation' in Alan Ford, J. I. McGuire and K. Milne (eds.), *As by law established: the Church of Ireland since the reformation* (Dublin, 1995), pp. 1–14.
　'The Church of Ireland, 1558–1634: a puritan church?' in A. Ford, J. I. McGuire and Kenneth Milne (eds.), *As by law established: the Church of Ireland since the reformation* (Dublin, 1995), pp. 52–68.
　'Dependent or independent? The Church of Ireland and its colonial context, 1536–1649', *The Seventeenth Century* 10 (1995), 163–87.
　'The reformation in Kilmore before 1641' in Raymond Gillespie (ed.), *Cavan: essays on the history of an Irish county* (Dublin, 1995), pp. 73–98.
　'The origins of Irish dissent' in Kevin Herlihy (ed.), *The religion of Irish dissent, 1650–1800* (Dublin, 1996), pp. 9–30.
　'James Ussher and the creation of an Irish Protestant identity' in Brendan Bradshaw and Peter Roberts (eds.), *British consciousness and identity: the making of Britain 1533–1707* (Cambridge, 1998), pp. 185–212.
　'James Ussher and the godly prince in early seventeenth century Ireland' in Hiram Morgan (ed.), *Political ideology in Ireland 1541–1641* (Dublin, 1999), pp. 203–28.
　'"Firm Catholics" or "loyal subjects"? Religious and political allegiance in early seventeenth-century Ireland' in D. George Boyce, Robert Eccleshall and Vincent Geoghegan (eds.), *Political discourse in seventeenth and eighteenth century Ireland* (2001), pp. 1–31.

'Criticising the godly prince: Malcolm Hamilton's *Passages and consultations*' in Vincent P. Carey and Ute Lotz-Heumann (eds.), *Taking sides? Colonial and constitutional mentalités in early modern Ireland* (Dublin, 2003), pp. 116–37.

'"That bugbear Arminianism": Archbishop Laud and Trinity College, Dublin in 1614' in Ciaran Brady and Jane Ohlmeyer (eds.), *British interventions in early modern Ireland* (Cambridge, 2005), pp. 135–61.

Forrestal, Alison, *Catholic synods in Ireland 1600–1690* (Dublin, 1998).

Foster, Andrew, 'A biography of Archbishop Richard Neile (1562–1640)', unpublished Oxford D.Phil. (1978).

'The function of a Bishop: the career of Richard Neile, 1562–1640' in Rosemary O'Daly and Felicity Heal (eds.), *Continuity and change* (Leicester, 1976), pp. 33–54.

'Church policies of the 1630s' in Richard Cust and Ann Hughes (eds.), *Conflict in early Stuart England* (1989), pp. 193–223.

'The clerical estate revitalised' in Kenneth Fincham (ed.), *The early Stuart church, 1603–42* (1993), pp. 139–60.

'Archbishop Richard Neile revisited' in Peter Lake and Michael Questier (eds.), *Conformity and orthodoxy in the English church c.1560–1660* (Woodbridge, 2000), pp. 159–78.

Foster, W. R., *The church before the covenants* (Edinburgh, 1975).

Gaffney, Declan, 'The practice of religious controversy in Dublin, 1600–1641' in W. J. Sheils and Diana Wood (eds.), *The churches, Ireland and the Irish*, Studies in Church History 25 (Oxford, 1989), pp. 145–58.

Gardiner, S. R., *The constitutional documents of the puritan revolution 1625–1660*, 3rd edn (Oxford, 1906).

Garstin, J. R., *The Book of Common Prayer in Ireland: its origin and history* (Dublin, 1871).

Giblin, Cathaldus, 'The *Processus Datariae* and the appointment of Irish bishops in the seventeenth century' in Franciscan Fathers (eds.), *Father Luke Wadding* (Dublin, 1957), pp. 508–616.

Gillespie, Raymond, *Colonial Ulster: the settlement of East Ulster, 1600–1641* (Cork, 1985).

'Funerals and society in early seventeenth century Ireland', *Journal of the Royal Society of Antiquaries of Ireland* 115 (1985), 86–91.

'The end of an era: Ulster and the outbreak of the 1641 rising' in Ciaran Brady and Raymond Gillespie (eds.), *Natives and newcomers* (Dublin, 1986), pp. 191–213.

'The trials of Bishop Spottiswood 1620–40', *Clogher Record* 12 (1987), 320–33.

'Destabilizing Ulster, 1641–42' in Brian Mac Cuarta (ed.), *Ulster 1641* (Belfast, 1993), pp. 107–21.

'The presbyterian revolution in Ulster, 1660–1690' in W. J. Sheils and Diana Wood (eds.), *The churches, Ireland and the Irish*, Studies in Church History 25 (Oxford, 1989), pp. 159–70.

'The religion of Irish Protestants: a view from the laity' in Alan Ford, J. I. McGuire and Kenneth Milne (eds.), *As by law established* (Dublin, 1995), pp. 89–99.

Thomas Howell and his friends: serving Christ Church Cathedral, Dublin 1570–1700 (Dublin, 1997).

'The crisis of reform, 1625–60' in Kenneth Milne (ed.), *Christchurch, Dublin: a history* (Dublin, 2000), pp. 195–217.

Goodare, Julian, 'The Statutes of Iona in context', *Scottish Historical Review* 77 (1998), 31–57.

Graham, B. J., 'The high middle ages c.1110–1350' in B. J. Graham and L. J. Proudfoot (eds.), *An historical geography of Ireland* (1993), pp. 58–91.

Green, Ian R., 'Career prospects and clerical conformity in the early Stuart Church', *P&P*, 90 (1981), 75–115.

Hagan, John (ed.), 'Miscellanea Vaticano-Hibernica', *Archivium Hibernicum* 3 (1914), 263–4.

Haigh, Christopher, *English reformations: religion, politics and society under the Tudors* (Oxford, 1993).

Heal, Felicity, 'Archbishop Laud revisited: leases and estate management at Canterbury and Winchester before the Civil War' in Rosemary O'Day and Felicity Heal (eds.), *Princes and paupers in the English church 1500–1800* (Leicester, 1981), pp. 129–52.

'Mediating the word: language and dialects in the British and Irish reformations', *JEH* 56 (2005), 261–86.

Healy, John, *History of the Diocese of Meath*, 2 vols. (Dublin, 1908).

Helmholz, R. H., *Roman canon law in Reformation England* (Cambridge, 1990).

Hibbard, Caroline, *Charles I and the Popish Plot* (Chapel Hill, NC, 1983).

Henry, Gráinne, 'Ulster exiles in Europe, 1605–41' in Brian Mac Cuarta (ed.), *Ulster 1641* (Belfast, 1993), pp. 37–60.

Hill, Christopher, *Economic problems of the church, from Archbishop Whitgift to the Long Parliament* (Oxford, 1956).

'Archbishop Laud and the English revolution' in Gordon J. Schochet, P. E. Tatspaugh and Carol Brobeck (eds.), *Religion, resistance, and civil war: papers presented at the Folger Institute Seminar 'Political thought in Early Modern England, 1600–1660'*, Proceedings of the Folger Institute Center for the History of British Political Thought 3 (Washington, DC, 1990), pp. 127–49.

Holloway, Henry, *The Reformation in Ireland: a study of ecclesiastical legislation* (1919).

Holmes, Finlay, *The Presbyterian Church in Ireland: a popular history* (Dublin, 2000)

Hoyle, David, 'A Commons investigation of Arminianism and Popery in Cambridge on the eve of the Civil War', *HJ* 29 (1986), 419–25.

Hughes, Seán F., '"The problem of Calvinism": English theologies of predestination c. 1580–1630' in Susan Wabuda and Caroline Litzenberger (eds.), *Belief and practice in Reformation England: a tribute to Patrick Collinson from his students* (Aldershot and Brookfield, VT, 1998), pp. 229–49.

Hunt, Arnold, 'The Lord's Supper in early modern England', *P&P* 161 (1998), 39–83.

Ingram, Martin, *Church Courts, sex and marriage in England* (Cambridge, 1987).

Jackson, Brian, 'The construction of argument: Henry Fitzsimon, John Rider and religious controversy in Dublin, 1599–1614' in Ciaran Brady and Jane Ohlmeyer (eds.), *British interventions in early modern Ireland* (Cambridge, 2005), pp. 97–115.

'Sectarianism: division and dissent in Irish Catholicism' in Alan Ford and John McCafferty (eds.), *The origins of sectarianism in early modern Ireland* (Cambridge, 2005), pp. 203–15.

Jefferies, Henry A., 'The Irish Parliament of 1560: the anglican reforms authorised', *IHS* 26 (1988), 128–41.

'Bishop George Montgomery's survey of the Derry diocese: a complete text from c. 1609', *Seanchas Ard Mhacha* 17 (1996–7), 44–76.

Priests and prelates of Armagh in the age of reformations, 1518–1558 (Dublin, 1997).

'Erenaghs in pre-plantation Ulster: an early seventeenth-century account', *Archivum Hibernicum* 53 (1999), 16–19.

'George Montgomery, first Protestant bishop of Derry' in Henry A. Jefferies and Ciarán Devlin (eds.), *History of the diocese of Derry from earliest times* (Dublin, 2000), pp. 140–66.

'The early Tudor Reformations in the Irish Pale', *JEH* 52 (2001), 34–62.

'Erenaghs and termonlands: another early seventeenth-century account', *Seanchas Ard Mhacha* 19 (2002), 55–8.

Jellett, Henry, *The Irish church and the articles of 1615* (1850).

Jenkins, Philip, 'The Anglican Church and the unity of Britain: the Welsh experience, 1560–1714' in S. G. Ellis and Sarah Barber (eds.), *Conquest and union: fashioning a British state, 1485–1725* (1995), pp. 115–38.

Jennings, Brendan, *Michael O Cléirigh, chief of the Four Masters, and his associates* (Dublin, 1936).

Johnston, T. J., Robinson, J. L and Jackson, R. Wyse, *A history of the Church of Ireland* (Dublin, 1953).

Jones, Norman, *The English reformation: religion and cultural adaptation* (Oxford, 2002).

Jourdan, G. V., 'The rule of Charles I' in W. A. Phillips (ed.), *The History of the Church of Ireland from the earliest times to the present day*, vol. 3: *The modern church* (Oxford, 1933), pp. 1–58.

Kearney, Hugh, *Strafford in Ireland, 1633–41* (Manchester, 1959; repr. Cambridge, 1989).

'Ecclesiastical politics and the Counter-Reformation in Ireland, 1618–1648', *JEH* 11 (1960), 202–12.

'Strafford in Ireland, 1633–40', *History Today* 39 (July 1989), 20–5.

Kelly, W. P., 'Ormond and Strafford, pupil and mentor?', *Journal of the Butler Society* 4 (1997), 88–106.

Kennett, White, *Impropriations* (1704).

Kenyon, J. P., *The Stuart constitution*, 2nd edn (1986).

Kilroy, Philomena, 'Sermon and pamphlet literature in the Irish reformed Church, 1613–1634', *Archivium Hibernicum* 33 (1975), 110–21.

'Bishops and ministers in Ulster during the primacy of Ussher', *Seanchas Ard Mhacha* 8 (1977), 284–98.

'Protestantism in Ulster, 1610–41' in Brian Mac Cuarta (ed.), *Ulster 1641* (Belfast, 1993), pp. 25–36.

King, Peter, 'The episcopate during the Civil Wars, 1642–1649', *English Historical Review* 83 (1968), 523–37.

Knox, R. Buick, *James Ussher, Archbishop of Armagh* (Cardiff, 1967).

Lake, Peter, 'Calvinism and the English church 1570–1635', *P&P*, 104 (1987), 32–76.

'Conformist clericalism? Richard Bancroft's analysis of the socio-economic roots of Presbyterianism' in W. J. Sheils and Diana Wood (eds.), *The church and wealth*, Studies in Church History 24 (Oxford, 1987), pp. 219–29.

'Protestants, Puritans and Laudians', *JEH* 42 (1991), 618–28.

'The Laudian style: order, uniformity and the pursuit of the Beauty of Holiness in the 1630s' in Kenneth Fincham (ed.), *The early Stuart church, 1603–1642* (1993), pp. 161–86.

'The Laudians and the argument from authority' in B. Y. Kunze and D. D. Brautigam (eds.), *Court, country and culture: essays on early modern British history in honour of Perez Zagorin* (Rochester, 1992), pp. 149–75.

'Retrospective: Wentworth's political world in revisionist and post-revisionist perspective' in J. F. Merritt (ed.), *The political world of Thomas Wentworth, earl of Strafford* (Cambridge, 1996), pp. 252–83.

Lawlor, H. J., 'Two collections of visitation reports in the library of T.C.D.', *Hermathena* 31 (1904/5), 319–31.

Fasti of St Patrick's, Dublin (Dublin, 1930).

Leerssen, J. T., 'Archbishop Ussher and Gaelic culture', *Studia Hibernica*, 22–3 (1982–3), 50–8.

Mere Irish and fíor-Ghael: studies in the idea of Irish nationality (Cork, 1996).

Le Neve, John, *Fasti ecclesiae anglicanae*, vol. IV, compiled by J. M. Horn and D. M. Smith (1975).

Lennon, Colm, *Richard Stanihurst: the Dubliner, 1547–1618* (Dublin, 1981).

'The counter-reformation in Ireland' in Ciaran Brady and Raymond Gillespie (eds.), *Natives and newcomers* (Dublin, 1986), pp. 75–92.

The lords of Dublin in the age of reformation (Dublin, 1989).

'The chantries in the Irish reformation: the case of St Anne's guild, Dublin, 1550–1630' in R. V. Comerford, Mary Cullen, Jacqueline R. Hill and Colm Lennon (eds.), *Religion, conflict and coexistence in Ireland* (Dublin, 1990), pp. 6–25.

Sixteenth-century Ireland: the incomplete conquest (Dublin, 1994).

The urban patriciates of early modern Ireland: a case-study of Limerick, the 28th O'Donnell Lecture (Dublin, 1999).

'The shaping of a lay community in the Church of Ireland, 1558–1640' in Raymond Gillespie and W. G. Neely (eds.), *The laity and the Church of Ireland, 1000–2000* (Dublin, 2002), pp. 49–69.

'Taking sides: the emergence of Irish Catholic ideology' in Vincent P. Carey and Ute Lotz-Heumann (eds.), *Taking sides? Colonial and constitutional mentalités in early modern Ireland* (Dublin, 2003), pp. 78–93.

Leslie, J. B., *Ardfert and Aghadoe clergy and parishes* (Dublin, 1940).

Armagh clergy and parishes (Dundalk, 1911).

Clogher clergy and parishes (Enniskillen, 1929).

Clergy of Connor (Belfast, 1992).

Biographical succession lists of the clergy of the diocese of Down (Dublin, 1937).

Succession lists of the diocese of Dromore (Belfast, 1933).

Derry clergy and parishes (Enniskillen, 1937)

Ferns clergy and parishes (Dublin, 1936).

Ossory clergy and parishes (Enniskillen, 1933).

Raphoe clergy and parishes (Enniskillen, 1940).

Levy, F. T., *Tudor historical thought* (San Marino, CA, 1967).

Little, Patrick, 'The earl of Cork and the fall of the earl of Strafford, 1638–41', *HJ* 39 (1996), 619–35.

'The English parliament and the Irish constitution, 1641–9' in Mícheál Ó Siochrú (ed.), *Kingdoms in crisis: Ireland in the 1640s: essays in honour of Donal Cregan* (Dublin, 2001), pp. 106–21.

'Discord in Drogheda: a window on Irish Church–State relations in the sixteen-forties', *Historical Research* 75 (2002), 355–62.

Lodge, John, *The peerage of Ireland*, ed. M. Archdall, 7 vols. (Dublin, 1789).

Loeber, R., 'Sculptured memorials to the dead in early 17th century Ireland: a survey from *Monumenta Eblanae* and other sources', *Proceedings of the Royal Irish Academy*, section C, 81, no. 11 (1981), 267–93.

Lotz-Heumann, Ute, 'The Protestant interpretation of the history of Ireland: the case of James Ussher's Discourse' in Bruce Gordon (ed.), *Protestant history and identity in sixteenth-century Europe*, vol. 2: *The later reformation* (Aldershot, 1996), pp. 107–20.

Lydon, James, 'The middle nation' in James Lydon (ed.), *England and Ireland in the later middle ages* (Dublin, 1981), pp. 1–26.

McAdoo, H. R., *John Bramhall and Anglicanism: 1663–1963* (Dublin, 1964).

McCabe, R. A., 'Making history: Holinshed's Irish Chronicles, 1577 and 1587' in David J. Baker and Willy Maley (eds.), *British identities and English renaissance literature* (Cambridge, 2002), pp. 51–67.

McCafferty, John, 'John Bramhall and the Church of Ireland in the 1630s' in Alan Ford, James McGuire and Kenneth Milne (eds.), *As by law established: the Church of Ireland since the reformation* (Dublin, 1995), pp. 100–11.

'"God bless your free Church of Ireland": Wentworth, Laud, Bramhall and the Irish Convocation of 1634' in J. F. Merritt (ed.), *The political world of Thomas Wentworth, earl of Strafford, 1621–1641* (Cambridge, 1996), pp. 187–208.

'St Patrick for the Church of Ireland: James Ussher's Discourse', *Bullán* 3 (1997–8), 87–101.

'"To follow the late precedents of England": the Irish impeachment proceedings of 1641' in D. S. Greer and N. M. Dawson (eds.), *Mysteries and solutions in Irish legal history* (Dublin, 2001), pp. 51–73.

'When reformations collide' in Allan Macinnes and Jane Ohlmeyer (eds.), *The Stuart kingdoms in the seventeenth century: awkward neighbours* (Dublin, 2002), pp. 186–203.

'Protestant prelates or godly pastors? The dilemma of the early Stuart episcopate' in Alan Ford and John McCafferty (eds.), *The origins of sectarianism in early modern Ireland* (Cambridge, 2005), pp. 54–72.

'*Mirabilis in sanctis suis*: the communion of saints and Catholic reformation in early seventeenth-century Ireland' in Robert Armstrong and Tadhg ÓhAnnracháin (eds.), *Community in early modern Ireland* (Dublin, 2006), pp. 199–214.

MacCarthy-Morrogh, Michael, *The Munster plantation* (Oxford, 1986).

McCavitt, John, 'The political background to the Ulster plantation, 1607–20' in Brian Mac Cuarta (ed.), *Ulster 1641* (Belfast, 1993), pp. 7–23.

'Lord Deputy Chichester and the English government's "mandates policy" in Ireland 1605–7', *Recusant History* 20 (1990), 320–55.

'An unspeakable parliamentary fracas: the Irish House of Commons, 1613', *Analecta Hibernica* 37 (1995–6), 223–35.

Sir Arthur Chichester, lord deputy of Ireland 1605–16 (Belfast, 1998).

Mac Craith, Mícheál, 'The Gaelic reaction to the Reformation' in Steven G. Ellis and Sarah Barber (eds.), *Conquest and union: fashioning a British state, 1485–1725* (1995), pp. 139–61.

'Creideamh agus athartha: idéoloaíocht pholaitíochta agus aos léinn na Gaeilge i dthús an seachtú haois déag' in Máirín Ní Dhonnchadha (ed.), *Nua-léamha: gnéithe de chultúr, stair agus polaitíocht na hÉireann, c.1600–c.1900* (Baile Átha Cliath, 1996), pp. 7–19.

Mac Cuarta, Brian, 'A planter's interaction with Gaelic culture: Sir Matthew De Renzy (1577–1634)', *Irish Economic and Social History* 20 (1993), 1–17.

MacCulloch, Diarmaid, *Tudor church militant: Edward VI and the English reformation* (1999).

McCullough, Peter, *Sermons at court* (Cambridge, 1998).

McGee, J. Sears, 'William Laud and the outward face of religion' in R. L. DeMolen (ed.), *Leaders of the Reformation* (1984), pp. 318–44.

McGuire, J. I., 'The Church of Ireland: a critical bibliography, 1641–90', *IHS* 28 (1993), 358–62.

'Policy and patronage: the appointment of bishops 1660–61' in Alan Ford, J. I. McGuire and Kenneth Milne (eds.), *As by law established: the Church of Ireland since the reformation* (Dublin, 1995), pp. 112–19.

Macinnes, Allan, *Charles I and the making of the Covenanting movement 1625–1641* (Edinburgh, 1991).

McMahon, G. I. R., 'The Scottish courts of High Commission, 1610–38', *Records of the Scottish Church History Society* 15 (1966), 193–210.

Mahaffy, J. P., *An epoch in Irish History* (1903, repr. New York 1970).

Maltby, Judith, *Prayer book and people in Elizabethan and early Stuart England* (Cambridge, 1998).

Mant, Richard, *History of the Church of Ireland*, 2 vols. (1840).

Marchant, R. A., *The Puritans and the church courts in the diocese of York, 1560–1642* (1960).

Marshall, Peter (ed.), *The impact of the English reformation 1500–1640* (1997). *Reformation England* (2003).

Maskell, William, *A second letter on the present position of the High Church party in the Church of England* (1850).

Mason, H. J. M, *Primitive Christianity in Ireland* (Dublin, 1836). *The catholic religion of St Patrick* (Dublin, 1822). *The life of William Bedell* (1843).

Mayes, Charles R., 'The early Stuarts and the Irish peerage', *English Historical Review* 73 (1958), 227–51.

Merritt, J. F., 'The historical reputation of Thomas Wentworth' in J. F. Merritt (ed.), *The political world of Thomas Wentworth, earl of Strafford, 1621–1641* (Cambridge, 1996), pp. 1–23.

'Power and communication: Thomas Wentworth and government at a distance during the personal rule' in J. F. Merritt (ed.), *The political world of Thomas Wentworth, earl of Strafford, 1621–1641* (Cambridge, 1996), pp. 109–32.

Millett, Benignus, 'The seventeenth century' in Réamonn Ó Muirí (ed.), *Irish Church history today* (Armagh, 1991), pp. 42–62.

Milton, Anthony, Review of Tyacke, *Anti-Calvinists*, *JEH* 39 (1988), 613–16.

'The Church of England, Rome and the true church: the demise of a Jacobean consensus' in Kenneth Fincham (ed.), *The early Stuart church* (1993), pp. 187–210.

Catholic and reformed: the Roman and Protestant churches in English Protestant thought, 1600–1640 (Cambridge, 1995).

'Licensing, censorship, and religious orthodoxy in early Stuart England', *HJ* 41 (1998), 625–51.

'The creation of Laudianism: a new approach' in Thomas Cogswell, Richard Cust and Peter Lake (eds.), *Politics, religion and popularity in Stuart Britain: eassys in honour of Conrad Russell* (Cambridge, 2002), pp. 162–84.

Moody, T. W., *The Londonderry plantation, 1609–41* (Belfast, 1939).

Mooney, Canice, 'Father John Colgan, OFM, his work, times and literary milieu' in Terence O'Donnell (ed.), *Father John Colgan OFM, 1592–1658* (Dublin, 1959), pp. 7–40.

Moran, P. F., *History of the Catholic archbishops of Dublin* (Dublin, 1864).

Morgan, Hiram, 'Writing up early modern Ireland', *HJ* (1988), 701–11.

'The end of Gaelic Ulster: a thematic interpretation of events between 1534 and 1610', *IHS* 26 (1988), 8–32.

'Hugh O'Neill and the Nine Years War in Tudor Ireland', *Historical Journal* 36 (1993), 21–37.

'"Faith & fatherland" in sixteenth-century Ireland', *History Ireland* 3:2 (1995), 13–20.

'Giraldus Cambrensis and the Tudor conquest of Ireland' in Hiram Morgan (ed.), *Political ideology in Ireland, 1541–1641* (Dublin, 1999), pp. 22–44.

Morrill, J. S., 'The National Covenant in its British context' in J. S. Morrill (ed.), *The Scottish National Covenant in its British context* (Edinburgh, 1990), pp. 1–30.

The nature of the English revolution (1993).

'The Britishness of the English revolution, 1640–1660' in R. G. Asch (ed.), *Three nations – a common history?* (Bochum, 1993), pp. 83–116.

'The attack on the Church of England in the Long Parliament' in J. S. Morrill (ed.), *The nature of the English revolution* (1993), pp. 69–90.

'A British patriarchy? Ecclesiastical imperialism under the early Stuarts' in A. Fletcher and P. Roberts (eds.), *Religion, culture and society in early modern Britain* (Cambridge, 1994), pp. 209–37.

'Three kingdoms and one commonwealth? The enigma of mid-seventeenth-century Britain and Ireland' in A. Grant and K. J. Stringer (eds.), *Uniting the kingdom? The making of British history* (1995), pp. 170–90.

Mullan, D. G., *Episcopacy in Scotland: the history of an idea* (Edinburgh, 1986).

Scottish puritanism 1590–1638 (Oxford, 2000).

Murray, James, 'The Church of Ireland: a critical bibliography, 1536–1603', *IHS* 28 (1993), 345–52.

'St Patrick's Cathedral and the university question in Ireland c.1547–1585' in Helga Robinson-Hammerstein (ed.), *European universities in the age of reformation and counter-reformation* (Dublin, 1998), pp. 1–33.

'The diocese of Dublin in the sixteenth century: clerical opposition and the failure of the Reformation' in James Kelly and Dáire Keogh (eds.), *History of the Catholic diocese of Dublin* (Dublin, 2000), pp. 92–111.

Napier, Joseph, *William Bedell* (Dublin, 1863).

Nicholls, K. W., 'The episcopal rents of Clonfert and Kilmacduagh', *Analecta Hibernica* 26 (1970), 130–57.

'Rectory, vicarage and parish in the western Irish dioceses', *Journal of the Royal Society of Antiquaries of Ireland* 101 (1971), 53–84.

Gaelic and gaelicised Ireland in the middle ages (Dublin, 1972).

Nicholson, William, *The Irish historical library* (Dublin, 1724).

Nye, Charles, 'John Bramhall', *Church Quarterly Review* 117 (1934), 267–91.

Ó hAnnracháin, Tadhg, *Catholic reformation in Ireland* (Oxford, 2002).

'"In imitation of that holy patron of prelates the blessed St Charles": episcopal activity in Ireland and the formation of a confessional identity, 1618–1653' in Alan Ford and John McCafferty (eds.), *The origins of sectarianism in early modern Ireland* (Cambridge, 2005), pp. 73–94.

Ó Buachalla, Breandán, 'Na Stíobhartaigh agus an t-aos léinn: cing Séamas', *Proceedings of the Royal Irish Academy*, section C, 83 (1983), 81–134.

'*Annála Ríoghachta Éireann* agus *Foras Feasa ar Éirinn*: an comhtheacs comhaimseartha', *Studia Hibernica* 22–3 (1982–3), 59–105.

'James our true king: the ideology of Irish royalism in the seventeenth century' in D. G. Boyce, Robert Eccleshall and Vincent Geoghegan (eds.), *Political thought in Ireland since the seventeenth century* (1993), pp. 7–35.

O'Connell, W. D., 'The Cahil Propositions of 1629', *Irish Ecclesiastical Record*, 5th series, 62 (1943), 118–23.

O'Connor, Thomas, 'A justification for foreign intervention in early modern Ireland' in Thomas O'Connor and Mary Ann Lyons (eds.), *Irish migrants in Europe after Kinsale, 1602–1820* (Dublin, 2003), pp. 14–31.

O'Dowd, Mary 'Gaelic economy and society' in Ciaran Brady and Raymond Gillespie (eds.), *Natives and newcomers* (Dublin, 1986), pp. 120–47.

Power, politics and land: early modern Sligo, 1568–1688 (Belfast, 1991).

Ó hÉaluighthe, D., 'St Gobnet of Ballyvourney', *Journal of the Cork Historical and Archaeological Society* 72 (1952), 43–61.

O'Grady, Hugh, *Strafford and Ireland*, 2 vols. (Dublin, 1923).

Ohlmeyer, Jane, *Civil war and restoration in the three Stuart kingdoms: the career of Randal MacDonnell, Marquis of Antrim, 1609–1683* (Cambridge, 1993).

'A failed revolution?' in J. H. Ohlmeyer (ed.), *Ireland from independence to occupation, 1641–1660* (Cambridge, 1995), pp. 1–23.

'Strafford, the "Londonderry business" and the "New British History"' in J. F. Merritt (ed.), *The political world of Thomas Wentworth, earl of Strafford, 1621–1641* (Cambridge, 1996), pp. 187–208.

'The Irish peers, political power and parliament, 1640–41' in Ciaran Brady and Jane Ohlmeyer (eds.), *British interventions in early modern Ireland* (Cambridge, 2005), pp. 161–85.

O Riordan, Michelle, 'The native Ulster mentalité as revealed in Gaelic sources, 1600–1650' in Brian Mac Cuarta (ed.), *Ulster 1641* (Belfast, 1993), pp. 61–91.

Orr, D. Alan, *Treason and the state: law, politics, and ideology in the English civil war* (Cambridge, 2002).

Osborough, W. N., 'Ecclesiastical law and the Reformation in Ireland' in R. H. Helmholz (ed.), *Canon law in Protestant lands* (Berlin, 1992), pp. 223–52.

'The Irish custom of tracts', *Irish Jurist* n.s. 32 (1997), 439–58.

Ó Siochrú, Mícheál, 'Foreign involvement in the revolt of Silken Thomas, 1534–5', *Proceedings of the Royal Irish Academy*, section C, 96 (1996), 49–66.

O'Sullivan, William, Review of R. Buick Knox, *James Ussher, Archbishop of Armagh*, *IHS* 16 (1968), 215–19.

'Ussher as a collector of manuscripts', *Hermathena* 88 (1956), 34–58.

'A finding list of Sir James Ware's manuscripts', *Proceedings of the Royal Irish Academy*, section C, 97 (1997), 69–99.

Oulton, J. E. L, 'Ussher's work as a patristic scholar and church historian', *Hermathena* 88 (1956), 3–11.

Oxford dictionary of national biography (Oxford, 2004).

Pawlisch, H. S., *Sir John Davies and the conquest of Ireland: a study in legal imperialism* (Cambridge, 1985).

Perceval-Maxwell, M., *The Scottish migration to Ulster in the reign of James I* (1972, repr. Belfast, 1990).

'Strafford, the Ulster Scots, and the covenanters', *IHS* 18 (1973), 524–41.

'The adoption of the Solemn League and Covenant by the Scots in Ulster', *Scotia* 2 (1978), 3–18.

'Protestant faction, the impeachment of Strafford, and the origins of the Irish civil war', *Canadian Journal of History* 17 (1982), 235–55.

'Ireland and the monarchy in the early Stuart multiple kingdom', *HJ* 34 (1991), 279–95.

'Ulster 1641 in the context of political developments in the Three Kingdoms' in Brian Mac Cuarta (ed.), *Ulster 1641* (Belfast, 1993), pp. 93–106.

The outbreak of the Irish rebellion of 1641 (Dublin, 1994).

Phair, P. B., 'Visitations of the seventeenth century', *Analecta Hibernica* 28 (1978), 79–102.

Phillips, W. A. (ed.), *History of the Church of Ireland*, 3 vols. (1933–4).

Pocock, J. G. A., 'The limits and divisions of British history: in search of the unknown subjects', *American Historical Review* 87 (1982), 311–36.

'British history: a plea for a new subject', *Journal of Modern History* 47 (1975), 601–21.

'History and sovereignty: the historiographical response to Europeanization in the two British cultures', *Journal of British Studies*, 31 (1992), 358–89.

Pogson, Fiona, 'Making and maintaining political alliances during the personal rule of Charles I: Wentworth's associations with Laud and Cottington', *History* 84 (1999), 52–73.

Pollard, A. M., *Dublin's trade in books, 1550–1800* (Oxford, 1989).

Prendergast, J. P., 'On the projected plantation of Ormond by King Charles I', *Transactions of the Kilkenny Archaeological Society* 1, no. iii (1849–51), 390–409.

Ranger, Terence, 'The career of Richard Boyle, 1st Earl of Cork, in Ireland 1588–1643', unpublished Oxford D.Phil. (1959).

'Richard Boyle and the making of an Irish fortune, 1588–1614', *IHS* 10 (1957), 257–97.

'Strafford in Ireland: a revaluation', *P&P* 19 (1961), 26–45.

Reeves, William, *The Book of Common Prayer according to the use of the Church of Ireland* (Dublin, 1871).

Reid, James Seaton, *Seven letters to the Rev. C. R. Elrington occasioned by animadversions in his life of Ussher* (Glasgow, 1849).

History of the Presbyterian Church in Ireland, new edn, 3 vols. (Belfast, 1867).

Rennison, W. H., *Succession list of the dioceses of Waterford & Lismore* (Waterford, 1920).

Rex, Richard, *Henry VIII and the English reformation* (Basingstoke, 1993).

Rice, Gerard, 'Thomas Dease of Meath and some questions concerned with the rights to ecclesiastical property alienated at the Reformation', *Ríocht na Midhe* 6 (1975), 69–89.

Richardson, John, *A short history of the attempts that have been made to convert the popish natives of Ireland*, 2nd edn (London, 1713).

Robinson, Philip, *The plantation of Ulster: British settlement in an Irish landscape, 1600–1670* (Belfast, repr. 1994).

Ronan, M. V., *The reformation in Ireland under Elizabeth 1558–1580* (1930).

Irish martyrs of the penal laws (1935).

Roots, Ivan, 'Union and disunion in the British Isles, 1637–60' in Ivan Roots (ed.), *Into another mould: aspects of the interregnum* (Exeter, 1991), pp. 5–23.

Ross, Linda, 'The legacy of John Bramhall as Laud's alter-ego' in Gerard O'Brien (ed.), *Derry and Londonderry: history and society. Interdisciplinary essays on the history of an Irish county* (Dublin, 1999), pp. 279–302.

Russell, Conrad, 'The theory of treason in the trial of Strafford', *English Historical Review* 80 (1965), 30–50.

'The British problem and the English civil war', *History* 72 (1987), 395–415.

'The British background to the Irish rebellion of 1641', *Historical Research* 61 (1988), 166–82.

The causes of the English Civil War (Oxford, 1990).

The Fall of the British monarchies, 1637–42 (Oxford, 1991).

'Composite monarchies in early modern Europe: the British and Irish example' in A. Grant and K. J. Stringer (eds.), *Uniting the kingdom? The making of British History* (1995), pp. 133–46.

'The reformation and the creation of the Church of England, 1500–1640' in John Morrill (ed.), *The Oxford illustrated history of Tudor and Stuart Britain* (1996), pp. 258–92.

Scarisbrick, J. J., *The reformation and the English people* (Oxford, 1984).

Schaff, Philip, *The creeds of Christendom*, 3 vols. (New York, 1877).

Schmidt, Leigh Eric, *Holy fairs: Scottish communions and American revivals in the early modern period* (Princeton, 1989).

Seymour, St John, *The succession of parochial clergy in the united dioceses of Cashel and Emly* (Dublin, 1908).

The diocese of Emly (Dublin, 1913).

Sharpe, Kevin 'Archbishop Laud', *History Today* 33 (1983), 26–30.

The personal rule of Charles I (New Haven, 1992).

Sharpe, Richard, *Medieval Irish saints' lives: an introduction to Vitae Sanctorum Hiberniae* (Oxford, 1991).

Shaw, Dougal, 'St Giles' church and Charles I's coronation visit to Scotland', *Historical Research* 77 (2004), 481–502.

Shaw, Duncan, 'The inauguration of ministers in Scotland: 1560–1620', *Records of the Scottish Church Historical Society* 16 (1968), 35–62.

Sheehan, A. J., 'The recusancy revolt of 1603: a reinterpretation', *Archivium Hibernicum* 38 (1983), 3–13.

Silke, J. J., 'Later relations between Primate Peter Lombard and Hugh O'Neill', *Irish Theological Quarterly* 22 (1955), 15–30.

'Primate Lombard and James I', *Irish Theological Quarterly* 22 (1955), 124–50.

Simms, Katherine, 'Frontiers in the Irish church – regional and cultural' in Terry Barry, Robin Frame and Katherine Simms (eds.), *Colony and frontier in medieval Ireland* (Woodbridge, 1995), pp. 177–200.

Sommerville, J. P., 'The royal supremacy and episcopacy iure divino', *JEH* 34 (1983), 548–58.

King James VI and I: Political writings (Cambridge, 1994).

Sparrow Simpson, W. J., *Archbishop Bramhall* (1927).

Spurr, John, *The Restoration Church of England* (Newhaven, 1991).

Stevenson, David, 'Conventicles in the Kirk, 1619–1637', *Records of the Scottish Church Historical Society* 18 (1974), 98–114.

Scottish covenanters and Irish confederates (Belfast, 1981).

Stieg, Margaret, *Laud's laboratory* (Lewisburg, PA, 1992).

Stokes, George, *Some worthies of the Irish Church* (1900).

Styles, Phillip, 'James Ussher and his time', *Hermathena* 88 (1956), 12–33.

Sykes, Norman, 'Ussher as a churchman', *Hermathena* 88 (1956), 59–80.

Tait, Clodagh, 'Adored for saints: Catholic martyrdom in Ireland c.1560–1655', *Journal of Early Modern History* 5 (2001), 128–59.

'Colonising memory: manipulation of death, burial and commemoration in the career of Richard Boyle, First Earl of Cork (1566–1643)', *Proceedings of the Royal Irish Academy*, section C 101, no. 4 (2001), 107–34.

Death, burial and commemoration in Ireland, 1550–1650 (2002).

Thomas, Keith, *Religion and the decline of magic* (1973).

Tighe, W. J., 'William Laud and the reunion of churches', *HJ* 30 (1987), 717–27.

Todd, J. H., *St Patrick apostle of Ireland* (Dublin, 1864).

Treadwell, Victor, 'The Survey of Armagh and Tyrone, 1622', *Ulster Journal of Archaeology* 23 (1960), 126–37; 27 (1964), 140–54.

'The House of Lords in the Irish Parliament of 1613–1615', *English Historical Review* 80 (1965), 92–107.

'Richard Hadsor and the authorship of "Advertisements for Ireland"', *IHS* 30 (1997), 305–53.

Buckingham and Ireland, 1616–28 (Dublin, 1998).

Trevor-Roper, H., *Archbishop Laud, 1573–1645*, 3rd edn (1988).

'James Ussher, Archbishop of Armagh' in *Catholics, Anglicans and Puritans: seventeenth century essays* (1987), pp. 120–65.

Tyacke, Nicholas, 'Puritanism, Arminianism and Counter revolution' in Conrad Russell (ed.), *The origins of the English civil war* (1973), pp. 119–43.

'The rise of Arminianism reconsidered', *P&P* 101 (1987), 201–16.

Anti-Calvinists: the rise of English Arminianism c. 1590–1640 paperback edn (Oxford, 1990).

'Archbishop Laud' in Kenneth Fincham (ed.), *The early Stuart church* (1993), 51–70.

'Anglican attitudes: some recent writings on English religious history, from the Reformation to the Civil War', *Journal of British Studies* 35 (1996), 139–67.

Aspects of English Protestantism, c. 1530–1700 (2001).

Usher, R. G., *The rise and fall of the High Commission* (repr. Oxford, 1968).

Walsham, Alexandra, *Church papists: Catholicism, conformity and confessional polemic in early modern England* (Woodbridge, 1993).

'The parochial roots of Laudianism revisited: Catholics, Anti-Calvinists and "parish Anglicans" in early Stuart England', *JEH* 49 (1998), 620–51.

Walshe, H. C., 'Enforcing the Elizabethan settlement: the vicissitudes of Hugh Brady, bishop of Meath, 1563–84', *IHS* 26 (1989), 352–6.

Watt, J. A., *The church and the two nations in medieval Ireland* (Oxford, 1970).

The church in medieval Ireland (Dublin, 1972).

'The disputed primacy of the medieval Irish church' in P. Linehan (ed.), *Proceedings of the seventh international congress of Medieval Canon Law, Cambridge 1984*, Monumenta Iuris Canonici, series C, Subsidia 8 (Vatican City, 1988), pp. 373–83.

Wedgwood, C. V., *Thomas Wentworth, first earl of Strafford, 1593–1641: a revaluation* (1961).

Westerkamp, M. J., *Triumph of the laity, Scots-Irish piety and the Great Awakening, 1625–1760* (Oxford, 1988).

Wheeler, Harvey, 'Calvin's case (1608) and the McIlwain–Schulyer debate', *American Historical Review* 61 (1956), 587–97.

White, Newport B., *Extents of Irish monastic possessions 1540–41* (Dublin, 1943).

White, N. J. D., *Catalogue of the manuscripts remaining in Marsh's Library, Dublin* (Dublin, 1913).

White, Peter, 'The rise of Arminianism reconsidered', *P&P* 101 (1983), 34–54.

'The *via media* in the early Stuart church' in Kenneth Fincham (ed.), *The early Stuart church* (1993), pp. 211–30.

Predestination, policy and polemic: conflict and consensus in the English church from the Reformation to the civil war (Cambridge, 1992).

Williams, Nicholas, *I bprionta i leabhar: na protastúin agus prós na Gaeilge, 1567–1724* (Baile Átha Cliath, 1986).

Winnett, Robert, 'The strange case of John Atherton', *Decies* 39 (1988), 4–17.

Wood, Herbert, *A guide to the records deposited in the Public Record Office of Ireland* (Dublin, 1919).

'The Public Records of Ireland before and after 1922', *Transactions of the Royal Historical Society*, 4th series, 13 (1930), 17–49.

Wooding, Lucy, *Rethinking Catholicism in reformation England* (Oxford, 2000).

Woolf, D. R., *The idea of history in early Stuart England* (Toronto, 1990).

Wormald, Jenny, 'The creation of Britain: multiple kingdoms or core and colonies?', *Transactions of the Royal Historical Society*, 6th series, 2 (1992), 175–194.

'Ecclesiastical vitriol: the kirk, the puritans and the future king of England' in John Guy and Alexander John (eds.), *The reign of Elizabeth I: court and culture in the last decade* (Cambridge, 1995), pp. 171–91.

Wright, W. Ball, *A great Yorkshire divine of the seventeenth century: a sketch of the life and work of John Bramhall D.D.* (York, 1899).

Yule, George, 'James VI & I: furnishing the churches in his two kingdoms' in Anthony Fletcher and Peter Roberts (eds.), *Religion, culture and society in early modern Britain* (Cambridge, 1994), pp. 182–208.

INDEX

Titles in the series